D0763476

HERALDRY IN AMERICA

HERALDRY IN AMERICA

A Guide with 1000 Illustrations

EUGENE ZIEBER

DOVER PUBLICATIONS, INC.
Mineola, New York

Bibliographical Note

This Dover edition, first published in 2006, is an unabridged republication of the work originally published by Bailey, Banks & Biddle Company, Philadelphia, in 1895. Two plates appearing on pages 218A and 254A have been reproduced in color on the inside covers.

International Standard Book Number: 0-486-44764-2

Manufactured in the United States of America
Dover Publications, Inc., 31 East 2nd Street, Mineola, N.Y. 11501

PREFACE.

Among civilized nations a knowledge of heraldry may properly be regarded as a desirable, and indeed a necessary, element in higher refinement and culture. Though such knowledge has at times been relatively neglected in the United States, coat-armor has always been in use here, and "recognized as a mark of social distinction," as John Gough Nichols remarks, "by the republicans of the New World quite as devotedly as by the patricians of the Old."

In America, quite as really as elsewhere, acquaintance with heraldic laws is indispensable to the architect, artist, and author, and to lovers of the fine arts and of literature. How many blunders in our art and absurdities in our literature might have been avoided had not Americans of a certain class assumed lofty indifference to a science they had taken little trouble to understand! Appreciation of the great works of the brush, the chisel, and the pen that come to us from or are studied by us in other lands must be largely impossible to persons who are unfamiliar with heraldry.

Aside from such practical questions, "it is always pleasant," as Boutell says, "to be familiar with the heraldic blazonry that appears upon the panels of aristocratic carriages. Nor is it less satisfactory when we chance to see a flag displayed and blowing out in the breeze, or when our eyes rest upon an heraldic seal, or when we discover a shield of arms in a book or on a monument, or amidst the decorative accessories of some building, to be·able to read what heraldry thus has written with her peculiar symbols."

This volume is designed to meet a felt want in America for a popular work upon heraldry. The writer has endeavored to group in a concise and intelligent manner all that is necessary to enable the student correctly to interpret and apply the manifold laws of the gentle science of Arms. In this respect the book is largely a compilation, as are all modern works upon the subject. It contains, in addition, a collection of material—gathered from the use of royal and other seals upon Colonial documents, and individual coat-

armor upon old tombstones, hatchments, tablets, family plate, wills, deeds, etc.
—showing an early practice and wide recognition of heraldry in America.
It also presents a view of the present practical application of heraldry in the
United States, particularly to the use of official, corporate, and personal seals,
and insignia of orders and societies.

The writer would be manifestly ungrateful if he failed to express his
appreciation to the many friends who have materially aided his work.   He
is under especial obligations to Rev. Henry C. McCook, D.D., for valuable
suggestions, and for free access to a large collection of heraldic seals.   To
Colonel J. Granville Leach acknowledgments are due, particularly for data
relating to Colonial and Revolutionary Societies and American Orders.   Mr.
William Nelson L. West also has the author's thanks for general and efficient
assistance.

In this volume heraldic experts may find something that is new : to
friends of heraldry in general the author ventures to hope it will prove
welcome.   From all readers he begs a generous indulgence.

E. Z.

PHILADELPHIA, December, 1894.

TABLE OF CONTENTS.

CHAPTER I.

CHAPTER II.

CHAPTER III.

CHAPTER IV.

CHAPTER V.

CHAPTER VI.

CHAPTER VII.

CHAPTER VIII.

CHAPTER IX.

CHAPTER X.

CHAPTER XI.

CHAPTER XII.

CHAPTER XIII.

CHAPTER XIV.

CHAPTER XV.

CHAPTER XVI.

CHAPTER XVII.

CHAPTER XVIII.

CHAPTER XIX.

GLOSSARY.

HERALDRY IN AMERICA.

CHAPTER I.

THE ORIGIN AND DEVELOPMENT OF HERALDRY.

IN determining the origin of heraldry, the modern writer is confronted with a confused mass of authorities on various sides of the question,—some ready to blazon the arms of Adam and Eve, others equally ready to assert that there was no heraldry in existence until the twelfth century.

Guillim, on the authority of Diodorus Siculus, traces the origin of the custom of bearing arms to Osyris, the grandson of Noah, who, in one of his great campaigns, bore on his shield "a Sceptre Royal, insigned on the Top with an Eye." His son Hercules, the captain of his army "in this so Ancient an Expedition of Wars," bore "a Lyon Rampant, holding a Battle-Axe." Certain authorities trace the origin of the custom to the Cimbri and Teutons; others to the distinctive symbols which Jacob gave to his children when he blessed them,—to Judah, a lion; to Issachar, an ass; to Benjamin, a wolf.— Gen. xlix. In Numbers ii. 2 we read, "Every man of the children of Israel shall pitch by his own standard, with the ensign of their father's house."

On the other hand, many hold that heraldry was not in existence at the time of the Norman Conquest, nor even at the time of the Crusades.

It is, however, certain that emblems closely resembling the devices of modern coats have been borne on the shields of warriors, as decorations or badges of distinction, from the very earliest ages. But armorial coats, strictly so called, were not in general use until much later, and it is only in comparatively modern times that they have become hereditary.

There can be little doubt that there is a relation between the early devices borne by warriors and the charges upon modern coats of arms. The only difficulty—for us an unimportant one—is to find exactly how close this relation is. Whether, as "the Ingenious Mr. Nisbet" says, the difference between early device bearing and modern heraldry is the same as that between early painting and the modern art; or whether, as modern writers seem to hold, the relation between the two can scarcely be discerned, we may rest assured that the early devices are the source from which many of our modern heraldic emblems are derived.

9

Much confusion has arisen from the different uses of the word heraldry, some making it synonymous with mere symbolism or bearing of devices; others using it to denote the modern system by which this early symbolism has been reduced to an exact science. Thus it happens that Boutell places the Bayeux tapestry " at the head of the early existing illustrations of the Heraldry of Britain," while Cussans, Hulme, and others point to it as a proof that no heraldry existed in England at the time of the Conquest, since its devices " are not at all heraldic in character."

On the whole, no better summary of the " rise and progress" of heraldry can be found than that given by Charles Boutell, M.A. It must be remembered that Boutell uses the word heraldry in the broadest sense, to mean any bearing of devices, however rude.

" An inquiry into the Heraldry of the past leads us back almost to the remote fountain-head of human history. From the very earliest periods, we find it to have been an usage universally prevalent amongst mankind for both individuals and communities to be distinguished by some *Sign, Device* or *Cognizance.* The idea of symbolical expression coupled with a love of symbolism appear, indeed, to constitute one of the component elements of the human mind, as well in the rude condition of savage life as in every progressive advance of civilization and refinement. Through the agency of such figurative imagery the mind is able both to concentrate a wide range of thought within a very narrow compass, and to give to the whole a visible form under a simple image. The mind thus speaks to the eye. By this symbolical blazonry a multiplicity of definite impressions are conveyed, in the simplest manner, and with poetic impressiveness. By such means, also, the mind is empowered to combine the imaginative with the real, and, while extending its speculations beyond the bounds of ascertained verities and actual facts, to impart a definite character to the visions of the imagination.

" The exercise of a faculty such as this, it is easy to conceive, would be held in the highest estimation in the primitive stages of human society. Men so circumstanced had much to say; but they had only rare opportunities for speaking, and they knew but few words in which to convey their meaning. They delighted, therefore, in an expressive symbolism, which might speak for them, laconically, but yet with emphasis and to the point. . . .

" War and the chase would naturally furnish the imagery that would first become prevalent. A man's physical powers or peculiarities, as a warrior or a hunter, or the issue of some exploit in which he might have been engaged, would determine his distinctive personal cognizance. If swift of foot, or strong of hand, or fierce in demeanour, or patient of hardship, he would naturally seek to symbolize himself under the form of some animal distinguished pre-eminently for one or other of those qualities. For, it is natural that man should find symbols of his own physical attributes in the inferior animals; because in mere swiftness or strength, or such like qualities, those animals are superior to man. The next thing would be to render this personal symbolism hereditary. A man's son would feel a natural pride in preserving the memorial of his father's reputation, by assuming, and also by transmitting, his device. It would be the same with the comrades of a chief, and with the subjects of a prince. Thus a system of Heraldry would arise and become established.

"And such is actually the process, which has produced and matured its own Heraldry amongst each of the various races and tribes of the earth. In the Far West, the Red Indian, from time immemorial, has impressed upon his person the *totem* of his people—the cognizance that his fathers bore, and by which they were distinguished before him. In the very constitution of his mind essentially a lover of symbolism, the Oriental revels, and he always has revelled, in a truly characteristic Heraldry. In the relics of the wonderful races that once peopled the valley of the Nile this Heraldry of the East is everywhere present. Another expression of the same semi-mystic symbolism was found, deep buried beneath the mounds of Assyria. Somewhat modified, it was well known in ancient Israel. In Europe, with the first dawn even of historical tradition, the existence of Heraldry may be distinguished. Nearly six hundred years before the Christian era, Æschylus described the heraldic blazonry of the chieftains who united their forces for the siege of Thebes. . . . The well-known Eagle of the Romans may be said to have presided over the Heraldry of Rome as their own Dragon has ever presided over that of the Chinese. The legendary annals of mediæval Europe abound in traces of a barbaric Heraldry, in the war-banners of the chiefs and in their personal insignia. The Bayeux tapestry of the Conqueror's Consort may be placed at the head of the early existing illustrations of the Heraldry of Britain. That celebrated piece of royal embroidery exhibits a complete display of the military ensigns in use at the period of the Conquest. . . .

"Illuminations in MSS. take up and carry on the Heraldic record. Seals, carvings in ivory, monumental memorials, stained glass, and the various productions of the architectural sculptor, gradually contribute their several memoirs, and lead us on to the full development of English mediæval Heraldry through the agency of the Crusades.

"The Crusades formed the armed followers of the different European princes into a military alliance for a common purpose, and also brought the rude yet gallant soldier of the West into contact with all that then existed in Eastern lands of the refinement, both military and social, of still earlier times. Among the many and important results of those strange and strangely romantic enterprises, were great changes in the weapons and armour of the Western chivalry; and these changes were accompanied with the introduction of an infinite variety of armorial devices. The Crusade confederacy itself would necessarily demand the adoption, by the allied sovereigns, of a more definite system of military standards and insignia than had been previously prevalent.

The use of the improved defensive armour, also, combined with a better system of organization and discipline in the armour-clad bands, rendered it necessary for each warrior of any rank to assume and wear some personal cognizance, without which he could not have been distinguished at a time when the ascertained presence of certain individuals was of such grave importance. And the device of each baron or knight would be assigned, with appropriate modifications, to their respective retainers and followers. In this manner, *Crests* were introduced, and placed on basinets and helms; and thus some recognized device or composition was displayed upon all knightly pennons and banners, and was emblazoned both upon the rich surcoats which the knights wore over their armour, and upon the shields which so long formed most important components of their defensive equipment. Such is the origin of *Shields-of-Arms* and *Coats-of-Arms*,—terms that we still retain, with the representations of the Shield, and with Crests, in our own Heraldry at the present day.

"In England, Heraldry may be considered to have first assumed a definite and systematic character during the reign of Henry III., A.D. 1216 to 1272; and at the close of the thirteenth century it may be said to have been recognized as a distinct science. The heraldic devices that were adopted in England in the thirteenth century, in common with those which were added to them during the century that followed, partook of the ideal character of all symbols, but at the same time they were distinguished by a simple and dignified expressiveness. And they were associated directly, and in a peculiar manner, either with individuals, families, establishments, potentates, or with the community at large: so that they may be considered after a definite method, their varieties readily admit of classification, their characteristics may be clearly elucidated and fully set forth, and they may be subjected to certain general laws and treated as forming a system in themselves. This classification and description, and the general laws themselves, we now unite with the devices and compositions under the common name of HERALDRY. And with the Heraldry of the thirteenth century we associate that of the fourteenth, and of succeeding centuries, and of our own era, assigning to the whole the same common title. For, as it happened in the instance of Architecture, when once it had been duly recognized in England, Heraldry rapidly attained to an advanced degree of perfection. Whatever the Heralds of Edward I. might have left to be accomplished after their time, their successors of the fourteenth century were not slow in developing. Under the genial influences of the long and brilliant reign of Edward III., mediæval Heraldry attained to its culminating point. The last quarter of the fourteenth century proved to be equally favourable to the Heralds. And again, during the Lancastrian era, and throughout the struggle of the Roses, English Heraldry maintained its reputation and its popularity. Its practical utility was felt and appreciated by the Plantagenets in their fierce social wars, as it had been before their time by the Crusaders. Then, with a general decline of the Arts, Heraldry declined. Its art-character, indeed, had shown signs of a coming degradation before the accession of the Tudors to the disputed throne of the realm. The next downward step seriously affected the early simplicity of the art-science, so that the Heraldry of the sixteenth, seventeenth, and eighteenth centuries can advance but comparatively slight claims upon our present consideration. And thus we are brought onwards to the great and general Art-Revival of our own times, in which Heraldry again appears in the act of vindicating its titles to honourable recognition, as an Art-Science that may be advantageously and agreeably studied, and very happily adapted in its practical application to the existing condition of things by ourselves."

USES OF ARMS. [1]

" *Firſt* then, They often ſhew from what Country, or Perſon, their Bearers did deſcend, and therefore (as *Mackenzie* doth well obſerve, Science of Heraldry, P. 3.) they are call'd *Teſſeræ Gentiltiæ.* Thus the *Maxwels* and *Ramſays* (ſays *Mackenzie*) bear the Eagle, to ſhew their Deſcent from *Germany :* The *Ruthwens* the Arms of Portugal, from which King they are ſaid to be deſcended : And the Name of *Majoribank* bear the Cuſhion, to ſhew that they were *Johnſtowns* originally. Thus the *Weems* and *Fyfe,* are known to be Cadets of *Mackduff;* and the *Colquhouns* and *McFarlans,* Cadets of the family of *Lennox;* and theſe (ſaith *Mackenzie*) are ſurer Marks of Conſanguinity than the Surname, as may be known by many Inſtances; and among others, the *Shaws* in the *North* are known to be *McIntoſhes* by their Arms.

" *Secondly,* They ſhew us the Alliance of their Bearers to other Families by the Heireſs from whom they deſcend, whoſe Arms are quartered by the Deſcendants; and by this Means the Memory of great Families, and even of Clans and Surnames in *Scotland,* ſaith *Mackenzie,* is only preſerved. Thus *Scotland* (adds he) by bearing a double Treſſure Flory Counter Flory, is remembered by their League betwixt *France* and them in the Reigns of *Achaius* and *Charlemaign;* and thus there are no Monuments (as he aſſerts of the *Scots,* by Instances, p. 3.) to preſerve the Memory of many ancient and worthy Families in *England,* but the quartering their Arms by their Succeſſors.

" *Thirdly,* Theſe Arms let us know, if the Bearers are Noblemen or Gentlemen, and what their Dignity is; that appearing by their Helmets, Coronets etc.

" *Fourthly,* The Shield, and oftentimes the Signet, made the Bearers who were killed in the Crowd to be known, that they might be honourably buried.

" *Fifthly,* They being appended informed us of the true Surnames of the Granters, which are become illegible; and thus, by the Seals, I have (ſaith *Mackenzie*) found ſome Charters to be granted by *Menzies* of *Weems,* when we could hardly read the Name ; and I have been (adds he) in Proceſſes, wherein Charters were alleged to be falſe and forged, becauſe the Granter's true Arms and Seal were not appended. For the *Scots* were very punctual in ſealing with their Arms, being enjoin'd by Law and Statutes in that Particular.

" *Sixthly,* By theſe Arms we are inſtructed of the right Originations and Writings of

[1] Sixth edition of Guillim (1724).

Surnames. And thus we know (fays *Mackenzie*) the Name of *Tarbet* to be wrong written, and that it fhould be written *Turbet*, feeing that they have three Turbets fretted for their Arms. He gives other inftances in p. 4.

"*Seventhly*, Thefe Arms fhew who have been Founders of Towns, Caftles, or Churches. Thus the Church of *Durham* is known to be built by the King of *Scotland*, and the Town of *Erfort* is known to be built by the *French* King, becaufe (Dreffer, p. 227.) they bear their Arms. And thus moft of our publick Buildings in *England*, fuch as our ancient Abbies, Churches and our Colleges in both Univerfities, do, for the moft Part, expofe to publick View the Arms of their Founders, as well as the ancient Seats of our Gentry do thofe of their Owners. Wherefore one of the late Editors of this Book did well obferve, that in cafe a Difpute fhould arife concerning the Right to any ruined building, or the like, he whofe Arms are found affix'd thereto, is moft interefted therein.

"*Eighthly*, Thefe Arms infer a prefumtive Right of Superiority, *Quando Arma in Portis, vel Curiis pinguntur, Bart. Tract. de infig. When they are painted in Gates and Courts.* And thus when the *Millaners* did engage to be Vaffals to the Emperor *Frederick* the Firft, they undertook to carry the Arms of the Empire upon the Steeple of their Chief Church, *Limn. de jure publ. cap. 6. num. 126.* And when *Orkney* and *Zetland* were fully refign'd to the Kings of *Scotland*, it was agreed, that the Arms of *Scotland* fhould be affix'd in their publick Courts: And thus the Dukes of *Venice* are known not to have an abfolute Jurifdiction, becaufe they are not allow'd to reprefent the Arms of their Family upon the Coin of the Publick, *Alberi, ad l. Si qui C. de oper. publ.* And one of their Dukes was feverely cenfured by the State, for having contravened this Rule in Heraldry, *Teffaur. decif.* 270. Arms do prefume Propriety in Moveables efpecially, to which Men have only right by Poffeffion, and not by Writ, *Hopping, c.* 13. And this is an ordinary Prefumption in all Judicatures, *Nam ficut ex fignis fignatum, ita ex infigniis Domini rerum cognofcuntur, Tufk. Tom. I. Concluf. 516. For as Signs declare the Thing fignified, fo Arms fhew the Owners of Goods.*

"*Ninthly*, By thefe the Ships of Enemies are known, and are accordingly confifcated, if taken at Sea; which Lawyers extend fo far, that if a Ship carry the Flag of an Enemy, it will be declared Prize, though it belong to a Kingdom in Amity with the Seizer, *Jafon, confil. 163 b. 19.*

"*Tenthly* and *laftly*, They are moft neceffary for figning Articles of Peace between Princes, Contracts and other Writs among private Perfons."

CHAPTER II.

THE HERALD.

THE herald was originally a messenger to hostile camps or one who proclaimed to the people the will and pleasure of his king. The antiquity of the office is indisputable, since reference is frequently made to it in Homer's Iliad, and in Daniel iii. 4 we have it recorded that a herald proclaimed the will and pleasure of Nebuchadnezzar, King of Babylon.

The office grew in dignity and honor as the pomp of warfare increased, and the herald came to be regarded as the representative of his sovereign; his person was held sacred and his position was considered one of the most honorable.

It was in the Middle Ages, when honor and chivalry were at their height, that this office attained its greatest dignity. A herald was created by the sovereign in person or by a special commission from him. According to Gerard Leigh, the ceremony was conducted in the following manner:

"The king asked the person to be so created whether he were a gentleman of blood or of second coat-armour; if he was not, the king gave him lands and fees, and assigned him and his heirs proper arms. Then, as the messenger was brought in by the herald of the province, so the pursuivant was brought in by the eldest herald, who, at the prince's command, performed all the ceremonies, as turning the coat of arms, setting the manucles thereof on the arms of the pursuivant, and putting about his neck a collar of SS, and when he was named, the prince himself took the cup from the herald, which was gilt, and poured the water and wine upon the head of the pursuivant, creating him by the name of *our herald*, and the king, when the oath was administered, gave the same cup to the new herald."

To appreciate the full significance of the office of the mediæval heralds, and thoroughly to understand the magnitude of their work, we must remember that its influence did not cease when the chivalric age ended, but that it lives and is of vital importance to-day. Those men and their successors instituted a system without which hopeless confusion would reign in regard to the origin of numerous social laws throughout Christendom, and it is owing entirely to the science of heraldry that the distinguishing signs of honors and privileges granted to warriors and statesmen have been preserved for the benefit of their descendants. A noted authority well says,—

"When the profession of arms became the profession of every gentleman, and the business of his life, at once employment and amusement; when martial exercises formed a part of every pageant, and the combat-camp became the court for love's disputants to decide their claims, and frequently the last supreme tribunal of appeal from the halls of justice; when man knew no other criterion of worth than the sword, and woman no other test of virtue, but cheerfully rested the justification of her arraigned innocence on the prowess of her champion, and her champion on her innocence all his hopes of victory; and when the Almighty was most frequently worshipped by the least amiable of the titles that man has given him, the God of battles,—in such a state of affairs when all that was dear and valuable so often depended on the issue of a combat, and life and fame, fortune and power, virtue and love were the stakes for which champions were daily entering the lists, it is natural that the whole proceedings should have been arranged with a caution proportionate to the importance of the event, that every possibility of unfair advantage should be precluded, and every obstacle removed to placing both parties on the most equal terms, and such laws formed as by an impartial observance of them should leave in the minds of the vanquished a full conviction of the unsoundness of their cause or resignation to the mysterious dispensations of that Providence, to whose especial care they fancied they had entrusted themselves, and by whose immediate interposition they believed it to be, that oppression should triumph and innocence be darkened for a while. To conduct the business of these proceedings required men of judgment and experience, and those to whom authority was first entrusted to arrange all matters of war and chivalry were men who had seen twenty years' service and generally such as had been disabled by their wounds. These when once possessed of such authority, could not fail to increase their own influence by creating, out of their knowledge, a system which none but the initiated could comprehend, and they bequeathed to their successors, not merely the result of their experience, but also the produce of their ingenuity: and as mystery in those times was considered essential to every science, Heraldry, among the rest, was not without its mysteries, which it was an impiety to divulge, and into which the sovereign himself had no right to inquire."

With the decay of mediæval knighthood and chivalry, the disuse of armor for defence, and the changes in the manner of warfare which attended the general employment of gunpowder, the necessity for the herald in the army was less strongly felt, and it became the custom for some inferior officer, chosen for the occasion, to bear the messages of the general to the opposing camp. The abandonment of the "trial by combat" or "wager of battle," as a means of settling disputes and suits at law, lessened the importance of the tournaments and turned them into mere pastimes, so that much of their dignity and solemnity was lost. With the disuse of knightly weapons in war, the skill in wielding them naturally declined, and even as amusements tournaments became less and less popular.

Cut off from his military office of messenger and no longer needed as a "blazoner" at tournaments, the herald gradually lost his prominence in public affairs, his duties became less known to the world, and he drifted into genealogical work. It was at this time that the clearness and simplicity of the early science were destroyed by the fantastic imagination of the age. New methods of blazoning were introduced; precious stones, the planets, the days of the week, and other curious systems were adopted for describing the tinctures of arms, instead of the simple metals and colors used in the early days. A great number of technical and frivolous rules were made, each herald differing from every other, until the whole system became confused and heraldry fell into discredit. It seems to be the general tendency of the present day to disregard this confused mass of rules, and return to the science as it existed in its purity.

In England, in modern times, armorial bearings have been regulated by the College of Arms or Heralds' College. At the head of this college is the Earl Marshal of England, and this office, of great antiquity and honor, is hereditary in the family of the Duke of Norfolk. It is the prerogative of the Earl Marshal to appoint and control all Kings-of-Arms, Heralds, and Pursuivants, except those of the Lyon Office, and through the various Kings-of-Arms he confirms arms and pedigrees, and grants new armorial bearings to those who are not entitled to them by descent, but who are nevertheless in a position to sustain the rank of gentleman. The granting of supporters to those below the rank of a Knight Grand Cross of the Bath does not come within the jurisdiction of the Earl Marshal. Such privileges are granted by the Sovereign only, as a mark of royal favor, in reward for important services to the state; in Scotland, however, they may be borne by the authority of the Lyon King-of-Arms.

The date at which the English College of Arms or Heralds' College was organized remains uncertain, but it is generally believed to have been during the reign of Henry V., though it was not incorporated until much later,—in 1483, by a charter from Richard III. The body then established varied from time to time until 1622, when it was limited to three Kings-of-Arms, six Heralds, and four Pursuivants. The GARTER KING-OF-ARMS, so called from his official connection with the Most Noble Order of the Garter, is the chief, and has jurisdiction over all England; under him, the CLARENCEUX KING-OF-ARMS, originally *Sorroy King-of-Arms*, has jurisdiction over England *South* of the Trent, and the NORROY KING-OF-ARMS, over England *North* of the Trent. The Heralds,—WINDSOR, CHESTER, YORK and LANCASTER were created by Edward III.; the RICHMOND HERALD was created by Edward IV., and the SOMERSET HERALD by Henry VIII. The official costume of a herald consists of an embroidered satin tabard or surcoat of the Royal Arms and a collar of SS.

The Pursuivants-of-Arms, whose duties, like those of the heralds, consist in tracing arms and genealogies and in regulating public feasts and processions, are,—ROUGE CROIX, the earliest created, and named "Red Cross" from the Cross of St. George; BLUE MANTLE, named by Edward III., on account of a blue French coat which he wore; ROUGE DRAGON, created by Henry VII., and named for one of the supporters of that king's arms; and PORTCULLIS, also created by Henry VII., and named for the portcullis which the king had adopted as one of his royal badges.

The present duties of the Heralds' College "comprise Grants of Arms; the Tracing and Drawing up of Genealogies; the Recording of Arms and Genealogies in the Registers of the Heralds' College; recording the Creation and Succession of Peers and others, with all similar matters, including the direction of Royal Pageants and Ceremonials."

The BATH KING-OF-ARMS, or, as he is sometimes termed, the *Gloucester King-of-Arms*, was created for the service of the Most Honorable Order of the Bath. He was soon after given jurisdiction over Wales and the power to grant arms to persons residing in that principality. Although not a member of the English Heralds' College, the Bath King is closely connected with it and takes precedence of Clarenceux and Norroy.

In Scotland, the duties of the English College of Arms are performed by the Lyon Office. Over this the LYON KING-OF-ARMS, or Lord Lyon, presides, and under him there were for many years six Heralds,—ROTHSAY, MARCHMONT, ISLAY, ALBANY, SNOWDON, and ROSS; six Pursuivants,—DINGWELL, BUTE, CARRICK, ORMOND, KINTYRE, and UNICORN; the LYON DEPUTE; the LYON CLERK and the LYON CLERK DEPUTE; and a PROCURATOR FISCAL; but by Statute (30 Vict. cap. 17) passed 3d of May, 1867, it was decreed that the Lord Lyon and the Lyon Clerk should discharge the duties of their respective offices in person, and hence the office of depute was abolished in both instances. By the same statute it was decreed that:—"No vacancy in the Office of Herald in Scotland shall be filled up by the Lyon King-of-Arms until the number of Heralds has, by death, resignation, or removal, fallen to below three, after which event the vacancies which may occur in said office shall be filled up, so that the number of Heralds shall in time coming be maintained at three." The same provisions are made for reducing the number of Pursuivants to three. The Heralds now are Rothsay, Marchmont, and Albany; the Pursuivants, Unicorn, Carrick, and Bute. The Lyon King-of-Arms is appointed by the Sovereign, and not by the Earl Marshal, as the other Kings-of-Arms are. His powers are in some respects greater than those of the Earl Marshal, particularly in the right to grant supporters, already noticed. In rank he is next to the Garter King-of-Arms, and occupies a position in the Most Noble and Most Ancient Order of the Thistle similar to that occupied by the Garter King in the Most Noble Order of the Garter. The Lyon Clerk is also appointed by the Sovereign, but the Heralds and Pursuivants, as well as a *Herald Painter* and a *Procurator Fiscal*, are appointed by Lord Lyon.

In Ireland the place of the Heralds' College is taken by the Office of Arms, whose duties are, according to late advices, discharged by the Ulster King-of-Arms and the Athlone Pursuivant. The Ulster King-of-Arms is the head of the office, and he is also officially connected with the Most Illustrious Order of St. Patrick.

In early times the heralds made periodical *Visitations* to the various provinces of the realm, and summoned all those bearing arms and those styling themselves Esquires or Gentlemen to appear before the proper officers and prove their right to the arms or titles. On these visitations pedigrees were inquired into, and arms were traced, and an accurate record was kept of both at the Heralds' College. Many of these records have come down to us, and in them are found the hereditary arms of the older English families. The first of these visitations was probably undertaken in the early part of the fifteenth century, but the records are fragmentary until a century later. From 1529 until 1687 the circuits of the kingdom were regularly made every twenty or thirty years, and these records of pedigrees and arms have proved invaluable to the genealogist and herald.

In following the development of the messenger between armies into the member of the College of Arms of the present day, one contrast cannot have failed to strike the mind of the most careless reader,—it is that between the herald of the Middle Ages, associated with the brilliant life of the mediæval camp and the gorgeous display of the tournament, and the modern herald, a man of peace, a scholar, and antiquarian.

CHAPTER III.

In the fine arts, heraldry occupies a prominent position, since, in most historical sculptures and paintings in which scenes or characters of the Middle Ages are displayed, the laws of heraldry must be closely followed, and the sculptor or painter requires to be familiar with the growth of the science and the forms in use at the different stages of its development. Historical accuracy is now deemed of great importance in all branches of art, and anachronisms are severely criticised. One example of an error of this sort exists in Leutze's well-known picture of Washington crossing the Delaware in December, 1776, in which the stars and stripes are displayed, when, in fact, the flag bearing them was not accepted until the fourteenth of the following June. In the picture of " The Boston Boys and General Gage," the British Union Jack is shown over the porch of the Providence House in the form which was not adopted until a quarter of a century after the occurrence depicted in the painting. The same mistake occurs twice in the frescoes in the Houses of Parliament. One of these represents the Mayflower sailing for America in 1620 with the Union Jack of 1801 flying! In another fresco, Charles II. is represented landing in England under the same flag.

Similar errors are very common in architecture also. One of the best known of these blunders is seen on the tomb of Elizabeth in the chapel of King Henry VII. There the arms ascribed to William the Conqueror are *impaled* with those of his wife. The system of impaling in its very earliest form, that of dimidiation, was not introduced until the time of Edward I., two hundred years later.

The most glaring anachronisms exist in the exemplification of American seals. We see documents with copies of State seals upon them which are intended to emphasize certain periods in America's history, but which were not designed until years after the dates they are supposed to commemorate. For instance; an example of the seal of New Jersey upon a colonial document bears the three ploughs, which were not adopted until 1776, the New Jersey seals having borne the various royal arms, and, previous to those, the arms of Berkeley and Carteret, as proprietors, and for six months after the Revolution the arms of Governor Livingston. In another illustration, the colonial seal of New Hampshire is depicted as bearing the ship upon the stocks. It is a matter of record that this device was not adopted until 1784. Representations of the French arms, supposed to be those borne by the French in America prior to the Revolution, are shown with the shield charged semé de lis, while it is of historical record that Charles V., in 1365, reduced the number of fleurs-de-lis in the French arms to three, and since then they have been so borne. In another representation, the arms of Maryland are included in a group of seals indicating the Revolutionary period, but instead of Lord Baltimore's crest, an eagle is shown.

Mr. W. H. Browne, of the Johns Hopkins University, Baltimore, in a letter dated October 28, 1880, states that "the legislature, some twenty-five or thirty years ago, swept away the Cap and Crest and put in their place an unmeaning eagle, which remained until about 1873 or 1874, when the ancient device was restored." Thus it is seen that the eagle did not appear in the Maryland arms until seventy-five years after the Revolution.

For the understanding of Gothic architecture in particular a knowledge of Heraldry is essential. A popular writer claims that "Every Gothic Architect ought to be a thorough Herald. Heraldry alone can enable him to render his works, in the noblest and most perfect sense, historic monuments. Without Heraldry, no lover of the great art, which has been so happily revived amongst us, is able to feel the full power of what the Gothic has transmitted to him from the olden time, or to realize all that it is now able to accomplish as a living Art."

An enthusiast has gone so far as to say of heraldry that "no one's education is complete until he shall have studied and mastered its laws and detail." While this assertion may not be accepted in its broad sense, it is true in the sense that the educated man who is acquainted with heraldry will derive much more pleasure and profit from history and literature than one who is not familiar with the science. In fact, heraldry is so closely connected with history that a certain amount of heraldic knowledge is indispensable for the historian. In the works of all early English writers, heraldic terms are constantly used; while in old ballads the personages are frequently called by their crests or devices, instead of by their proper names. Many parts of Shakespeare's historical plays would be almost unintelligible without an heraldic commentary, and Scott's works, both prose and verse, abound in allusions which must be entirely lost upon those of his readers who are deficient in heraldic learning. Many of the romances of the Middle Ages contain descriptions of tournaments, and Scott's "Ivanhoe" has made the spectacle a familiar one to every reader of English. In Chaucer's "Knight's Tale" the gorgeous accessories of the lists are described, and the combat for the hand of Emelie is precisely such as would have taken place in Chaucer's time. During the reign of Richard II., such ceremonies were conducted with the greatest pomp, and in Shakespeare's play the preliminaries are well described. Lohengrin appears as the champion of Elsa's innocence in a trial of this kind in Wagner's opera.

A few quotations, chosen at random from English literature, as illustrations of the use of heraldic terms by our best authors, may interest the reader.

Richard III., when the tide has turned against him at the battle of Bosworth, eagerly seeks Richmond, so that by killing him he may destroy the hope of the enemy, and at last exclaims,—

> " I think there be six Richmonds in the field ;
> Five have I slain to-day instead of him."
>
> *Richard III.*, Act V., Scene 4.

This is an allusion to the practice of having several knights bear in battle the devices of their lord in order to mislead the enemy.

Henry Bolingbroke, afterwards King Henry IV., on his return from banishment, tells of his degradation by Richard II.:

> " From my own windows torn my household coat,
> Raz'd out my impress, leaving me no sign,
> Save men's opinions and my living blood,
> To show the world I am a gentleman."
>
> *Richard II.*, Act III., Scene 1.

Frequent reference is made to the badge of the Beauchamps, Earls of Warwick, inherited by the Neville family, Earls of Salisbury and Warwick,—

FIG. 1.

> "*Clif.* Might I but know thee by thy household badge.
> *War.* Now, by my father's badge, old Nevil's crest,
> The rampant bear chain'd to the ragged staff,
> This day I'll wear aloft my burgonet,
>
> *   *   *   *   *   *   *   *
>
> Even to affright thee with the view thereof."
>
> *Second Part of King Henry VI.*, Act V., Scene 1.

Richard Plantagenet, in the same scene, means the Nevilles—father and son—where he cries,—

> " Call hither to the stake my two brave bears,
> That with the very shaking of their chains
> They may astonish these fell-lurking curs :
> Bid Salisbury and Warwick come to me."

In the Third Part of King Henry VI., Edward congratulates himself on the security of his throne, and refers to the Earl of Warwick, " The King-Maker," and his brother, the Marquis of Montague, as among the noble slain :

> " With them the two brave bears, Warwick and Montague,
> That in their chains fetter'd the kingly lion."
>
> Act V., Scene 7.

The cognizance of Richard III. was a white boar, and it is to him that Hastings alludes when he says,—

> " To fly the boar before the boar pursues
> Were to incense the boar to follow us,
> And make pursuit where he did mean no chase."
>
> *King Richard III.*, Act III., Scene 2.

Gloster, afterwards King Richard III., refers to the badge of Edward IV. —the *sun in splendor*—when he says at the opening of the play,—

FIG. 2.

> " Now is the winter of our discontent
> Made glorious summer by this sun of York."
>
> *King Richard III.*

Henry VI., following the custom introduced by Edward III., bore the Royal Arms of France in the first and third quarters of his arms, to show that the English kings claimed the crown of France. Henry IV. changed the French quarters in the Royal Arms of England from France Ancient to France Modern, since this change had been made in the French Arms about forty years before by Charles V. (See Figs. 538 and 539.) It is to the decline of English success in the French wars, after the death of King Henry V., that the messenger refers when he exclaims,—

> " Awake, awake, English nobility !
> Let not sloth dim your honours, new-begot :
> Cropp'd are the flower-de-luces in your arms ;
> Of England's coat one-half is cut away."
>
> *First Part of King Henry VI.*, Act I., Scene 1.

In the same play the noble Talbot cries at a moment when defeat seems imminent,—

> " Hark, countrymen ! either renew the fight
> Or tear the lions out of England's coat ;
> Renounce your soil, give sheep in lions' stead."
>
> Act I., Scene 5.

The famous badges, the white rose of York and the red rose of Lancaster, are frequently referred to. Near the close of the scene in the Temple Garden, in which the roses were adopted as emblems, Somerset (Lancaster) cries,—

FIG. 3.

> " Ah, thou shalt find us ready for thee still ;
> And know us by these colours for thy foes,
> For these my friends, in spite of thee, shall wear."

Plantagenet (York),—

FIG. 4.

" And, by my soul, this pale and angry rose,
    As cognizance of my blood-drinking hate,
    Will I forever, and my faction, wear,
    Until it wither with me to my grave,
    Or flourish to the height of my degree."

First Part of King Henry VI., Act II., Scene 4.

The Tudor Rose, formed by the union of the roses of York and Lancaster, was borne as a badge by Henry VII., to symbolize the union of the two factions by his marriage with Elizabeth of York. Thus Henry, after his success at Bosworth, says,—

FIG. 5.

" We will unite the white rose and the red."

King Richard III., Act V., Scene 5.

Scott refers to the same cognizance:

" Let merry England proudly rear
    Her blended Roses bought so dear."

In Canto First of Scott's " Marmion," we have a description of Marmion in armor, with his arms emblazoned on his shield. It will be noticed that the rule that " color shall not be placed upon color " is violated by the *falcon sable* on an *azure* field. Sir Walter, however, defended himself against the charge of false heraldry by declaring that the rule was of comparatively recent date, and in earlier times there were few strict rules, so that a knight bore the tinctures which pleased him best.

FIG. 6.

" Well was he arm'd from head to heel,
    In mail and plate of Milan steel;
    But his strong helm, of mighty cost,
    Was all with burnished gold emboss'd;
    Amid the plumage of the crest
    A falcon hover'd on her nest,
    With wings outspread, and forward breast:
    E'en such a falcon, on his shield,
    Soar'd sable in an azure field:
    The golden legend bore aright,
    ' Who checks at me, to death is dight.'
    Blue was the charger's broider'd rein;
    Blue ribbons decked his arching mane;
    The knightly housing's ample fold
    Was velvet blue, and trapp'd with gold."

*   *   *   *   *   *   *   *

" On high his forky pennon bore ;
Like swallow's tail, in shape and hue,
Flutter'd the streamer glossy blue,
Where, blazon'd sable, as before,
The towering falcon seem'd to soar.
Last, twenty yeomen, two and two,
In hosen black, and jerkins blue,
With falcons broider'd on each breast,
Attended on their lord's behest."

FIG. 7.

In Canto IV. we have a description of the Scottish camp :

" A thousand streamers flaunted fair,
    Various in shape, device, and hue,
    Green, sanguine, purple, red, and blue,
Broad, narrow, swallow-tail'd, and square,
Scroll, pennon, pensil, bandrol, there
    O'er the pavilions flew.
Highest, and midmost, was descried
The royal banner floating wide ;
    The staff, a pine-tree, strong and straight,
Pitch'd deeply in a massive stone,
Which still in memory is shown,
    Yet bent beneath the standard's weight
    Whene'er the western wind unroll'd,
    With toil, the huge and cumbrous fold,
And gave to view the dazzling field,
Where, in proud Scotland's royal shield,
The ruddy lion ramp'd in gold."

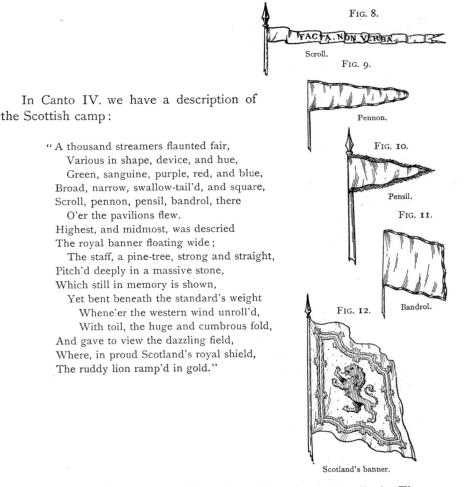

FIG. 8.

FACTA. NON VERBA.

Scroll.

FIG. 9.

Pennon.

FIG. 10.

Pensil.

FIG. 11.

Bandrol.

FIG. 12.

Scotland's banner.

In Canto Sixth a carving of the arms of Douglas is described. The arms were anciently *azure, three stars argent*, but the *crowned heart* was added by the successors of the Black Douglas to commemorate his pilgrimage to the

Holy Land bearing the heart of Bruce.   The arms are now blazoned, *Argent,
a heart gules, ensigned with an imperial crown proper; on a chief azure, three
mullets of the field.*

FIG. 13.

" Above the rest, a turret square
    Did o'er its Gothic entrance bear,
    Of sculpture rude, a stony shield ;
    The Bloody Heart was in the field,
    And in the chief three mullets stood,
    The cognizance of Douglas blood."

The procession preceding " Lord Lyon King-at-Arms" is thus described :

" First came the trumpets, at whose clang
    So late the forest echoes rang ;
    On prancing steeds they forward press'd,
    With scarlet mantle, azure vest ;
    Each at his trump a banner wore,
    Which Scotland's royal scutcheon bore :
    Heralds and pursuivants, by name
    Bute, Islay, Marchmount, Rothsay, came
    In painted tabards, proudly showing
    Gules, argent, or, and azure glowing,
    Attendant on a king-at-arms."

Sir David Lindsay, one of the most famous of the Lyon Kings, follows his
Heralds and Pursuivants, and his accoutrements are minutely chronicled :

" On milk-white palfrey forth he paced ;
    His cap of maintenance was graced
        With the proud heron-plume.
    From his steed's shoulder, loin, and breast
        Silk housings swept the ground,
    With Scotland's arms, device, and crest
        Embroidered round and round.
    The double tressure might you see,
        First by Achaius borne,
    The thistle and the fleur-de-lis,
        And gallant unicorn.
    So bright the king's armorial coat,
    That scarce the dazzled eye could note,
    In living colors, blazon'd brave,
    The lion, which his title gave."

In " The Lay of the Last Minstrel," the *Lion passant argent*, the badge of
the Duke of Norfolk, is thus vaunted :

" For who in field or foray slack
    Saw the blanche lion e'er fall back ?"
                                        Canto IV.

The war-cry of the Homes, which has now become the motto of the family, occurs in its older use in " The Lay of the Last Minstrel":

> " Nor list I say what hundreds more,
> From the rich Merse and Lammermoor,
> And Tweed's fair borders, to the war,
> Beneath the crest of old Dunbar,
> And Hepburn's mingled banners come,
> Down the steep mountain glittering far,
> And shouting still, ' A Home ! A Home !' "

William Dunbar, in " The Thistle and the Rose" (1503), refers thus to the Scottish lion:

> " This awfull beist full terrible of cheir,
> Persing of luke and stout of countenance,
> Ryght strong of corpes, of fassoun fair, but feir,
> Lusty of shap, lycht of deliverance,
> Reid of his cullour as the ruby glance.
> In field of gold he stude full myghtely
> With floure de lucis sirculit lustely."

The tradition is that the badge of the Prince of Wales, three ostrich plumes and the motto " Ich Dien," was won by the Black Prince from John, King of Bohemia, at Crécy, and adopted as an emblem of his victory. It is to this that Aleyn refers:

FIG. 14.

> " There lay the trophie of our chivalry,
> Plumed of his ostridge feathers, which the Prince
> Tooke as the ensign of his victory,
> Which he did after weare and ever since
> The Prince of Wales doth that atchievement beare,
> Which Edward first did win by conquest there."

FIG. 15.

> " Upon his breast a bloodie Cross he bore,
> The deare remembrance of his dying Lord,
> For Whose sweet sake that glorious badge he bore,
> And dead, as living, ever Him adored ;
> Upon his shield the like was also scored,
> For sovereign hope which on His help he had."
>
> SPENSER.

Chaucer, in " The Rime of Sir Thopas," describes the armor of the knight:

> " And over that his cote armour,
> As whit as is a lilye flour,
> In which he wol debate.[1]

[1] Fight.

> " His sheeld was al of gold so reed
> And ther-inne was a bores hed,
> A charbocle [1] bisyde."

In " The Knight's Tale," after the battle in which Theseus captures Thebes, Palamon and Arcite are found among the heaps of slain :

> " And so bifel, that in the taas [2] they founde,
> Thrugh-girt with many grevous blody wounde,
> Two yonge knightes, liggynge by and by,[3]
> Bothe in oon armes wroght ful richely :
>
> *　　*　　*　　*　　*　　*　　*　　*
>
> " Nat fully quyke, ne fully dede they were.
> But by here cote-armures, and by hir gere,
> The heraudes knewe hem best in special,
> As they that weren of the blood roial [4]
> Of Thebes, and of sustren [5] two yborn."

DRAYTON.

FIG. 16.

> " Upon his surcoat valiant Neville bore
> A silver saltire upon martial red."

> " Behold the eagles, lions, talbots, bears,
> The badges of our famous ancestors."

> " A Raven sat on Corbet's armed head."

In many old ballads the characters are called by their badges rather than by their names ; thus, in " The Battle of Towton," the Rose stands for the Earl of March, the Ragged Staf for the Earl of Warwick, the Fisshe Hoke for Lord Fauconberg, the Cornysshe Chowghe for Lord Scrope :

> " The way unto the North contre, the Rose ful fast he sought ;
> Wt him went ye Ragged Staf, yt many men dere bought ;
> The Fisshe Hoke came into the feld wt ful egre mode,
> So did the Cornysshe Chowghe and brought forth all hir brode."

" The Rising of the North Countree :"

> " Now spread thine Ancyent [6] Westmorland,
> Thy Dun Bull faine would we spye ;
> And thou, the Earle of Northumberland,
> Now raise thy Half-Moone up on hye."

---

[1] Carbuncle.　　[2] Heap.　　[3] Lying side by side.　　[4] Royal.　　[5] Sisters.
[6] *Ancyent,* a sort of banner.　See dictionary.

The badge of the Percys, Earls of Northumberland, a *crescent argent*, is referred to in another ballad:

> " The minstrels of thy noble house
> All clad in robes of blue,
> With silver Crescents on their arms,
> Attend in order due."

In a ballad in Scott's " Minstrelsy of the Scottish Border," the old blazon for a *lion passant guardant*, a *leopard*, or *libbard*, appears in referring to the lions of England. The victory of the English is graphically symbolized by the boast that the " Libbards " on England's banner shall tear the Scottish Lion from the golden field on which he is displayed.

> " There shall the lion lose the gylte
> And the libbards bear it clean away
> At Pinkyn Cleutch, there shall be spilt
> Much gentle bluid that day."

In " Owen Glyndwr's War Song" Felicia Hemans mentions the comet or " blazing star" which appeared in 1402 and was interpreted as favorable to the Welsh cause. Owen Glyndwr assumed the name of " The Dragon" in imitation of Uthyr, the father of King Arthur, who bore as his cognizance, during the wars against the Saxons, a star with a dragon beneath it, since such a star, appearing near the beginning of the strife, was regarded as an omen of his success.

> " Saw ye the blazing star?
> The heavens look down on freedom's war,
> And light her torch on high:
> Bright on the dragon crest,
> It tells that glory's wing shall rest
> When warriors meet to die."

Among writers, none have used heraldic language with more beautiful effect, and none probably more correctly, than Tennyson. In " Merlin and Vivien" a particularly attractive verse is presented:

> " And Merlin lock'd his hand in hers and said,
> ' I once was looking for a magic weed,
> And found a fair young squire who sat alone,
> Had carved himself a knightly shield of wood,
> And then was painting on it fancied arms,
> Azure, an Eagle rising or, the Sun
> In dexter chief; the scroll " I follow fame."
> And speaking not, but leaning over him,
> I took his brush and blotted out the bird,
> And made a Gardener putting in a graff,
> With this motto, " Rather use than fame."
> You should have seen him blush; but afterwards
> He made a stalwart knight.'

FIG. 17.

The care of Lancelot's shield by Elaine forms the first verse of the popular poem:

> " Elaine the fair, Elaine the lovable,
> Elaine, the lily maid of Astolat,
> High in her chamber up a tower to the east
> Guarded the sacred shield of Lancelot;
> Which first she placed where morning's earliest ray
> Might strike it, and awake her with the gleam ;
> Then fearing rust or soilure, fashion'd for it
> A case of silk, and braided thereupon
> All the devices blazon'd on the shield
> In their own tint, and added, of her wit,
> A border fantasy of branch and flower."

When Lancelot lies hidden, ill of his wound received at the tournament of the diamond, and King Arthur has despatched a knight in search of him, this messenger finds his shield in the possession of Elaine and recognizes it:

> " And when the shield was brought, and Gawain saw
> Sir Lancelot's azure lions, crown'd with gold,
> Ramp in the field, he smote his thigh, and mock'd ;
> ' Right was the King ! our Lancelot ! that true man !' "

The suggestion of a *fesse* or a *bend*, charged, is contained in the following:

> " And out of this she plaited broad and long
> A strong sword-belt, and wove with silver thread
> And crimson in the belt a strange device,
> A crimson grail within a silver beam ;
> And saw the bright boy-knight, and bound it on him."
> *The Holy Grail.*

A knight of " The Last Tournament" is thus described:

> " An ocean-sounding welcome to one knight,
> But newly-enter'd, taller than the rest,
> And armor'd all in forest green, whereon
> There tript a hundred tiny silver deer,
> And wearing but a holly-spray for crest,
> With ever-scattering berries, and on shield
> A spear, a harp, a bugle—Tristram—late
> From overseas in Brittany return'd."

One verse of " Gareth and Lynette" calls to mind the statement of an old writer, that a shield was borne without any device or decoration, until, owing to some valiant or meritorious action, the bearer was granted distinguishing marks:

" For, midway down the side of that long hall
 A stately pile,—whereof along the front,
 Some blazon'd, some but carven, and some blank,
 There ran a treble range of stony shields,—
 Rose, and high-arching overbrow'd the hearth.
 And under every shield a knight was named :
 For this was Arthur's custom in his hall ;
 When some good knight had done one noble deed,
 His arms were carven only ; but if twain
 His arms were blazon'd also : but if none
 The shield was blank and bare without a sign
 Saving the name beneath ; and Gareth saw
 The shield of Gawain blazon'd rich and bright,
 And Modred's blank as death."

THE WAYSIDE INN.

" But first the Landlord will I trace :
 Grave in his aspect and attire,
 A man of ancient pedigree,
 A Justice of the Peace was he,
 Known in all Sudbury as " The Squire."
 Proud was he of his name and race,
 Of old Sir William and Sir Hugh,
 And in the parlor, full in view,
 His Coat-of-Arms, well framed and glazed,
 Upon the wall in colors blazed ;
 He beareth gules upon his shield,
 A chevron argent in the field,
 With three wolf's heads, and for the crest
 A wyvern part-per-pale addressed
 Upon a helmet barred ; below,
 The scroll reads, " By the name of Howe,"
 And over this, no longer bright,
 Though glimmering with a latent light,
 Was hung the sword his grandsire bore
 In the rebellious days of yore,
 Down there at Concord in the fight."

FIG. 18.

LONGFELLOW.

" His sev'n-fold Targe, a *field of gules* did stain
 In which two swords, he bore his word ; Divide and reign."

P. FLETCHER.

" Follow thy drum ;
 With man's blood paint the ground *gules, gules*."

SHAKESPEARE.

Like a hawk which feeling herself freed,
 From *bells and jesses* which did let her flight."

SPENSER.

" Between the *increscent* and *decrescent* moon."

TENNYSON.

" *Two gemels silver between two griffins passant.*"

STRYPE.

" On sounding wings a *dexter* eagle flew."

POPE.

" The *lion of England* and the *lilies of France* without the *baton sinister*, under which, according to the laws of heraldry, they were *debruised* in token of his illegitimate birth."

MACAULAY.

" Whose nether parts, with their bases, were of watchet cloth of silver, *chevroned* all over with lace."   B. JONSON.

" The King gave us the arms of England to be borne in a *canton* in our arms."

EVELYN.

" Not like those steps on heaven's *azure*."

MILTON.

" Yonder *argent* fields above."

POPE.

" *Standards* and *gonfalons* 'twixt van and rear,
Stream in the air."   MILTON.

" A battered *morion* on his brow."

SIR WALTER SCOTT.

" Hang up your *ensigns*, let your drums be still."

SHAKESPEARE.

" His obscure funeral :
No trophy, sword or *hatchment* over his bones."

SHAKESPEARE.

" The *tressured fleur-de-luce* he claims
To wreath his *shield*."

SIR WALTER SCOTT.

" Turns thither his *regardant* eye."

SOUTHEY.

" The fierce lion in his kind which goeth *rampant* after his prey."

GOWER.

" The lion *rampant* shakes his brinded mane."

MILTON.

" The deer is *lodged ;* I have tracked her to her covert."

ADDISON.

" Now put your shields before your hearts and fight,
With hearts more proof than shields."

SHAKESPEARE.

" The *lozenged* panes of a very small latticed window."

C. BRONTË.

CHAPTER IV.

HERALDRY IN AMERICA.

THE bearing of coats of arms in this country has been sometimes faulted, but there is surely no reason why any individual in America should be deterred, by ignorant or malicious criticism, from preserving, for himself or his children, the heraldic devices which were borne by his ancestors, even though in his own land such devices have no governmental recognition, and are not of official record in any herald's office. The fact that arms were borne here during Colonial times creates of them American arms, and is sufficient authority for their use by descendants of the old families. It is an historical fact that the early settlers did not emigrate to this country with the view of severing family connections, or discarding the customs of their various nations. The love they bore their mother-country was evinced by the loyalty with which they adhered to home customs, and by the fact that nearly all their villages and cities were named after, or were similar in name to, those from which they came.

Cussans, in his recent edition, very justly remarks: "It is no matter of surprise that Americans, particularly those of the Eastern States, with all their veneration for Republican principles, should be desirous of tracing their origin to the early settlers; and of proving their descent from those single-hearted, God-fearing men who sought in a foreign land that religious liberty which was denied them at home." Many seals, engraved with the arms of these early settlers, are now in the possession of their descendants or exhibited by various American historical societies.

An interesting group of individual seals may be described as follows:

In Massachusetts, the civil commissions bore the seal of the Province. The commissions of the military officers were from the Governor, who, as commander-in-chief and vice-admiral of the forces of the Province, signed them as such, and under his seal-at-arms. Examples of the gubernatorial seals are with few exceptions quite common; the one which is deemed the most rare is that of Governor Samuel Shute, 1716–1723, affixed to a military commission. There is but one known impression of this seal, which is in the possession of Walter Kendall Watkins, Esq., Assistant Librarian of the New England Historical Society.

The following examples are from the report of the Massachusetts House of Representatives, April 29, 1885:

FIG. 19.

Sir William Phipps,
Governor, 1691-1694.

FIG. 20.

William Stoughton,
Lieutenant-Governor, 1694-1699.

FIG. 21.

Earl of Bellomont,
Governor, 1699-1701.

FIG. 22.

Joseph Dudley,
Governor, 1702-1715.

FIG. 23.

Samuel Shute,
Governor, 1716-1722.

FIG. 24.

William Dummer,
Lieutenant-Governor, 1723-1728.

FIG. 25.

William Burnet,
Governor, 1728-1729.

FIG. 26.

Jonathan Belcher,
Governor, 1730-1741.

FIG. 27.

William Shirley,
Governor, 1741-1757.

FIG. 28.

Thomas Pownall,
Governor, 1757-1760.

FIG. 29.

Francis Bernard,
Governor, 1760-1769.

FIG. 30.

Thomas Hutchinson,
Governor, 1769-1774.

THE HISTORICAL SOCIETY OF PENNSYLVANIA.[1]

If doubt exists in the mind of any one as to the use of heraldry in the early days of America, such doubt may be readily dispelled by a visit to the Historical Society of Pennsylvania, Thirteenth and Locust Streets, Philadelphia. Here are found carefully preserved documents of Colonial and post-Revolutionary times, bearing their heraldic seals, official and individual, still distinct enough to be interpreted.

Old books in endless numbers contain engravings of arms and heraldic devices in book-plates of ancient pattern. Notable is the Bible of William Penn, dated 1698, containing a book-plate of the Penn arms. A book-plate of General Washington is also shown in one of the cases, and musty old army commissions still bear the clear impressions of their seals in paper or wax.

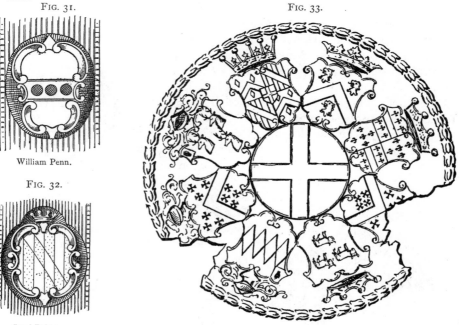

FIG. 31.

William Penn.

FIG. 32.

Lord Baltimore.

FIG. 33.

In the study an old example of the *American eagle, displayed*, executed in gold relief, supports the national shield upon his breast, and on the chief are *three mullets*, suggestive of the arms of Washington.

The arms of Penn are executed in bold relief in iron-work upon the front windows, and an illuminated cast of the same arms is hung upon the inner walls.

These arms are again seen hanging side by side with those of Lord Balti-

[1] The author notes the valuable assistance rendered by Frederick D. Stone, Esq., and John Woolf Jordan, Esq.

more, where it is noted that the tinctures are not correctly indicated (Figs. 31 and 32). The originals are upon stones upon either side of Mason and Dixon's Line.

Upon the same wall we see the great seal of the lord proprietors of the Province of Carolina, the reverse of which bears a grouping of their individual arms (Fig. 33). Their fac-simile signatures are appended in the following order:

Clarendon (Lord Clarendon).
Albemarle (General Monk, Duke of Albemarle).
Craven (Lord Craven).
Will Berkeley (Sir William Berkeley, Governor of Virginia).
Ashley (Lord Ashley Cooper, afterwards Earl of Shaftesbury).
Carteret (Sir George Carteret).
John Berkeley (Lord Berkeley).
Jno. Colleton (Sir John Colleton).

FIG. 34.

The old seal of the United States, as shown in Fig. 274, is distinctly impressed upon a document, signed by George Washington, appointing *David Lenox* marshal of Pennsylvania District.

Benjamin Franklin's seal of office (Fig. 34) is attached in wax to the appointment of *Richard Bache, Esq.*, "for Secretary, Comptroller and Receiver General of the General Post Office," and a fine example of an ecclesiastical seal (Fig. 35) is boldly impressed upon a grant,

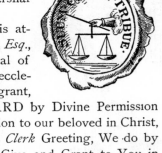

FIG. 35.

viz.: "RICHARD by Divine Permission Bishop of London to our beloved in Christ, *Richard Peters, Clerk* Greeting, We do by these Presents Give and Grant to You in whose Fidelity, Morals, Learning, Sound Doctrine and Diligence we do fully confide our Licence & Authority (to continue only during our pleasure) To perform the Office of a Priest in the United Churches of Christ Church and Saint Peters in the City of Philadelphia in North America," etc. etc.

Great interest is aroused by the old heraldic flag (Fig. 36) which was made by the Pennsylvania Volunteers while on their way to Mexico, and under which they fought so gallantly; beside this flag are also exhibited two embroidered banners bearing the American eagle and severally the inscriptions, "First Regiment

Pennsylvania Volunteers," "Second Regiment Pennsylvania Volunteers." These flags were presented to
the troops, upon the heights of Mexico, by General

FIG. 36.

Scott. Here too is what may be called
a genuine American helmet, a rusty old
morion, a true relic of the colonial soldier, which was dug up on the banks
of the Susquehanna (Fig. 37).

FIG. 37.

It would be useless to attempt to mention the
Society's wealth of literary treasures pertaining to the
heraldry of America, which are of such great value,
alike to the genealogist and heraldist. The books contain enough book-
plates alone to furnish months of interesting study, and the various historical
works upon the seals, arms, and coins of America are replete with facts and
illustrations.

INDEPENDENCE HALL.

FIG. 38.

In Independence Hall, Philadelphia, a very odd
coat of arms in proper colors is seen upon the genealogy of *Cæsar Rodney*, one of the signers of the Declaration of Independence, and Governor of Delaware.
These arms are doubly interesting from the fact that
they bear three crests, and the tincture *purpure* appears
in the devices. They may be properly described as
follows: ARMS: *Or, three eagles displ. purp.* CRESTS:
1. *A boar's head sa. couped gu.* 2. *Out of a ducal
coronet or, an eagle rising, purp.* 3. *A demi-talbot arg.*
eared and langued gu. ducally gorged or (Fig. 38).

In the same room are collected the coats of arms of
the thirteen original States, painted in proper colors upon
shields; the seal of Penn, a jug bearing the Washington
arms, Colonial flags, etc.; and a moulded coat of arms
surmounts the portrait of Thomas Cushing, and forms a
portion of the frame (Fig. 39). ARMS: *Quarterly, I. and
IV. gu. an eagle displ. arg.*, II. and III. *gu. two dexter
hands bendways couped. A canton chequy or and az.*
CREST: *Two lion's gambs erased sa. supporting a ducal
coronet or, from which hangs a human heart gu.*

FIG. 39.

Other proofs that heraldry was early practised in
America, and that its use was not entirely abandoned
after the Revolution, are to be found on tombstones and
memorials throughout New England, the Middle and Southern States, and
probably exist in other parts of the country as well. In old graveyards are
specimens of heraldic carving in which coats of arms are displayed, and some

of them are well executed and in a remarkable state of preservation. Exact blazoning is, however, impossible, since the color lines are frequently omitted and some of the minor details are incorrect. In both cases the fault has probably been with the sculptors in their evident desire to produce effects. A number of the carvings are strongly cut in bold relief, and the quiet dignity of the tombs cannot fail to impress the spectator. It is with regret that the writer, in referring to the important factor " detail," and in showing examples of monumental heraldry in this country, has been obliged to place before the reader so many instances in which charges and tinctures have been slighted, or else obliterated by time. Such incompleteness is unfortunate, since in heraldry every charge or tincture has its distinct value. The coats of arms found in our burying-grounds are to a great extent of assistance in the compiling of genealogies ; but the uncertainty as to the tinctures and other points, which are of vital consequence in substantiating claims to coats of arms by different branches of families of the same name, would have been removed in many cases if the attention of the designer or sculptor had been drawn to the necessity of a closer following of heraldic laws.

The following coats of arms are copied exactly as they now exist, and no attempt has been made to supply any deficiencies. Under the heading of Miscellaneous are shown other examples copied from various church records, genealogies, etc. Many of these specimens are now illegible upon their tombstones, others are not to be found, and some tombstones have through neglect sunken so far into the ground that their inscriptions and heraldic carvings cannot be seen.

OLD CHRIST CHURCH, PHILADELPHIA, PENNSYLVANIA.

It is due to the courtesy and kind interest of Rev. C. Ellis Stevens, LL.D., D.C.L., the Rector of Christ Church, Philadelphia, that the writer was given access to the valuable heraldic objects within that historic old building, and in

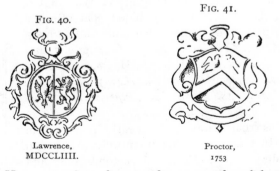

FIG. 40.

Lawrence,
MDCCLIIII.

FIG. 41.

Proctor,
1753

its graveyard. Here a number of coats of arms are found, but several of the slabs are so much worn and defaced by time and weather that it is impossible to decipher them, and the carving on others is barely legible.

Upon the tomb of Thomas Lawrence appears the outline of what must have been very finely executed arms. The shape of the shield and peculiar style of mantling are readily recognized as belonging to the Colonial period. Beneath the arms is the inscription, but so indistinct that reference to the church records becomes necessary to insure correctness. This is one of the few examples of impaled arms found upon monuments in this country, and is most interesting (Fig. 40).

Merely a suggestion of the carving (Fig. 41) remains upon the slab bearing the name of Richard Proctor; enough, however, to permit one to form an idea of what the arms originally were. The inscription is entirely obliterated, and this name is also taken from the church records.

Another coat is here found, under the name of Baynton; although of much later date, it is the least legible of the arms that have been deciphered. The outlines are quite indistinct and a *bend* of some combination is just perceptible. The arms are probably those of the English family of Baynton: *Sa. a bend lozengy arg.* (Fig. 42).

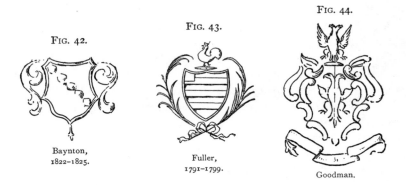

FIG. 44.

FIG. 43.

FIG. 42.

Baynton,
1822–1825.

Fuller,
1791–1799.

Goodman.

The best-preserved arms are those upon the slab bearing the names of Benjamin and Rebecca Fuller (Fig. 43).

The inscription upon another monument proves that it was erected to Captain Walter Goodman, who died August 26, 1782. A perpendicular line indicates that the shield was *parted per pale*. The crest is indistinct, but appears to have been a *double-headed eagle, displayed*, as on the shield. If this presumption is correct the arms would coincide with the blazon in Burke: "*Per pale erm. and or, an eagle displ. with two heads sa.* CREST: *An eagle as in the arms*" (Fig. 44).

It is in the church that the more interesting heraldic specimens are to be found, and each one contains its lesson. Entering the doorway, the eye is attracted by a beautiful memorial window erected to Bishop White. It is rich in ecclesiastical decoration, and contains, in the lower centre, the bishop's arms (Fig. 45).

FIG. 45.

Memorial window to Bishop White.

FIG. 46.

Head of George II.

FIG. 47.

Atlee.

In the Tower Room, and executed in a very quaint style, is a carving of the head of George II., which was formerly upon the outside of the building; artistic scrolls, boldly cut, form a framework, and give the appearance of a shield; surmounting the whole is the royal crown, handsomely carved, no detail being neglected, the cross having evidently been broken off (Fig. 46).

Upon the south wall, over a tablet are the arms of Colonel Samuel John Atlee (Fig. 47), which are faithfully executed, and surmounted by a helmet, but marred by the absence of the crest, which, with a portion of the wreath, has been omitted. The family book-plate is also designed in this way, though no reason can be given for it. What appears to be a border is evidently the result of the sculptor's attempt to produce effect. The tinctures are indicated; the blazon being, *Az. a lion ramp. arg.* According to Burke the crest is, "*Two lion's heads addorsée ppr.*"

A perfect gem of an old heraldic achievement (Fig. 48) is found upon a tomb in the north aisle. It is in the form of impaled arms surmounted by a helmet and crest, and is surrounded by a mantling of beautiful scroll-work.

FIG. 48.

Welsh.

The coat of arms upon the dexter is that of Welsh, *Az. six mullets or, three, two, one,* and so proved by a careful glass inspection of the tomb. Beneath the achievement is the scarcely legible inscription, " Here lies the body of Samuel Welsh deceased January 1702 aged 70." The changes upon the sinister are identical with those of the families of Glover, Palmer, or Withers, although the church records reveal no connection of any one of the three with the family of Welsh; and as the color indications are worn away, it remains an interesting subject for future investigation. The crest surmounting the impaled arms is evidently a demi-unicorn, but so much worn by footsteps that this is not positively clear.

Another very valuable relic is a wood carving in bold relief of the royal arms of the reign
of William and Mary, which decorated the state
pew of the governors. Despite its great age,
its features are still distinct, though it is naturally
much discolored and cracked. (See Fig. 49.)

FIG. 49.

A very rare specimen is a hatchment which
hangs in the Tower Room, and contains the
inscription, " Frederick Smyth Died 5th May
1806 aged 65 Be Virtuous & be Happy." This
was originally prepared upon the decease of his wife, as the *sable* in the sinister
side indicates. The example is shown in Fig. 914. Frederick Smyth was the
last royal Chief Justice of New Jersey.

Carvings of bishops' mitres appear upon several chairs. A copy of the
arms of the thirteen original States hangs in the belfry, and is said to have
been presented by General Washington.

Wondrous old books are carefully preserved in the library of this church;
and their vellum bindings, iron clasps, and odd type prove some of them to
have been printed in the early days of the art of
printing. Engraved portraits of various clergymen
appear in frontispieces, to which in several instances
are added exceedingly fine examples of ecclesiastical
arms; particularly noticeable are those of Bishop
Sanderson.

FIG. 50.

William Penn Esq. Proprietor
of Penfylvania :1703

Reduced fac-simile of William
Penn's book-plate.

In other volumes, book-plates adorn the inside of
the covers, and the names Preston, Chambres, and
Penn appear frequently beneath them. In the case
of the latter, an original book-plate is found of the
private library of the first Pro-
prietor of Pennsylvania, whose
family were long connected
with this church, where some
of their tombs are still to be found.

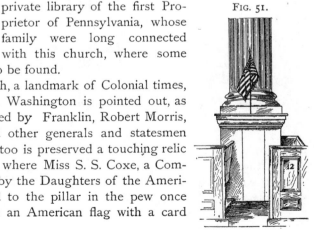

FIG. 51.

It is in this old church, a landmark of Colonial times,
that the pew of General Washington is pointed out, as
well as the pews occupied by Franklin, Robert Morris,
Francis Hopkinson, and other generals and statesmen
of the Revolution; here too is preserved a touching relic
of the first " Flag Day," where Miss S. S. Coxe, a Committee of one appointed by the Daughters of the American Revolution, fastened to the pillar in the pew once
occupied by Betty Ross an American flag with a card
bearing the inscription :

"In honor of Elizabeth Claypole who made the first American Flag [stars and stripes], and who at one time occupied this pew.

"Placed here Flag Day June 14th 1891 by a member of the 'Daughters of the American Revolution.'"

In Old Swedes' Church-Yard, Wilmington, Delaware, a monument, recently erected, bears, over the names of Noah Platz Burr (Fig. 52) and Rebecca Bulkley (Fig. 53), his wife, the arms of the two families in shields, side by side.

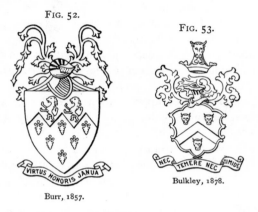

FIG. 52.

FIG. 53.

Burr, 1857.

Bulkley, 1878.

The helmets are placed to face each other for the sake of artistic effect, and hence the one over the Burr coat of arms faces to the *sinister*.

In the church-yard on Market Street near Tenth in the same city, a monument in memory of Gunning Bedford, a friend of Benjamin Franklin, who died in 1812, bears on one side an escutcheon charged with *three lion's gambs couped* and *erect within a bordure* (tincture not indicated)   For crest: *A lion's gamb couped and erect* (Fig. 54).

FIG. 54.

FIG. 55.

FIG. 56.

Bedford.

Bedford.

Drake.

On the opposite side of the shaft there is carved the design shown in Fig. 55, which seems to be two representations of another crest (*a leopard's head*) placed side by side.

An exceptionally fine example is found in the church-yard of Old St. David's at Radnor, Pennsylvania (Fig. 56).   Sculptured on a monument over the names of Richard Drake (died 1808) and Mary Fearon, his wife (died 1812), appears the well-known *wyvern* of the Drake family, and for a crest a *castle of three towers embattled, surmounted by a wyvern.* (The wyvern on the shield corresponds with that on the arms of John Drake, who settled in Boston in 1630, and the two families are probably connected.)

In the Evergreen Cemetery at Gettysburg, Pennsylvania, two coats of arms are found, not as finely executed as that on the Drake monument, but quite well preserved. One is a representation of the Mac-Pherson arms (Fig. 57) over the name of Robert McPher-son (died 1749). *Per fesse or and azure, a lymphad with her sails trussed up, and oars in action of the first. In the dexter chief point a hand couped grasping a dagger, point upwards gu.; in the sinister chief a cross-crosslet fitchée of the last.* CREST: *A cat sejant ppr.* MOTTO: *" Touch not the cat, but a glove."* [1] The color lines are not indicated and the carving is somewhat inaccurate. On another tomb the Buchanan arms appear over the name of Andrew Buchanan (died 1780): *Or, a lion rampant sable, armed and langued gules, within a double tressure flory counterflory of the second.* CREST: *A hand holding up a ducal cap, tufted on the top with a rose gules, within a laurel branch, disposed orleways proper.* MOTTO: *" Audaces juvo clarior hinc hones."* [2] The supporters seem to be two parrots. The indications of the tinctures are omitted in this coat of arms also (Fig. 58).

FIG. 57.

MacPherson, 1749.

FIG. 58.

Buchanan, 1780.

In the Old South Church in Boston, below the portrait of Col. William Henshaw, Adjutant-General of Massachusetts Militia in 1775, are represented

FIG. 59.   FIG. 60.   FIG. 61.

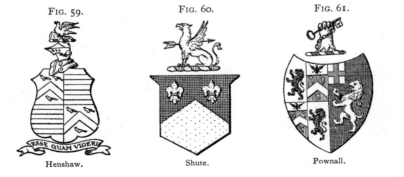

Henshaw.   Shute.   Pownall.

his arms as shown in Fig. 59. In the Old State House in the same city hang paintings of the arms of Col. Samuel Shute, Governor and Commander-in-Chief in 1716 (Fig. 60), and those of Thomas Pownall, Governor and Commander-in-Chief in 1757 (Fig. 61).

[1] Burke.   [2] Burke.

Copp's Hill Burying-Ground, formerly called the Old North Burying-Ground, Boston, was the second one established in that town, and was used for interments as early as 1660. The names of many illustrious dead can here be found, among them those of Andrew and John Elliot, Cotton Mather, and Edmund Hart, builder of the frigate " Constitution."

Among the coats of arms still preserved are

FIG. 62.

Mountfort, 1724.

FIG. 63.

Greenwood, 1722.

FIG. 64.

Browne, 1771.

FIG. 65.

St. Mary's Church-Yard in Burlington, New Jersey, one of the early settlements on the Delaware, contains several specimens of ecclesiastical heraldry worthy of special mention. A very elaborate *pastoral staff* is to be seen on the tomb of William Henry Odenheimer, who died August 14, 1879; also a finely carved bishop's mitre upon the same tomb, every detail of which is depicted by the sculptor, leaving no room for speculation or doubt as to any portion (Figs. 65, 66).

FIG 66.

On another tomb is seen a beautiful specimen of the bishop's mitre (Fig. 67) with the inscription:

FIG. 67.

Washington Doane
D.D., LL.D.
for XXVII years Bishop of N. J.

Here are also seen the arms of Bayntone, who died A.D. 1743 (Fig. 68).

FIG. 68.

Bayntone, 1743.

While these arms are apparently incorrectly represented upon the tomb, there is no doubt that they are those of the same family (or of a branch of it) whose arms are seen upon a slab in Old Christ Church Burying-Ground in Philadelphia (Fig. 42).

A very curious instance of the misappropriation of arms, most likely unintentional, is found in Maplewood Cemetery, Freehold, New Jersey. Upon a tomb bearing the name of

Bennett is the coat of arms of Rhode Island with some slight variations. This mistake was evidently committed through ignorance on the part of the sculptor or, having the knowledge perhaps that the family originally came from Rhode Island, he has copied the design of the arms of the State, embodying the anchor and motto, "Hope," for want of a better emblem, without regard to its legitimacy.

FIG. 69.

Newberry, 1704.

The coat of arms shown in Fig. 69 is taken from a tomb found upon Greenberry farm, opposite Annapolis, one of the early plantations, and gives rise to the opinion that this was formerly a very old burying-ground. Portions of blue-granite tombs, which are now and then brought to the surface, together with the bricks (evidently of foreign make) used in supporting the slabs, strengthen this belief.

Among other examples found by the writer are those of

ST. PETER'S CHURCH-YARD, PINE STREET NEAR THIRD, PHILADELPHIA, PENNSYLVANIA.

FIG. 70.

Wallace, 1783.

FIG. 71.

Sims, 1773.

FIG. 72.

FORTIS ET FIDIS.

Lachlan, 1802.

FIG. 73.

Nordeek, Baron de Rabenau, 1782.

BURYING-GROUND, CHARLESTOWN, MASSACHUSETTS.

FIG. 74.

Fowle, 1711.

FIG. 75.

Dows, 1725.

FIG. 76.

Chambers, 1743.

FIG. 77.

Eckley.

FIG. 78.

Freke.

FIG. 79.

Foster, 1774.

FIG. 80.

Greaves, 1747.

FIG. 81.

Cheever, 1744.

FIG. 82.

Wood, 1762.

FIG. 83.

Jenner, 1725-1765.

FIG. 84.

Cary, 1740.

FIG. 85.

Lemmon, 1724.

The Granary Burying-Grounds, Boston, Massachusetts.

FIG. 86.

Tothill.

FIG. 87.

Perkins, 1796.

FIG. 88.

Sears of Chatham.

FIG. 89.

Checkley, 1737.

FIG. 90.

Lyde.

FIG. 91.

Hubbard.

FIG. 92.

Leverett, 1724.
From tomb in the old burying-ground at Cambridge, Mass.

Mount Bethal Cemetery, Columbia, Pennsylvania.

FIG. 93.

From tomb of William Campbell, an English prisoner of war.

St. Ann's Church-Yard, Annapolis, Maryland.

FIG. 94.

Tasker, 1768.

FIG. 95.

Garrett, 1727.

FIG. 96.

Dulaney-Smith.

FIG. 97.

Bladin, 1718.

FIG. 98.

Reed, 1732.

FIG. 99.

Ambler, 1836.

FIG. 100.

Bassett.

FIG. 101.

Alston.
From tombstone, Georgetown, South Carolina.

FIG. 102.

Mayo, 1740.
Powhatan, near Richmond, Virginia.

FIG. 103.

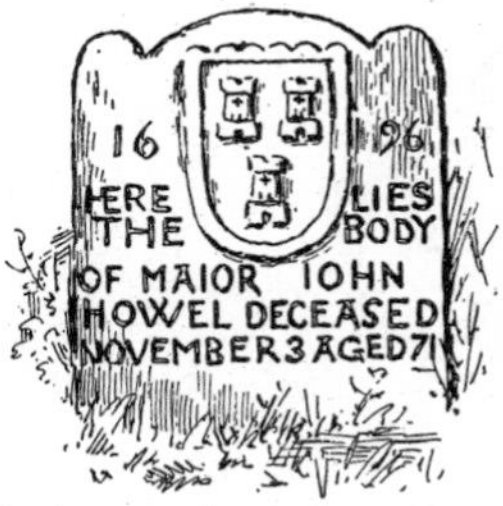

Tombstone at Southampton, Long
Island.

DENBIGH CHURCH, WAR-
WICK COUNTY, VIRGINIA.

FIG. 104.

Harrison—Digges.

FIG. 105.

PATRICK HOUSTOUN
Baronet Prefident of his
Majeftys Council of Georgia
died 5ᵗ Febʸ 1762 Aged 64

LAdy HOUSTOUN HisWidow
ed 16ᵗʰ Febʸ 1775 Aged 60

Tombstone formerly in old cemetery,
Savannah, Georgia, now at
Bonaventura.

FIG. 106.

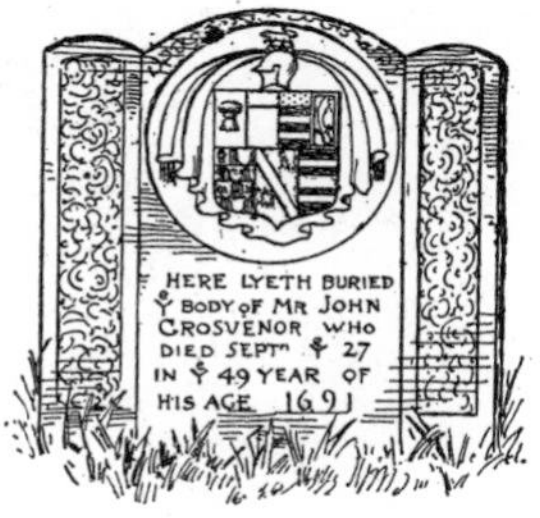

HERE LYETH BURIED
Y BODY OF MR JOHN
CROSVENOR WHO
DIED SEPTᵇ Y 27
IN Y 49 YEAR OF
HIS AGE 1691

Tombstone, Boston, Massachusetts.

MONUMENTAL HERALDRY.—MISCELLANEOUS EXAMPLES.

GRANARY BURYING-GROUND, BOSTON, MASSACHUSETTS.

FIG. 107.

Winslow, 1753.
Bonner, 1804.

FIG. 108.

Faneuil.

FIG. 109.

Lasinby, 1774.

FIG. 110.

Jackson.

FIG. 111.

Bowdoin.

FIG. 112.

Southac.

FIG. 113.

Cushing.

FIG. 114.

Bulkley, 1748.

FIG. 115.

Bulkley, 1713.

OLD IPSWICH BURYING-GROUND, MASSACHUSETTS.

FIG. 116.

Denison, 1747.

FIG. 117.

Emerson, 1712.

FIG. 118.

Wainwright, 1711.

FIG. 119.

Appleton, 1725.

FIG. 120.

Richards, 1680.

Old Dorchester Church-Yard, Massachusetts.

Fig. 121.

Poole, 1674.

Fig. 122.

Stoughton.

Fig. 123.

Royall, 1724.

Fig. 124.

Dudley.

Fig. 125.

Wheelwright, 1740.

Fig. 126.

Gedney.

Fig. 127.

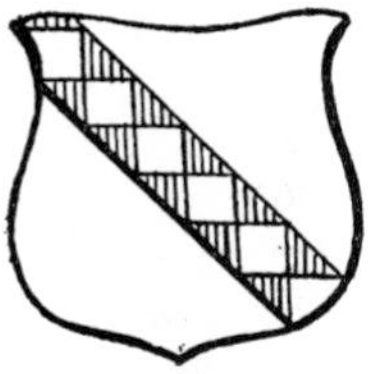

Winslow.

Fig. 128.

Trail.

Fig. 129.

Pain, 1704.

Fig. 130.

Shirley.

Fig. 131.

Apthorp, 1758.

Fig. 132.

Greene.

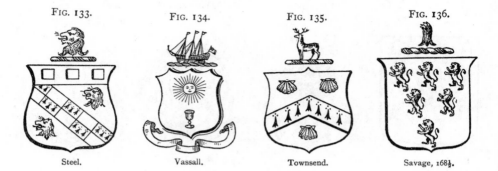

FIG. 133.

Steel.

FIG. 134.

Vassall.

FIG. 135.

Townsend.

FIG. 136.

Savage, 168½.

FIG. 137.

Dawes, 1809.

FIG. 138.

Bromfield, 1734.

FIG. 139.

Loring, 1744.

FIG. 140.

Clap, 1690.

FIG. 141.

Ewing.

FIG. 142.

Wendell, 1761.

FIG. 143.

Vincent, 1800.

FIG. 144.

Bell, 1808.

FIG. 145.

Salisbury, 1818–26.

FIG. 146.

Winthrop, 1649.

FIG. 147.

Lloyd, 1810.

FIG. 148.

Hall, 1777.

FIG. 149.

Hoar, 1773.

FIG. 150.

Barrett, 1779.

OLD NORTH BURIAL-GROUND, PROVIDENCE, RHODE ISLAND.

FIG. 151.

Harris, 1723.

FIG. 152.

Andrews, 1751.

FIG. 153.

Fenner, 1751.

FIG. 154.

Young, 1738.

FIG. 155.

Tew, 1751.

FIG. 156.

Gibbs, 1757.

FIG. 157.

Arnold, 1770.

ST. JOHN'S CHURCH-YARD, PROVIDENCE, RHODE ISLAND.

FIG. 158.

Merrett, 1770.

TRINITY CHURCH-YARD, NEWPORT, RHODE ISLAND.

FIG. 160.

FIG. 159.

Gibbs, 1767.

Gidley, 1727.

FIG. 161.

FIG. 162.

FIG. 163.

Bell, 1737.

Wanton, 1735

Goulding, 1742.

OLD BURYING-GROUND NEAR NORTHERN END OF THAMES STREET, NEWPORT, RHODE ISLAND.

FIG. 165.

FIG. 164.

FIG. 166.

Bayly, 1723.

Cranston, 1680.

Sanford, 1721.

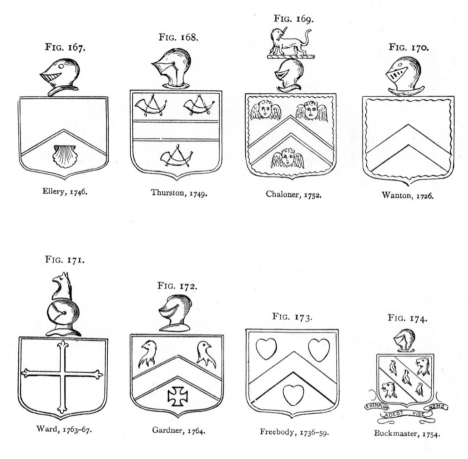

FIG. 167.

Ellery, 1746.

FIG. 168.

Thurston, 1749.

FIG. 169.

Chaloner, 1752.

FIG. 170.

Wanton, 1726.

FIG. 171.

Ward, 1763–67.

FIG. 172.

Gardner, 1764.

FIG. 173.

Freebody, 1736–59.

FIG. 174.

Buckmaster, 1754.

GRAVEYARD AT SALEM, MASSACHUSETTS.

FIG. 176.

FIG. 175.

Brown, 1687.

Lynde, 1752.

FIG. 177.

Pickman, 1761.

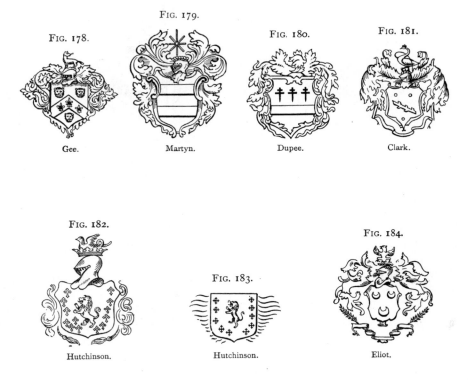

FIG. 178.

FIG. 179.

FIG. 180.

FIG. 181.

Gee.

Martyn.

Dupee.

Clark.

FIG. 182.

FIG. 183.

FIG. 184.

Hutchinson.

Hutchinson.

Eliot.

WICKETAQUOC, STONINGTON, CONNECTICUT.

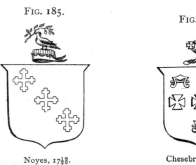

FIG. 185.

FIG. 186.

Noyes, 17⅛⅞.

Chesebrough, 1782.

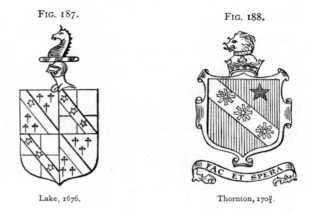

FIG. 187.

Lake, 1676.

FIG. 188.

Thornton, 170⁹⁄.

Nowhere perhaps on the American continent is to be seen such a magnificent display of sculptured coats of arms as upon the battle-field of Gettysburg, Pennsylvania, where monuments bear the arms of the States by which they have been erected.

Many of these States, whose regiments took part in the battle commemorated, seem to have vied one with another in erecting handsome and costly monuments to the memory of their honored dead. As one pauses on the summit of Little Round Top and looks down into the valley of the Cumberland, one is impressed by the great numbers of monuments dotting the valley as far as the eye can reach, standing out in sharp contrast to the green background. In most cases, as just said, they are embellished with the coats of arms of the State which they represent.

Upon the 136th New York Infantry monument on the Taneytown road, as upon that erected to the 121st Infantry of the same State on Little Round Top, are the arms of the State of New York, finely executed in bronze.

The arms upon the monument to Berdan's Sharpshooters of New York are also worthy of mention. The arms of Michigan modelled in bronze are placed upon the base of the memorial of the 5th Michigan Infantry near "the loop."

A plain but substantial monument is that in honor of the 2d Rhode Island Volunteers on Sedgwick Avenue; the arms of the State are clear and finely cut, the details being exceptionally well sculptured.

The beauty of the plain, massive stone of the 20th Connecticut Infantry on Culp's Hill is greatly enhanced by the arms of that State.

The arms of Pennsylvania are in nearly every instance cast in bronze upon an oblong panel, as on the remarkably fine specimen shown in Fig. 189.[1] The large cross to the 142d Pennsylvania on Reynolds Avenue, as well as the

---

[1] From photograph furnished by Colonel John P. Nicholson.

very imposing one to the 2d Pennsylvania Cavalry on Meade Avenue, bears the arms in this same manner.

The arms of Maryland form the prominent feature of the Confederate monument on Culp's Hill.

The writer could fill pages in the enumeration and description of the State arms upon the memorials dotting this famous battle-field; suffice it to say that the comparative newness of these monuments has an especial attraction to those interested in a correct delineation of armorial insignia, as they are examples of what is being accomplished to-day, and clearly show that the science is not degenerating, but that the laws of heraldry are becoming more clearly understood and more closely followed.

ARCHITECTURAL HERALDRY.

Coats of arms are frequently seen forming a portion of the decoration of public buildings in the United States.

On the Public Buildings of Philadelphia the arms of Pennsylvania are placed high over the south entrance. The carving is well executed and accurate in detail even to the indications of the tinctures; but the position of the horses (supporters) is incorrect. They should be rampant. Above the

FIG. 190.   FIG. 191.

other three doorways are the arms of Philadelphia, which, while finely carved, are marred by the incorrect drawing of the fesse (excepting one at the north entrance) and the position of the supporters.

Upon the front of that quaint old building, Carpenters' Hall, appears a carving of the armorial insignia of the Carpenters' Company. (See Fig. 192.) This is identical with the arms of the Worshipful Company of Carpenters of London. Two old flags bearing the same device, and which were carried in processions in 1788 and 1832, are displayed upon the inside walls. The arms of the thirteen States in proper colors are also upon these walls.

FIG. 192.

This building is memorable in history as the place where the First Continental Congress met.

FIG. 193.

FIG. 194.

An instance of a coat of arms used for interior decoration is furnished in the Redwood Library at Newport, Rhode Island, where the arms of William Redwood (Fig. 193) are displayed in a large and finely-executed piece of carved work placed above the doorway. This adds to the artistic effect of the quaint old building, and at the same time stands as a memorial of the beneficent founder of this old and valuable library.

In the vestibule of Old Trinity Church, Newport, are seen the coat of arms of the Chevalier de Ternay (Fig. 194). These are executed upon a black marble tablet erected to his memory.

FIG. 195.

FIG. 196.

The shield and crest of Judge Richard Peters of Revolutionary fame are executed in stucco upon the ceiling of Belmont Mansion, Fairmount Park, Philadelphia (Figs. 195, 196).

In the Capitol at Harrisburg the carved arms of Pennsylvania enter very extensively into the decoration, and a representation of these arms in mosaic is placed on one of the main paths leading to the building. In the mosaic work, however, heraldic accuracy is sacrificed to artistic beauty.

FIG. 197.

Washington contains among its many examples of American heraldry some fine specimens of arms of the States, both in stained and painted glass, but more frequently they are found in sculptured work.

On the ceiling in the hall of the House of Representatives are seen the arms of the States, illuminated in proper colors. This ceiling is of glass, and with the lights above produces a very beautiful effect.

In this hall is the time-honored mace, the Speaker's symbol of authority; it is very similar to the Roman fasces frequently borne as a charge in heraldry, and is composed of a number of sable rods bound together with transverse bands of silver; at the top is a silver globe surmounted by the American eagle in silver. The mace is held aloft by the sergeant-at-arms when he is required to execute the commands of the Speaker.

In other portions of the Capitol are representations of the escutcheon of the American arms, the dome itself of this magnificent edifice being surmounted by the figure of Liberty supporting the national shield.

The Washington Monument, one of the main attractions of

our capital, contains upon the inside the arms of many of the States, sculptured upon different varieties of marble and placed in the walls of the monument. The greater number of these are the productions of clever sculptors, but are incorrectly executed; as is often the case with this class of work in the United States.

George R. Howell, M.A., in an interesting paper upon heraldry, thus describes several coats sculptured in the Capitol at Albany, New York. The carvings are placed in ornamental spaces overlooking the court, as shown in Fig. 203, from photograph lately secured: "Above the six dormer windows that open on the court, and that are in the story above the chambers of the Senate and Assembly, are sculptured the arms of six families that have become more or less distinguished in the history of the State. The vertical length of these arms as sculptured is about four feet, and, as they are placed so high, from any possible point of observation this is none too large to enable one to distinguish their several devices. It may be difficult to make on stone such a carving as will indicate the color or tincture of the various objects employed in coat armor, and to preserve their proper and relative proportions. This may account for some variations between the arms as they are sculptured and as they are engraved on book plates or blazoned in works of heraldry. The carving, so far as a good field-glass enables one to inspect it, appears to be admirably well done. The names of the families that have been thus commemorated in the lofty court of the capitol are Stuyvesant (Fig. 198), Schuyler (Fig. 199), Livingston (Fig. 200), Jay (Fig. 201), Tompkins (Fig. 202), and Clinton (Fig. 203). Had there been one more window we doubtless would have seen over it the arms of Hamilton, to whom perhaps, more than to any one man, we are indebted for the strength of the form of our National government."

Fig. 198.	Fig. 199.	Fig. 200.

FIG. 201.

FIG. 202.

FIG. 203.

Artistic effects have been produced by coats of arms which enter into the

FIG. 204.

ornamentation of the grill-work of gates. In America fine examples were executed during the Colonial period. Notable among these may be mentioned the Byrd arms in the gate at Westover, Virginia (Fig. 204).

FIG. 205.

The mansion of Provost William Smith, D.D. (1727–1803), was erected at Falls of Schuylkill in 1760. A brass plate on the massive gate-post bore his crest. (See Fig. 205.) The plate is in the possession of a descendant.

Upon the gate-posts at the entrance to Harvard College grounds are the arms (Fig. 206) which are depicted in the seal of the college, cast upon an

FIG. 206.

oblong iron panel and set into the brick-work, giving the front that picturesque appearance so often seen in European countries, where it has been the custom to place armorial bearings upon the entrance to cities, baronial estates, and public buildings.

The arms of Pennsylvania (Fig. 207), sculptured in white marble, set in the brick-work above the western door of the State House in Philadelphia, are a notable example of this old style of architectural decoration.

The oldest specimen perhaps to be found on this continent is the Spanish

FIG. 207.

FIG. 208.

coat of arms (Fig. 208), surrounded by the insignia of the Order of the Golden Fleece, upon the old fort at St. Augustine, Florida. This beautiful example of architectural heraldry is shown in "St. Nicholas," 1894, and the building upon which it appears is described as the most interesting feature of St. Augustine. "This is the old fort of San Marco, which, since it came into the possession of our government, has been re-named Fort Marion.

"The old fort is not a ruin, but has the style of fortifications of the Middle Ages. We cross the moat and the drawbridge, and over the stone doorway we see the Spanish Coat of Arms, and under it an inscription stating that the fort was built during the reign of King Ferdinand VI. of Spain, with the names and titles of the dons who superintended the work."

The decadency of the custom of introducing heraldic decoration was noticeable at the discontinuance of Colonial styles of architecture. However, with the very marked revival of Colonial forms in building it has again at times been found necessary to introduce coats of arms upon prominent portions of the edifices, to complete that old-fashioned effect, which is so pleasing to eyes accustomed to the many varied styles of architecture seen in our day.

MEMORIAL WINDOWS.

The decided leaning toward the antique, and with it, necessarily, the introduction of heraldic devices, such as shields, fleurs-de-lis, lions rampant, griffins,

FIG. 209.

dragons, etc., in our modern architecture, is very
perceptible even to the casual observer, and indeed it
is an attempt to rob heraldry of a great portion of
its time-honored glory to say that without it many
of the pleasing and harmonious effects to be seen on
our modern buildings could be obtained.

The trend among designers of church architecture of the present day is in this direction, and the
beauty of many of our churches is due to the fact
that they are modified forms of old cathedrals and
abbeys of European countries, wherein heraldry
forms an integral part of the decorations, and the
imposing effect of their great stained windows, with
heraldic devices depicted in brilliant colors, lends an
additional loveliness to the stately whole.

In this country we have numerous examples of
such memorial windows, but attention is only directed to those that have come under the personal
observation of the writer. A most beautiful window
is seen in St. Mark's Church, Philadelphia, erected "in
memory of a branch of the Mifflin family." The design is plain, extremely
artistic, and the coloring is in perfect harmony. The well-known Mifflin arms
appear in the lower portion of this window, as shown in Fig. 209. It is

FIG. 210.

gratifying to note in another window of this church the care and correctness
with which the heraldic tinctures of the shields and charges are delineated
(Fig. 210).

In the Old Swedes' Church at Wilmington, Delaware, is a very handsome window, placed there some years ago, in memory of James Asheton Bayard (1799–1880) and Anne Francis Bayard (1802–1864). It is one of the finest pieces of stained glass work known to the writer; the coloring is exquisite, and the design is graceful, simple, and in good taste. A very important feature is the display of the arms and crest of Bayard and Francis, placed side by side. For BAYARD: *Azure, a chevron or, between three escallops argent.* CREST: *A demi-horse argent.* For FRANCIS: *Per bend sinister sable and or, a lion rampant counterchanged.* CREST: *Out of a ducal coronet or, a demi-lion sable, holding between his paws a garb erect of the first* (Fig. 211).

FIG. 211.

Another example of heraldic work in stained

FIG. 212.

glass is found in St. Peter's Church in Philadelphia. In the lower part of a window erected in memory of Joseph R. Evans, by his grandson, Joseph R. Evans, Jr., appears the achievement shown in Fig. 212.

In the First Reformed Church of Philadelphia can be seen the arms of Zwingli, the great Swiss reformer, on a window surmounting a brilliantly diapered background and embodying the word "Zwingli" in a panel (Fig. 213).

Very close to this is a copy of a seal bearing the inscription, "Synod of the German Reformed Church in the U. S." (Fig. 214).

FIG. 213.

FIG. 214.

An example of amateur heraldic work, comparing very favorably with work of professionals, is shown in Fig. 215. This window was designed and executed by Eugene Devereux, Esq., formerly of Philadelphia, and appeared in his De Lancey Place home for several years.

Fig. 216 is copied from illustrations of windows, of the old church at Albany, said to be now in the possession of the Dudley and Van Rensselaer families.

FIG. 215.

FIG. 216.

Thus from Colonial days to the present time there is a continuous line of architectural and memorial carvings of heraldic devices, which bears witness that the value of the art has been appreciated by many.

FIG. 217.   FIG. 218.

WASHINGTON'S SEALS.

From letter to Bouquet, 1758.   Private seal, 1783
From " Harper's Magazine" for May, 1891.

Additional proof that the custom of bearing arms was not thrown aside at the time of the Revolution is furnished by the fact that numerous instances may be cited of officials in high life who retained in use their family arms, seals, and signet-rings, impressions of which appear with their signatures upon many documents of state, as well as upon papers of a private nature, now in

FIG. 220.

FIG. 219.

FIG. 221.

THE ARMS OF WASHINGTON as borne upon his carriage. From a print in Old South Church, Boston.

A copy of the book-plate of John Quincy Adams in the Old State House at Boston.

ARMS OF SHIPPEN. From old iron seal in possession of Dr. Edward Shippen, descendant, Philadelphia.

the possession of their heirs. George Washington, the first Chief Magistrate of the United States, bore arms, an etching of which is shown in Fig. 918. These facts alone seem sufficient to warrant the use of arms by those entitled to bear them, and refute the false notion that the heraldic idea is inconsistent with republican principles; General Washington's opinion on this question is a matter of record, and is as follows:

" HERALDRY AND REPUBLICANISM."

" It is far from my design to intimate an opinion, that Heraldry, Coat-Armor, etc., might not be rendered conducive to public and private use with us; or that they can have any tendency unfriendly to the purest spirit of

Republicanism. On the contrary, a different conclusion is deducible from the practice of Congress, and the States; all of which have established some kind of *Armorial Devices*, to authenticate their official instruments."[1]

FIG. 223.

ARMS OF CLEMENT PLUMSTED, MAYOR OF PHILA-DELPHIA, 1723. From old silver in possession of the Devereux family, descendants, Philadelphia.

FIG. 222.

ARMS OF MIFFLIN. From the seal of John Mifflin in possession of James Mifflin, Esq., descendant, Philadelphia.

FIG. 224.

ARMS OF MICHAEL HILLEGAS (FIRST TREASURER OF THE UNITED STATES) AND WIFE, HENRIETTA BOUDE. From old silver in possession of descendant, Captain Henry Hobart Bellas, U.S.A.

FIG. 225.

THE ALLEN ARMS. From photograph (of tombstone at Windsor) in possession of Francis Olcott Allen, Esq., Philadelphia.

FIG. 226.

THE WAYNE ARMS. From old seal-ring in possession of Miss Mary Wayne, Philadelphia, descendant of Captain Anthony Wayne (first settler).

FIG. 227.

CREST OF JASPER YEATES (1745–1817), JUDGE OF THE SUPREME COURT OF PENNSYLVANIA. From lid of snuff-box now in possession of his great-grandson, Dr. John H. Brinton, Philadelphia.

FIG. 228.

ARMS OF THE RITTENHOUSE FAMILY. From the "Rittenhouse Genealogy."

[1] Extract from "Maxims of Washington, Political, Social, Moral, and Religious," page 22, by John Frederick Schroeder, D.D.

FIG. 229.

IMPALED ARMS OF COX-GREEN-
LEAF. From old painting in posses-
sion of descendant, Dr. Charles
Harrod Vinton, Philadelphia.

FIG. 230.

ARMS OF JOHN MASON (1670),
DEPUTY GOVERNOR OF CONNECTI-
CUT.

From copies of seals from the Archives of Connecticut, at Hartford, in
possession of their descendant, Rev. C. Ellis Stevens, LL.D., D.C.L.,
Philadelphia.

FIG. 231.

ARMS OF WILLIAM PITKIN,
GOVERNOR OF CONNECTICUT, 1766.

FIG. 232.

ARMS OF ABERCROMBIE. From
old glassware in possession of Mrs.
Clifford Stanley Sims, descendant,
Burlington, New Jersey.

FIG. 233.

ARMS OF SHEEPSHANKS.
From old gold seals in possession of the Sproat family, descendants, West-
town, Pennsylvania.

FIG. 234.

ARMS OF SPROAT.

FIG. 235.

ARMS OF THE LOGANS OF STEN-
TON. From old silver in possession
of descendant, A. Sydney Logan,
Esq., Philadelphia.

FIG. 236.

ARMS OF THE DE PEYSTER FAM-
ILY. From the original seal of silver,
brought to America by Johannes De
Peyster, the first of the family in
this country, and in the possession
of his descendant, General J. H.
Watts De Peyster, New York.

FIG. 237.

THE SPARHAWK ARMS (Pep-
perell in pretense). From painting
of Colonel Nathaniel Sparhawk,
by John Singleton Copley, now in
Boston Art Museum.

FIG. 238.

FIG. 239.

FIG. 240.

THE BOND ARMS.

From signet-ring of Phineas Bond.   From old silver of Lady Erskine.
In possession of
descendant,   nephew,
Travis Cochran, Esq., Philadelphia.

LOGAN CREST. From old silver
in possession of Miss Elizabeth P.
Smith and Mr. Horace Smith, descendants, Philadelphia.

FIG. 241.

FIG. 242.

THE CUTHBERT CREST. From old china in possession of descendant, George Cuthbert Gillespie, Esq.,
Philadelphia.

PENINGTON ARMS. From old silver in possession of
descendant, Mrs. James de W. Cookman, Philadelphia.

FIG. 243.

FIG. 244.

THE PEMBERTON ARMS. From old steel seal in
possession of descendant, Henry Pemberton, Esq.,
Philadelphia.

THE NORTH ARMS. From old painting on wood in
possession of Edwin North Benson, Esq., descendant,
Philadelphia.

THE NECESSITY OF HERALDRY.

As an argument that heraldry is a necessity, and consequently has its uses in America, let us consider that the United States has in its coat of arms a beautiful and thoroughly heraldic device, that its flag is heraldic, as are also the seals of its various Departments. The seals of the war-ships are heraldic; their flags are likewise heraldic. The seals of the States and Territories are either heraldic, or symbolic of the various State resources or products. State flags bear coats of arms. Our money is stamped with the arms of the Treasury Department or with the national arms, and the private seal of the chief executive of the nation is practically a reduced fac-simile of the great seal of the United States. Colonial and other societies have heraldic insignia, historical and heraldic devices and seals. Corporations, charitable institutions, and colleges often find heraldry a necessity in order to emphasize certain features or objects; and individuals display their family devices in various ways. The statement made by certain persons that heraldry has no place in a republic, or that it is an assumption of nobility, is, ninety-nine times out of one hundred, made by those who do not understand this noble science and who speak at random; while many who do understand condemn because of the abuse in America. But if the abuse of heraldry is any argument against its proper usage, it may as well be discontinued throughout the entire world, and what will be found to fill its place?

It may be fairly stated that, at the present day, heraldry and genealogy are ignored only by those who have no ancestors in whom they can take pride, or who have not given the questions just and proper attention. The love of ancestry has been deep-rooted in men's minds for centuries, and no educated man will affect to despise a long line of illustrious descent, or the emblems which bespeak the bravery, wisdom, and honor of his race. And while many who possess such records and heirlooms may not wish to display them, their pride therein is none the less deep and sincere.

During the last few years the spirit of genealogical research has increased greatly. The organization of the various Colonial societies, in which lineage forms an indispensable consideration in all applications for membership, has been largely instrumental in forwarding this movement; and the effect on American society has been and will be beneficial. Genealogy and heraldry have been important factors in the formation of society in the past; and, at a time when so much pride is taken and so much patient labor expended in seeking for points of family history, it is not to be wondered at that family arms should be sought out and reproduced with careful accuracy.

In this connection it is interesting to note the great interest in heraldry which has been developed by the formation of the several historic organizations, to which a later chapter will be devoted. Many members and applicants for membership, in tracing their genealogies, are daily bringing to light seals, book-marks, and other heirlooms whereon family arms are engraved, which their ancestors had brought with them from the Old World, and cherished as evidences of ancient lineage and social distinction.

It should be noticed also, that these proofs that heraldry was practised during the Colonial period and later have encouraged many persons, hitherto opposed to the display of arms, to institute investigations, which, in some instances, have resulted in the identification of shields and crests, and in the discovery of valuable items of family history, establishing descents and connections where actual genealogical information was wanting.

It is, therefore, safe to say that before many years heraldry will be better understood and appreciated in the United States, and will even enter into the decoration of houses. Heraldic frescoing, painting, and carving are already attempted; but the results are, as a rule, discouraging, since the designs are often executed by men who, though skilled artisans, are totally ignorant of heraldic laws. A brilliant exception to the general ill success of heraldic decoration in America was seen in the elaborate and remarkably handsome display of heraldry at the Columbian Fair held in Chicago. Every nation represented decorated its head-quarters with a varied assortment of banners, paintings, carved or modelled arms, and heraldic devices. There was the painting which depicted the United States seal of 1782, and which was intended by the Department of State to be "the pivotal feature of the entire exposition," and to make the people familiar with the device of the nation. In the Liberal Arts Building, forming a beautiful border, the arms of the United States, *accolé* with those of each other nation, afforded a most interesting study to the lovers of the art. The arms of the different States of the Union, as well as of foreign nations, executed in the varied branches of the fine arts, formed an important part of the decoration, both exterior and interior, of other buildings, and the general excellence in execution and the attention given to every detail were remarkable, particularly in the English display. Noticeable throughout the exhibit was the plain form of the shield (spoken of elsewhere in this book) which, with but few exceptions, figured in the heraldic compositions. A display so magnificent, and, moreover, so accurate in detail, is encouraging to Americans interested in heraldry; and the excellence of the workmanship did credit to the ability of the heralds who designed, and to the skill of the artists who executed it. Probably the

FIG. 245.

ARMS OF COLUMBUS.
From original grant.

most interesting feature of all was the original grant of arms to Columbus, dated 1496, and signed by King Ferdinand and Queen Isabella. This is executed upon parchment, and, while much worn and defaced, clearly shows an illumination of the coat of arms. A noticeable error in designing is shown in Fig. 246 in the fourth quarter. On the original grant the anchors are charged fessways, as in Fig. 245, while

FIG. 246.

souvenir copies, prints, etc., all bear them in pale, as in Fig. 246, without one exception known to the writer.

SYMBOLISM.

Many members of American families entitled to bear arms have hesitated to do so because the devices of their ancestral coats are commonplace, or because an interpretation derogatory to the original bearer has been placed on the symbols by the fancy of some writers. The folly of this course is evident. Coats of arms were never intended as marks of disgrace, and it is absurd to say that the camel on one man's shield symbolizes slothfulness, or the fly on another's "a shameless or impudent person, over-bold at each man's table." The real signification of these creatures is frequently hard to ascertain; many of them, doubtless, had no symbolical meaning when bestowed. One thing is, however, clear,—that in former times animals and their characteristics were looked upon in a way very different from that now customary. Guillim truly says, " All sorts of Animals borne in Arms or Enfigns muft in Blazoning be interpreted in the beft senfe, that is, according to their moft generous and noble Qualities, and fo to the Greateft Honour of their Bearers, For Example: The Fox is full of Wit, and withal given wholly to filching for his Prey; if then this be the Charge of an Efcutcheon, we must conceive the Quality represented, to be his Wit and Cunning but not his Pilfering and Stealing."

The griffin, phœnix, dragon, unicorn, and other mythical creatures were just as real in mediæval minds as the camel and elephant are to us, and the belief in the existence of several such monsters was not entirely destroyed until the last century. This is evidenced by the care which a writer of that time takes to refute stories of the marvellous powers of some animals, and even the existence of such creatures as the wyvern and unicorn. He says the " *Wyvern* is a kind of flying serpent, the upper part resembling a dragon, and the lower an adder or snake; some derive it from *Vipera* and so make it a winged viper; others say it owes its being to the heralds and can boast no other creation." He describes the unicorn at some length, but in closing assures the reader that, " after the most diligent inquiry made by the most judicious travellers in all parts of the world, there is no such creature to be found." Of the salamander he remarks, "that a Salamander can live in and not be burned by fire is without foundation of truth, for the experiment has been tried." He also cautions the reader against the notions about the porcupine: " The opinion of its being able to dart its quills at its enemies is now universally allowed to be fabulous."

Again, the conception of the distinguishing characteristics of particular animals has, no doubt, changed. The donkey, once the emblem of the Christian virtue patience, has become to the modern mind the emblem of stupidity and stubbornness.

Since devices were at first assumed by the voluntary choice of the wearers, it is natural that in many cases the nature of the animal was not considered, but it was adopted as a badge for some chance reason, or, perhaps, merely from caprice. It might be an animal which the bearer had just killed, or one which was calculated by its fierce looks to inspire terror in the minds of his enemies, or, again, it might be one suggested by the fact that it had a name similar to that of the knight, or possibly one given to some warrior by the sovereign to commemorate and reward some heroic deed. In all these cases the attributes of the animal would have had no relation to those of the warrior who bore it as a crest. We can hardly imagine a chieftain adopting a goose as his badge with any idea that the modern conception of that bird would symbolize his character.

The manner in which devices sometimes came to be adopted may be explained by the following : [1]

" The feudal age was a time also when leaders of armies, even kings themselves, engaged in personal conflict on the battle-field, and in the mêlée were often in imminent personal danger. That was the opportunity for the nearest man to win his spurs and his coat armor, by interposing his shield between the steel of the enemy and his sovereign's body. Thus, at the battle of Hastings a shield of one William several times saved the life of a greater William, the Norman duke and the English king. After the battle the king said to him, ' Forte scutum salus ducum.' Whereupon he assumed the name of Fortescue and was granted a coat of arms with a shield for a crest.

"Sometimes the peril came to the king or liege lord in the hunt. As when David II., King of Scotland, was hunting with a few followers in Stocket forest, in his eagerness to attack a wolf that had been the terror of the neighboring shepherds, becoming separated from his men, he was suddenly confronted by the beast. The wolf with a powerful spring seized the throat of the horse with such fury that after rearing and plunging violently it rolled over upon its master. The king was now helpless and would have fallen an easy prey to the beast had not help been at hand. A young man coming up succeeded, by a vigorous use of the skene or dagger, after a desperate fight, in killing the wolf. After releasing the king he was asked his name. ' Robertson,' said the man. ' Henceforth then,' answered the king, ' be thou called Skene, in memory of the weapon which thou knowest so well how to use.' In addition to lands, the sovereign granted him, to bear on his shield, wolves' heads and daggers to commemorate this event."

At the battle of Hastings (1066) Ferrers, the Master of Horse to William the Conqueror, bore as his arms, *argent, six horse-shoes, sable*, and the Ferrers family still retain the horse-shoe as a bearing. While a horse-shoe may not be considered a classic device, yet in the Ferrers arms it speaks of an old and noble family and perpetuates the glory of the founder of the house.

After the reign of Richard II., the king granted all coats of arms, and no new bearing could be lawfully adopted by a knight without the consent of the sovereign. Since devices were bestowed as marks of honor only, no charge would be given to which any idea of disgrace was attached in the mind of either king or vassal.

For these reasons alone no one should discard or despise a coat of arms because of the modern interpretation of its devices.

[1] From paper by George R. Howell, M.A.

THE MISAPPROPRIATION OF ARMS.

No error is more common than the idea that heraldry is a completed science, and that crests, devices, and coat-armor are only to be found in the musty pages of old records. Heraldry is an exact, living, and progressive ~~art~~ *science.* The Heralds' College almost daily grants new arms and augmentations of existing ones, whose very devices show their modern origin: the mill-wheel, the spindle, and other charges indicating competency amassed by honorable toil, are not infrequent in the official records of old as well as recently granted arms.

In England a man who occupies the position of a gentleman, in the conventional meaning of the word, may apply to the Heralds' College and have granted to him, and confirmed in his heirs, some heraldic composition *different* from any other coat of arms. This correct manner of procuring arms is very often ignored, and the practice of misappropriating arms is almost as common in England and on the Continent as it is in the United States. Since the rules for the regulation of armorial bearings are sanctioned by the European governments, and new coats of arms can be legally secured, it becomes a matter of surprise that such a condition of affairs as the wholesale assumption of arms should exist there; and it ceases to be a wonder that this practice exists in America, where there has been no law for the protection of those who are rightfully entitled to the use of armorial bearings. Certain it is that the custom of individuals assuming the arms of another family of the same name has done much to injure the cause of heraldry among all nations, and is one that cannot be too strongly condemned.

There is no reason why any American should not bear arms, if entitled to them; in fact, there is every reason why he should bear them, particularly as arms have become in this country the badge of the family and the mark of lineage. But when borne at all, arms should be in accordance with heraldic law, and the fact that great care is necessary in proving them cannot be too strongly impressed on the mind. The Rev. Beverly R. Betts has remarked, —and not too severely,—"As the right to bear Arms is an incorporeal hereditament, it follows that Arms are property. The practice of appropriating other people's Arms at one's own will is one that cannot be too strongly reprehended. Apart from its peculiar heinousness, in the eyes of the genealogist, in corrupting descents and obscuring pedigrees, its immorality is obvious. A man who steals his neighbor's Arms is no better than he would be if he were to 'convey,' as Ancient Pistol says, the spoons and forks on which the proprietor chooses to engrave them."

The necessity of some regulation for the bearing of coats of arms in

America is commented upon by the eminent English writer, Mr. Cussans, in an extended chapter on American heraldry in the last edition of his "Handbook of Heraldry." "Unfortunately, there is not in the United States of America any Institution analogous to our College of Heralds; the consequence is, there are probably more *Assumptive Arms* borne in that country than anywhere else. Nor are the bearers of such Arms to be so much blamed as the unscrupulous self-styled Heralds who supply them. The advertising London tradesmen who profess to find arms, are for the most part less anxious to give themselves the trouble of examining the requisite documents—even if they possess the necessary ability to do so, which many certainly do not—than they are of securing the fee. If, therefore, they cannot readily *find* in the printed pages of Burke, they do not hesitate to draw from the depths of their imagination. Many American gentlemen consequently engrave their plate, and adorn the panels of their carriages, with heraldic insignia to which they have no right whatever: and this, too, though they may have an hereditary claim to Arms as ancient and honorable as those of a Talbot or a Hastings."

"The number of privately printed Genealogies which have been issued during the past few years conclusively shows that the commendable pride of Ancestry has a great hold on Americans—as, indeed, it has on any one who values the reputation of his parents—and that it would be a national boon if some incorruptible authority, analogous to our College of Heralds, could be established among them."

Mr. Cussans' suggestions are surely worthy of more than passing consideration, particularly at the present time, since the study of heraldry, stimulated by the results of genealogical researches, has led the American to place a greater value upon coats of arms than heretofore, and some means should be devised whereby the bearer of arms in this country may be protected in the use of his individual or family property.

THE USE OF THE CREST IN AMERICA.

"What custom sanctions becomes a law."

With the love of ancestry which exists in the hearts of all true Americans, it is very natural that they should cling with tenacity to the relics and heraldic insignia of their forefathers. Coats of arms have, as a rule, been used in the form in which they were first brought to this country by the early settlers. The descendants have cherished the family arms as they appear upon old documents, seals, etc., deeming it almost sacrilegious to alter them or omit any portion of the heraldic composition. Thus it has become usual for all the members of a family to bear the same crest and arms, without modification or distinction.

In England, on the contrary, coats of arms are subjected to changes. The head of the family alone is entitled to bear the full coat of arms without modifications; each son has his "mark of cadency;" the wife bears the shield, and the daughters the devices of the shield in a lozenge, the *crest* being omitted in the two latter instances. Permanent changes are introduced by marriage with an heiress, and temporary ones by almost every other marriage. The system is so perfect, when rigidly carried out, that a heraldic decoration upon note-paper, for instance, at once reveals the position of the writer, whether man or woman; if a man, whether the head of the family, a son, or a connection; if a woman, whether an heiress, or a wife not an heiress, a maid or a widow. (See Figs. 871 to 880.)

The absence of any central heraldic authority in the United States has naturally led to an indifference to heraldic laws and customs, and the crest and arms have, from long usage, become the badge of the family, not of the individual. Thus it has been the American custom for a woman to bear the full arms or crest of her husband or ancestor, and it may possibly be claimed that "what custom sanctions becomes a law." In other countries, however, the heraldic rule is absolute that "*no woman except the Sovereign may bear a crest.*" This rule is founded on the idea that the crest was originally the individual decoration of a warrior; it was worn upon his helmet in battle, to distinguish *him* personally from others. Hence it is natural that, in times of peace also, it should be borne by him alone. In later days, however, the crest, while hardly an integral part of the arms, became hereditary, and passed from father to son. At this point the development ceased in England, but in the United States, as we see, it has gone even further; the crest has become as much a part of the coat of arms as the charges on the shield, and the arms without the crest have been until lately seldom used. Although the rule that "no woman except the Sovereign may bear a crest" prevails in England and other countries, it is doubtful whether a change so sweeping as would be necessary in order to conform thereto can be made in a custom which has been established in America for so many years, although there is no doubt as to the proper course to be pursued.

RULES TO GOVERN HERALDRY IN AMERICA.

THE ENGLISH RULES PREFERRED.

It is not within the province of this book to dictate rules for the government of an American heraldry; that, indeed, would be "assumptive and presumptive" in the superlative degree. But it may be permissible to make such suggestions as will have a tendency to direct the attention of those interested to the necessity of some system by which the bearing of arms in this country shall be regulated. The difficulty in formulating such a plan is apparent.

In England the population is homogeneous, and therefore governed by a common heraldic rule; and so of Germany, France, Russia, Italy, Spain, etc. But in the United States the population is heterogeneous and composed of the descendants of ENGLISH ancestors who settled throughout the country, of the patriotic FRENCH who gave such valuable aid in establishing American independence, of the DUTCH who settled along the Hudson, of the SWEDES and DANES upon the Delaware, of the SPANIARDS in Florida, and of GERMANS who came here about the time of the Revolution. The living descendants of these early settlers are Americans, and we may presume that they bear the arms of their ancestors exactly as such came into their possession.

It is very evident that, as the English rule has, in a measure, heretofore guided Americans of English descent, they will not depart from it. It may be assumed that if an arms-bearing German takes up his residence here, he is entitled to bear his devices according to the rule which established them. And it is very natural that if a Frenchman, Italian, Spaniard, or Russian of long residence here should desire to trace his family arms and bear them, he would do so in accordance with the heraldic rule of his own country, if he were to follow any rule at all.

This all forms a very good theory, but, like many other theories, it is not confirmed in practice. For there have been in America no rules to follow; and it is certain that the rules of all nations cannot govern the heraldry of one. The result of this absence of a general rule, and the assumption of arms *ad libitum*, places the heraldry of America in practically the same position as the heraldry of the eleventh century, and for some time later, when no law or order regulated the bearing of arms, and each man adopted such devices as best pleased his fancy, or copied from others. This method naturally produced much confusion as the number of arms increased; the same devices were borne by several knights, and the necessity of some regulation became apparent. Out of this chaotic condition of affairs grew system and order only as nations adopted certain rules to regulate the use of arms and protect those who were entitled to them. It is an indisputable fact that from the assumptive arms came many of the coats of arms of the nobility of the Old World.

The question now arises, how can the bearing of arms be regulated in America? And it admits of the suggestion that the English rules, which are clear, precise, and positive, should govern American heraldry as far as possible. By this proposal it is intended to convey the idea that the peculiar conditions of the United States forbid a blind following of the heraldic laws of any *one* country, and the bearing of arms here can only be governed by a general knowledge of heraldry, an appreciation of circumstances, and the exercise of sound judgment and good taste in the treatment of each individual case. Any treatment must be guided by certain laws, usages, and customs. For example, let us say that the general rules of English heraldry shall fundamentally govern heraldic bearings in America,—to this there will be the exceptions providing for due recognition of Continental arms, which should be treated apart if necessary; but as far as possible they also should yield priority to English laws. Three reasons are offered for this course:

1. It is agreed that the time has come, owing to the increasing popularity of heraldry and the consequent much greater usage than heretofore, that some system should be established for guidance, if in any way possible; otherwise chaos must still reign, the confusion increase, and the science fall into disrepute.

When rules conflict, some must yield. When Continental peculiarities can be simply engrafted without conflict, that may be done; but it is apparent that in forming a system out of discordant elements something must give way.

2. Probably ninety per cent. of the descendants of armiger ancestors in America are of British origin. Majority rules!

3. Each of the original thirteen Colonies forming the American Union was at the time of the Revolution an English possession, under English law as to ranks, degrees, titles, etc., and the heraldry was governed accordingly. Of this ample proof exists. *The original heraldic laws of this country were British*, and there are to-day more English, Scotch, and Irish arms borne here than those of all other nations combined. Our legal as well as our blood ancestry is British, and we are in a manner required to recognize the fact. Of course the French and Spanish colonists were under laws governing those nations; and in the Southwest and South they still have representatives who undoubtedly will be glad to bear their arms as Americans,—rules once established,—for Americans they are. Persons who *have come into the country since its national origin* ought not to change the fundamental principles. The cases of such persons should be exceptional.

An example of the practical superiority of the English rule may be in place. The German rule, following custom, that charges and crests may face dexter or sinister, which of course would result in the helmets facing either way, might be adversely commented upon by the French; for, according to Palliot (1661), the French helmet when borne alone and turned to the sinister is a mark of illegitimacy. The English in all cases turn their crests and charges to the dexter. It is here that the adoption of the English rule is certainly preferable for American application, for if crests and charges all face the dexter they will be in conformity with the heraldic laws most approved by all nations, and thus be open to no justly unfavorable criticism.

The Germans permit color upon color. When it appears so in France it is excused by the term *cousu* (sewed to); while the English follow the original idea of distinctness, and consider color on color a great fault, for it is very confusing.

Then there are occasions where the English rule *cannot* affect the American arms, and we are thrown entirely upon our own resources. In England the eldest son is the shining light, and a mark of cadency upon his coat of arms so testifies. In America all sons are equal, and thus the rules of cadency can never be applied to the use of arms in the United States, the marks of cadency here appearing in many instances as an integral part of the arms, as a result of the custom of bearing arms and transmitting them as first brought to this country. In fact, the constitutional abrogation and prohibition of the law of primogeniture has introduced into American heraldry a factor little short of revolutionary.

The marshalling of arms by quartering is comparatively unknown in the United States, but in other countries it is often faithfully executed, and thus preserves a record of marriages of the male line with heiresses or otherwise. The correct marshalling of arms in America would be difficult and almost impossible (wholly impossible in some instances), a difficulty due to the confusion caused by the occasional bearing of the paternal arms by the female as well as by the male descendants.

For these reasons the following suggestions are offered, and it is hoped may not be amiss:

1. Apply the English rules to heraldry in America whenever it is possible to do so, especially as to the following:

2. Metal upon metal, color upon color, should be avoided.

3. All charges and crests should face the dexter.

4. Men should avoid the bearing of such helmets as designate technically a rank not possessed by them. The use of the esquire's helmet is permissible and advised.

5. Great care should be taken against the bearing of the coronet of an *English duke*, a *French count*, a *German prince*, or other foreign nobleman. Coronets indicate the rank of the bearers. The crest coronet (ducal coronet) is the exception.

6. For individual use omit supporters. If belonging to an ancestor they may be portrayed in an original copy of his arms, but upon personal seals, plate, etc., they would be out of place, as they indicate a rank. In England, with few exceptions, supporters are borne by peers, and inherited by the eldest son *only*.

7. The garter decoration, which is peculiar to Knights of the Garter, around arms, should not be used by those not members of that Order.

8. Retain original marks of cadency if desired, in cases where they have been borne in the family arms for several generations, and thus have practically become part of the arms.

9. A husband may impale the arms of his wife. The impaled arms can be borne by both, or by the survivor of either, but these arms should not be borne in the form of impalement by the children.

10. If the tintures of a coat of arms have long been reversed in accord-

ance with heraldic law, do not change them. The arms are possibly thus differenced for some just purpose. If they are unintelligibly reversed, it is better to conform them to the original blazon.

11. Ladies who desire to conform to the laws of English heraldry will omit the helmet and crest at all times, and unmarried ladies, or widows, will bear their heraldic devices in a lozenge. Mottoes are also denied ladies by heraldic law, the Sovereign alone excepted. In both cases the English rule is advised.

12. A widow may bear her husband's arms in a lozenge, either separately or impaled with her own; but if she marries again, the arms of her late husband should be discarded.

13. In the United States, in which it has been the custom for all branches of a family to bear the same coat of arms without change or modification, and in which a coat of arms may be said to be preserved as a family tradition, the coat of arms of the mother as well as the father is sometimes used and cherished by the children, male and female, and their descendants, without question. Thus, in America, coats of arms of maternal ancestors (not heiresses) are occasionally borne by descendants as paternal arms, simply because they have been handed down the paternal line for several generations.

By prescriptive right, it may be considered proper to continue the bearing of such arms. But to search out a mother's coat and adopt it as one's own is contrary to heraldic laws, unless she was an heiress.

14. In carving, engraving, or designing arms, *for any purpose*, the tinctures should be indicated by heraldic marks and lines, unless the device is borne *proper*. Failure to thus indicate the tinctures will create *false heraldry*.

15. Do not guess at any thing. Be sure your crest is a *martlet*, not a *Cornish chough*, or that a charge is a *trefoil*, not a *cross*, etc. Charges and crests are often changed by misinterpretation, and create different arms. The distinctions in some instances are very trifling, but important enough to demand careful attention.

16. Do not assume the arms of another simply because the names are similar, or relationship is *imagined*. *Do not take unlawful possession of the property of another*. When heraldry is better understood such action will prove embarrassing.

17. If you are uncertain of your claim to a coat of arms, apply to any competent genealogist. If he cannot trace the connection, do not bear arms.

ARMS OF PENNSYLVANIA FAMILIES.

Whilst it is not within the province of this book to publish, even in part, a roll of American arms, the following illustrations from coats of arms borne by descendants of some of the families who resided in Philadelphia and vicinity, prior to the Revolution, are considered of value to the student, inasmuch as they will acquaint him with heraldic devices which may be recognized as in almost daily use, and prove, with other arms herein shown, the statement that " Coat Armor has been continuously borne in the United States as a mark of social distinction, from early colonial days to the present time."

FIG. 249.

ATLEE (of Lancaster) (Fig. 249): *Azure, a lion rampant argent.* CREST (see Fig. 47).

FIG. 250.

BOND (Fig. 250): *Argent, on a chevron sable three bezants.* CREST: *A demi-pegasus azure winged and semée of estoiles or.*

FIG. 251.

CADWALADER (Fig. 251): *Azure, a cross formée fitchée or.*

FIG. 252.

CARPENTER (Fig. 252): *Argent, a greyhound passant and chief sable.* CREST: *A greyhound's head erased, per fesse sable and argent.*

FIG. 253.

CHEW (of Cliveden) (Fig. 253): *Gules, a chevron or, on a chief of the second three leopard's faces proper.* CREST: *A leopard rampant guardant proper.*

FIG. 254.

CUTHBERT (Fig. 254): *Vert, a fesse engrailed between four mullets argent, over all an arrow in pale, point downward proper.* CREST: *A demi-lion rampant azure.*

HAMILTON (of the Woodlands) (Fig. 255): *Gules, three cinquefoils or.* CREST: *Out of a ducal coronet argent an oak-tree fructed and penetrated transversely in the main stem by a frame saw proper, the frame gold, upon the blade the word "through" sable.*

Fig. 256.

LLOYD (of Dolobran) (Fig. 256): *Azure, upon a chevron between three cocks argent, a crescent sable.* CREST: *A goat rampant argent, charged on the neck with a crescent sable.*

Fig. 257.

LOGAN (of Stenton) (Fig. 257): *Or, three passion nails gules conjoined in point piercing a man's heart proper. In base a lion passant of the third.* CREST: *A stag's head proper gorged and chained or.*

FIG. 258.

MIFFLIN (Fig. 258): *Or, a chevron azure, in sinister chief a mullet of six points gules.* CREST: *A dove holding in its beak an olive branch proper.*

FIG. 259.

NORRIS (of Fairhill) (Fig. 259): *Argent, upon a chevron gules between three falcon's heads erased sable, a mullet or.* CREST: *A falcon's head erased sable.*

FIG. 260.

PEMBERTON (Fig. 260): *Argent, a chevron sable between three water bougets of the second hooped and handled or.* CREST: *A dragon's head couped proper.*

FIG. 261.

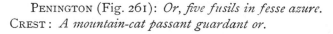

PENINGTON (Fig. 261): *Or, five fusils in fesse azure.* CREST: *A mountain-cat passant guardant or.*

FIG. 262.

FIG. 263.

FIG. 264.

FIG. 265.

PLUMSTED (Fig. 262): *Ermine, three chevronels sable, on the uppermost three annulets argent.* CREST: *Out of a ducal coronet a griffin's head argent.*

RAWLE (Fig. 263): *Sable, three swords in pale, two with points in base, the middle one in chief, argent.* CREST: *An arm embowed in armor proper holding in the gauntlet a sword argent hilted or.*

SHIPPEN (Fig. 264): *Argent, a chevron between three oak leaves gules.* CREST: *A raven sable holding in its beak an oak leaf gules.*

TILGHMAN (Fig. 265): *Per fesse sable and argent, a lion rampant reguardant doublequeued counterchanged, crowned or.* CREST: *A demi-lion issuant and statant sable, crowned or.*

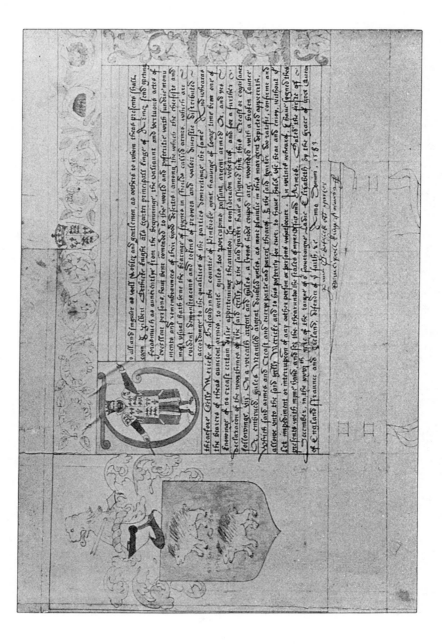

To all and singular as well Nobles and gentlemen as others to whom these presents shall come &c. Wilbt Dethick knight als Garter principall Kinge of Armes, send greeting. Forasmuch as auncientlie from the beginninge the valiaunt and vertuous actes of excellent persones have bene comended to the world and posteritie with sundrie monumentes and remembraunces of their good Desertes: among the which the chiefeste and most usuall hath bene the bearinge of signes in Shieldes called armes, which are evident demonstracons and tokens of prowes and valor: Diverslie distributed accordinge to the qualities of the persones somtimes the same...

Therefore I Garter Kinge of Armes in the countie of &c. In the bearers of these auncient armes to witt, Gules two porcupines passant argent armed Or, and yet knowinge of no juste cleate Wilbe appertaininge thereunto, In consideracon whereof, and for a further Declaration of the worthines of the said Gules, to the said parties have assigned him this Creast or cognisance followinge, viz: On a wreath argent and gules, a demi Lion couped arg. mounted with a Gorget Laurer Which said armes and Creast and turrey park and parcell thereof, to the said parties do ratifie, confirme and allowe unto the said parties, and to his posteritie for ever, to have hold use beare and enjoy, without let impediment or interruption of any other person or persons whatsoever. In witnes whereof I have signed these presentes with my hand and fett the subscribinge the seale of mine office and Armes. Geven the first of December, in the xxvij yere of the raigne of o[ur] soueraigne Ladie Elizabeth, by the grace of god Queene of Englande Fraunce and Irelande Defendo[ur] of faith &c. Anno Domini, 1583.

William Dethick Garter of armes

FIG. 266.

WAYNE (Fig. 266): *Quarterly; I. and IV. gules, a chevron ermine between three inside gauntlets or,* for *Wayne; II. and III. Azure, a lion rampant argent,* for *Atlee.* CREST: *A stag's head erased proper.*

FIG. 267.

WHARTON (Fig. 267): *Sable, a maunche argent within a bordure or, charged with eight pairs of lion's paws saltireways erased, gules.* CREST: *A bull's head erased argent armed or gorged with a ducal coronet per pale of the second and gules.*

A GRANT OF ARMS.

A rarity in America is an original grant of arms, as, with but few exceptions, such documents have not been brought to our shores. Fig. 268 is a reduced fac-simile of the grant to Sir Gelly Mericke in 1583. This original grant is now in the possession of a descendant, John Vaughan Merrick, Esq., Philadelphia.

CHAPTER V.

AMERICAN FLAGS, SEALS, AND COINS.

THE same rules that apply to a shield are also observed in the blazoning of armorial devices upon a flag, and the colors are indicated in precisely the same manner, although the system is seldom applied in America.

The effect upon the mind of an English herald would be difficult to imagine

FIG. 269.

if he should possibly see the manner in which flags are sometimes designed in this country. The American flag, for instance, indicated with dots and lines thus: *A field or, " stripes" azure, canton sable, stars of the first*, or his own beloved flag, with the heraldic lines indicating the following colors in the crosses alone: *sable, gules, azure, vert, purpure.*

We also note the frequent and incorrect use of stars upon the chief of the American shield and the indifferent use of lines, which indicate at various times the entire list of heraldic tinctures. The idea of *" stripes" or and azure, upon a chief gules thirteen stars of the first*, is simply ridiculous. Let us at least emblazon our national emblems correctly, and not mislead or confuse people of other countries who, while possibly not acquainted with the details of our national devices, are capable of interpreting heraldic notation correctly.

The length of a flag from the staff to the end is called the *Fly*, and the depth the *Hoist* or *Dip*. Charges upon the field of a flag must face the staff (excepting when contourné). This system is necessary to distinctness, as flags are generally transparent, and each part of a device should cover the identical part of the same device on the reverse side.

Coats of arms have been borne upon flags in America from the date of

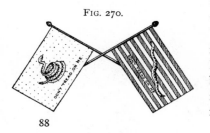

FIG. 270.

the country's settlement, and from the time of the Revolution the flags of the United States and the flags of many individual States have been charged with heraldic devices. One of the earliest emblems for the American Colonies was the rattlesnake. It was borne on flags, and frequently accompanied by the expressive

88

motto, " Don't tread on me." Two of these " rattlesnake flags" are preserved at the State House in Philadelphia, where they are placed over the door of the east room, in which the Declaration of Independence was adopted (Fig. 270).

Hon. Samuel W. Pennypacker directs attention to an interesting group of heraldic flags,—those carried by the Associators of Pennsylvania.[1]

1. A lion erect, a naked scimitar in one paw, the other holding the Pennsylvania scutcheon. Motto: Patria.

2. Three arms, wearing different linen,—ruffled, plain, and checked,—the hands joined by grasping each other's wrist, denoting the union of all ranks. Motto: Unita Virtus Valet.

3. An eagle, the emblem of victory, descending from the skies. Motto: A Deo Victoria.

4. The figure of Liberty sitting on a cube, holding a spear with the cap of Freedom on its point. Motto: Inestimabilis.

5. An armed man with a naked falchion in his hand. Motto: Deus adjuvat Fortes.

6. An elephant, being the emblem of a warrior always on his guard, as that creature is said never to lie down, and hath his arms ever in readiness. Motto: Semper Paratus.

7. A city walled round. Motto: Salus Patriæ Summa Lex.

8. A soldier with his piece recovered, ready to present. Motto: Sic Pacem Quærimus.

9. A coronet and plume of feathers. Motto: In God we Trust.

10. A man with a sword drawn. Motto: Pro Aris et Focis.

11. Three of the associators marching with their muskets shouldered, and dressed in different clothes, intimating the unanimity of the different sorts of people in the Association. Motto: Vis Unita Fortior.

12. A musket and sword crossing each other. Motto: Pro Rege et Grege.

13. Representation of a glory, in the middle of which is wrote, Jehovah-Nissi; in English, The Lord our Banner.

14. A castle, at the gate of which a soldier stands sentinel. Motto: Cavendo Tutus.

15. David as he advanced against Goliath and slung the stone. Motto: In Nomine Domini.

16. A lion rampant, one paw holding up a scimitar, another a sheaf of wheat. Motto: Domine, Protege Alimentum.

17. A sleeping lion. Motto: Rouse me if you dare.

18. Hope represented by a woman standing clothed in blue, holding one hand on an anchor. Motto: Spero per Deum Vincere.

19. Duke of Cumberland as a general. Motto: Pro Deo et Georgio Rege.

20. A soldier on horseback. Motto: Pro Libertate Patriæ.

[1] The works of Franklin, by Jared Sparks.

The first of these flags has been adopted by the Society of Colonial Wars in the Commonwealth of Pennsylvania, and is recognized as very appropriate for the purpose intended. A paper read before the Society[1] contains the following information in reference to it:

FIG. 271.

"In 1747, during the 'War of the Spanish Succession,' the Spaniards came up the Delaware to Newcastle. The vessels and towns were in alarm. The Assembly of Pennsylvania declined to provide any means of defence. Dr. Franklin issued his 'Plain Truth,' arousing the citizens of Philadelphia. Twelve hundred signed 'Articles of Association,' and, finally, ten thousand became subscribers to the pledge of the Associators and organized. Their wives and daughters raised money for arms and bought silk for flags. Dr. Franklin made devices for them, of which the first one was 'a lion erect, in one paw a naked scimitar, the other holding the Pennsylvania escutcheon— motto, Patria.' As this motto was different from that on Penn family arms, 'Dum clarum teneam,' and from the motto on Penn arms as used officially in the Province, 'Mercy & Justice,' and as the organization, equipment, and efficient drill of the 'Associators' was without the previous knowledge or consent of the Proprietaries and filled them with alarm (which was finally pacified into toleration), and as the newspapers (Pennsylvania Gazette, January 12th and April 16th, 1748) of the date distinctly say *that this device was carried through the city under Col. Abram Taylor's* command, we may be justified in calling this the prophecy of an independence of British influence, and the flag bearing this device as a Provincial flag of Pennsylvania, if not *the* Provincial or Colonial flag of Pennsylvania. These views and conclusions having been submitted to Rev. Dr. Stevens, Dr. Charles J. Stillé, Mr. Frederick D. Stone, Mr. John W. Jordan, Dr. William H. Egle, Mr. Charles R. Hildeburn, Col. J. Granville Leach, Judge Pennypacker, and Mr. Taylor Dickson, the consensus of their opinions (I feel justified in saying) was expressed by Mr. Hildeburn, viz.: 'You have undoubted historical ground for using the device mentioned,' and by Dr. Egle in saying, 'If any object to your conclusion, let them prove what *was* the Provincial flag of Pennsylvania.' "[2]

In Fig. 272 is shown the banner of the First Troop Philadelphia City Cavalry, a body formed on the 17th of November, 1774, by the association of twenty-eight of Philadelphia's leading citizens: Abraham Markoe, Andrew Allen, Samuel Morris, James Mease, Thomas Leiper, William Hall, Samuel Penrose, Samuel Howell, Jr., James Hunter, James Budden, John Dunlap, John Mease, Robert Hare, William Pollard, Henry Hill, John Boyle,

William Tod, John Mitchell, George Campbell, Samuel Caldwell, Andrew Caldwell, Levi Hollingsworth, Blair McClenachan, George Graff, Benjamin Randolph, Thomas Peters, George Fullerton, and William West, Jr. The flag was presented to the troop by the first captain, Abraham Markoe, and is of bright yellow silk, emblazoned with a complete heraldic achievement composed of shield, crest, supporters, and motto. The dexter chief is charged with a canton, *barry of thirteen azure and argent*, and the border of running vine and the fringe are of silver bullion. It is still carefully preserved by the Philadelphia City Troop, and possesses a particular historical value, since, according to Preble,

FIG. 272.

it is the first American banner upon which thirteen stripes were displayed, and is believed by many to have suggested the design for the " Stars and Stripes."

Though many theories have existed as to the origin of the American flag, the ascertained facts of history seem to be as follows : The American colonists were accustomed to the use of the flag of Great Britain. This was the flag which they carried to victory in their Colonial battles against Indians, the Spaniards, and the French. It floated over all their public buildings, and was honored and loved until the Revolution. It was a flag of red, white, and blue, and bore a canton in the corner. When hostilities broke out against the crown, a flag came into use which was the British flag differenced only by the placing of a series of white stripes across the red of the mother-country. This was so arranged as to divide the red into thirteen alternate stripes of red and white, symbolizing the thirteen Colonies. Such is the origin of the present stripes in the American flag. The canton of England, with its crosses of St. George and St. Andrew, was retained. Of course there was nothing especially appropriate in this retention of the two crosses that stood for England and Scotland. Yet the design is of importance as showing the gradual development of the new flag from the old. The next stage was the action of Congress providing for the present banner. Of the committee appointed to arrange for the making of the final design, Washington was a member. The committee waited on Mrs. Betsy Ross, in her upholstering shop on Arch Street, Philadelphia, and it is related that Washington drew the outlines of the work. The canton and stripes were continued, and the only change made was the introduction of thirteen stars on a blue field, in place of the two crosses. As the Washington coat of arms contained stars, or mullets, and bars of alternate red and white, it is not improbable that Washington had these, to him, familiar details in his mind as

FIG. 273.

he did his drawing, and that this explains the retention of the stripes and the addition of the stars, which has given rise to the tradition that the design had its origin in his coat of arms. The facts seem to be that the American flag is the old flag of Colonial times transformed into a national ensign, which now stands for all the States in the number of its stars, and for the original thirteen in the number of its stripes. The matter is of special significance, for the flag thus records the history of American political life from the days of the Colonial settlement to the addition of our latest new State.

It may be apropos for the author to here record the origin of "Flag Day," which was first celebrated upon June 14, 1893. This was at the suggestion of Col. J. Granville Leach, and "The Pennsylvania Society of the Colonial Dames of America inaugurated the movement to have the 14th day of June known as Flag Day, and the same forever hereafter observed by the display of the American flag from every home in the land."

The committee in charge of the first celebration were as follows: Mrs. E. D. Gillespie, Chairman, Mrs. G. Dawson Coleman, ex officio, Mrs. J. P. Mumford, Miss Magee, Mrs. Wm. D. Winsor, Mrs. James D. Winsor, Miss Anne Hollingsworth Wharton, Miss Ellen Emlen.

SEALS.

Seals were at first used to furnish marks of attestation to contracts, when the contracting parties were unable to write their names. This practice led to the introduction of the signet-ring, which was made of gold or other metal, and often mounted with precious stones. The ancient Egyptians practised the art of seal engraving, and in later times the Romans and their emperors bore on seals devices which symbolized the tastes, fancies, and superstitions of the people and era. Each of the early English kings had his seal, and in English law it was necessary that, on formal contracts, the *seal* of each party as well as his signature should appear. Upon the warrant to execute Charles I. appear fifty-nine individual seals opposite their owners' respective signatures. The older custom of impressing each seal with its owner's device has fallen into disuse, and a small, plain paper seal, or even a mere scroll made on the paper by the pen of the scrivener, is now sufficient in most cases to comply with the legal form. Every incorporated body, however, has its own seal, bearing particular devices, with which all its formal acts are attested, and such devices may be assumed at pleasure.

With the decline of the necessity for individual seals bearing distinctive emblems in legal transactions, the use of them has gradually been abandoned, except for closing letters; and the introduction of modern envelopes has rendered even this practice an ornament rather than a necessity. There has been in late years, however, a tendency toward a revival of the custom of using seals on letters of a social character, and consequently signet-rings have again become popular.

The necessity for some formal attestation early led to the adoption of a seal by the English kings; and the changes in the Great Seal with each successive sovereign form a very interesting study. Mr. W. H. Whitmore remarks: " The use of national coats-of-arms and seals is of great antiquity. The convenience of such a national emblem has led to a continuance of the custom, and most modern communities have promptly assumed flags and seals as an assertion of sovereignty.

" In England the use of royal seals is continuous from the time of Edward the Confessor; and from the time of Richard I. three lions passant have been regarded as the arms of England. The fleur-de-lys or lilies of France; the lion rampant within a double tressure, flory, of Scotland; the harp of Ireland: have all become familiar in our literature. Under a monarchy the national arms and seal are those of the King; but it is to be noted that when James of Scotland became King of England, the English arms occupied the first place in his emblazonment. Since that time, although the royal family had the paternal arms and added them to the shield, under Queen Victoria the royal arms bore only the insignia of England, Scotland and Ireland.

" When the colonies in America were established under the authority of Great Britain, it was found convenient to devise armorial seals for them, examples of which are to be found in our local histories. Several of these colonies, like Massachusetts, received special and peculiar seals; but when they became royal provinces a new rule was adopted. The British arms were granted, but with a difference, usually the addition of a motto specifying that the arms were those of the province. . . .

" After the Revolution the use of an armorial seal, and thus of a state coat of arms, was continued in Massachusetts as well as in the other original colonies, and the custom has been imitated in all the states since added to our nation. Other corporate bodies, as cities, colleges and societies, have followed the same course, finding heraldic seals to be at once the simplest, most expressive and best defined symbols obtainable.

" The terms of heraldry are few and exact, and the advantage of an heraldic seal is that the description in heraldic terms is understood by all skilled in the art, and every herald is thereby able to produce the same representation. It is a convenient short-hand, of universal precision; and as it is of the highest importance that a state seal or symbol should always be represented in the same manner, there is every reason that it should be established in accordance with heraldic rules."

It is, however, unfortunate that with but comparatively few exceptions the devices upon the seals of our various States are susceptible to criticism from a heraldic stand-point. In many cases no attempt has been made to approach the heraldic standards of simplicity and accuracy. The devices are numerous, and consequently too small and crowded to be distinct on even the best impressions, and the introduction of perspective into heraldic designs is wholly improper. The State seals leave much to be desired, not only because of the frequently unheraldic nature of their devices, but on account of their indistinctness. In many of these seals it is evident no thought of heraldry has been in the minds of the designers, and the seals of the Western States particularly symbolize the resources of their respective countries.

It is to be regretted that in many of the older States only imperfect records of the early seals have been preserved. Even the date of the adoption of the seal now in use is uncertain in some cases, and in others the seal was used for many years before it was officially approved. This uncertainty appears particularly unfortunate when we consider that the seals of other countries are of great value to the antiquary and historian, since they record events from the rise and fall of monarchies to the "landmarks" in individual family history. A pleasing illustration is to be found in the Great Seal of Queen Anne, which was devised after the union of England and Scotland. The rose of England and the thistle of Scotland grow from one stem, and are surmounted by the crown of England. The seal will thus ever bear witness that the union took place during the reign of Queen Anne. Such evidence can always be credited, since no error could have remained undiscovered in a seal in almost daily use.

AMERICAN SEALS.

In the preparation of what follows it has been the author's object to secure as much information, hitherto unpublished, as possible, together with examples of seals not before shown, that this work may be truly termed up to date,—though it is not improbable that there have been omissions. All reproductions of these seals are from direct impressions, furnished by the Governors and Secretaries of the States and Departments, to whom the author desires to express his acknowledgments for the uniform courtesy extended to him at all times.

It is but fair that the author should assume no responsibility for the heraldic correctness of these illustrations, which are reproduced exactly from the original seals.

THE GREAT SEAL OF THE UNITED STATES.

Among the most heraldic American seals may be classed those of the government, with the seal of the United States in first place in point of correctness and appropriate symbolism. Several papers have been written upon this seal. The most recent and authentic[1] was published by the Department of State in 1892, from which the following information is taken:

[1] By Mr. Gaillard Hunt, Washington, D.C.

" On July 4, 1776, after the Declaration of Independence had been read in the Continental Congress, it was ' *Resolved*, That Dr. Franklin, Mr. J. Adams and Mr. Jefferson be a committee, to prepare a device for a Seal of the United States of North America.'

FIG. 274.

Original seal.

FIG. 275.

FIG. 276.

Present seal.

Reverse.

" The committee reported on August 10 as follows : ' The great seal should on one side have the arms of the United States of America, which arms should be as follows :

" ' The shield has six Quarters, parts one, coupé two. The 1st Or, a Rose enamelled gules and argent for England : the 2nd Argent, a Thistle proper for Scotland: the 3d Vert a Harp Or for Ireland: the 4th Azure a Flower de luce Or for France: the 5th Or the Imperial Eagle Sable for Germany; and the 6th Or the Belgic Lion Gules for Holland, pointing out the countries from which these States have been peopled. The Shield within a border Gules entwined of thirteen Scutcheons Argent linked together by a chain or, each charged with the initial letters Sable, as follows: 1st N. H., 2nd M. B., 3d R. I., 4th C., 5th N. Y., 6th N. J., 7th P., 8th D. C., 9th M., 10th V., 11th N. C., 12th S. C., 13th G., for each of the thirteen independent States of America. Supporters, Dexter the Goddess of Liberty in a corselet of Armour, alluding to the present times, holding in her right hand the Spear and Cap and with her left supporting the shield of the States; Sinister, the Goddess Justice bearing a sword in her right hand and in her left a Balance. Crest, the Eye of Providence in a radiant Triangle whose Glory extends over the shield and beyond the Figures. Motto: E Pluribus Unum. Legend round the whole

FIG. 277.　　　　　　　　　　　　　　　FIG. 278.

atchievement, Seal of the United States of America MDCCLXXVI. On the other side of the said Great Seal (Fig. 278) should be the following device: Pharaoh sitting in an open Chariot, a Crown on his head and a sword in his hand passing through the divided waters of the Red Sea in pursuit of the Israelites: Rays from a pillow [pillar] of Fire and the Cloud, expressive of the devine Presence and Command, beaming on Moses who stands on the shore and extending his hand over the Sea causes it to overwhelm Pharaoh. Motto: Rebellion to Tyrants is Obedience to God.'

"Two features of this design were preserved in the seal as finally adopted —the Eye of Providence in the triangle, which now appears upon the reverse, and the motto E pluribus unum. The latter was a familiar quotation to the colonists as the motto of the Gentleman's Magazine, and naturally suggested itself as the most appropriate description of the new order of things, when the several colonies united in their opposition to Great Britain. . . .

"The device of this committee did not meet with a favorable reception, and no drawing of it appears to have been submitted. The report was laid on the table, and nothing further was done until March 25, 1779, when the matter was referred to a new committee, composed of James Lovell, of Massachusetts; Scott, of Virginia; and William Houstoun, of Georgia. Lovell had been a teacher in the Latin School of Boston, master of another New England school. After he came to Congress he took a part of some prominence as a member of the Committee of Foreign Affairs. Houstoun, the brother of Governor John Houstoun, was a lawyer with an English education. The committee reported May 10, 1780, the original report reading as follows: 'The Seal (Fig. 279) to be 4 inches diameter. On one side, the Arms of the United States, as follows: The Shield charged on the Field with 13 diagonal stripes alternate red and white. Supporters, dexter, a Warriour holding a sword; Sinister, a figure representing Peace bearing an Olive Branch. The

FIG. 279.   FIG. 280.

Crest, a radiant constellation of 13 stars. The Motto BELLO VEL PACI. The legend round the atchievement SEAL OF THE UNITED STATES.

"'On the Reverse—The Figure of Liberty seated in a chair holding the staff and cap. The Motto SEMPER. Underneath MDCCLXXVI' (Fig. 280).

"This report was modified so as to make the seal three inches in diameter. It advocated also 'a miniature of the face of the Great Seal to be prepared of half the Diameter, to be affixed as the less seal of the United States.'

"In this device appéared for the first time the constellation of the thirteen stars and the thirteen alternate red and white stripes; but the latter were here diagonal, whereas they finally appeared as perpendicular. The idea followed naturally the design of the national flag, which Congress had adopted June 14, 1777.

"After debate the report was ordered to be recommitted to a new committee, composed of Middleton and Rutledge, of South Carolina, and Boudinot, of New Jersey.

"Two years later the records show activity in the effort to evolve a suitable device, and in the meantime the committee reports had been referred to the Secretary of Congress, Charles Thomson. The name of Arthur Lee, who had returned from France and was now a member of Congress from Virginia, also appears as one of the members to whom the designs were submitted. It was at this time that the assistance of William Barton, A.M., a prominent resident of Philadelphia, was sought. He submitted the following: 'Device for an *Armorial Atchievement* for the Great Seal of the United States of America, in Congress assembled; agreeable to the Rules of Heraldry—proposed by William Barton A.M. ARMS: Barry of thirteen pieces, Argent & Gules; on a Canton, Azure, as many stars disposed in a Circle, of the first: a Pale, Or, surmounted of another, of the third; charged, in Chief, with an Eye surrounded with a Glory, proper; and, in the Fess-point, an Eagle displayed on the Summit of a Doric Column which rests on the base of the Escutcheon, both as the Stars.

"'CREST: On the Helmet of Burnished Gold damasked, grated with six Bars, and surmounted of a Cap of Dignity, Gules, turned up Ermine, a Cock armed with gaffs, proper:

"'SUPPORTERS: On the dexter side: the Genius of America (represented by a Maiden with loose Auburn Tresses, having on her head a radiated Crown, of Gold, encircled with a sky-blue fillet spangled with silver stars; and clothed in a long, loose, white garment, bordered with Green: from her right shoulder to her left side, a scarf semé of Stars, the Tinctures thereof the same as in the Canton; and round the Waist a purple Girdle fringed Or; embroidered, Argent, with the word "Virtue":)—resting her interior Hand on the Escutcheon, and holding in the other the proper *Standard of the United States*, having a Dove, argent, perched on the top of it. On the sinister side: a Man in complete Armour, his sword-belt, Azure, fringed with Gold; the Helmet inscribed with a Wreath of Laurel, and crested with one white and two blue Plumes: supporting with his dexter Hand the Escutcheon and holding, in the exterior, a Lance with the point sanguinated; and upon it a Banner displayed, Vert,—in the Fess-point an Harp, Or, stringed with Silver, between a star in Chief, two Fleurs-de-lis in Fess, and a pair of Swords in Saltier, in Bass, all Argent. The Tenants of the Escutcheon stand on a Scroll, on which the following Motto: "DEO FAVENTE," which alludes to the Eye in the Arms, meant for the *Eye* of Providence. Over the crest, in a scroll, this motto—"VIRTUS SOLA INVICTA"—which requires no comment.

"'The thirteen pieces, barways, which fill up the field of the Arms, may represent the several States; and the same Number of Stars upon a blue Canton, disposed in a Circle, represent a new Constellation, which alludes to the new Empire, formed in the World by the Confederation of those States. Their Disposition, in the form of a circle, denotes the perpetuity of its continuance, the Ring being the Symbol of Eternity. The Eagle displayed is the symbol of Supreme Power & Authority, and signifies the Congress; the Pillar, upon which it rests, is used as the Hieroglyphic of Fortitude and Constancy; and it's being of Doric order, (which is the best proportioned and most agreeable to nature) & composed of several Members or parts, all, taken together, forming a beautiful composition of Strength, Congruity & Usefulness, it may with great propriety signify a well planned Government. The Eagle, being placed on the summit of the Column, is emblematical of the Sovereignty of the Government of the United States; and, as further expressive of that Idea, those two charges or figures are borne on a Pale, which extends across the thirteen pieces, into which the Escutcheon is divided. The signification of the Eye has been already explained.

"'The Helmet is such as appertains to Sovereignty and the Cap is used as the Token of Freedom & Excellency. It was formerly worn by Dukes "Because," says Guillim, "*They Had a more worthy Government than other subjects.*" The Cock is distinguished for two most excellent Qualities, necessary in a free country, viz: *Vigilance & Fortitude.*

"'The genius of the American Confederated Republic is denoted by her blue Scarf & Fillet, gilittering with Stars, and by the flag of Congress which she displays. Her dress is white edged with green colours, emblematical of Innocence and Youth. Her *purple* girdle and radiated *crown* indicate her sovereignty: the word "*Virtue*" on the former is to show, that *that* should be her principal ornament, and the *radiated* Crown, that no *Earthly* Crown shall rule her. The Dove on the Top of the American Standard denotes the mildness and lenity of her Government.

"'The Knight in Armour with his bloody Lance represents the military Genius of the American Empire, armed in Defence of its just Rights. His *blue* Belt and *blue* feathers indicate his Country, & the White Plume is in Compliment to our gallant Ally. The Wreath of Laurel round his helmet is expressive of his success. The Green Field of the Banner denotes Youth and Vigor; the Harp is emblematical of the several States acting in Harmony and Concert; the Star, *in Chief,* has reference to America, *as principal* in the contest; the two fleurs-de-lis are borne as a grateful Testimonial of the support given to her by France; and the two swords, crossing each other signify a state of War. This Tenant and his Flag relate totally, to America at the time of her Revolution. '. . .

"'WILLIAM BARTON.'

"It is here that the eagle appears for the first time.

"Barton submitted another device of a similar character, so far as the obverse is concerned: 'Device for an Armorial Atchievement & Reverse of a Great Seal, for the United States of America: proposed by William Barton, Esq., A.M. (Fig. 281).

"'Blazoned according to the Laws of Heraldry:—Barry of thirteen pieces,

FIG. 281.

Argent & Gules; on a pale, Or, a Pillar of the Doric Order, Vert, reaching from the Base of the Escutcheon to the Honor point; and from the summit thereof, a Phœnix in Flames with Wings expanded, proper; the whole within a Border, Azure, charged with as many stars as pieces barways, of the first. CREST: On a Helmet of Burnished Gold, damasked, grated with six Bars, a Cap of Liberty, Vert; with an Eagle displayed Argent thereon holding in his dexter Talon a Sword, Or, having a wreath of Laurel suspended from the point; and in the sinister, the Ensign of the United States, proper.

" ' SUPPORTERS: On the dexter side, the Genius of the American Confederated Republic: represented by a Maiden, with flowing Auburn Tresses; clad in a long, loose white Garment, bordered with Green; having a sky-blue scarf, charged with Stars as in the Arms, reaching across her waist from her right shoulder to her left Side; and, on her Head, a *radiated* crown of Gold, encircled with an azure Fillet spangled with Silver Stars; round her Waist, a purple Girdle, embroidered with the word " Virtus" in silver :—a Dove, proper, perched on her dexter Hand. On the Sinister Side, an American Warrior, clad in an uniform Coat, of blue faced with Buff, and in his Hat a Cockade of black and white Ribbons; in his left hand, a Baton Azure semé of stars Argent. Motto over the crest—" IN VINDICIAM LIBERTATIS." Motto under the arms—" VIRTUS SOLA INVICTA." Reverse of the seal: (Fig. 282) A Pyramid of thirteen Strata (or Steps) Or. In the Zenith, an eye, surrounded with a Glory, proper. In a Scroll, above—or in the Margin " DEO FAVENTE." The Exergue " PERENNIS."

FIG. 282.

" ' REMARKS: The Imperial Eagle of Germany (which is Sable, and with two Heads) is represented with a sword in one Talon, and a sceptre in the other. The Phœnix is emblematical of the expiring Liberty of Britain, revived by her Descendants in America. The Dove (perched on the right Hand of the Genius of America) is Emblematical of Innocence and Virtue. The Sword (held by the Eagle) is the Symbol of Courage, Authority and Power. The Flag or Ensign denotes the United States of America, of the sovereignty of which the Eagle is expressive. The Pillar is the Hieroglyphic of Constancy and Fortitude, and is likewise emblematical of Beauty, Strength and Order. The Pyramid signifies Strength and Duration.'

" Here the first design of the reverse of the seal is clearly fixed; it being the same as the one finally adopted, except for the motto.

" The next device was by the Secretary of Congress, Charles Thomson:

"'Device for an Armorial Atchievement and Reverse of a Great Seal for the United States in Congress Assembled (Fig. 283).

"'ARMS: On a field Chevrons composed of seven pieces on one side & six on the other, joined together at the top in such wise that each of the six bears against or is supported by & supports two of the opposite side, the pieces of the chevrons on each side alternate red and white. The shield borne on the breast of an American Eagle, on the Wing and rising proper. In the dexter talon of the eagle an olive branch & in the sinister a bundle of arrows. Over the head of the Eagle a constellation of stars surrounded with bright rays and at a little distance clouds. In the bill of the Eagle a scroll with the words " E PLURIBUS UNUM."—Reverse: A pyramid unfinished. In the zenith an eye in a triangle surrounded with a glory, proper.

FIG. 283.

"'Over the eye these words, "ANNUIT CŒPTIS." On the base of the pyramid the numerical letters, "MDCCLXXVI," and underneath these words, "NOVUS ORDO SECLORUM."

"'N.B. the Head and tail of the American bald Eagle are White, the body and wings of a lead or dove colour.'

"Here, it will be observed, a step further was made. The eagle bearing the shield on its breast, grasping the olive branch and arrows, and the constellation surrounded by clouds appear as they now actually are. The motto, too, is the same, and is held in the same way. The reverse appears as it was finally adopted.

"The words 'Annuit cœptis novus ordo seclorum' have commonly been taken as one motto, meaning 'the new series of ages is favorable to our undertakings;' but, from the 'remarks and explanation' accompanying the description of the seal as finally adopted (p. 102), it is evident that the intention was to have two mottoes—'annuit cœptis,' meaning 'it (the Eye of Providence) is favorable to our undertakings,' and 'novus ordo seclorum,' meaning simply 'a new order of centuries.'

"The words were probably adapted from two passages in Virgil—'Audacibus annue cœptis' (favor my daring undertaking), and 'Magnus ab integro seclorum nascitur ordo' (the great series of ages begins anew). The former is found in the Æneid, book 9, verse 625 (also in the Georgics, I. 40), and the latter in the fourth eclogue, fifth verse. Although the form 'seclorum' was adopted, the more approved form is ' sæclorum;' and the word is spelled with the ' æ' in all or nearly all the best modern editions of Latin authors.

"The next report is endorsed 'Mr. Barton's improvement on the Secretary's device,' and describes a device almost identical with the one finally agreed upon :

"'Device for an Armorial Atchievement for the United States of North America, blazoned agreeably to the Laws of Heraldry—proposed by Wm. Barton, A.M.

"'ARMS: Paleways of thirteen pieces, Argent and Gules; a Chief Azure: —The Escutcheon placed on the Breast of an American (the bald-headed) eagle, displayed, proper, holding in his Beak a Scroll, inscribed with this motto, viz., "E PLURIBUS UNUM"—And in his dexter Talon a Palm or an Olive Branch—in the other a bundle of 13 Arrows; all proper. FOR THE CREST: Over the Head of the Eagle, which appears above the Escutcheon, a Glory, Or; breaking through a cloud, proper, and surrounding thirteen Stars forming a Constellation, Argent, on an Azure Field. In the Exergue of the Great Seal—" JUL. IV. MDCCLXXVI"—In the margin of the same—" SIGIL. MAG. REIPUB. CONFŒD. AMERIC."

"'REMARKS: The Escutcheon is composed of the Chief & Pale, the two most honourable ordinaries: the latter represent the several States; all joined in one solid, compact Entire, supporting a Chief, which unites the whole and represents Congress.—The Motto alludes to this Union.—The Colours or Tinctures of the Pales are those used in the Flag of the United States—White signifies Purity and Innocence; Red, Hardiness and Valour. The Chief denotes Congress—Blue is the Ground of the American uniform, and this colour signifies Vigilance, Perseverance and Justice. The meaning of the Crest is obvious, as is likewise that of the Olive Branch and Arrows.

"'The Escutcheon being placed on the Breast of the Eagle displayed is a very antient mode of bearing, and is truly imperial. The Eagle *displayed* is an Heraldical figure; and, being borne in the manner here described, supplies the place of supporters and Crest. The American States need no supporters but their own Virtue, and the Preservation of their Union through Congress. The Pales in the Arms are kept closely united by the Chief, which last likewise depends on that Union and the strength resulting from it, for its own support —The Inference is plain.

"'June 19th, 1782. W: B.'

" The legend as proposed by Barton was left out finally.

" On June 20, 1782, the seal was finally decided upon.[1]

" On report of the Secretary, 'to whom were referred the several reports on the device for a great seal, to take order:

"'The device for an armorial achievement and reverse of the great seal for the United States in Congress assembled, is as follows:

"'ARMS. Paleways of thirteen pieces, argent and gules; a chief, azure; the escutcheon on the breast of the American eagle displayed proper, holding in his dexter talon an olive branch, and in his sinister a bundle of thirteen

[1] Journals of Congress, vol. iv. p. 39.

arrows, all proper, and in his beak a scroll, inscribed with this motto, " E pluribus Unum."

" ' For the CREST. Over the head of the Eagle, which appears above the escutcheon, a glory, or, breaking through a cloud, proper, and surrounding thirteen stars, forming a constellation, argent, on an azure field.

" ' REVERSE. A pyramid unfinished.

" ' In the zenith, an eye in a triangle, surrounded with a glory proper. Over the eye these words, " *Annuit cœptis.*" On the base of the pyramid the numerical letters MDCCLXXVI. And underneath the following motto, " *Novus Ordo Seclorum.*" '

" Accompanying the report and adopted by Congress, was the following :

" ' REMARKS AND EXPLANATION. The Escutcheon is composed of the chief and pale, the two most honourable ordinaries. The pieces, paly, represent the several States all joined in one solid compact entire, supporting a Chief, which unites the whole and represents Congress. The Motto alludes to this union. The pales in the Arms are kept closely united by the chief and the chief depends on that Union and the strength resulting from it for its support, to denote the Confederacy of the United States of America and the preservation of their Union through Congress. The colours of the pales are those used in the flag of the United States of America; White signifies purity and innocence, Red, hardiness and valour, and Blue, the colour of the chief signifies vigilance perseverance & justice. The Olive branch and arrows denote the power of peace and war which is exclusively vested in Congress. The Constellation denotes a new State taking its place and rank among other sovereign powers. The Escutcheon is born on the breast of an American Eagle without any other supporters, to denote that the United States ought to rely on their own Virtue.

" ' REVERSE : The pyramid signifies Strength and Duration : The Eye over it and the motto allude to the many signal interpositions of providence in favour of the American cause. The date underneath is that of the Declaration of Independence and the words under it signify the beginning of the New American Æra, which commences from that date.

" ' Passed June 20, 1782.'

" The new seal was cut in brass soon after it had been decided upon, and it is found on a commission date September 16, 1782, granting full power and authority to General Washington to arrange with the British for exchange of prisoners of war. The commission is signed by John Hanson, President of Congress, and countersigned by Charles Thomson, Secretary, the seal being impressed upon the parchment over a white wafer fastened by red wax, in the upper left hand corner, instead of the lower left hand corner, as is now the custom.

" This seal continued in use for fifty-nine years. The present seal differs from it only in details of execution. The first seal, being contemporaneous with its adoption, was in all probability cut in Philadelphia, and it may be presumed under the immediate supervision of the authors of the device.

"The reverse of the seal was not cut then, nor has it ever been cut since, but has been allowed to go unnoticed officially to the present day. The

FIG. 284.

second seal was cut in 1841, Daniel Webster being Secretary of State. It will be observed that this seal, which continued in use up to 1885, contained but six arrows, and its dimensions were smaller than the present seal. (See Fig. 284.)

"The seal now in use was cut in 1885, Frederick T. Frelinghuysen being the Secretary of State, after the design had been submitted by the Department to several historical scholars and authorities on heraldry and had been approved by them.

"In many countries, at the present day, the authenticity of a treaty with another power is attested by a large pendant wax seal, the cords which run through the paper of the treaty being carried through the wax. As the wax would otherwise be certain to break and the cords become detached, a metal box—usually of gold or silver—is used to contain the wax impression. Our own seal was thus attached to treaties up to 1869, when the practice was finally abandoned; and the impression upon the paper itself, with a thin white wafer, is used upon treaties, as well as upon all other documents to which the seal is affixed.

"When the Federal Government of the United States was formed under the Constitution, Congress passed a law on September 15, 1789, creating the Department of State. Sections 3 and 4 of the act read (1 Stat., 68):

"'SEC. 3. . . . That the seal heretofore used by the United States in Congress assembled shall, and hereby is declared to be, the Seal of the United States.

"'SEC. 4. . . . That the said Secretary [of State] shall keep the said seal and shall make out and record, and shall affix the said seal to all civil commissions, to officers of the United States, to be appointed by the President by and with the advice and consent of the Senate, or by the President alone, *Provided*, That the said seal shall not be affixed to any commission, before the same shall have been signed by the President of the United States, nor to any other instrument or act, without the special warrant of the President therefor.'

"The Secretary of State, therefore, is the custodian of the seal, but has no power to affix it to any paper that does not bear the President's signature.

"In 1803 Chief Justice Marshall, in delivering an opinion of the Supreme

Court, used the following language relative to the seal. It may be considered applicable to all instruments to which the seal is affixed, except that the President's signature is considered a warrant in itself for affixing it to commissions and exequaturs. All other legal instruments require a separate warrant, signed by the President, authorizing the seal to be used.

" ' The signature [of the President] is a warrant for affixing the great seal to the commission, and the great seal is only to be affixed to an instrument which is complete. It attests, by an act supposed to be of public notoriety, the verity of the presidential signature.

" ' It is never to be affixed till the commission is signed, because the signature which gives force and effect to the commission is conclusive evidence that the appointment is made.

" ' The commission being signed, the subsequent duty of the Secretary of State is prescribed by law, and not to be guided by the will of the President. He is to affix the seal of the United States to the Commission, and is to record it.' (1 U. S. Reports, 374.)

" As the duties of the Government have expanded, the impracticability of having the seal of the United States attached by the Department of State to the commissions of officers who are under some other Department has been recognized by Congress. By the Act of March 18, 1874, the commissions of postmasters were directed to be made out under the seal of the Post-Office Department; the Act of March 3, 1875, placed the commissions of officers of the Interior Department under that Department; and by Act of August 8, 1888, all judicial officers, marshals, and United States attorneys were ordered to be appointed under the seal of the Department of Justice. At the present time the seal of the United States is affixed to the commissions of all Cabinet officers and diplomatic and consular officers who are nominated by the President and confirmed by the Senate; all ceremonious communications from the President to the heads of foreign governments; all treaties, conventions, and formal agreements of the President with foreign powers; . . . all proclamations by the President; all exequaturs to foreign consular officers in the United States who are appointed by the heads of the governments which they represent; to warrants by the President to receive persons surrendered by foreign governments under extradition treaties; and to all miscellaneous commissions of civil officers appointed by the President, by and with the advice and consent of the Senate, whose appointments are not now especially directed by law to be signed under a different seal."

THE PRESIDENT'S SEAL [1] (Fig. 285).

The seal of the President of the Continental Congress was a small oval cluster of thirteen stars, surrounded by clouds, and was almost identical in

---

[1] For seal impression acknowledgments are tendered Henry T. Thurber, Esq., Private Secretary to President Cleveland.

FIG. 285.

design with the crest of the seal of the United States (the Great Seal). It was used to attest the verity of the President's signature until the latter was adopted and superseded it. The design was afterwards changed, and it was made to conform closely to the Great Seal; the only differences being that in the President's seal the eagle's head is turned towards the sinister, and the stars are differently distributed. It is used simply in sealing envelopes containing communications from the President to Congress, the official seal for all Presidential acts being the seal of the United States, or, if the law permits it, of one of the Executive Departments.

DEPARTMENT SEALS.[1]

In addition to the Senate and House of Representatives, each Department of the government has its individual seal. The Department of State has a seal much like that of the United States, with thirteen stars placed on the chief of the shield. The seal of the Department of Agriculture contains a sheaf of wheat. The Post-Office Department has as its device a mounted mail-carrier or "post rider," a design used by Franklin. The eagle appears on the seals of the Departments of Interior and Justice, and it is combined with an anchor and a ship on that of the Navy. The War Department has a group of military flags and a cap of liberty between a spear and a musket, and above these a serpent. The seal of the Treasury Department appears on our paper money, and is quite heraldic in character. The shield may be blazoned, from the representation on the Treasury notes: *Or, on a chevron azure, between a pair of scales in chief and a key in base, proper, thirteen stars argent.* The color is marked in the field and on the chevron and stars. Round the shield, in a circle, is the legend, *Thesaur Amer. Septent. Sigil.*

UNITED STATES SENATE.[2]

In this seal the American shield, surmounted by the liberty cap, and supported by an olive branch upon the dexter and an oak branch upon the sinister (emblematic of peace and strength), forms the central feature. The common error of omitting tincture lines is noticeable in the field and chief, and the shading of the "stripes" indicates that the field is charged with six pales, whereas the American shield is paly of thirteen.[3] The stars and motto are entirely out of place.

---

[1] The seals of the Executive Departments, unless where the law otherwise specifies, were prescribed by the heads of the Departments in accordance with the general authority conferred by the Act of July 27, 1789.

[2] Impression from which seal is copied was furnished by the courtesy of Hon. A. E. Stevenson, Vice-President of the United States.

[3] For explanation of this point see Fig. 666.

The Secretary has the custody of the seal, and uses "the same for the authentication of process, transcripts, copies, and certificates whenever directed by the Senate; and may use the same to authenticate copies of such papers and documents in his office as he may lawfully give copies of."

FIG. 286.　　　　　　　　　　　　　　　FIG. 287.

HOUSE OF REPRESENTATIVES.[1]

"The seal is in the custody of the Clerk of the House. It is affixed to resolutions. The design represents the Capitol at Washington, as it existed before the statue of Liberty surmounted the dome, with the legend "House of Representatives United States" underneath. In the exergue are twenty-four stars. There is no law prescribing the seal."

DEPARTMENT OF STATE.[2]

This seal was adopted September 15, 1789, and the device was probably intended to be a copy of that represented upon the Great Seal of the

FIG. 288.　　　　　　　　　　　　　　　FIG. 289.

United States. The field and chief bear the color lines (*gules* and *azure*), but for some reason, or perhaps no reason, the eagle faces the sinister, the sinister

[1] Seal impression from Mr. Gaillard Hunt, State Department.
[2] Seal impression from letter of Mr. W. W. Rockhill, Chief Clerk.

claw holds but three arrows instead of the symbolic thirteen, and the stars are unevenly distributed, the cloud being omitted.

DEPARTMENT OF AGRICULTURE.[1]

The seal of this Department has been in use for some time, but the date of its adoption is not known, and no record of any law governing its use exists at this writing.

POST-OFFICE DEPARTMENT.[2]

A disregard of the English custom of facing all charges to the dexter is apparent in this seal, which was adopted upon May 1, 1837, when it was ordered, "That the seal of the Post Office Department shall hereafter be a post horse in speed, with mail bags and rider, encircled with the words, ' Post Office Department, United States of America.'"

Between the years 1825 and 1837 no seal appears to have been used, but simply a wafer was affixed to papers without any impress being made thereon.

FIG. 290.   FIG. 291.

DEPARTMENT OF THE INTERIOR.[3]

" The act of March 3d, 1849, created the Department of the Interior, and the device of the seal which is now in use was soon afterwards adopted. There were no specific legal provisions."

In this device several " artistic liberties" taken with the national emblems may be commented upon as follows : The shield is but paly of ten, the arrows are in the dexter claw instead of the sinister, and number but four, and the eagle faces to the sinister, while but five leaves of the olive branch are shown, and it is held in the wrong claw. The positions of eagle and shield are also incorrect.

[1] Hon. J. Stirling Morton, Secretary of the Department of Agriculture, furnished impression from which example is taken.

[2] For seal impression acknowledgments are due Mr. George A. Howard, Chief Clerk.

[3] Seal impression from letter of Commissioner D. M. Browning.

NAVY DEPARTMENT.

The Board of Admiralty, which was organized in the Continental Congress by resolution of October 28, 1779, adopted a seal May 4, 1780, which was cut soon afterwards. The historian Lossing thus describes it:

FIG. 292.

"An escutcheon on which was a chevron with a blue field and thirteen perpendicular and mutually supporting bars, alternate red and white. Below the chevron was a reclining anchor, proper. The crest was a ship under sail. The motto, 'Sustentans et Sustentatum'—Sustaining and Sustained. The legend, 'U. S. A. Sigil. Naval.'"

Later, by resolution of February 7, 1781, Congress provided for a Secretary of Marine, and he was authorized to have a seal. Naval functions were, however, performed by an agent of Marine, until they passed under the Superintendent of Finance, and there was no change in the device of the seal.

It remained the same after the adoption of the Constitution, when the Navy was under the War Department, until, by act of April 30, 1798, the Navy Department was formed. A new seal was then adopted, but the law made no specific provisions therefor. A copy of the present seal is shown in Fig. 292.

NAVY BUREAUS AND DEPARTMENTS.[1]

Lately seals have been adopted for the bureaus and all subordinate branches of the Navy Department and for ships, the same in all cases except that the legend of the border specifies the bureau, subordinate department, or ship for which used. These seals are supplied in accordance with Article 1646 of the Navy Regulations. Those for the heads of departments at navy-yards are marked (in addition to the words "Department of the Navy") "Yards and Docks," "Equipment," etc., as the case may be. For ships the seals are marked thus: "U. S. S. Miantonomah."

FIG. 293.

"The following are the specifications: The seal to be 1⅜" in diameter, and made in conformity with the design as submitted to the Bureau of Equipment. To be engraven on brass with copper counterpart, and fixed in lever press with nickel-plated handle; to be placed in small walnut box, lined with velvet and fastened with lock and key, and to have German silver engraved plate

---

[1] For information thanks are extended to Hon. H. A. Herbert, Secretary of the Navy, Paymaster-General Edwin Stewart, U.S.N., and Mr. Gaillard Hunt.

on the top of the box designating the name of the bureau, vessel or yard department to which the seal belongs. Every seal should bear in its upper semicircle the words 'Department of the Navy,' the words in the lower semicircle differ and should be as follows :"

(That is, according to the bureau, ship, or yard department to which the seal belongs.)

DEPARTMENT OF JUSTICE.[1]

The Act of September 24, 1789, provided for an Attorney-General of the United States, and June 2, 1870, the Department of Justice was created

FIG. 294.

with the Attorney-General as its head. Section 353 of the Revised Statutes (March 5, 1872) declares : "The seal heretofore provided for the office of the Attorney-General shall be, with such change as the President shall approve, the seal of the Department of Justice."

The seal now in use, therefore, is substantially the same as the one adopted by the Attorney-General before the Department was formed. No device was ever prescribed by law.

This, like other seals, is also susceptible to criticism, inasmuch as the shield is but paly of eleven, the stars are on the chief, and the eagle's position is wholly incorrect.

WAR DEPARTMENT.[2]

Lossing, in his article on " Executive Departments and Seals," states :

" A new Board of War and Ordnance was authorized in October, 1777, to consist of three persons not members of Congress. These were chosen on the 7th of November, and consisted of General Thomas Mifflin, Colonel Timothy Pickering, and Colonel Robert H. Harrison. The two first named soon entered upon their duties, and on the 17th of the same month Messrs. Dana and J. B. Smith were added to the members of the Board. A few weeks later a seal for the use of the Board was adopted, having for its device a group of military trophies, with the Phrygian cap, the emblem of freedom, between a spear and a musket. Over this was a serpent. Beneath the trophies was the date, 'MDCCLXXVIII.' Around the seal were

FIG. 295.

---

[1] Seal impression from letter of Mr. Cecil Clay, Chief Clerk.
[2] Letter of Hon. Daniel S. Lamont, Secretary of War.

the words, 'BOARD OF WAR AND ORDNANCE. UNITED STATES OF AMERICA.' This was the origin of the present seal of our War Department, which yet bears precisely the same device. The date is omitted. Within the curve of the serpent are the words, 'WILL DEFEND;' and around the seal the legend, 'UNITED STATES OF AMERICA. WAR OFFICE.'"

TREASURY DEPARTMENT.[1]

"On September 26, 1778, the Continental Congress resolved 'That a committee of three be appointed to prepare a seal for the treasury and for the navy.'

"The Navy at that time was under the jurisdiction of the Board of Admiralty, and the Treasury under that of the Committee on Finance, or Board of Treasury.

"The said committee made a report as to the device for a seal for the Navy, but no record can be found of a report for the Treasury. A seal, however, was adopted, impressions of which may be found on original papers now in the files of the Office of the Register of the Treasury. Some minor changes have been made from time to time,

FIG. 296.

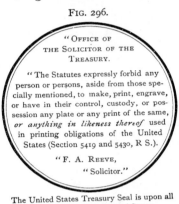

"OFFICE OF THE SOLICITOR OF THE TREASURY.

"The Statutes expressly forbid any person or persons, aside from those specially mentioned, to make, print, engrave, or have in their control, custody, or possession any plate or any print of the same, *or anything in likeness thereof* used in printing obligations of the United States (Section 5419 and 5430, R S.).

"F. A. REEVE, "Solicitor."

The United States Treasury Seal is upon all paper money of the United States.

but the seal adopted was substantially the same in device and legend as the seal of the Treasury Department at this day." In 1849 it was decided to make a new seal, the old one having become worn. The die-cutter was informed that the design must be copied exactly " In accordance with the law." " Diligent efforts have been made by numerous interested parties to locate the law referred to, but, so far as I am informed, without avail.

"The legend on the Treasury Department seal is 'Thesaur. Amer. Septent. Sigil.,' being an abbreviation of the Latin sentence, 'Thesauri Americana Septentrionis Sigillum,' meaning 'The Seal of the Treasury of North America.' The inference drawn from the history of those times would be that, in event of success by the Colonies, the whole of North America would be represented by the symbol."

DEPARTMENT OF INDIAN AFFAIRS.[2]

The seal of the Department of Indian Affairs forms a fair example of the many ways in which our national device is ill-treated, notwithstanding the fact that there is but one correct way of drawing it, and any departure from the set form is abuse pure and simple.

In this seal the eagle faces the sinister, stands upon the American shield, clasps in his claws (the wrong claws at that) but a small sprig of olive, and

---

[1] Letter of Hon. D. N. Morgan, Treasurer of the United States.
[2] Thanks are extended to Commissioner D. M. Browning and Josephus Daniels, Esq., for information.

FIG. 297.

but four arrows. The entire significance of the United States arms is thus lost and changed to that which is suggestive of disruption. It matters not whether the device of our nation is intended for government, corporate, or individual purposes, where the American eagle, shield, olive branch, arrows, and stars appear, they should be in conformity with heraldic law, and as prescribed by national law, which provides for the magnificent symbol of a great and united country. In one of our State seals, which will be described later, the eagle appears above the olive branch, which lies upon the ground. If this device was placed in the eagle's claw, to symbolize peace, there can be but one interpretation attached to his act when he casts it from him.

The seal of the Department of Indian Affairs was authorized by Act of July 26, 1892.

ALABAMA.

By an Act approved December 29, 1868, the Governor was directed to have prepared a seal, to be known as the "'Great Seal of the State,' and which shall be of the following character: the seal shall be circular, and the diameter thereof two and a quarter ($2\frac{1}{4}$) inches. Near the edge of the circle shall be the word 'Alabama,' and opposite this word at the same distance from the edge shall be the words, 'Great Seal.' In the centre of the seal there shall

FIG. 298.

be a representation of an eagle and a shield and upon such part of the seal as the Governor may direct there shall be the words 'Here we rest.'" [1]

This seal bears a well-drawn eagle, but is subject to about the same criticisms as have been applied to other State seals which bear the American arms

The seal and coat of arms in use previous to 1868 "was the representation of an outline map of the State, posted on a tree, with the word 'Alabama' on the face, but this was never adopted as a seal or coat of arms, being used as such by some official at an early date." [2]

FIG. 299.

[1] Letter of Hon. J. D. Barron, Secretary of State.
[2] Letter of Mr. W. Brewer.

ALASKA.

Nothing is known about the history of the seal of Alaska, excepting "that it was made for the use of the first governor" (Fig. 299).

ARKANSAS.

The seal of Arkansas is described as follows: "An eagle at the bottom, holding a scroll in its beak, inscribed 'Regnant Populi,' a bundle of arrows in one claw and an olive branch in the other; a shield covering the breast of the eagle, engraved with a steamboat at top, a bee-hive and plow in the middle, and sheaf of wheat at the bottom; the Goddess of Liberty at the top, holding a wreath in her right hand, a pole in the left hand, surmounted by a liberty cap, and surrounded by a circle of stars, outside of which is a circle of rays; the figure of an angel on the left, inscribed 'Mercy,' and a sword on the right hand, inscribed 'Justice,' surrounded with the words 'Seal of the State of Arkansas.'" [1]

FIG. 300.

The same emblems and devices are borne upon the seals of State offices, with the proper change of surrounding words; on the Secretary's seal,—"Seal of the Secretary of State, Arkansas;" on the Auditor's seal,—"Seal of the Auditor of State, Arkansas," etc.

ARIZONA.

The original seal [2] of Arizona is thus described: "The territorial seal is two and one-fourth inches in diameter, surrounded by the legend, 'SEAL

FIG. 301.

FIG. 302.

---

[1] Act of May 3, 1864. Mansfield's Digest, 1884, Chapter CXXXVI. For seal impression thanks are extended to Governor Fishback.

[2] Design from Hough's "American Constitutions."

OF THE TERRITORY OF ARIZONA, " 1863."' The device is a miner, dressed in a miner's shirt and trousers and broad-leaved hat, leaning on his pick and spade. In the distance, mountains; and below his feet the motto 'Ditat Deus,' in Roman capitals"[1] (Fig. 301). The present seal is described as follows:

"The Seal of this Territory shall be of the size of two and one quarter inches in diameter, and of the following design: A view of San-Francisco mountain in the distance, with a deer, pine trees, and columnar cactus in the foreground: the motto to be 'Ditat Deus.' The date on said seal to be 1863, the year of the organization of the Territory"[2] (Fig. 302).

CALIFORNIA.[3]

When the Constitutional Convention met in Monterey in 1849, the question of designing the Great Seal was agitated, and some time later a drawing was submitted. It represented the figure of Minerva, with the Golden Gate, and a ship in full sail in the foreground and the Sierra Nevada range in the background, with the word "Eureka" above. The design was referred to a committee, and on September 29, 1849, the report of the committee was considered by the Convention. After various amendments had been suggested, the matter was laid on the table. On October 2 the report of the committee was again considered, and adopted. This design was also adopted as the arms of the State of California.

FIG. 303.

In 1858 the State seal was damaged so that it failed to give a true impression, and a bill was introduced in the Senate to authorize the Secretary of State to procure a new seal, to be engraved on steel, and to be substituted for and used instead of the seal then in existence; and requiring him to destroy the then State seal in the presence of the Governor and Controller. The bill was accompanied with a design which reduced the size of the seal a twelfth part of an inch, and to admit of this contraction some of the details of the original design were omitted. The bear was made to crouch submissively at the feet of Minerva, the miner's cradle was left out, and the miner was brought nearer the water. On March 10, 1858, the Senate amended the bill providing that the design and size should be the same as in the then seal; and on April 16 another amendment was adopted, that "the design of the present seal shall

[1] Preble, p. 634.

[2] From Act relating to same, Chap. 28, Par. 3120, Sec. I., R. S. Letter of Francis B. Devereux, Esq., Assistant Secretary, Arizona.

[3] From description furnished by Hon. E. G. Waite, Secretary of State, California.

be preserved intact in the new one, but the size thereof shall be reduced six-tenths of an inch, so that the new seal, when completed, shall be three and three-tenths of an inch in diameter." The bill with this amendment passed the Senate on the 31st, but it was not considered in the House.

Designer's description of seal:

"Around the bend of the ring are represented thirty-one stars, being the number of States of which the Union will consist upon the admission of California. The foreground figure represents the Goddess Minerva, having sprung full grown from the brain of Jupiter. She is introduced as a type of political birth of the State of California, without having gone through the probation of a Territory. At her feet crouches a grizzly bear, feeding upon the clusters from a grapevine, emblematic of the country's peculiar character-istics. The sheaf of wheat and bunch of grapes were adopted as emblems of the Agricultural and Horticultural interests of the State. A miner is engaged, with his rocker and bowl at his side, illustrating the golden wealth of Sacramento, upon whose waters are seen shipping typical of commercial greatness; and the snow-clad peaks of the Sierra Nevada make up the background, while above is the Greek motto, 'Eureka' (I have found it), applying either to the principle involved in the admission of the State, or the success of the miner at work."

Colorado.[1]

"The seal of the State shall be two and one-half inches in diameter, with the following device inscribed thereon: An heraldic shield bearing in chief, or upon the upper portion of the same, upon a red ground, three snow-capped mountains; above, surrounding clouds; upon the lower part thereof, upon a golden ground, a miner's badge, as prescribed by the rules of heraldry; as a crest above the shield, the eye of God, being golden rays proceeding from the lines of a triangle; below the crest and above the shield, as a scroll, the Roman fasces bearing upon a band of red, white and blue the words, 'Union and Constitution;'[2] below the whole the motto, 'Nil Sine Numine;' the whole to

Fig. 304.

be surrounded by the words, 'State of Colorado,' and the figures 1876."[3]

The Territorial seal of Colorado was the same as the present State seal, excepting that the wording in the exergue was as follows: "Sigillum Territorii Coloradensis, 1861."

---

[1] The author acknowledges the assistance of Hon. Nelson O. McClees, Secretary of State, and M. Lorentz, Esq.

[2] Upon the impressions received these words are not visible.

[3] Chapter XC., General Laws, approved March 15, 1877; in force June 13, 1877.

CONNECTICUT.[1]

"In a paper hitherto unprinted, written in 1759 by Roger Wolcott, some-time Governor, he tells us that his step-father, Daniel Clark, informed him

FIG. 305.

that the seal was given to the Colony by George Fenwick. Mr. Clark was likely to be well informed on the subject, for he was born about 1623, and was Secretary of the Colony for several years between 1658 and 1666. Mr. Fenwick was agent for the proprietors of Connecticut under the Warwick patent of 1631. Perhaps he gave the seal when the Colony bought of him Saybrook Fort, etc., in 1644, and it may be that the seal was used by the said proprietors. There is in the State Library a pretty fair impression of this seal on wax, affixed to the commission of John Winthrop as magistrate at Nameock (New London), dated October 27, 1647.

"This seal represents a vineyard of fifteen vines, supported and bearing fruit. Above the vines a hand issuing from clouds holds a label with the motto 'Sustinet qui transtulit.' The seal is slightly oval in form and has a beaded border. There remain, besides the one above mentioned, but three impressions of it among the State archives; all are on wax and all poor.

"After the receipt of the charter, the first General Assembly held under it, October, 1662, ordered that the seal that formerly was used by the General Court should still remain and be used as the seal of this Colony until the court saw cause to the contrary; and the Secretary was to keep it and use it on necessary occasions for the Colony.

FIG. 306.

"In October, 1662, the General Assembly laid claim to West-chester as being within the chartered limits of Connecticut, and sent down a copy of their vote certified under the Colony seal, which is thus curiously described by Mr. Richard Mills, who had the document in his custody: 'The signal of the seal above is come to the inhabitants of Westchester, absolute, made in red wax; the motto I suppose to be the arborated craggy wilderness and the flying cloudes.'

[1] From article by Charles J. Hoadly in "Connecticut State Register and Manual for 1889." Acknowledgments are due to Frank D. Rood, Esq., for assistance.

"The first printed revision of the statutes of Connecticut, Cambridge, 1673, had, by order of the General Court, an impression of the Colony seal upon the title page. All other editions of the statutes during our Colonial period had the royal arms instead.

"When Sir Edmund Andros took the government of the Colony in October, 1687, the public seal disappeared. Gershom Bulkeley, in his book 'Will and Doom,' says that 'The Secretary (John Allyn), who was well acquainted with all the transactions of the General Court, and very well understood their meaning and intent in all, delivered their common seal to Sir Edmund Andros.' Whether the seal was broken or what became of it we know not; certain it is that the seal used after the resumption of the charter government in 1689 differs considerably from the first one :—it was not so well cut, is a trifle larger, the hand bends downward, and the motto reads, 'Sustinet qui trastulit.' I am inclined to doubt whether the new seal had been procured in 1690, for of five or six impressions on commissions which I have seen, made in that year, all are so very bad that it would seem as though some temporary substitute, made of wood, perhaps, had been used.

"No further change was made until 1711, when, at a meeting of the Governor and Council, October 25th, it was agreed, ordered, and resolved, that a new stamp should be made and cut of the seal of this Colony, suitable for sealing upon wafers, and that a press be provided, with the necessary appurtenances for that purpose, as soon as may be, at the cost and charge of the Colony, to be kept in the Secretary's office.

"This seal was considerably larger than its predecessors, measuring 2⅛ inches in length and 1¾ in breadth. Instead of fifteen vines there are but three, and there is a hand, about midway on the dexter side, pointing to them. The motto, which is on a label below the vines, is 'Qui transtulit sustinet,' and around the circumference is the legend, 'Sigillum coloniæ connecticensis.' In October, 1747, the General Assembly voted, that the public seal of the Colony be altered and changed from the form of an oval to that of a circle, and that the same should have cut and engraved upon it the same inscription, motto and device, that are on the present seal, with a correction of such mistakes as happened in the spelling and letters in the inscription of the present seal, and the Secretary was to procure such alterations. Nothing seems to have been done.

"The press, becoming worn through age, was replaced by a more powerful one in the Secretary's office, and after doing duty for some time in the Treasurer's office, was relegated to the cellar, where it was probably left when the State abandoned the old State House in 1879.

"Wax seems to have been generally used until within about a century. The few impressions upon paper preserved among the Colonial documents are all poor.

"In May, 1784, the General Assembly passed the following resolution:

" ' Whereas the circumscription of the seal of this State is improper and inapplicable to our present constitution, Resolved by this Assembly, that the Secretary be and he is hereby empowered and directed to get the same altered from the words as they now stand to the following inscription, namely, " Sigill. Reip. Connecticutensis." '

" The inscription was, however, cut without abbreviation, though in its shortened form it appears in engravings of that period. At the October session in 1784, the new seal was approved and ordered to be lodged with the Secretary to be used as the seal of this State as the law directs. The size of this seal was 2⅜ inches in length by 1⅞ in breadth. It was engraved on a silver plate soldered to a brass shoe or base. The silver plate was given to Yale College after a new seal was procured, and the brass base is at this moment serving the writer as a paper weight.

" Article fourth, section eighteenth, of the constitution adopted in 1818 declares that the seal of the State shall not be altered : but it is singular that neither in that instrument nor in any law or resolution is the seal ascertained or described. In 1840, it was resolved, ' That the Secretary of State be instructed to ascertain the proper seal and bearings of this State, and report to the next General Assembly ; and also, whether any legislative enactment is required for a proper description of said seal.' Mr. Hinman was at that time Secretary, but, as the subject would have required considerable investigation, he made, as he informed the writer, no report at all.

" At present there are two State seals in use : one for sealing with wax or wafer, which was procured in accordance with a resolution passed October, 1842, which directed that it should be similar to the one then in use. The resolution as originally drawn up provided that the new seal might be of smaller dimensions and circular instead of oval ; but these provisions were struck out in the House of Representatives, probably upon constitutional grounds, and the seal was made of similar form and size with the preceding one, except that it is a trifle broader ; the workmanship also is better ; there are three clusters of grapes on each vine, whereas the old one had four on each of the upper and five on the lower one. It is engraved on brass. The hand had been omitted from the seal of 1784. The other seal is used for making an impression upon paper without the use of wax or other tenacious substance, which mode was declared, by an act passed in 1851, to be a sufficient sealing. This seal is supposed to have been procured in 1882, under authority of a resolve passed in 1864.

" The armorial bearings of Connecticut in heraldic language would be blazoned thus : Argent, three vines supported and fructed proper : that is, the field is white or silver, and the vines of their natural colors. The blazon of the first seal would be : A field argent semé with vines supported and fructed proper. In chief a hand issuing from clouds, proper, holding a label inscribed with the motto. The number of vines on the old seal was doubtless arbitrary ;

that on the present seal has no special significance, but is the more usual number when a charge is repeated.

"The first issue of bills of credit was made by Connecticut in 1709. The General Assembly ordered that they should be stamped with such stamps as the Governor and Council should direct, and the latter body at a meeting June 14, 1709, directed that they should be all stamped with the arms of the Colony, or such a figure as was drawn in the council book representing three vines. On the small bills issued in 1777 the seal represented has but one vine, and a seal having but one vine has been used in the Secretary's office for sealing letters.

"The vines symbolize the Colony brought over and planted here in the wilderness. We read in the 80th Psalm: 'Thou hast brought a vine out of Egypt; Thou hast cast out the heathen and planted it:'—in Latin, Vineam de Ægypto transtulisti, Ejicisti gentes et plantasti eam; and the motto expresses our belief that He who brought over the vine continues to take care of it—Qui transtulit sustinet."

DAKOTA.—NORTH DAKOTA.

When Dakota came to be admitted as a State it was divided into North and South Dakota. North Dakota retained the devices of the Territorial seal, altering the legend, date, and number of stars.

FIG. 307.

Following is the description:[1] "A tree in the open field, the trunk of which is surrounded by three bundles of wheat; on the right a plow, anvil and sledge; on the left a bow crossed with three arrows and an Indian on horseback pursuing a buffalo toward the setting sun; the foliage of the tree arched by a half circle of forty-two stars, surrounded by the motto, 'Liberty and Union now and forever, one and inseparable,' the words 'Great Seal' at the top, the words 'State of North Dakota,' at the bottom; 'October 1st' on the left and '1889' on the right. The seal to be two and one-half inches in diameter" (Fig. 307).

SOUTH DAKOTA.

"SEAL AND COAT OF ARMS. The design of the Great Seal of South Dakota shall be as follows: A circle within which shall appear in the left foreground a smelting furnace and other features of mining work. In the left background a range of hills. In the right foreground a farmer at his plow. In the right background a herd of cattle and a field of corn. Between the

[1] Section 207 of the Constitution. Letter of W. O. De Puy, Esq., Deputy Secretary.

FIG. 308.

two parts thus described shall appear a river bearing a steamboat. Properly divided between the upper and lower edges of the circle shall appear the legend 'UNDER GOD THE PEOPLE RULE,' which shall be the motto of the State of SOUTH DAKOTA. Exterior to this circle and within a circumscribed circle shall appear in the upper part, the words, 'STATE OF SOUTH DAKOTA.' In the lower part the words 'GREAT SEAL,' and the date in Arabic numerals of the year in which the State shall be admitted to the Union."[1]

DELAWARE.

"On the 24th of March, 1770, it was enacted by the Hon. John Penn, Esqr: with His Majesty's Royal approbation, Lieut. Governor and Counselor in Chief of the Counties of New Castle, Kent and Sussex Upon Delaware, and province of Pennsylvania, under the Hon. Thos. Penn and Richard Penn, Esqrs, and one and absolute Proprietaries of the Said Government and Province, by and with the advice and consent of the Representators of the Freemen of the Said Government in General Assembly met, and by the authority of the same, that whereas these Counties before the 24th day of August in the year of our Lord 1682, were under the jurisdiction and government of the Province of New York, and the lands within the same were granted by the Governor and Commander in Chief of said Province; and many of the orders of the Governors, minutes of council, warrants, surveys, patents and deeds for the same were filed and recorded in the Secretary's office there :—

"SECTION II. And whereas the said original papers are entered in the books and records in the said office promiscuously with other original papers for, and relating to lands, tenements, and hereditaments, lying within that province, so that the said original papers and records cannot be obtained from and hence, and

"SECTION III. Whereas considering the grievous hardships encountered in procuring such original papers and records ; The Assembly of this Government has procured as many of the orders of Governors, minutes of Council, surveys, patents, deeds, wills and original papers, as in any wise related to lands, tenements, &c., within these Counties, and could be there found by him, to be transcribed under the direction of Thomas McKean, one of the members of said assembly ; and being compared with the originals, and properly authen-

[1] Article XXI., Section 1, Constitution. Design is from seal impression furnished by Governor Sheldon.

ticated and sworn to by the Deputy Secretary, Attorney at Law, before His Excellency Henry Moore, Baronet, Captain General, and Governor in Chief of the said Province of New York &c. Under the *Great Seal of the Province*, certified and signed by the said Thomas McKean &c."

"The object in reciting the above law is to show that until the 24th August, 1682, the seal of the Province of New York was used to authenticate all public and private papers requiring its use.

"The following extracts from the 'Notes and Proceedings of the House of Representatives of the Province of Pennsylvania (*Printed* by *Benj. Franklin* and *D. Hall, A.D. 1752*)' show that the form of government framed by William Penn, April 25th, 1682, was sealed with his own 'Broad Seal':

"Also, that at an Assembly of Representatives from the six counties, Bucks, Chester, Philadelphia, New Castle, Kent and Sussex, held in Philadelphia February 3rd, 1682, 'it was Resolved that all Laws should be passed under the "Great Seal of the Province." '[1]

"On the 24th August, 1682, in the 34th year of Charles Second, James, Duke of York and Albany &c. &c., granted a Deed of Feoffment of New Castle and the land within a twelve miles circle northward to William Penn, Esqr., and also a Deed of a tract of Land South of New Castle to the Whorekills; both which were sealed with the Seal of James, Duke of York &c. In the year 1683, an act was passed directing that all grants of inheritance from the Proprietary William Penn, shall be sealed with the 'Court Seal.'[2]

Fig. 309.

Arms of George II.

"In the year 1700 in the 12th year of William III., it was enacted that all grants of lands from the Proprietary shall henceforth be sealed with the great seal of this province and territories."

In the year of George II., A.D. 1751, an act was passed which provides that a certain silver seal in the then Governor's custody, with the arms of the King of Great Britain engraved thereon, and the inscription " Delaware" around it, was, by an act establishing a " Great Seal" for this government, directed to be the " Great Seal of Government in these Counties and Territories"—"and whereas upon receiving the said Seal it is found that the

---

[1] See same Notes and Proceedings also at an Assembly held at Chester, *alias* Upland, October 6, 1682: " an Act of Union was made by William Penn and Sealed with his ' Broad Seal.' " See Appendix to same book.

[2] See page 15 of the Appendix to the copy of " Laws of the State of Delaware," printed by John & Samuel Adams, 1797.

[3] See the Duke of York's " Book of Laws and Charter and Laws of the Province of Pennsylvania" published by the Legislature of Pennsylvania, 1879, for an engraving of this seal of Pennsylvania, which was the seal adopted by William Penn.

inscription ' Dellovvare' is thereon cut around the same instead of the word
' Delaware,' in the said act mentioned; therefore for presenting any doubt or
controversaries that may arise by reason thereof; it was enacted by the Hon.
James Hamilton Esqr; with his Majesty's Royal approbation Lieut. Governor
and Commander in Chief of Counties of New Castle, Kent and Sussex, upon
Delaware, and province of Pennsylvania, by and with the advice and consent
of the Representatives of the freemen of the Said Counties in General Assembly met; and by the authority of the same it was directed that Jehu Curtis,
Benjamin Chew and Abraham Wyncoops, Gentlemen, or any two of them

FIG. 310.

FIG. 311.

FIG. 312.

are hereby authorized to provide at the expense of this Government, with all
possible speed, a silver Seal, to be made of the diameter of two inches, to be
engraved with the Arms of the King of Great Britain and an inscription of
words, ' COUNTIES ON DELAWARE,' and the figures 1751, around the same;
which shall be the ' Great Seal of this Government;' and any two of the
above named persons shall cause the Great Seal now in use to be broken and
defaced in their presence."

"It would appear, then, that in the year 1751 the *first* great seal of the
' Three Counties on Delaware' was provided. This seal remained unchanged
until ' In the Constitution or System of Government agreed to and resolved
upon by the Representatives of the Delaware State in full Convention, which

state was formerly styled, "the Government of the Counties of New Castle, Kent and Sussex upon Delaware,"[1] the said Representatives being chosen by the freemen of the said State for that express purpose (Article XIX.), it is declared "that the Legislative Council and Assembly shall have the power of making the Great Seal of this State, which shall be kept by the President, or in his absence by the Vice-President, to be used by them as occasion may require. It shall be called the 'Great Seal of the Delaware State, and it shall be affixed to all Laws and Commissions.'"[2] This was the Constitution adopted September 20, 1776.

"The Constitution of 1792 recognizes a Great Seal as then *existing.* In 1793 it was enacted 'that the seal heretofore used (to wit, the seal decided in the Constitution of 1776) shall be, and is hereby declared to be the *Great Seal* of the State,' and it was also enacted, February 2, 1793, 'That the Secretary of State shall cause a *Great Seal* to be made of such device as the Governor shall approve, which shall hereafter be used for the same purposes for which the said seal, herein first mentioned is directed to be used ; and when such New *Great Seal* shall be made, the seal first mentioned aforesaid shall be broken, and no longer used.'

FIG. 313.

This seal was used in 1846 on Dr. Henry F. Hall's certificate of appointment as brigadier-general by Governor Murell.

"This seal was used until the adoption of the seal of 1847; it was enacted 'that the Secretary of State be empowered to procure a New Seal, to be used as the Great Seal.'

"The proceedings connected with the adoption of the device for the Great Seal of the State of Delaware were as follows :

"'October 30th, 1776. The "House Assembly" requested the Council to appoint a committee to confer with the committee of the "House" on the subject matter of making a Great Seal of the State ; and withdrew.

"'The Council, taking the same into consideration, resolved, that Messrs. Sykes and Von Dyke be appointed a Committee to confer with a committee of the House of Assembly on the subject of forming a device and making a Great Seal of the State. Nov 2nd, 1776. The Report of the Committee on a device for a Great Seal, was read in the House, and reported to the Council as follows :

"'*Resolved,* that a committee of one member from each House be appointed to procure, as soon as possible a silver Seal of the Diameter of three inches, and of a circular form, and that there be engraved, "Britania" upon the Right side thereof, and upon the left side opposite to her, "Liberty" in the

---

[1] For seals see Figs. 310, 311, 312.
See Appendix to the "Laws of Delaware" as aforesaid, page 87, vol. i.

usual shape, with a label proceeding from "Britania" to "Liberty" in these words, "Go to America;" and there be engraven on the top, the shape of a Book, having these words thereon, "The Bill of Rights;" and at the bottom another Book, having these words thereon, "The System of Government;" and that there shall be an inscription around the same, near the edge or extremity thereof in the following Capital letters, "THE GREAT SEAL OF THE STATE OF DELAWARE," with the figures "1776." That Mr. McKean be appointed on the part of this "House," for the purpose above mentioned.

"'On motion, *Resolved*, that Mr. Sykes be appointed on the part of the Council to procure a Great Seal of the State as aforesaid.

"'January 16th, 1777. Mr. Sykes, the Committee appointed on the part of the Council to procure a Great Seal, agreeably to the Resolution of this House of November 2nd 1776, made the following Report; The Committee to get a skillful engraver to make a Great Seal for this State, which was agreed upon by both Houses, now Report, that they could procure no person capable of executing the work at this time, being engaged in other very important business for the safety of the Country, That upon consulting an ingenious gentleman in the Art of Heraldry, your Committee are of the opinion that the Great Seal agreed upon would be more suitable for a medal, than the Seal of a State; and therefore submit the same to the consideration of both Houses; which having been considered to the satisfaction of the Council, the Committee was discharged, this was agreed to by the House.

"'January 13th, 1777. In the House of Assembly Messrs. Robinson and McKean were appointed a Committee to confer with a Committee of the Council on the subject of a device for a Great Seal of the State; and also to fix upon a seal which shall be used pro tempore, until the Great Seal of the State be agreed upon by both Houses, shall be made.'

"The seal of New Castle County was decided upon and used as a Great Seal after the Declaration of Independence. This seal was afterwards captured and carried away by the British; and not having been recovered at the time of the meeting of the Legislature, in 1777, it was resolved that the ancient seal of the County of Kent, dated 1683, be the Great Seal of the State, *pro tempore*, until the New Great Seal be prepared and delivered to the Commander-in-Chief of the State; John McKinley, President of the State, being held a prisoner by the British, Messrs. Cantwell and Wiltbank were appointed a Committee of the Council to confer with a Committee of the House of Assembly on the subject of forming a seal.

"'January 17th, 1777. The above Committee brought in their Report; which was accepted and adopted; and it was Resolved N. C. D. that Mr. McKean be a committee to employ a skillful workman to make a silver seal of the Diameter of three inches, and of a circular form, and that there be engraven thereon a sheaf of wheat and an ear of Indian Corn, and an Ox of full stature in a shield, with a river dividing the wheat sheaf and ear of Indian Corn from that which is to be cut on the nether part of the shield below the River; that the supporters be an American Soldier under arms, on the right, and a husbandman with a hoe in his hand on the left; and that a ship be the Crest; and that there shall be an inscription around the same near the edge or extremity thereof in the words following, in Capital letters: THE GREAT SEAL OF THE DELAWARE STATE, with the figures 1777, which shall after the delivery thereof be the Great Seal of the State, and still farther as follows; to be emblazoned as follows: Party per fess, or and argent, the first charged with a Garb (wheat sheaf) in bend dexter; and an ear of maize in bend sinister; both proper; the second charged with an ox statant ruminating, proper, Fess, wavy azure. Supporters, on the dexter a husbandman with hilling hoe, on the sinister a rifleman armed and accoutered, at ease; Crest, on a wreath azure and argent, a ship under full sail, proper;

FIG. 314.

1847 seal.   Same as recommended January 17, 1777.

with the words, Great Seal of the State of Delaware and also the words Liberty and Independence, engraved thereon. When procured the Secretary shall break and destroy the Seal now used (*to wit the Seal of 1793*) as the Great Seal of the State of Delaware.' This is the present seal of the State of Delaware,—to wit, the seal of 1847. As far as can be ascertained, the first Great Seal of this State (then called the Three Counties on Delaware) was provided by enactment in 1751. The next Great Seal was provided by Constitution of September 20, 1776. The third Great Seal was ordered in 1793; and the fourth and last, in 1847.' " [1]

FIG. 315.

DISTRICT OF COLUMBIA.[2]

The design of seal for the District of Columbia was approved August 3, 1871, and is thus described:

"The device to the left of the figure, looking at its face, appears to be a sunrise, and a train of cars on a bridge over a stream leading from a larger body of water in the foreground. Back of the eagle's wing is a barrel on its side, a sheaf of wheat, another barrel on end, and two bags of grain. To the right, from the

[1] For the above information acknowledgments are tendered Captain Henry B. Nones, U.S.N.

[2] Obligations are noted for assistance rendered by Marshal Daniel S. Ransdell and William Tindall, Esq., Secretary.

same point of view, is the Capitol, with the Potomac River in the background, and the heights on the right bank of the river on the horizon. The legend on the scroll is 'Justitia Omnibus.' The date within the wreath is 1871, and the letters on the side of the book in the arms of the female figure are those of the word 'Constitution,' arranged in three lines of four letters each. The left hand of the male figure rests on a fasces representing the union of the States, and his right hand on a sword."

FIG. 316.

FLORIDA.[1]

"When Florida was admitted into the Family of States, in 1845, the Legislature authorized the governor to adopt a Seal and he adopted the State (with its present boundaries). After Reconstruction the Legislature, in 1868, I think, adopted the present State Seal."

GEORGIA.[2]

The first Great Seal of the State of Georgia is described in the Constitution of 1777 as follows:

"The Great Seal of this State shall have the following device: On one side a scroll, whereon shall be engraved, 'THE CONSTITUTION OF THE STATE OF GEORGIA;' and the motto, '*pro bono publico*,' on the other side, an elegant house, and other buildings; fields of corn, and meadows covered with sheep

FIG. 317.   FIG. 318.

and cattle, a river running through the same with a ship under full sail; and the motto, '*Deus nobis hæc otia fecit.*' "[3]

Fig. 317 represents the Confederate seal of 1861. This is now used by the Secretary of State as the seal of his office.

[1] Letter of Mr. John L. Crawford, State Librarian.
[2] Letter of Governor W. J. Northen.
[3] Marbury's "Digest," p. 13.

PRESENT GREAT SEAL (Fig. 318): The Constitution of 1789 (see Marbury's Digest, pp. 16, 17; Prince's Digest, p. 909) provided that "the Great Seal shall be deposited in the office of the Secretary of State, and not affixed to any instruments of writing but by order of the Governor, or of the General Assembly." This referred to the old seal described above. The Act of February 8, 1799, described a device for a new seal, made provision for the making of the same, and ordered the old seal broken in the presence of the Governor.[1]

IDAHO.

The Territorial seal of Idaho [2] shown in Fig. 319 was adopted on the 5th of March, 1866, and is described as follows:

FIG. 319.

"*Shield.* A view of the Shoshone River, with the mountains of Owyhee at the left; and a distant view of the mountains of Pannock and Bannock on the right, with a new moon in the sky, and a steamer on the river. *Supporters.* Liberty with her sword at the right, and Peace with her palm branch on the left. *Crest.* An elk's head to the neck, with full antlers. *Motto.* '*Salve*' (Welcome to the miner, to the farmer, to the merchant). Around the seal is the legend, 'SEAL OF THE TERRITORY OF IDAHO.'"

The State seal as shown in Fig. 320 was taken from an original impression kindly sent by Governor Wm. J. McConnell.

The Great Seal of the State of Idaho, adopted March 14, 1891, by the First State Legislature of Idaho, was designed by Miss Emma Edwards, of

FIG. 320.

Stockton, California, a daughter of Hon. John C. Edwards, a pioneer of San Joaquin County, California, and formerly Governor of the State of Missouri.

The explanation of the seal is as follows: "The female figure represents Justice and Liberty, typifying a just and liberal State Government. By her side grows a tall bunch of grain, representing the immense vegetable growth of the upper Palouse agricultural section of Idaho. The figure of the Miner is represented with the pick on his shoulder and one hand resting on

---

[1] For description of the new (present) seal, see Prince's "Digest," p. 753 *et seq.*, where will be found the Act of February 8, 1799, and a supplementary Act upon the same subject. Description may also be seen in Irwin's "Code of Georgia," 1868, Section 81, page 22, and in the present Code (1882), Section 86, and in the Constitution of 1877, given in the present Code as Article V., Section III., Paragraph 1.

[2] Hough's "American Constitutions."

the spade, ready to delve into the rocky ledge beside him for the wonderful riches of gold and silver which have established Idaho's fame as a mining State.   Horticulture is represented by two cornucopias filled with fruits and resting at the feet of both figures.   Agriculture by a sheaf of wheat placed below the shield.   Above the shield is the deer's head, emblematic of the proud position Idaho expects to take in the roll of States.

"Upon the face of the shield, directly in the foreground is represented a farmer plowing the soil; while beyond him on the right of the Snake River, which flows toward the front, is a large quartz mill.   On the right side stands an immense fir tree, illustrating the timber interests of the State.   In the background [1] loom the snow-covered summits of the Saw Tooth mountains, while rising behind them, and gilding their tops, is seen the glory of the morning sun, typical of the rising glory of the young State of Idaho.

"On a scroll above the Deer's head is the Latin motto ' Esto Perpetua,' signifying the perpetuity of Statehood."

The above description of the Great Seal of Idaho was written by its designer, Miss Edwards.

ILLINOIS.[2]

"The Great Seal of State was provided for by the act of February 19th, 1819.   Under this act the first governor of the state, Shadrach Bond, and the

FIG. 321.

first justices of the Supreme Court, procured a permanent state seal.   Who designed the signet is not now known.   The original seal then procured was used until the general assembly met in 1867, when by an act approved March 7 of that year, the secretary of state was ' authorized and required to renew the great seal of state, and to procure it as nearly as practicable of the size, form and intent of the seal now in use, and conforming with the original design, as follows: " American eagle on a boulder in prairie—the sun rising in distant horizon," and scroll in eagle's beak, on which shall be inscribed the words: " State Sovereignty," " National Union," to correspond with the original seal of state in every particular.'

"The old state seal had borne the motto: ' State Sovereignty and National Union.'   Inspired by the strong national spirit then prevailing, and informed in every effort by zeal to emphasize the late ascendency of the federal govern-

---

[1] The introduction of perspective into heraldic designs may be criticised as wholly improper.

[2] The author extends his thanks for seal impression and information furnished by Hon. William H. Hinrichsen, Secretary of State, and Captain Brand Whitlock, Chief of Index Department in the office of Secretary of State.

ment, the majority wing of the legislature sought to transpose the old motto, that the future generations of Illinois might read the sentiment of the state to be ' National Union *and* State Sovereignty.' But the determined opposition which the bill provoked in the Democratic party forced the assembly to cling to the ancient seal, and the bill was finally amended to read after the manner already quoted. The sentiment was left as it was when first expressed by the first governor and his venerable associates. But even with the sanction of a legislative enactment, the old seal was not immutable. It was not reproduced with exactness. The Secretary of State, resorting to a clever expedient, in executing the provisions of the act, so altered the poise of the eagle on that boulder in the prairie, that the federal end of his pennant was flaunted uppermost, and upon the present seal, the motto of the commonwealth must be read inversely to be read aright."

INDIANA.[1]

FIG. 322.

"A bill passed the General Assembly in 1816 and approved December 13th of that year providing for a State Seal as follows : ' A Forest and the Woodman felling a tree. A Buffalo leaving the forest and fleeing through a plain to a distant forest and the Sun setting in the West, with the word Indiana bottom of Seal.' "

Changes in the drawing of this seal have occurred from time to time, but are said to have been of no importance.

INDIAN TERRITORY.

Through the kindness of Commissioner D. M. Browning and of the several chiefs, original impressions of the seals of the civilized Indian nations were obtained.

The seal of the Osage nation (Fig. 323) bears a buffalo and tree in the foreground, and in the distance the sun rising behind a mountain.

The Chickasaw nation bears as its device (Fig. 324) an Indian affronté, holding in his dexter hand two arrows, and leaning upon a bow in his sinister.

A sheaf of wheat and plough form central figures in the seal of the Muscogee nation (Fig. 325), and a bow and arrows and tomahawk are grouped in that of the Choctaws (Fig. 326). The Seminole seal (Fig. 327) represents a factory on the shore, probably emblematic of civilization, and an Indian in a canoe paddling toward it. The Cherokees (Fig. 328) use a star of seven points surrounded by a wreath. Around each of these seals is appropriate wording and the name of the nation to which it belongs.

[1] Letter of Myron D. King, Esq., Private Secretary.

FIG. 323.

FIG. 324.

FIG. 325.

FIG. 326.

FIG. 327.

FIG. 328.

Iowa.[1]

The Great Seal of the State of Iowa was authorized by an Act of February 25, 1847, which is as follows:

Fig. 329.

"Be it enacted by the General Assembly of the State of Iowa, That the Secretary of State be, and he is, hereby authorized to procure a seal, which shall be the Great Seal of the State of Iowa, two inches in diameter, upon which shall be engraved the following device, surrounded by the words, 'The Great Seal of the State of Iowa'—a sheaf and field of standing wheat, with a sickle and other farming utensils, on the left side near the bottom; a lead furnace and pile of pig lead, on the right side; the citizen soldier, with a plow in his rear, supporting the American flag and liberty cap with his right hand, and his gun with his left, in the center and near the bottom; The Mississippi River in the rear of the whole, with the steamer Iowa under way; an eagle near the upper edge, holding in his beak a scroll, with the following inscription upon it; 'Our liberties we prize, and our rights we will maintain.'"

Kansas.

The seal of the State of Kansas "was adopted in May, 1861, by the Legislature of the State at its first session.[2] The design embraces a prairie landscape, with buffalo pursued by Indian hunters, a settler's cabin, and a ploughman with his team, a river with a steamboat, a cluster of thirty-four stars, surrounding the legend, 'Ad Astra per Aspera;' the whole encircled by the words, 'Great Seal of the State of Kansas, 1861.' This seal was adopted on the recommendation of a conference committee of the two houses of the Legislature."

Fig. 330.

"This State seal, however, much resembles a wood engraving in the centre of the head of the newspaper called 'The Herald of Freedom,' one of the first papers published in Kansas Territory, the first issue of which in Kansas is dated January 6, 1855, published at Lawrence."

[1] The author's acknowledgments are extended to Governor Boies, Hon. W. M. McFarland, Secretary of State, and Frank M. Carrell, Esq.

[2] Letter of F. G. Adams, Esq., Secretary of the Kansas State Historical Society.

A description of the seal of Kansas Territory, as published in the Easton (Pennsylvania) "Argus" in January, 1855, is as follows:

"We have just seen the seal of the Territory of Kansas, engraved by Robert Lovett of Philadelphia, according to the design of Governor Reeder. It consists of a shield with two supporters, surmounted by a scroll motto, and is emblematic of the life of the pioneer and the agriculturist. The lower compartment of the shield contains the buffalo and the hunter; the upper contains the implements of agriculture. The left hand supporter is a pioneer with his smock frock, leggings, rifle and tomahawk; whilst on the right is the Goddess Ceres with her sheaf; at their feet and between them lies a fallen tree and an axe. The motto is a beautiful allusion to the principle on which the Territory was organized, and consists of 'Populi Voce,' thus translated— 'Born of the popular will.'"[1]

KENTUCKY.

This seal was authorized by an Act of the Legislature of Kentucky on December 20, 1792, to wit:

"Be it enacted by the General Assembly, That the Governor be empow-

FIG. 331.

ered and he is hereby required, to provide, at the public charge, a Seal for this Commonwealth; and procure the same, to be engraved with the following device, viz. Two friends embracing, with the name of the State over their heads; and round about them the following motto, 'United we stand, Divided we fall.'"

What became of this seal is not known; but, as the State House has been several times destroyed, it is presumed the seal was also lost by fire. An impression of what is thought to have been this seal, attached to an old document, conforms generally to the one now in use, though much more crudely engraved.

The present law prescribes that the seal shall have upon it the device two friends embracing each other, with the words "Commonwealth of Kentucky" over their heads, and around about them the words, "United we stand, Divided we fall."[2]

LOUISIANA.

When forwarding an impression of the seal, Mr. George Spencer, Assistant Secretary of State, writes that "the statute which was passed in the year 1855

---

[1] For assistance the author notes his obligation to Hon. Lorenzo D. Lewelling, Governor.

[2] Letter of Edward O. Leigh, Esq., Assistant Secretary of State.

has no particular reference to the seal, except
that it instructs the Governor to make a suitable seal."

FIG. 332.

The seal of Louisiana is described as follows:[1]

"The seal of Louisiana is circular, and one
and three-quarter inches in diameter. On its
white or silver circular shield is represented a
pelican standing on her nest filled with young
ones in the attitude of protection and defence,
and in the act of feeding them, all sharing
alike her maternal assiduity. This device
occupies the whole of the shield. Over the head of the bird hang the scales
of justice evenly balanced, and a circle of eighteen stars around the upper
part of the shield signifies the number of States in the Union in 1812, at the
time of the admission of Louisiana. Over these stars, on the outer edge of
the shield, is the motto, 'Union, Justice, and Confidence,' and around the
lower edge the legend, 'State of Louisiana;' both the motto and legend are
in Roman capital letters, and separated by two white five-pointed stars."[2]

MAINE.

"The State of Maine was known as the District of Maine up to 1820, when
it became a State. As it was governed by Massachusetts from 1678, the seals
used on its legal documents were those of the
mother State.

FIG. 333.

"One of the earliest Acts of the first Legislature was to establish the arms and a seal for
the new State," June 9, 1820, as follows:

"A Shield argent charged with a Pine
Tree: a Moose Deer at the foot of it recumbent. Supporters: on dexter side an husbandman resting on a scythe; on sinister side a
seaman resting on an anchor.

"In the foreground, representing sea and
land, and under the shield the name of the
State in large Roman capitals, to wit: MAINE.
The whole surmounted by a Crest, the North Star. The motto in small
Roman capitals in a label interposed between the shield and crest, viz., DIRIGO.

---

[1] It will be noted that the copy of the present seal, as shown in Fig. 332, differs from this description, and it is to be regretted that the difficulty in procuring information leaves it a question of
doubt whether the changes were intentionally made, or the stars, shield, and scales carelessly omitted
in cutting the new seal.

[2] Preble.

"Explanation: The Moose Deer (Servus alces) is a native of the forests of Maine. When full grown it is scarcely inferior to a horse in size. It has a neck short and thick, a large head, horns dilating almost immediately from the base into a broad palmated form, a thick heavy upper lip hanging very much over the lower, very high shoulders and long legs. The color is a dark grayish brown, much paler on the legs and under part of the body. The hair is coarse and strong, and much longer on the top of the shoulders and ridge of the neck than on other parts. The eyes and ears are large, the hoofs broad and the tail extremely short. The greatest height of the moose deer is about seventeen hands and the weight of such an animal about twelve hundred and twenty pounds. In deep snows they collect in numbers in pine forests.

"The MAST PINE (*Americana quinis ex uno jolliculo setis*), leaves five together, cones cylindrical, imbricated, smooth, longer than the leaves or needles. . . . It is as well the staple of the Commerce of Maine as the pride of her forests. It is an evergreen of towering height and enormous size. It is the largest and most useful of American Pines and the best timber for masts.

"*Application of the Emblems:*

"NAME. The territory embraced by the limits of the State bears the name MAINE. CREST. As in the Arms of the United States a cluster of stars represents the States composing the Nation, the NORTH STAR may be considered particularly applicable to the most Northern member of the Confederacy, or as indicating the local situation of the most Northern State in the Union. MOTTO. Dirigo—*I direct* or *I guide.* As the Polar Star has been considered the Mariner's *guide* and *director* in conducting the ship over the pathless ocean to the desired haven, and the center of magnetic attraction; as it has been figuratively used to denote the point to which all affections turn, and as it here is intended to represent the State, it may be considered the citizen's *guide* and the object to which the patriot's best exertions should be *directed.* SHIELD. *The Pine Tree.* The stately pine with its straight body, erect head and evergreen foliage, and whose beauty is exceeded only by its usefulness, while it represents the State, will excite the constant prayer of its Citizens, *Semper viridis. The Moose Deer.* A native animal of the State, which retires before the approaching steps of human inhabitancy, in his *recumbent* posture and undisturbed situation denotes the extent of unsettled lands, which future years may see the abode of successive generations of men, whose spirit of independence shall be untamed as this emblem and whose liberty shall be unrestricted as the range of the moose deer. THE SUPPORTERS OF THE SHIELD. A Husbandman with a scythe represents Agriculture generally, and more particularly that of a grazing country; while a Seaman resting on an anchor represents Commerce and Fisheries; and both indicate that the State is *supported* by these primary vocations of its inhabitants."

The early Proprietors of the District of Maine affixed their personal seals to important documents. Among them Thomas Gorges, Sir Ferdinando Gorges, Thomas Jenner, Richard Vines, Edward Godfrey, George Cleeve.[1]

MARYLAND.[2]

" The Great Seal of Maryland presents a marked contrast to those of the other States of the American Union in that its device consists of armorial bearings of a strictly heraldic character, being in fact the family arms of the Lords Baltimore which were placed by the first Proprietary upon the Seal of the Province at the time of its founding.

" Most of the States have upon their seals emblems indicative of agriculture and commerce, plenty and prosperity, or kindred subjects, represented in a more or less pictorial or allegorical manner. The colonies that were governed directly under the British Crown formerly had seals upon which were symbols of the royal authority; but these were discarded at the time of the Revolution, and in their stead were adopted devices more in harmony with the new order of affairs. The New England Colony and Virginia, for example, had seals bearing upon the obverse the effigy of the sovereign and upon the reverse the royal arms of Great Britain. The Seal of Carolina had depicted on one side horns of plenty and other symbols of a youthful colony, and upon the other the arms of the eight Lords Proprietors. But this seal like those of the royal colonies, has become a thing of the past.

" Maryland, like the other States, put aside shortly after the Revolution the seal in use during the colonial period and adopted one supposed to be more in consonance with the spirit of republican institutions; but after a while the historic interest attaching to the old Provincial Seal came to be recognized, and the ancient coat-of-arms was finally, by legislative enactment, restored to the Seal of the State.

" The seal, which was sent to the Province by Cecilius Lord Baltimore, by the hands of Captain William Stone, is the first Great Seal of Maryland of which there is a recorded description. This seal was sent to replace one which having been stolen in 1644, during the rebellion of Richard Ingle, was subsequently lost or destroyed; and a minute description of it is contained in the letter of commission, dated August 12th, 1648, by which it was accompanied. No impressions of the first Great Seal, which was in use only during the brief period intervening between the date of the settlement of the colony and the year 1644, can be found. Its exact device is therefore unknown. The seal of 1648 was, however, described by the Lord Proprietary as differing but

[1] Letter of H. W. Bryant, Esq., Maine Historical Society. Seal is from impression furnished by E. C. Stevens, Esq., Secretary to Governor Cleaves.

[2] From paper on " The Great Seal of Maryland," by Clayton C. Hall, Esq., of the Maryland Historical Society, Baltimore, and published by that Society in 1886.

Copy of seal (Fig. 340) is from impression furnished by Governor Brown.

little from its predecessor. In 1652, four years after the sending out cf the second seal, it, with the government of the Province passed into the hands of Commissioners appointed by Parliament; and it was not until March 24th, 1657–8, that the Lord Proprietary's authority was re-established. In November, 1657, in anticipation of the restoration of his authority, negotiations for which were already in progress, Lord Baltimore deemed it necessary, in accordance with his intention previously expressed in letters the record of which has been preserved,[1] to provide a third Great Seal for the Province. Of this third seal, which was sent to the Province in the charge of Captain Josias Fendall, no description was given; but in the letter of instruction which accompanied it authority was given to Fendall, who was appointed ' Lieutenant and Keeper of the Great Seal,' to pass grants in his Lordship's name under the new seal, and particular directions were given, in relation to a certain grant that had been promised, that if no record could be found of its having been passed under the former seal, then the grant was to be made under the new one.[2]

Fig. 334.   Fig. 335.

" It is, perhaps, impossible now to determine which seal remained subsequently in use in the Province. It would be natural to conclude that it must have been the third one sent out in 1657; but it is by no means certain that such was the case, and for some reasons it appears probable that the seal of 1648 was continued in use.

" On the obverse of this seal (Fig. 334) was the equestrian figure of the Lord Proprietary, symbolizing his personal authority. He was represented arrayed in complete armor, and bearing a drawn sword in his hand. The caparisons of the horse were adorned with the family coat-of-arms. On the ground below were represented some flowers and grass growing. The entire figure was admirably designed and full of life. On the circle surrounding this side of the seal was the inscription, [' Carolus . Absolu . Dms . Terræ . Mariæ . et . Avaloniæ . Baro . de . Baltemore.']

---

[1] Archives of Maryland; Proceedings of the Council, 1636–1667, pp. 325, 329.
[2] Ibid., p. 335.

"On the other, or reverse, side of the seal was Lord Baltimore's hereditary coat-of-arms. The first and fourth quarters represented the arms of the Calvert family, described in heraldic language as *paly of six pieces, or and sable, a bend counterchanged.* The second and third quarters showed the arms of the Crossland family which Cecilius inherited from his grandmother, Alicia, daughter of John Crossland, Esquire, of Crossland, Yorkshire, and wife of Leonard Calvert, the father of George, first Lord Baltimore. This coat is quarterly, *argent and gules, a cross bottony counterchanged.* Above the shield was placed an earl's coronet; above that a helmet set full faced; and over that the Calvert crest, *two pennons, the dexter or, the other sable, staves gules, issuing from a ducal coronet.* The supporters upon this seal were a *plowman* and a *fisherman,* designated respectively by a spade and a fish held in the hand. The motto was that adopted by the Calvert family,—Fatti maschi parole femine. Behind and surrounding both shield and supporters was depicted an ermine-lined mantle; and on the circle about this side of the seal were the words ' Scuto bonæ voluntatis tuæ coronasti nos.' The arms thus described have become the historic Arms of Maryland.

" Such was the Great Seal of Maryland under the Proprietary government of the Lords Baltimore. During the sway of the Royal Governors, from 1692 to 1715, while the jurisdiction of the Proprietaries was superseded by the Crown, other seals came into use. The first of these was frequently designated in the papers to which it was affixed as the *Broad* Seal of the Province. This seal was formally adopted by the Council at a meeting held at the City of St. Mary's, on the first day of October, 1692, Lionel Copley, Esq., being Governor. But this action was not taken without the direct sanction of royal authority; for, as the record [1] shows, ' His Majesty's Warrant dated the 7th day of January, Anno Domini 1691-2 for making use of the new Broad Seal appointed for this province' was first ' produced and read.' No description of this seal was entered on the minutes at this time, and no impression from it has been found. The royal warrant above quoted has however been preserved in the Public Record Office in London, and it contains a full description of the seal. Upon the obverse were the royal arms of England with this inscription upon the border : ' Gulielmus III. et Maria II. Dei Gratia Mag. Brit. Fran. et Hiber. Rex et Regina Fidei Defensores.' On the reverse was the royal cypher, surmounted by a Crown, and these words upon the circumference: ' Sigillum Provinciæ de Maryland in America.'

" This seal continued in use until 1706, four years after the accession of Queen Anne to the throne of England, when it was returned to that country by the hands of Evan Evans, to be delivered by Colonel Nathaniel Blakiston, agent for the Province, to the Lords of Trade and Plantations. [2]

---

[1] Proceedings of the Council, Liber K., 1692–1694, fol. 47.
[2] Proceedings of the Council, Liber C. B., 1704–1708, fol. 56.

"The seal next in use appears to have been adopted with scant formality. Among the proceedings at a meeting of the Council, held September 22d, 1706, the following entry appears: 'The Seals for Govern^r & Councill Provinciall Court & Twelve Countys were brought by Mr. Evan Thomas & well approved off, and Ordered that he be allowed forty shilling for each Seale to be paid by the publiq & recommended to the Comittee for allowance.

"'Also Order that the sd Seals be used in ye Councill Prov^ll & County Courts.'

"In less than a year after the accession of George I. the government of the Province was restored to the Proprietary. The title was then vested in Charles, fifth Baron of Baltimore, a minor, for whom Lord Guilford was guardian. The old seal now once more became the great Seal of the Province.

"On Sunday, November 3d, 1776, the Convention assembled at Annapolis to devise a form of government for what was now become the State of Mary-

FIG. 336.　　　　　　　　　　　　　　　FIG. 337.

land, adopted a Declaration of Rights; and on the Friday ensuing, November 8th, the Constitution and Form of Government were agreed to. By the thirty-sixth article of the Constitution the power to make the Great Seal of the State was vested in the Governor's Council, and at a meeting of the Council held March 31st, 1777, this authority was exercised by the adoption of an order recorded among their proceedings as follows:

"'The Council being empowered by the Constitution and Form of Government to make the Great Seal of this State, do make and declare the Great Seal of Maryland heretofore used, the Great Seal of this State, and as such to be used in future until a new one can be devised and executed, which cannot be done for immediate service.'[1]

"Under the authority of this order of the Council the seal of the Province was continued in use until the year 1794. In that year the Council adopted a new seal. This seal, like its predecessor was affixed pendant to documents.

[1] Proceedings of the Council, 1777-1779.

Upon the obverse was a female figure representing Justice, holding aloft the scales in her left hand, and in her right an olive branch. Rays of light emanated from behind and surrounded the figure. Below were the *fasces* and an olive branch crossed, and upon the border were graven the words 'Great Seal of the State of Maryland.' (Fig. 336.) On the reverse side was depicted a tobacco hogshead standing upright, with bundles of leaf tobacco lying thereon. Two sheaves of wheat stood in the foreground, and in the background could be seen a ship approaching shore, with fore and main topsails set, the other sails furled. At the base was a cornucopia. On the circle about this side were the words 'Industry the Means and Plenty the Result.'

"This seal was formally adopted by the Council on February 5th, 1794, and a proclamation, publishing the fact of its adoption, was issued by the Governor.

"This seal continued in use only for twenty-three years. Its size, three and a half inches in diameter, and its pendent form were probably deemed inconveniences; for it was superseded by a much smaller one, which was made, as have been the subsequent seals, to be used with a press and stamped in the papers to which it was affixed.

"The order for the new seal is recorded by the following entry among the Council Proceedings under date of March 14th, 1817.[1]

"'Ordered that the Great Seal of the State be altered and changed and that the Register in Chancery cause a new seal to be made of the diameter of one inch and a quarter, that the device on the same be the Coat of Arms of the United States surrounded with the words 'Seal of the State of Maryland,' and that the same when completed shall be and is hereby declared to be the Seal of the State of Maryland.' (See Fig. 338.)

FIG. 338.

"The seal prepared under this order was engraved on steel. Its device was merely the American Eagle, as the order of Council required, with thirteen stars in a semicircle above, and surrounded by a border ornamented with thirteen points.

"The formal adoption of this seal by the Council occurred on June 9th, 1817, and on the following day a proclamation publishing the fact was issued by the Governor, Charles Ridgely of Hampton.

"This rather insignificant seal was used until 1854 when an attempt was made to restore the arms of the State to their place upon the Great Seal. . . . Governor Lowe brought the subject to the attention of the General Assembly. In his message to the Legislature, at the session of 1854, he said: 'The Great Seal is much worn by long use. I do not think that it is appropriate. It

[1] Proceedings of the Council, 1813–1817.

should in my judgment consist of the arms of the State, and not of a device which has no significant relation to its local history. I recommend that another be provided.'

"In accordance with this recommendation an act was passed by the Legislature providing for the procuring of a new seal bearing 'the arms of the State as heretofore known and accepted,' and the motto 'Crescite et Multi-

FIG. 339.

plicamini.' (See Fig. 339.) The act required that the new seal should be used on May 1st, 1854, on which day the old seal should be broken.[1] The intention of the Legislature in respect to the restoration of the arms of the State was not successfully carried out at this time. In the preparation of the seal recourse was evidently had to a rough wood-cut printed on the title page of Bacon's Laws of Maryland in 1765, and some errors which it contained were reproduced in the seal. For example, the Calvert arms were made *paly of five pieces* instead of *six*, and the portions of the cross in the second and third quarters of the shield which are properly red, were represented as black. These departures were not only errors in fact, but they were in violation of the ordinary rules of heraldic drawing and coloring. The errors did not end here. The coronet, helmet, and crest were correctly represented in the wood-cut; but in their stead a spread eagle was placed upon the seal. The story is told that the gentleman,—an officer of the State government at that time,—to whom was entrusted the task of preparing the new seal, deemed it imprudent to restore the coronet, lest the Whigs, then in opposition in the State, should use the circumstance upon the hustings, and by accusing the Democrats of an intention to restore aristocratic institutions, secure their defeat at the next election. He, therefore, of his own motion and for these prudential considerations, disregarded the directions of the act of the Assembly which required the restoration of the Arms 'as heretofore known,' and substituted for the ancient crest the familiar figure of the American Eagle.

"At the session of the Legislature held in 1874, attention having been by that time attracted to the errors in the existing Great Seal, a joint resolution was adopted directing its correction; but in this resolution reference was made to the wood-cut in Bacon's Laws as the model to which the corrected seal should conform. When it was recognized that the copying of that wood-cut would result in re-producing some of the errors which it was intended to correct, the Governor, James Black Groome, concluded to take no action under the resolution, and brought the matter to the notice of the Legislature

---

[1] The old seal, defaced as the law directed, was found November, 1885, and is now preserved in the Land Office in Annapolis.

in his message at its next session, in 1876. A carefully prepared resolution was then adopted in which was embodied a full description of the arms intended to be restored, so as to guard against the possibility of errors in the future. The restoration of the Italian motto and the legend upon the circle was also directed. In the preparation of this resolution Lord Baltimore's letter of commission for the seal of 1648, and old impressions of the seal itself, were taken as the guides to be followed, and the arms upon that seal were distinctly designated as the Arms of Maryland.

"It was not until 1880 that the succeeding Governor, John Lee Carroll, reported to the Legislature that the new seal was completed and had 'been in use for the last year.' From a note addressed by Richard C. Hollyday, Esq., Secretary of State, to the Maryland Historical Society, presenting to the Society the first impression of the new seal, it appears that it was first used February 27th, 1879.

"This seal (see Fig. 340) was engraved upon brass, and executed in Paris, under the order of Governor Carroll. It was not attempted, in preparing a new design, to reproduce the style of the old seal; but the directions contained in the resolution were departed from only in the introduction, not inappropriate in itself, of the figures '1632' (the year in which the charter of Maryland was signed) at the base of the circle. On the new seal the pennons forming the crest are represented flowing toward the dexter side, as upon the lesser seal used by Frederick, Lord Baltimore. There is no inscription upon this seal to indicate that it is the Great Seal of the State, none having been prescribed in the resolution under which it was prepared.

FIG. 340.

"By the adoption of this seal in 1876 the ancient arms of Maryland were finally restored in their integrity to the Great Seal of the State. The equestrian figure upon the obverse of the old seal, which symbolized the personal authority of the Proprietary, ceased to be appropriate after the downfall of the Proprietary government. But the arms upon the reverse side, which had become identified with the Province, and did not change either in form or significance with changing administrations, are retained as the symbol of the State."

MASSACHUSETTS.

"The Colony of Massachusetts was authorized by its charter of 4th March, 1628-9, as follows: 'And further that the said "Governor and Companye and their successors maie have forever one common seale, to be used in all causes and occasions of the said Company, and the same seale maie alter, chaunge, breake and newe make, from tyme to tyme, at their pleasures." '[1]   In April, 1629, the Governor in England wrote to the colonists here that he had sent over 'the Companyes seale in silver, by Mr. Samuell Sharpe, a passenger.'[2]

"This seal bears the device of an Indian, as shown in the impression (Fig. 341), and this seal was the only one used for over fifty years, or until the abrogation of the first charter, in 1684.[3]

"When King James II. formed a new government for New England, in 1686, with Sir Edmund Andros as Governor, a new seal was found necessary and was furnished. This seal had two sides, and therein differs most essentially from the first seal.

"A representation of it is as follows (Fig. 342):

FIG. 341.   FIG. 342.

Seal under James II.

"It might be held that the Indian of the earliest seal was really the arms of the Colony; but in this second seal, the armorial part consists of the royal arms, duly distinguished therefrom by the addition of the words 'Sigillum Novæ Angliæ in America.'

"With the downfall of King James in 1689 came a new state of affairs; the Second Charter, for the province of Massachusetts, being granted in 1692. This act provides[4] that all laws &c. 'as shall be soe made and published under our Seale of our said Province,' shall be duly observed. And also that all laws 'be, by the first opportunity after the makeing thereof, sent or Transmitted unto us, Our Heirs and Successors, under the publique Seal to be appointed by us, for Our or their approbation or Disallowance.'

---

[1] Mass. Rec., vol. i. p. 10.

[2] Ibid., vol. i. p. 397.

[3] In this example attention is directed to the color of the Indian, which is indicated by lines vert. This is an exact copy of cut published in the pamphlet issued by the Massachusetts House of Representatives. There is no doubt that the Indian should be in proper colors, and that this is an error of the maker of the original cut.

[4] Acts and Res., i. 16, 17.

"The seal thus adopted for Massachusetts was the royal arms, with a motto showing that it appertained to the province. The following examples show the two forms in use from 1692 to the Revolution. The second style was adopted about 1728, and on the accession of George III. his name was substituted (Fig. 344).

FIG. 343.   FIG. 344.

Seal under George I.   Seal under George II.

"In 1775 the temporary government adopted the seal whose design is shown in Fig. 345, and this continued in use for five years. When Massachusetts became a State, however, action was taken by the Legislature on the subject of a State seal, and under date of 13th December, 1780, we have the following record: 'Ordered That Nathan Cushing Esqr. be a Committee to

FIG. 345.   FIG. 346.

prepare a Seal for the Commonwealth of Massachusetts, who reported a Device for a Seal for said Commonwealth as follows viz. *SAPPHIRE, an Indian dressed in his Shirt; Moggosins, belted proper, in his right Hand a Bow TOPAZ, in his left an Arrow, its point towards the Base; of the second, on the Dexter side of the Indian's head, a Star; PEARL,* for one of the United States of America.

" ' CREST. *On a Wreath a dexter Arm cloathed and ruffled proper, grasping a Broad Sword, the Pummel and Hilt TOPAZ* with this Motto. ENSE PETIT PLACIDAM SUB LIBERTATE QUIETEM—And around the Seal—SIGILLUM REIPUBLICÆ MASSACHUSETTENSIS (Fig. 346).

" ' Advised that the said Report be Accepted as the Arms of the Commonwealth of Massachusetts.'

" This report was sent up for approval by the Governor and Council, and it seems that no further action was taken on it. The seal was, however, made and used for many years, inaccuracies were introduced by different designers, until in 1885 it was thought necessary to pass the following Statute :

" ' SECTION 1. The great seal of the Commonwealth shall be circular in form, and shall bear upon its face a representation of the arms of the Commonwealth, with an inscription round about such representation, consisting of the words " Sigillum Reipublicæ Massachusettensis ;" but the colors of such arms shall not be an essential part of said seal, and an impression from an engraved seal according to said design, on any commission, paper or document of any kind, shall be valid to all intents and purposes whether such colors, or the representation of such colors by the customary heraldic lines or marks, be employed or not.

" ' SECT. 2. The arms of the Commonwealth shall consist of a shield, whereof the field or surface is blue, and thereon an Indian dressed in his shirt and moccasins, holding in his right hand a bow, in his left hand an arrow, point downward, all of gold; and in the upper corner above his right arm a silver star with five points. The crest shall be a wreath of blue and gold, whereon is a right arm bent at the elbow, and clothed and ruffled, the hand grasping a broadsword, all of gold. The motto shall be " Ense petit placidam sub libertate quietem." ' " [1]

FIG. 347.

MICHIGAN.[2]

" The Great Seal of the State of Michigan was presented by the Hon. Lewis Cass to the Convention which framed the first Constitution for the State, in session at the city of Detroit, on the 2d day of June, 1835.

" The Latin motto on the seal, ' Si quæris peninsulam amœnam circumspice,'—' If you

---

[1] From pamphlet entitled " Great Seal of the Commonwealth," No. 345, published by the House of Representatives of Massachusetts. Cut of present seal of Massachusetts was furnished by Charles Warren, Esq.

[2] Letter of Mrs. Mary C. Spencer, State Librarian. Seal is from impression supplied by Governor John W. Jochim.

wish to see a beautiful peninsula, look around you,'—was doubtless suggested by the inscription upon a tablet in St. Paul's Cathedral, London, to the memory of Sir Christopher Wren, its renowned architect, Si quæris monumentum circumspice,'—'If you wish to see his monument, look around you,' referring to the great masterpiece of architecture, by him designed, as the most fitting tribute to his memory."

MINNESOTA.[1]

"The first official record of a State seal is in the message of Governor Ramsey to the first Territorial Legislature, September 9, 1849, in which he says, 'A temporary great seal of the territory of Minnesota has been adopted, an impression of which will be submitted. I preferred consulting the legis-

FIG. 348.   FIG. 349.

lative assembly upon the adoption of a permanent great seal, and I herewith lay before you the design of one, to which I ask your attention, and if you approve it, or suggest its modification, it will be placed in the hands of an artist and engraved, and thenceforward supersede the seal now in use.' On October 31, Mr. James Boal, from the committee appointed to draft a device for the Territorial seal, reported having adopted for 'a device, an every-day scene, consisting of an Indian family with their lodge, canoe, etc., and a single white man visiting them, with no other protection than the feeling of hospitality and friendship existing between the two people. The white man is receiving from the Indian the pipe of peace,' etc. This report was adopted, and an Act providing for the use of the seal was duly passed and became a law. But, for some reason, the seal so authorized was never used.

"In place of it one was adopted, just how or by whom there is no record now, and which was used as 'the great seal of Minnesota' until 1858. It bears the date at the bottom '1849.' The device is much the same as the

---

[1] Information and seal impression from Governor Nelson.

present State seal. A farmer is ploughing in the foreground, but facing to the west. His rifle, powder-horn, etc., are leaning on a stump near him; in the distance, to the left, is the Falls of St. Anthony, and an Indian on horseback riding rapidly eastward towards what appears to be a rising sun. Over the device is the motto, 'Quo sursum velo videre,' the third word a misprint for volo, the whole meaning, 'I wish to see what lies beyond.' This motto was selected by Hon. H. H. Sibley, while delegate in Congress.

"This seal was ridiculed more or less by journalists, who said it represented 'a man plowing one way and looking another,' or 'an astonished Indian and a scared white man,' etc. But it was used until 1858.

"At the first session of the State Legislature the subject of a State seal was taken up. Hon. Charles F. Dowe, a member of the Constitutional Convention in 1857, had drafted (by Mr. Buechner, an artist of St. Paul) a design for a State seal which he had hopes that the first State Legislature would adopt. It was generally considered very suitable.[1] Article fifteen of the State Constitution, adopted on October 13, 1857, provided that 'The legislature shall provide for an appropriate device and motto for said seal.' The first legislative session (which assembled December 2, 1857), however, does not seem to have done so, and when the State government came into operation in May, 1858, there was still no 'State seal' for use on documents. Governor Sibley authorized the Secretary of State to continue the use of the old Territorial seal for the present. At the adjourned session of the Legislature, in June, Governor Sibley referred to the subject, and a special committee was appointed to report the design for a seal, of which W. H. C. Folsom was chairman. This was done on June 30. Mr. Folsom had secured an elaborate design from an artist of St. Paul, Dr. R. O. Sweeny, fully described in his report. A joint resolution adopting the design was passed and duly signed on July 16.

"Several months appear to have elapsed before the new seal was engraved and put into use, and when it was, it was found that the elaborate design proposed in Mr. Folsom's report had not been adopted, but that the device of the old Territorial seal had been used, with a little change. The equestrian Indian was represented as riding westward, and the farmer ploughing eastward. No other change was made, except the use of the word 'State' instead of 'Territory,' and adding the date of its admission, '1858.' The motto was 'L'Etoile du Nord' (the North Star). The 'Minnesotian' newspaper ridiculed this latter in a series of vituperative articles, declaring that Governor Sibley had used a French motto simply because he spoke that tongue. But the seal soon came into general use, and has been the only one used officially for twenty years. Mr. Folsom in his book says, 'There seems to be no evidence that it was ever legally adopted, and the question may well be raised as to its validity.'

---

[1] An engraving is given of it on page 658 of W. H. C. Folsom's "History of the Northwest."

MISSISSIPPI.

The most correct representation of the national device, so far noted, in State seals is here shown, but open to criticism, inasmuch as but three arrows instead of thirteen appear, and they are held in the dexter claw, the olive branch in the sinister. The olive branch also should contain the symbolic thirteen in its leaves.

FIG. 350.

"The State of Mississippi has never adopted a Coat of Arms. In 1861 the State Convention, which is denominated the 'Secession Convention,' adopted a Coat of Arms and Flag for the State, but when the star of the Confederacy went down the Coat of Arms and State Flag went down with it, and since that time the State of Mississippi has had neither Coat of Arms nor State Flag.

"The Seal, an impression of which I send herewith, has been in use ever since the admission of Mississippi into the Union as a State."[1]

MISSOURI.

Fig. 351 is a representation of the Seal of Missouri as it exists, and Fig. 352 a representation of the seal as it should be, to conform to the statute and as it is printed upon official stationery. The difference between the two designs is explained by the following description:

FIG. 351.   FIG. 352.

"The device for an armorial achievement for the state of Missouri shall be as follows, to wit: Arms, parted per pale; on the dexter side, gules, the white or grizzly bear of Missouri, passant guardant, proper, on a chief engrailed, azure, a crescent argent; on the sinister side, argent, the arms of the

[1] Letter of Governor Stone.

United States, the whole within a band inscribed with the words, 'United we stand, divided we fall.' For the crest, over a helmet full-faced, grated with six bars, or, a cloud proper, from which ascends a star argent, and above it a constellation of twenty-three smaller stars, argent, on an azure field, surrounded by a cloud proper. Supporters on each side, a white or grizzly bear of Missouri, rampant, guardant proper, standing on a scroll inscribed with the motto 'Salus populi suprema lex esto,' and under the scroll the numerical letters MDCCCXX. And the great seal of the state shall be so engraved as to present by its impression the device of the armorial achievement foresaid, surrounded by a scroll inscribed with the words, 'THE GREAT SEAL OF THE STATE OF MISSOURI,' in Roman capitals, which seal shall be in a circular form and not more than two and a half inches in diameter." [1]

It will thus be seen that in the seal now in use the dexter impalement is divided *per fesse*, the engrailed line is omitted or illegible, and the arrangement of the stars does not conform to the blazon.

In both seals the bear wrongly faces the sinister, and in Fig. 351 is *passant*, and not *passant guardant* as described.

The seal as in Fig. 352 contains a line *invected*, which should be *engrailed*, and the shield upon the eagle's breast is charged with stars, which are again duplicated above him.

The seal as Fig. 351 was prescribed by an "Act approved January 11th, 1822." [2]

Montana.[3]

The Territorial seal of Montana is shown in Fig. 353, the State seal in Fig. 354. The latter was approved by an Act of March 2, 1893, as follows:

FIG. 353.   FIG. 354.

---

[1] Laws of Missouri, vol. ii. p. 721.

[2] Preble, page 645. It is here noted that the design shown in Preble does not coincide with the blazon. Hon. A. A. Lesueur, Secretary of State, in forwarding impression of seal directs attention to these irregularities.

[3] Seal is designed from impression furnished by Hon. L. Rotwitt, Secretary of State.

"Be it enacted by the Legislative Assembly of the State of Montana: SECTION 1. There shall be a great Seal of the State of Montana, which shall be of the following design, namely: A central group representing a plow, a miner's pick and shovel; upon the right a representation of the great falls of the Missouri River; upon the left mountain scenery, and underneath, the words 'ORO-Y-PLATA.' The Seal must be two and one-half inches in diameter, and surrounded by these words, 'THE GREAT SEAL OF THE STATE OF MONTANA.' SECTION 2. All Acts and parts of Acts in conflict with this Act are hereby repealed. SECTION 3. This Act shall take effect and be in force from and after its passage."

NEBRASKA.[1]

"The territorial seal of Nebraska was never adopted by any act of the legislature; but as it existed in fact, was two and one-half inches in diameter, and bore the following devices: 'In the centre a chart, inscribed "The Constitution," supported on the right hand by a man in citizen's dress, and on the left hand by a man in a hunting frock, holding a gun resting on his left arm,—both of these supporters pointing to an American ensign waving over the chart. On the right of the citizen a locomotive, plow, and other agricultural emblems. On the left of the hunter a river, steamboat, and sheaf of wheat. The sun's rays are seen behind the folds of the American flag. Over these devices the motto, "Popular Sovereignty," under them, the word "Progress." '"[2]

FIG. 355.

In 1867 Nebraska was admitted into the Union as a State, and then adopted the seal shown in Fig. 355, and described as follows: "The eastern part of the circle to be represented by a steamboat ascending the Missouri River; the mechanic arts to be represented by a smith with hammer and anvil; in the foreground, agriculture to be represented by a settler's cabin, sheaves of wheat, and stalks of growing corn; in the background a train of cars heading towards the Rocky Mountains, and on the extreme west, the Rocky Mountains to be plainly in view; around the top of this circle, to be in capital letters, the motto, 'Equality Before the Law,' and the circle to be surrounded with the words, 'Great Seal of the State of Nebraska, March 1st, 1867.'"[3]

---

[1] Seal impression was furnished by Hon. Lorenzo Crounse, Governor, and information by Hon. John C. Allen, Secretary of State.

[2] Preble.

[3] General Statutes of Nebraska, 1873, Chapter lxxiii.

NEVADA.

"An Act of the Legislature of 1861 provided for a Territorial Seal, designed as follows:

FIG. 356.

"Mountains with a stream of water coursing down their sides and falling on overshot wheel of a quartz mill at the base. A miner leaning on his pick and upholding a United States flag, with a motto expressing the two ideas of loyalty to the Union and the wealth to sustain it: Volens et potens.

"Several designs were made and submitted for a State Seal, none of which proved acceptable. The Legislature in 1866 passed an Act providing for 'a Seal of State for the State of Nevada.' It is described in the Act as follows: 'The Great Seal of the State of Nevada,' the design of which shall be as follows, to wit: In the foreground two large mountains, at the base of which, on the right there shall be located a quartz mill, and on the left a tunnel penetrating the silver leads of the mountain, with a miner running out a carload of ore and a team loaded with ore for the mill. Immediately in the foreground there shall be emblems indicative of the agricultural resources of the State: a plow, a sheaf, and a sickle; in the middle ground a train of railroad cars passing a mountain gorge; also a telegraph line extending along the line of the railroad. In the extreme background a range of snow-clad mountains, with the rising sun in the east; thirty-six[1] stars to encircle the whole group in an outer circle, the words, "The Great Seal of the State of Nevada," to be engraven, with these words for the motto of the State: "All for our country."'"[2]

NEW HAMPSHIRE.[3]

SOME SEALS OF THE PROVINCE OF NEW HAMPSHIRE.

"A grant was made in 1622 to Mason and Gorges of land from the Merrimack to the Kennebec River, and in the next year the first settlement was made at Portsmouth, and one at Dover, New Hampshire. In 1629 this grant was divided and a separate one made to Mason of the part west of the Piscataqua River, called New Hampshire, and to Gorges that east of the river, called Maine.

"In 1641 Massachusetts claimed jurisdiction over New Hampshire, and

---

[1] Impression from which design No. 356 is taken contains thirty-nine stars.

[2] Biennial Report of the Secretary of State of Nevada, by Hon. O. H Grey.

[3] For information and seal impressions the author pays acknowledgments to Walter Kendall Watkins, Esq. Obligations are also expressed for the assistance of Hon. Ezra S. Stearns, Secretary of State, and Mr. Kimball, of the State Library.

maintained it until 1679, when it was decided by the English court of appeal that the authority exercised by Massachusetts was illegal, and New Hampshire was made a separate Province.

" John Cutt was appointed the first President, his commission bearing date 18th September, 1679, and on the 1st of January, 1679–80 he received his commission and the seal first used by the Province.

" The motto on this seal read as follows: ' SIGILLUM PRÆSIDENTIS ET CONSILIS DE PROVINCIA NOVÆ HAMPTONIÆ IN NOVA ANGLIA;' the arms used were the royal ones of that period. This was used by John Cutt and his successor, Richard Waldron, in 1680 and 1681. On the accession of Edward Cranfield, in 1682, who was commissioned lieutenant-governor, the motto was changed to ' SIGILLUM PROVINCIÆ NOSTRÆ NOVÆ HAMPTONIÆ IN NOVA ANGLIA.'

" This was also used by Walter Barefoote, Deputy Governor, who succeeded Cranfield in 1685, till the following year, when New Hampshire, Maine, Massachusetts, and Narragansett (Rhode Island) were united under a single Royal Province, with President Joseph Dudley at the head for a year, until Sir Edmund Andros was appointed Governor in 1687. On his overthrow in 1689, when Massachusetts resumed under her old charter, she took New Hampshire under her protection with Simon Bradstreet as Governor.

" In 1692 Massachusetts received her second charter, and New Hampshire was re-established as a separate Province with John Usher as Lieutenant-Governor, acting for Samuel Allen, of London, the Governor.

" The seal used at that time bears the motto, ' SIG : PROVIN : N'RÆ : NOVÆ : HAMPTON : IN : NOV : ANGLIA.'

" Fortunately for antiquarians and students of heraldry, the die of this interesting seal is in existence and deposited in the custody of an institution, where it may be inspected by those interested in the subject. Its owners are the Misses Getchell, of Newburyport, descendants of the Pillsbury family, a noted one in Colonial times. Through the indefatigable research and labors of Mr. James Rindge Stanwood, of Portsmouth, New Hampshire, this gem of the engraver's art has been identified and preserved, and now is exhibited in the chamber of the old State House, Boston, in the keeping of the Bostonian Society.

" The motto encircles a crown, surmounting the British shield of William and Mary's time, which includes the arms of Nassau with those of France, Scotland, and Ireland.

" Surrounding the shield is the familiar motto in the garter of ' Honi soit qui mal y pense,' while outside the garter appear the monogram of William and Mary on one side, and R. R. (Rex, Regina) on the other.

" We refer more fully to this seal, as the die is still in existence, and will pass over the changes wrought in the royal arms on its successors and dwell on one more interesting to the American public as an example of ' native

FIG. 357.

blazoning,' as it might be termed. We refer to the seal adopted by the Colony of New Hampshire in 1776. The seal displayed a codfish, five arrows bound together, and a pine-tree. The motto, 'COLONY OF NEW HAMPSHIRE. VIS UNITA FORTIOR' (Fig. 357).

"This is the first example on her seal of native emblems, the codfish of her coast and the pine-tree of her interior being represented, while the five arrows represents the then five counties of her jurisdiction, and her 'united strength the stronger.'

"The die of this interesting specimen of 'native heraldry' has fortunately survived the century and more of the existence of New Hampshire as an independent State, and is preserved as a precious relic of the Revolutionary period in the cabinet of the New England Historic-Genealogical Society in Boston. This die was used only in the year 1776, being superseded by a similar device with the motto 'SIGILL : REIPUB : NEO : HANTONI : VIS : UNITA FORTIOR.'

FIG. 358.

"In 1784 the familiar ship on the stocks appears on the State seal, with a rising sun, which in a design accepted in 1785 was omitted, and the motto now used, 'SIGILLUM REIPUBLICÆ NEO HANTONIENSIS,' is the legal one adopted February 12, 1785.[1]

"The present seal of New Hampshire was adopted in November, 1784, but owing to some irregularity in the proceeding it was thought necessary to confirm it in February, 1785. The description then made was, '*A field encompassed with laurels ; round the field, in capital letters, " Sigillum Reipublicæ Neo Hantoniensis," on the field, a rising sun, and a ship on the stocks, with the American banners displayed.*'" This seal has not been changed since then.

NEW JERSEY.[2]

"Of Colonial seals, properly used and to be used in the State of New Jersey, a very early allusion thereto, which is at the same time quaint and curious, is that concerning the seal of New Albion (Figs. 359, 360). Regard-

---

[1] This bare synopsis of the history of New Hamshire's seals has perhaps an interest to many readers, who may add greatly to their knowledge of the subject by a perusal of Mr. J. R. Stanwood's account of "The Province Seal of New Hampshire under William and Mary."

[2] From paper by Francis Bazley Lee, Esq., of New Jersey Historical Society. Acknowledgments are also expressed for the valuable assistance of Governor Werts, Hon. Henry C. Kelsey, Secretary of State, General William S. Stryker, Vice-Chancellor Robert S. Green, and William John Potts, Esq.

ing the history of the semi-fabulous expedition by Plowden to the shores of the Delaware, Mr. Gregory B. Keen, of Philadelphia, has given a full and succinct account.[1] As one of the phases of this elaborate attempt to found an earldom in what was later West Jersey, Edmund Plowden essayed a seal for his colony in or about the year 1648, which appears in Beauchamp Plantagenet's 'Description,' and was at this time printed in London. The 'Order, Medall and Riban of the Albion Knights, of the Conversion of 23 Kings,

FIG. 359.   FIG. 360.

their support' may be thus described. The medal bears on its face a coroneted effigy of Sir Edmund Plowden surrounded by the legend 'Edmvndvs . Comes · Palatinvs · Et · Gvber · N · Albion.' Upon the reverse are two coats of arms impaled, the dexter those of the Province of New Albion, viz.: the open Gospel, surmounted by a hand dexter issuing from the parti-line grasping a sword erect, surmounted by a crown: the sinister those of Plowden himself, a *fesse dancettée* with two *fleurs-de-lis* on the upper points: supporters two bucks rampant gorged with crowns; the whole surmounted by the coronet of an Earl Palatine, and encircled with the motto 'Sic Svos Virtvs Beat,' and the order consisting of this achievement encircled by twenty-two heads couped and crowned held up by a crowned savage kneeling—the whole surrounded with the legend 'Docebo Iniquos vias tuas, et impii ad te convertentur.' Other Latin mottoes appear, as do the verses:

> 'True virtue mounted aloft on Honour high
> In a Serene Conscience as clear as skie.'

> 'All power on life and death the Sword and Crown
> On Gospel's truth shineth Honour and Renown.'

"Previous to the English conquest of 1664, the Dutch claimed all of what is now the State of New Jersey, but colonized only the northeast portion thereof. Whatever claims they may have had to the Zuydt Rivere (Delaware) shores were in virtual abeyance until 1655 when the Hollanders broke down

---

[1] From Winsor's "Critical and Narrative History," vol. iii. p. 462.

the power of Sweden. Thus all the Dutch settlements in New Jersey were a part of New Netherlands, and as such the seal of the Province had full force and effect in the plantations and towns on the west of Hudson's River. The seal of the colony is thus blazoned: '*Argent*, a beaver proper: *Crest*, a coronet: *Legend*, Sigillvm Novi Belgii.' Van Der Donk alludes to this seal in one of his papers, when the historian says that New Netherland was called

FIG. 361.[2]

a province because it was invested by their High Mightinesses with the arms of an earl.[1] This seal was used until 1664. Occupying, upon the Delaware, a position analogous to the Dutch on the Hudson, were the Swedes, who during their occupancy of the Zuydt Rivere extended colonization operations into West Jersey from 'The Falls' at Trenton to the Cohanzey. This was during the fourth, fifth, and sixth decades of the XVII. century. Most of these attempts were abortive, except in the counties of Camden, Gloucester and Salem. Inasmuch as the Dutch confined their claims to quarrelling with the Swedish Governors, until the bloodless war of 1655, it is to be taken for granted that all Swedish commissions and state papers designed for the West Jersey settlements would bear the seal of the Province of New Sweden.

"In 1664 the English conquered New Amsterdam, and with this Anglo-Saxon occupancy fell the rule of both Dutch and Swedes in New Jersey. Charles II. soon granted New Jersey, and much adjacent territory, to his brother James, Duke of York, who in turn re-granted practically what is now called New Jersey to Lord John Berkeley and Sir George Carteret, who somewhat later partitioned the grant between them. What may well be termed their Great Seal has fortunately been preserved.

FIG. 362.

Arms of Sir George Carteret: also used by Governor Philip Carteret.[3]

---

[1] "Documentary History of the State of New York."

[2] Seal upon document at Historical Society of Pennsylvania, signed by Christina at Stockholm.

[3] From "New Jersey Archives," vol. i. p. 60. This design contains several palpable errors, but, like other illustrations, is copied exact and the reference noted. The fusils should not be voided and the canton should be argent, the hand *gules*.

"The arms of Berkeley in duplicate with those of Carteret (Fig. 363) and surrounded by the motto 'Sigillvm Provinciae Cesareae Novae' appear in the commission of Robert Vauguillin to be surveyor of New Jersey. This document, now preserved in the New Jersey Historical Society, is believed to have this only impression of the arms which were 'Given vnder our seale of our said Province y^e Tenth day of ffebruary in the yeare of our lord one thousand six hundred sixtie and foure.'

FIG. 363.

Seal of Berkeley and Carteret.[1]

"Carteret and Berkeley at a later time disposed of their interests, each division passing into the hands of Proprietors. In 1683 the Board of Proprietors came into existence and as such their great seal appears. Upon the 11th of May, 1685, in a confirmation of orders sent to Governor Barclay it is recited that 'For the Just encouragement of those who travell dilligently for the good of the Publique and for the fixing of due Authoritie in them, That all commissions Instruments, Orders and Instructions whatsoever, and every of them, that shall hereafter have the Seale of the Province affixed thereunto, and the Hands of five whole Proprietors.' William Dockwra of London was instructed to 'affixe the Seale' and be a subscriber.

FIG. 364.[2]   FIG. 365.[3]

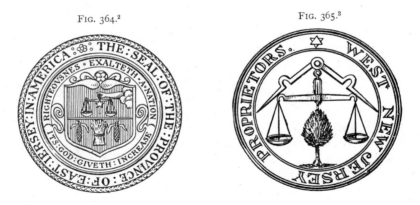

"Fig. 364 shows the seal of the Eastern Proprietaries in use before 1701.

"The two mottoes of the seal of the Eastern Proprietaries in letters of *sable*, 'RIGHTEOVSNES · EXALTETH · A · NATION,' 'ITS : GOD : GIVETH : IN-

---

[1] From " New Jersey Archives," vol. i. p. 27.

[2] Ibid., vol. i. p. 488.

[3] Ibid., vol. ii. p. 199.

CREASE,' and around the whole ' The : Seal : of : the : Province : of : East : Iersey : in : America : This seal was probably destroyed upon the surrender of the government in 1702.

" The Western Proprietors took origin about 1676.

" Fig. 365 is the seal of the Western Proprietors and is the earliest seal discovered.

" The seal of the Western Proprietaries has no motto.

" In a quit rent authority by both East and West Jersey Proprietors to Rip Van Dam (December 14, 1697), appears the ' Publique Seal' of the Province of West New Jersey as is here shown.

" The attempt of James II. to annul the grants of East and West Jersey which he himself, as Duke of York, had delivered to Carteret and Berkeley, is well known. The project had long been considered by the King and bore fruit in 1688 in a commission to Governor Andros dated April 7 of that year to include New York and the Jerseys in his jurisdiction, which jurisdiction, up to that time, had only circumscribed practically what is now New England. As early as September 18, 1685, Governor Thomas Dongan wrote that ' A New Seal of this Province is very much wanting,' to which Secretary Sunderland, from the Court at Windsor, August 16, 1687, replied. The King appointed a seal for ' Our Province of New York and the Territorys depending there upon in America,' thus including the Jerseys. The seal is thus described, in a warrant, under date of August 14, 1687, ' being engraven on the one side with Our Royal Effigies on Horsback in Arms over a Land-skip of Land & Sea, with a Rising Sun and a Scrole containing this Motto *Aliusq et Idem*, and our Titles round the circumference of the said Seal. There being alsoe engraven on the other side Our Royal Arms with the Garter, Crown, Supporters & Motto, with this Inscription round yᵉ Circumference *Sigillum, Provinciæ Nostræ Novi Eboraci &c in America* . . . and that it bee to all intents and purposes of the same force & validity as any former seal within our said Province, or as any other seal whatsoever appointed for the use of any of Our Plantations in America is or hath been.' This seal was ordered defaced on the 16th day of April, 1688, and in its place the Great Seal of New England be used. An order was issued to Governor Dongan to deliver his seal to Sir Edmond Andros, which was broken in New York City in September of that year.

" Governor Andros and his council went to Elizabeth and Burlington. Both East Jersey and West Jersey ' shewed their great satisfaction in being under his Maᵗⁱᵉˢ immediate Govʳ' writes Mr. Randolph to the Lords of Trade, which would be valuable history—were it true ! Both the Jerseys, under their own Proprietary government, disowned Andros, and in so far as he was concerned gave the lie to Director Stuyvesant's statement written a quarter of a century before, that the Englishman in sight of the great seal ' commonly gapes as at an idol.'

"The Andros government foisted upon the Jerseys was repudiated, and whilst *de nomine* the Great Seal of New England was presumed to be used in the Eastern and Western divisions, it is doubtful if it were ever recognized *de facto*. The accession of William and Mary saw the effectual re-establishment in 1689 of the seals of the Proprietors.

"Upon the union of the Jerseys in the year 1702 Edward Hyde, Lord Cornbury, was appointed by his cousin, Queen Anne, Governor of New York and the Jerseys. Upon the 3d day of May, 1705, a warrant for a new seal for the 'Province of New York and the Territories depending thereon in America' was issued. It was engraven upon one side with the royal effigies, with two Indians kneeling and offering presents, with the royal titles around the circumference, and upon the other side with the royal arms, garter, crown, supporters, motto *Semper Eadem*, and this inscription, 'Sigillum · Provinciæ · Nostræ · Novi · Eboraci · in · America.' Whilst this seal was in preparation Lord Cornbury, on the 8th of July, 1705, requests from the Lords of Trade a new seal as 'the old one is very much worn.' A seal had already been sent for New Jersey, as Secretary William Papple so advised on the 28th of July, 1705.

"Upon July 24, 1710, Governor Hunter returned the seal of New Jersey broken in council, which was laid before Queen Anne late in October or early in November of that year.

"A curious fact appears in Governor Hunter's 'State of the Quit Rents' relative to Provincial seals. This shows that in land patents that both Dongan and Andros, who assumed, the former by virtual implication, the latter by commission, a certain gubernatorial authority in the Jerseys, used their seal at arms and the ducal seal.

"In July, 1718, Governor Robert Hunter received the new seals for New Jersey, which had been issued by a warrant from George I. to Governor Hunter, dated Hampton Court, October 8, 1717, wherein the King directs the Governor on receipt of the 'new Seals' to cause 'the former Seal to be broke before you in Council and then to transmit the said former Seal so broken to our Com^rs for Trade and Plantations to be laid before Us in Council as usual.'

"This seal was engraven with the Royal Arms, Garter, Supporters, Motto and Crown, with this inscription round the same, '*Sig : Provinciæ nostræ de Nova Cæsarea in America.*'

"From New York on the 11th of July, 1718, Governor Hunter transmitted the old seal which was broken at 'a Council in the Jerseys,' and which, 'according to His Ma'tys Commands and by the Same Ship (which is still here by Contrary winds),' is sent to the Lords of Trade and Plantation.

"This seal of George I. lasted until the accession of his successor. Upon the 17th of November, 1727, a warrant was issued from the Board of Plantations to 'Mr. Rollos His Majesty's Seal Cutter to prepare new Seals for His Majesty's Plantations in America.'

"The order from council included all the colonies and plantations in

America. The general direction commanded the insertion of the King's particular arms and foreign titles as in the Great Seal of the Kingdom. To the seal cutter discretion was given in contracting words. The seal was the same as that of 1717, with this addition, 'in an outward Circle' 'Georgicus II DEi Gratia Magnæ Britaniæ Franciæ Et Hib: Rex Fid: DEfensor Brunsvici et Luneburgi Dux, Sacri Romani Imperij Archi Thesaurarius et Elector.' The ship bearing this seal was cast away, and the symbol of authority lost. However, under date of December 17, 1731, another was ordered.

"The 20th day of October, 1760, in Court at Saville House, George III. directed Governor Thomas Boone, through an order from the Secretary, William Pitt, that His Excellency continue the use of the former seal. Upon the 29th of the same month a circular letter was addressed from the Lords of Trade to the Governors in North America informing them that warrants for using the old seals were in preparation, together with proclamations for continuing officers at their employments, orders for the alteration of the liturgy, and the like. A general order was issued from Whitehall, December 2, 1760, from John Pownall, Secretary of the Lords of Trade and Plantations, and directed to Mr. Major, engraver of seals, that he engrave 'new ones for the Colonies.' With the exception of 'Georgicus Tertius' for 'Georgicus Secundus' the seal of New Jersey underwent no change.

"William Franklin, the last colonial governor of New Jersey, writing from Burlington under date of October 6, 1767, acknowledges to the Earl of Shelburne the receipt of a new seal for New Jersey and a warrant for the use thereof. The old seal was returned, and was defaced at Saint James on the 20th of April, 1768, together with the seals of some of the West Indies, South Carolina, Georgia, Nova Scotia, New York, and Massachusetts Bay.

"From 1702 until 1738, when New Jersey was separated from New York, the seals of the two colonies were identical in obverse and reverse. After 1738 New Jersey assumed *Nova* Cæsarea in place of Novi Eboraci."

"THE GREAT SEAL OF THE STATE OF NEW JERSEY.

"Upon the 27th day of August, 1776, the Legislature of the State of New Jersey met in the town of Princeton, within the classic walls of her famous college. The General Assembly forthwith chose John Hart, Speaker, the Council (Senate) selecting John Stevens as its presiding officer. This was the incipiency of the new political life of the commonwealth, and the formal institution of New Jersey's share in national liberty. Desirous of some symbol whereby the power and authority of the new-born State should be recognized, active measures were taken to prepare a great seal, ending in a formal resolution of the Council, bearing date the sixth day of September, 1776, wherein it was ordered that 'Mr. *Smith* and Mr. *Cooper* be a Committee to meet a Committee of the House of Assembly in order to form a great Seal for the State and to make report thereof to this house.'

" Mr. Richard Smith was of the county of Burlington, whilst Mr. John Cooper was from Gloucester County. Mr. William Paterson, of Somerset County, was directed by Council to inform the Lower House of the selection. Upon the same day the Assembly chose Mr. Samuel Dick, of Salem, Mr. Ephraim Harris, of Cumberland, Mr. John Covenhoven, of Monmouth, and Mr. Charles Coxe, of Hunterdon, as a committee to act with Council ' in order to form a Great Seal for the State.'

" Council was informed of the action of the Assembly by Mr. Joseph Holmes, Jr., of Monmouth, and Mr. Joseph Newbold, of Burlington.

" On September 10, 1776, Senator John Fell, of Bergen, brought to the Lower House a resolution from Council, who ' having taken into Consideration that it will necessarily take up some Time to get a Proper Great Seal prepared for the Sealing of such Commissions as have usually passed under the Great Seal and that it will be necessary for the publick Good that Sundry Commissions should issue before such Great Seal can be made : therefore

" ' *Resolved :*—That the Seal of Arms of His Excellency *William Livingston*, Esquire, Shall be deemed and taken as the Great Seal of this State till another shall be made.'

" In which the Assembly concurred, and Messrs. Dick and Covenhoven acquainted Council thereof.

" The Joint Committee of the 6th of September through its chairman, Mr. Richard Smith, reported to both Houses on the 3rd of October, ' That they have considered the Subject and taken the Sentiments of several intelligent Gentlemen thereon : and are of Opinion that *Francis Hopkinson*, Esq., should be immediately engaged to employ proper Persons at Philadelphia to prepare a Silver Seal, which is to be round, of two and a half Inches diameter, and three-eighths of an Inch thick, and that the Arms shall be three Ploughs in an Escutcheon ; the Supporters, Liberty and Ceres, and the Crest, a Horse's Head; these words to be engraved in large Letters round the Arms *videlicet*, " THE GREAT SEAL OF THE STATE OF NEW JERSEY" ' (Fig. 366).

FIG. 366.

The present Great Seal of New Jersey.

" Mr. Hopkinson was ordered to ' draw on the Treasurer of this State for the Expence' of the Great Seal. Mr. William Woodhull, of Morris, and Mr. Peter Tallman, of Burlington, were instructed to acquaint Council of the engagement of Mr. Hopkinson in this service. To this Council assented, and Mr. Andrew Sinnickson, of Salem, advised the Assembly of the concurrence of the Upper House.

" In the office of the Honorable Henry C. Kelsey, Secretary of the State, at Trenton, is the silver seal designed by Du Simitiere, and with it the carefully preserved report of the 6th of September, 1776. Upon a comparison of the two it will be seen at a glance that the artist deviated not a little from the wording of the report. From his note-book it is learned that he drew the design in India ink during October, 1776, having finished the Great Seal of Virginia in August and preparing for the artistic execution of the seals of Georgia and Delaware, which he finished in November, 1776, and January, 1777, respectively. When the drawings for the great seal of New Jersey came from the brush of this artist-archeologist—Pierre Eugene Du Simitiere—he had placed beneath the crest of the horse's head an earl's helmet, and had inserted below the escutcheon 'MDCCLXXVI.' No legislative sanction exists for these alterations, which may well be traceable to the eccentricities of the designer. That Du Simitiere did exceed his authority is shown by the fact that in many of the printed representations of the great seal, as upon the title-pages of State laws, the printers discarded both helmet and date and made their own designs based on the report of 1776. It is worthy of note that the late seal of the State Department of Insurance follows the letter of the law.

" Throughout the range of New Jersey's official publications no less than a score of designs of the great seal are to be found. The supporters are often reversed, whilst the horse's head faces either dexter or sinister over the escutcheon. The widest liberties were taken with the supporter Ceres, her cornucopia being in all imaginable positions. Often the representations border the ludicrous, as in many cases the supporters are clad in what appear to be bombazine petticoats. Not until Morton A. Stilles' edition of the laws of 1854 is there any attempt toward artistic execution of the seal on the part of State printers.

" A variety of mottoes occur; but among the earliest is that used in the Joseph Justice edition of the laws (1821), wherein the words 'Liberty and Prosperity' are found. This is now the recognized motto of New Jersey when such is used.

" In the ' Life of William Livingston,' Revolutionary Governor of New Jersey,[1] a most interesting reference is made to the arms of William Livingston, which it will be remembered were used as the Great Seal of New Jersey from October, 1776, to May, 1777. The original emigrant Robert Livingston, the virtual baron of the manor, was compelled to return to England in 1694. In this voyage, taken to advance business interests, he was shipwrecked in Portugal and reached the mother country by a continental journey. To commemorate the event, it is said the American family at this early period altered the Scottish crest, a demi-savage, to a ship in distress, and changed the motto *Si je puis* to *spero meliora*.

" Among the papers of General Henry Livingston of Ancram, New York, was found, in 1811, a letter from William Livingston dated December 13, 1698,

---

[1] By Theodore Sedgwick, Jr.

from Edinburgh. Writing to the American family, he notes their genealogy and thus blazons the arms of the family : ˙

"' Quarterly 1st and 4th Argent three gilliflowers gules, slipped Propper within a double tressure umber florevest, the name of LIVINGSTON: 2nd quartered 1st and last Gules a chifron Argent, a rose between two lyons counter rampant of the field 2nd and 3rd Argent three Martletts Gules, the name of HEPBURN of Waughtenn 2nd quarter Sable a bend between six billets Or the name of CALLENDER, your liveries is green faced up w^h whytt and red green and whytt passments.

FIG. 367.

"' I would cause cutt you a seal with this coat-of-arms, having one James Clark, a very honest man, who is graver to our mint-house here, and the most dexterous in that art, but could not get a steel block to cut upon.'

" Sedgwick considers that this excerpt contains 'heraldic blunders.' Further on the biographist quotes a letter from the Governor addressed to Colonel Livingston in Holland and dated June 10, 1785. His Excellency reiterates the fact of the alteration of crest and motto and adds, 'These have been retained by all the family except myself who not being able without ingratitude to Providence to wish for more than I had, changed the former (crest of a ship in distress)

ARMS OF LIVINGSTON FAMILY. From collection of book-plates at Historical Society of Pennsylvania.

into a ship under full sail and the latter (spero meliora) into " Aut Mors aut vita decora."' A book-plate, probably engraved when William Livingston was an entered student-of-law in Middle Temple about the year 1742, shows the alterations made by himself.

" In the commissions signed by the Governor between October, 1776, and May 10, 1777, the quartered seal was not used."

FIG. 368.

NEW MEXICO.

" Although the impression (Fig. 368) has been used as the great seal of New Mexico almost since the organization of the Territory, yet it was not formally adopted as such, by law, until the 27th session of the legislature, held in 1887, when that body passed an act entitled 'An Act adopting and establishing the coat of arms and great seal of the territory,' which was approved by the then Governor, Edmund G. Ross, on the first day of February, of that year. The first section of which reads as follows:

"'The coat of arms of the territory of New Mexico shall be the Mexican Eagle grasping a serpent in its beak, the cactus in its talons, shielded by the American eagle with outspread wings, and grasping arrows in its talons. The date MDCCCL, under the eagles, and above that, on a scroll, the motto: *Crescit Eundo.* That the great seal of the territory have the coat of arms thereon, being the same seal now used by the secretary of the territory, and that the same be adopted and established as the official seal and coat of arms of the territory of New Mexico.'"[1]

NEW YORK.[2]

"I.—SEAL OF NEW NETHERLAND.

FIG. 369.

First seal of Province: seal of New Netherland, 1623–1664.

"This is the first public seal of the Province, and is thus described: '*Argent*, a Beaver, proper; *Crest*, a Coronet; *Legend*, SIGILLVM · NOVI · BELGII.' In a paper by Van der Donck, entitled 'Further Observations on the Petition of the Commonalty of New Netherland,' it is stated, that 'New Netherland was called a Province because it was invested by their High Mightinesses with the Arms of an Earl.' The engraving is copied from an impression of the seal in the office of the Secretary of State. It was in use until 1664, and afterwards, we presume, under Governor Colve in 1673–4.

"II.—SEAL OF THE DUKE OF YORK.

"This is a copy of the Royal arms of the House of Stuart, which Burke thus describes: 'Quarterly, first and fourth, FRANCE and ENGLAND quarterly; second, or, a lion rampant, within a double tressure, flory counter flory, gu. SCOTLAND; third, az. a harp, or, stringed, ar. IRELAND. *Motto,* "Honi · Soit · Qui · Mal · y · Pense."

FIG. 370.

Great Seal of the Province of New York, 1670–1673, 1674–1687.

---

[1] Letter of Hon. W. T. Thornton, Governor of New Mexico.

[2] New York is one of the few States that possess complete records of Colonial and other seals. The "Documentary History of New York" furnishes the examples of Colonial seals from which the cuts in this book are taken, and most valuable papers by Henry A. Homes, LL.D., New York State Library, give an exceptionally interesting and complete history of the seal which was adopted after the Revolution.

Legend, "Sigill · Provine Novi · Eborac." *Crest,* a Coronet composed of crosses and fleur de lis, with one arch;' which, Burke adds, the Duke of York was directed to use, by a Royal Warrant dated 9th Feb. 1662. There are several impressions of this seal in the first Vol. of Land Papers, in the Secretary's office. They are incumbent, but those to the patent of Renselaerwyck (1685) and to the charter of the city of Albany (1686) are pendent. The earliest impression in the Secretary's office is to a patent dated 20th August, 1670, and from the fact that the patents issued by Governor Nicolls are sealed only with his signet, it is inferred that the Great Seal now reproduced was received in October, 1669, at the same time as the seal presented by Governor Lovelace to the city of New York. It was in use until 1687, with the exception of Colve's brief administration in 1674.

"III.—SEAL OF JAMES II.

"We have not been able to find an impression of this seal, the warrant for which bears date 14th August, 1687. It is described therein as having ' on the one side our Royal effigies on Horseback in Arms over a Landskip of Land and Sea, with a Rising Sun, and a Scrole containing this motto, Aliusq : et Idem. And our Titles round the circumference of the said Seal; There being also engraven on the other side Our Royal Arms with the Garter, Crown, Supporters and Motto, with this Inscription round ye Circumference Sigillum Provinciæ Nostræ Novi Eboraci etc., in America.' Despatches of the above date were received in New York on the 21st November following; the seal was in use, it is supposed, until Leisler's usurpation in June, 1689.[1]

"IV.—SEAL OF KING WILLIAM AND QUEEN MARY.

"The warrant for this seal, which was brought over by Governor Sloughter, bears date 31st May, 1690. It served as the model for all the Great Seals of New York subsequently received from England, and has, on one side, the effigies of the King and Queen, and two Indians kneeling offering as presents—the one, a roll of Wampum, the other a Beaver-skin. Around the circumference are their Majesties' titles: Gvliemlmvs III · et · Maria · II · Dei · Gra · Mag · Brit · Fran · Hib · Rex et Regina · Fid · Def. On the reverse are the Royal arms with the garter, crown, supporters, and motto, and this inscription: Sigillvm : Provinc : Nostr : Nov : Ebor : etc : in : America. These arms are, it will be remarked, the same as those on the Stuart seal, with the

FIG. 371.

Great Seal of the Province of New York, 1691–1705.

---

[1] The seal of James II. is shown in the seals of Massachusetts (Fig. 342). The wording, of course, is different.

addition, however, of an escutcheon of pretence, containing a Lion rampant, for the arms of Nassau, of which house King William was a member. It has some peculiarities worthy of attention. Much importance has been attached to this seal from the fact that it was affixed to several patents in this country after the King's death. But the objections made to the validity of those patents, on that account, must disappear when the fact is understood that this seal was not superseded until September, 1705, —three years and a half after the King's demise. The engraving is from the seal attached to the original charter of Trinity Church, New York, 1697, in the State Library, and to the commission of Johannis Abeel, Mayor of Albany, 1694, in the Albany Institute.

"V.—SEAL OF QUEEN ANNE.

"There were two Great Seals for the Province in this reign.

"1. The first, the warrant for which bears date the 3rd May, 1705, was brought out by Col. Nott, of Virginia, and was received on 6th September

FIG. 372.

Great Seal of the Province of New York,
1705-1710.

following, when that of William and Mary was defaced, and sent back to England broken. On the one side are the Queen's effigy and the Indians offering their tokens of submission, as before, with the Royal titles Anna · Dei · Gra · Mag · Brit · Fran · et · Hib · Regina · Fid · Defen. On the reverse, the Stuart arms as already described (see II.)—the escutcheon of Nassau having been removed on the death of the King—with crown, garter, supporters, and motto, and this Inscription: Sigillvm · Provinciæ · Nostræ · Novi · Eboraci · in · America. Motto, Semper Eadem. The engraving is copied from the seal in the State Library to a patent of Anne Bridges and others for a tract in Westchester County, dated 25th Sept., 1708.

"2. The Union between England and Scotland, in 1706, rendering a new seal requisite, a second one was ordered on 29th October, 1709, and received on the arrival of Governor Hunter, 14th June, 1710, when that of 1705 was broken. The Queen's effigy, the Indians with the Royal titles, are the same as on the first seal; on the reverse, the Royal arms, now changed in consequence of the Union; on the first and fourth quarters Eng-

FIG. 373.

Great Seal of the Province of New York,
1710-1718.

land empales Scotland; on the second are the lilies of France; on the third the Harp for Ireland, and the former motto, Semper Eadem. Around the circumference is the inscription Sigillvm · Provinciæ · Nostræ · Novi · Eboraci · in · America. This seal was not superseded until July, 1718, four years after the Queen's death.

"VI.—SEAL OF GEORGE I.

"This seal was ordered 8th October, 1717, and received 'by Hopkins' on 1st July, 1718, when that of Queen Anne was broken and returned to the

FIG. 374.

Board of Trade. On the one side are the effigy of his Majesty, two Indians offering presents; and around the circumference the royal titles: 'Georgivs · D · G · Mag · Brit · Fran · et · Hib · Rex · Brvn · et · Lvn · Dvx · Sa · ro · Im · Arc · Thes · et · Prin · Elec.' On the reverse, the Royal arms, garter, crown, supporters, and motto, and this inscription: 'Sigillvm · Provinciæ · Nostræ · Novi · Eboraci · in · America.' The 'Semper Eadem' of the last seal is replaced by *Dieu et Mon Droit;* and on the escutcheon we have, first, the arms of England empaling those of Scotland; second, France; third, Ireland; fourth, gu. two lions passant

Great Seal of the Province of New York, 1718.

guard. in pale or, for Brunswick; impaling, or, semée of hearts gu. a lion ramp. az., for Lunenburgh, on a point in point gu. a horse courant ar., for Saxony; on the centre of the fourth quarter an escutcheon gu. charged with the Crown of Charlemagne, or, as Arch-Treasurer of the Holy Roman Empire.

"VII.—SEAL OF GEORGE II.

"This seal is a finer specimen of the arts than the last, and exhibits a progressive change in the dress and drapery of the principal figure. The

FIG. 375.

Great Seal of the Province of New York.

kneeling Squaw is introduced here for the first time *nude*, and great care is bestowed in delineating the skin she offers, in which we can almost trace the perfect outline of the animal to which it belonged. There is another improvement worthy of remark,—the inscriptions on this and the next seal are on the sides opposite to those they heretofore occupied. The words 'Sigillvm · Provinciæ · Nostræ · Novi · Eboraci · in · America' are appropriately on the side representing American gifts; whilst the Royal titles, 'Georgius · II · D · G · Mag · Bri · Fr · et · Hib · Rex · F · D · Brun · et · Lun · Dux · S · R · I · Arc ·

Th · et · Pr · El.', surround the Royal arms on the reverse side. These arms are the same as those last described, but their design and finish are immensely superior. This engraving is, also, from an impression in the State Library.

FIG. 376.

Great Seal of the Province of New York,
1767 to the Revolution.

" VIII.—SEAL OF GEORGE III.

" The warrant for this seal bears date 9th July, 1767 ; it was received on the following 3d October (seven years after the death of George II.), and the preceding seal was returned to the Colonial office. The principal side, where the Indians are offering their gifts to the King, is surrounded by the inscription ' Sigillum · Provinciæ · Nostræ · Novi · Eboraci · in · America ;' on the reverse are the Royal arms (as last described) with the royal titles : ' Georgius III · D · G · Mag · Bri · Fr · et · Hib · Rex · F · D · Brun · et · Lun · Dux · S · R · I · Ar · Thes · et · El.' This was the Great Seal of the Province of New York down to the Revolution.

" NEW YORK STATE.

" The first Great Seal of the State of New York was devised by a committee consisting of Messrs. John Jay, Gouverneur Morris, and John Sloss Hobart, appointed by the Constitution of the State in 1777. It was thus described :

FIG. 377.

" ' A rising sun, over three mountains ; motto underneath, " Excelsior ;" legend, " THE GREAT SEAL OF THE STATE OF NEW YORK." The reverse is a huge rock rising out of the sea, and the legend, " Frustra, 1777." '

" In 1798 a new pendent seal was adopted, having for a device the arms of the State. The third seal, which is still in use, was adopted in 1809, and is incumbent."

The drawings of the State arms have differed materially from each other, and in 1880 a commission was appointed to examine into the matter and to fix upon a design for the arms which should be definitely adopted by the Legislature. The result of this committee's work is shown in Fig. 377. The committee's design for the arms has been severely criticised, however, by the Rev. Beverly R. Betts in an article in " The New York Genealogical and Biographical Record" for October, 1885, in which he states that the meadow and vessels in the foreground do not belong to the arms. He gives as his authorities, among others, the seals of 1798 and 1809 and the flag of the Third New York Regiment, in the possession of the family of Mrs. Abraham Lansing, of Albany, New York. The design which the Commissioners recommended was based largely on a design which formed the interior of the initial letter of military commissions of Revolutionary times.

North Carolina.[1]

"The first legislation upon record since the adoption of the State Constitution relative to the Great Seal of State is to be found in an ordinance ratified the 22nd day of December, 1776; that is to say, four days after North Carolina ceased to be a colony.

"This ordinance appointed William Hooper, Joseph Hews, and Thomas Burke 'Commissioners to procure for this State for the use of the Governor for time being a Great Seal to be affixed to all grants, proclamations and other public acts.' It was further ordained that until a Great Seal could be procured the Governor should use his own private seal.

Fig. 378.

"So far as appears these Commissioners failed to procure a seal; at least, in April, 1778, by act of Assembly, William Tisdale was appointed to cut and engrave a seal under the direction of the Governor for the use of the State, to be called the Great Seal of the State of North Carolina. A seal was made under this act, and used until the year 1794. From a seal pendent to a commission as major-general of the Third Division of Militia in the State to William Richardson Davie (the impressions on which were taken from the seal of 1778) its design is described. It had two faces or sides, and made its impression upon a cake of beeswax covered with paper, three inches in diameter and near a quarter inch thick, and was the last State seal so made, the succeeding ones having one face only, and being applied directly to the face of the paper-writing to be sealed. This indeed had come to be the practice on ordinary occasions years before. Governor Tryon states in one of his dispatches that since 1750, at the request of the inhabitants living remote from the Secretary's office, paper had been substituted for parchment for grants of land and impressions on the faces of the grants for the heavy pendent wax seals. The bulk and weight of the grants to be sent out, if of parchment with pendent wax seals, caused 'great inconveniency and expense' in delivery to remote settlers, whereas if of paper with seals impressed thereon, 'one or

---

[1] From letter to Governor Jarvis by Secretary of State W. L. Saunders, January 30, 1883.

Governor Carr, S. F. Telfair, Esq., Private Secretary, and J. C. Ellington, Esq., State Librarian, have the author's acknowledgments for assistance rendered.

two horsemen would take up to them all the grants issued at a court of claims.' It had been found from experience too, he said, in this climate, that parchment was more liable to destruction by insects and little vermin than paper.

"On one face of the new seal appears a figure supposed to be a female. . . . Her left hand is extended, and plainly grasps a sword. Her right arm abruptly disappears at the elbow, leaving no trace whatever of forearm or hand. It is supposed that the hand in its palmy days held a well-adjusted pair of scales. . . . This impression was taken in 1794, after the new seal of 1793 had been ordered into use, but failed to work for want of a proper screw. Hard by stands a forked tree. . . . It does not show any sign of being a pine. Between the tree and the lady is a cow peacefully browsing, or drinking it may be, in front of and seemingly with her hip against the sword. The cow is of some dwarf species, and does not reach higher than the line of the lady's knee. Enclosing the whole is the legend, 'O FORTUNATOS NIMIUM, SUA SI BONA NORINT,' which being liberally interpreted may read: 'How happy are they if they only knew which side their bread was buttered.'

"On the other side is Liberty, with her pole and cap in one hand and a scroll in the other inscribed with the word 'Constitution.' Enclosing all is the legend, 'The Great Seal of the State of North Carolina.' Beneath Liberty is the further legend, 'IN LEGIBUS SALUS.' The legend beneath the other lady is 'Independence, MDCCLXXVI.' When this seal was made is not known; it is known, however, that Governor Caswell in 1787 used his private seal.

"In 1791 the Governor was again requested, by act of Assembly, to procure a seal for the State. The order for the new seal was given by Governor Alexander Martin, but it was not filled until the second year of Governor Spaight's administration. It was designed in Philadelphia under the supervision of Colonel Abesha Thomas, the State's agent in Philadelphia for the settlement of North Carolina's Revolutionary claims against the Federal Government, aided by the skill and learning of Dr. Hugh Williamson, then in Philadelphia as a member of Congress from this State.

"Governor Martin himself was not satisfied with the old seal of 1778, and he accordingly designed a new one. This design he sent to Colonel Thomas with instructions to the artist to correct the disposition of the figures and give them such ornaments as they might need and the proper classic drapery, and is as follows:

"The Great Seal is laid off into quarters. The first sinister is intended for a sheaf. . . . The first dexter is intended for Amalthea with her cornucopia heaped with Indian corn; the corn is falling out, representing the great planting interests of Roanoke and the northern part. The second dexter is filled with hogshead, barrels, and bales of goods, representing the commerce of the State. The fourth sinister contains a pine-tree, representing the timber, pitch, tar, and turpentine productions of the southern part, and Liberty standing under the shade with her cap on a staff held by her right hand and the Constitution held by her left. The motto, ' His Cresco,' to be done in the shape of a riband or label at the bottom. The diameter of the seal to be three inches.

"Under date of January 30, 1793, Colonel Thomas wrote to Governor Spaight that it was agreed on all hands, in Philadelphia, that the design sent by Governor Martin would not do. Nor was Governor Martin himself satisfied with it, for he had directed Colonel Thomas to procure an artist to sketch something for his design and send to him for approbation. Colonel Thomas did so, but the sketch proved equally unsatisfactory, and the Governor gave orders to stop further proceedings in the premises.

"Along with Governor Martin's design Colonel Thomas sent Governor Spaight the artist's sketch from it, which is as follows :

"'The figures are Minerva in the act of introducing Ceres, with her horn of plenty, to Liberty, who is seated on a pedestal holding in her right hand a book on which is inscribed the word "Constitution." In the background are introduced a pyramid, denoting strength and durability, and a pine-tree, which relates immediately to the produce of the State.'

"It was objected that the first was too complex to be executed on so small a scale, besides, the men of science said it was not conformable to the rules of heraldry to quarter the arms on the seal of a single sovereign State.

"Governor Spaight, under date of 11th February, 1793, wrote back to Colonel Thomas, professing to be perfectly ignorant of the science of heraldry, and for that reason said he would not presume to give any particular directions respecting the seal. He preferred, however, the sketch of the artist by far to Governor Martin's. He thought Governor Martin's too large and the objects too crowded and diminutive. He thought that the fault in the artist's sketch, viz., its lack of reference to commerce, might be easily amended by adding a ship (in the most proper part), which, in his opinion, was the most sublime emblem of commerce, and would stand for boxes, bales, tobacco, hogsheads, pitch, tar, and turpentine, barrels, and a thousand other minute articles, the basis of commerce. In conclusion he left the business wholly to Colonel Thomas, as he was in a city where the arts and sciences were understood, and where he could get the necessary information and assistance.

"The press of business pertaining to his agency prevented anything being done toward cutting the seal until 1st of July, after which date it was made, and Colonel Thomas brought it home with him in time for the meeting of the Legislature in November following.

"By act of Assembly in 1793, the new seal was 'approbated' and ordered into use. But not even an act of Assembly will make a seal, great or small, work, if its screw is wrong, which happened to be the case with this. Another act of Assembly was therefore passed in 1794 authorizing the use of the old seal of 1778 until the screw of the new seal could be put in order.

" Unfortunately in the act ' approbating' the seal in 1793 no description of it was set forth, and there is consequently nothing in the statute books to show what the seal was, or if there be, a faithful search has failed to discover it.

" From impressions, however, made from this seal it is known to have been simple in its design, presenting only two figures, viz.: Liberty sitting on a pedestal with her pole in her right hand, and her cap on the pole; in her left hand, as if exhibiting it to Plenty, is a scroll with the word ' Constitution' upon it. Plenty is standing to the left and front of Liberty, with her horn in her right hand, its mouth turned upward; in her left is a sheaf of wheat. Enclosing all is the legend, ' The Great Seal of the State of North Carolina.'

" The seal of 1793 lasted until the winter of 1834–35, when the Legislature, after bearing preambulatory testimony to its long service, passed an act directing the Governor to get a new seal with suitable devices. This seal, while it preserved the unity of the design of its predecessor, changed the disposition of the figures. Liberty is now standing up, with the Constitution in her right hand and her pole and cap in the left, while Plenty is sitting down, with her left hand on her cornucopia, from the mouth of which its contents are running out at her feet; in her right hand are three heads of wheat. Enclosing all is, of course, the legend, ' The Great Seal of the State of North Carolina.' And this is the seal of to-day also.

" There can be little doubt, however, that in its main design the seal finally chosen was suggested by the Colonial seal. Under date of 9th of July, King George sent out to Governor Tryon a new Great Seal, the principal figures of which on one side were Liberty and Plenty, and the Royal Effigies, nor was there any reason against it. All that was needed was to substitute the scroll of the Constitution for the Royal Effigies, call it ' The Great Seal of the State of North Carolina,' instead of ' The Great Seal of the Colony of North Carolina,' and the work was done !

" In the Revised Statutes a general provision was inserted requiring the Governor to procure a new seal whenever the old one became unfit for use, and this provision has been brought forward through the Revised Code to Battle's Revisal. Since the Revised Statutes it is believed there has been no special legislation relating to the Great Seal of the State."

Following is a copy of " An Act to establish a State Motto. WHEREAS, Contrary to the usage of nearly all the States of the American Union the Coat-of-Arms and the Great Seal of this State bear no motto ; and whereas, a suitable motto, expressive of some noble sentiment and indicative of some leading trait of our people, will be instructive as well as ornamental, and the State should also keep in perpetual remembrance the immortal Declaration of Independence made at Charlotte ; now therefore,

" The General Assembly of North Carolina do enact:

" SECTION 1. That the words ' *Esse quam videri* ' are hereby adopted as the motto of this State, and as such shall be engraved on the Great Seal of North

Carolina and likewise at the foot of the Coat-of-Arms of the State as a part thereof.

"SEC. 2. That on the Coat-of-Arms, in addition to the motto at the bottom, there shall be inscribed at the top 'May the 20th, 1775.'

"SEC. 3. That this act shall be in force from and after its ratification.

"Ratified the 21st day of February, A.D. 1893."

OHIO.[1]

"The present Arms and Seal which were established by Acts passed April 16, 1867,[2] are described as follows:

"'SEC. 15. The coat of arms of the State of Ohio shall consist of the following device: A shield, in form a circle. On it, in the foreground on the right, a sheaf of wheat; on the left a bundle of seventeen arrows, both standing erect; in the background and rising above the sheaf and arrows a mountain range, over which shall appear a rising sun.

FIG. 379.

"'SEC. 16. All official seals shall have engraved thereon the coat of arms of the State, as described in the preceding section. The great seal of the State shall be two and one-half inches in diameter, and shall be surrounded by these words: "The great seal of the State of Ohio."'"

OKLAHOMA TERRITORY.[3]

"An Act to establish a permanent Grand Seal for the Territory of Oklahoma was effected March 10, 1893, as follows:

FIG. 380.

"'Under the motto "Labor Omnia Vincit" shall be Columbia, as the central figure, representing Justice and Statehood. On her right is the American pioneer farmer, on her left is the aboriginal American Indian. These two representatives of the white and red races are shaking hands beneath the scales of Justice, symbolizing equal justice between the white and red races of Oklahoma, and on the part of the Federal Government. Beneath the trio group is the cornucopia of plenty and the olive

[1] The impression from which design is made was furnished by Governor M'Kinley.

[2] Laws, vol. lxv. p. 175. From letter of Robert Clarke, Esq.

[3] The cut of seal is taken from an original impression sent by Governor Renfrow and from a copy of his letter-head, sent by him as an example of "the correct arms of the Territory."

branch of peace, and behind is the sun of progress and civilization. Behind the Indian is a scene depicting the barbarous, nomadic life of the aborigines— tepees, emigrants' train, grazing herds, etc., representing Oklahoma in her primeval wildness. Behind the white man is a scene depicting the arts of civilization—farmer plowing, rural home, railroad train, compress mills, elevator, manufactories, churches, schools, capitol and city.

"'The two scenes are symbolic of the advance of the star of empire westward; the peaceful conquests of the Anglo-Saxon and the decadence of the red race. Under all shall be the words, "Grand Seal Territory of Oklahoma."'"

OREGON.[1]

FIG. 381.

The seal of Oregon is as shown in Fig. 381, and the description is from the statutes:

"The seal of the State of Oregon shall be an escutcheon, supported by thirty-three stars, and divided by an ordinary, with the inscription, 'The Union.' In chief—mountains, an elk with branching antlers, a wagon, the Pacific Ocean, on which a British man-of-war departing, an American steamer arriving. The second—quartering with a sheaf, plow, and a pick-ax. Crest—the American eagle. Legend —State of Oregon."

PENNSYLVANIA.

Records relating to the Colonial Seal of Pennsylvania are not known to exist, and it is doubtful if any other than that of Penn was ever in use. The Penn Charter, signed by Charles II., instructs William Penn to use his own seal, and documents bearing the personal devices of the Proprietor are still in

FIG. 382.   FIG. 383.

---

[1] Impression of seal and copy of statutes was supplied by the Secretary of State, Hon. George W. McBride.

existence. Two of these are preserved in the Historical Society of Pennsylvania. Here the Great Seal is pendent from a commission dated 1702, appointing Penn's "well beloved friends Edward Shippen, John Guest, Samuel Carpenter, William Clark, Thomas Story, Griffith Owen, Phineas Pemberton, Samuel Finney, Caleb Pusey and John Blunston, to be my Council of State for the Government of the Said Province of Pennsylvania." The lesser seal appears in sealing wax upon a paper dated 1682, appointing "Justices of the peace and Court of Judicature for the town of Newe Castle." The obverse and reverse of the Great Seal are shown in Figs. 382 and 383.

Until lately but little has been known of the seal adopted after the Revolution, and readers are indebted to the researches of Dr. William H. Egle, State Librarian, for the following information:

"THE ARMS AND SEAL OF THE STATE.

"Although the general Convention which adopted the first Constitution establishing the Commonwealth of Pennsylvania, on the 28th of September, 1776, provided that 'all commissions shall be in the name, and by the authority of, the freemen of the Commonwealth of Pennsylvania, sealed with the State Seal,' no provision was made what that seal should be, and yet it is here that we ought to find the first record of the arms of the State.

"On the 20th of March following, however, an act was passed for emitting bills of credit for the defence of the State; and on the 10th of April, 1777, currency was issued upon which was engraved a shield with the Arms. These Arms consisted of the same armorial bearings now officially recognized as those of the Commonwealth, and may be described as follows:

FIG. 384.

"A plough between two barrulets; in chief, a ship under full sail; and in base, three garbs (Fig. 384).

"There is, however, neither crest, motto, nor supporters. We have no knowledge to whom we are indebted for this design; and yet it would seem to have been a composition made up from the Provincial seals of the three original counties; for, we find that on the crest which surmounts the Penn Coat of Arms on that of Philadelphia, in 1683, a ship under full sail; on the seal of Chester County, a plough; while on that of Bucks County was probably a sheaf of wheat; of the latter we have no description. The seal of Sussex County (now in Delaware) of the same period seems to have had for its crest a sheaf of wheat, while the seal of the city of Philadelphia in 1701 had upon its quartered arms a sheaf of wheat and a ship under full sail.

"In 1778 we find an engraving of the Coat of Arms in type metal (Fig.

385), printed on a broadside, in which, in addition, is the motto, ' Virtue,

FIG. 385.

Liberty, and Independence,' the eagle as a crest, as also the supporters, two horses rearing, caparisoned for draught, including the stock of maize and an olive branch as additional devices. A fac-simile of this publication of the Arms of the State is given in this connection. The State Arms were first cut in printer's metal by Caleb Lownes, who was directed by the Supreme Executive Council, on the 19th of April, 1779, to be paid therefor. Various reproductions of this plate, as to size, were prepared and in use upon imprints of laws, proclamations, commissions, and other public documents, down to the year 1805, when we have the first innovation made by the engraver. One of the early plates was in good preservation and in use occasionally as late as 1865, when by the burning of the Telegraph printing-office in Harrisburg it, with many other relics of the craft, was destroyed. That this was one of the original plates there can be no doubt, because, as early as 1782, there appeared upon the laws printed by F. and R. Bailey, a 'battered' plate of the Coat of Arms. This is especially noticeable in the mane of the horse on the dexter side of the shield, impressions of which are in existence down to the period of its destruction. Neither can there be any doubt that the Arms of Pennsylvania, as engraved originally by Lownes, were those adopted by the authority of the State. No record, however, of this appears, and yet, it will be perceived by the sketch of the Great Seal of the Commonwealth, hereafter presented, that it had official recognition.

"As referred to, the first innovation made upon the Arms proper was in 1805 or thereabouts. A rude engraving of the Arms was used, omitting the stocks of maize in the rear of the supporters and also the harnessing of the horses. The olive branch is also omitted. Various changes were made from that period down to the year 1874. In all instances the engraver left off the harness; while in some cases two white horses were in proper position; again we find one black and one white horse; at another time both horses were in a semi-recumbent position; and, more frequently, each in different posture. It appeared to be impossible for any two engravers to give the same design for the Arms, from the fact that so many innovations had been made coming down for almost three-quarters of a century, that scarcely any one knew what was really the authorized Arms of the Commonwealth.

"The attention of the Legislature of 1874 having been called to this matter, a joint resolution approved the 30th day of April, 1874, directed the appointment of a commission ' to correct the Coat of Arms of the Commonwealth,' and ' to have the same recorded in the State Archives.' The preamble of that resolution sets forth that,—

" ' Whereas, There is no record of the Coat of Arms of the Commonwealth to be found in any Department of the Government; and whereas, such armorial ensigns are frequently used, attached to or copied upon public documents of various kinds, as also upon banners upon State occasions, such as are very likely to arise during the approaching centennial celebration, and in other ways displayed or issued from the seat of Government, wherein correctness and regularity are desirable; and whereas, the Arms now in use, from their style and from their approach to uniformity, are evidently founded upon and derived from the devices composing the Great Seal of the State, now of correct record in the State Department, thus conferring what would seem to be sufficient authority upon the said armorial bearings by common consent and custom, though more specific authority be not known to exist, or having existed, has been lost.'

" This commission were authorized ' to have the present Arms of the State, as far as ascertained, the same being derived from the Great Seal, corrected of such errors or anomalies as may be therein discovered, by careful comparison with and consultation of the science of the rules of heraldry, and as soon as may be practicable, to have a copy of the said Arms, so corrected, carefully emblazoned and described so as to be of record in the State Department for future reference; the description to be in manner similar to the description of the Great Seal now of record in said Archives.'

" The Commissioners at first delegated their authority to two gentlemen well versed in heraldry, to report any suggestions or recommendations. Unfortunately, these gentlemen transcended their authority and reported at first a Coat of Arms with the following heraldic devices:

" ' Escutcheon—Party, per fess, azure, and vert; on field azure, a ship sailing proper, with canton Arms of Penn, argent, fess sable with three plates; on the fess, Or, a plough; on field vert, three garbs, Or.

" ' Crest—On an escroll sustained by a keystone, an eagle, rousant, proper.

" ' Supporters—Two horses, sable, rearing, respecting, caparisoned for draught.

" ' Motto—" Virtue, Liberty, and Independence." '

" Another modification of the escutcheon was suggested, as follows.

" ' Party per fess, Or, azure and vert; on field azure, a ship sailing, proper; on a field vert three garbs, Or, over the fess on an escutcheon of pretence, argent, fess sable with three plates.'

" The foregoing was thus recommended, to the surprise of every one who was familiar with the history of the early seal of the State, and also with the resolution of the Legislature, which directed that ' the present Arms of the State' as ' derived from the Great Seal' be ' corrected of such errors or anomalies as may be therein discovered' and ' carefully emblazoned and described, so as to be of record.' In their report, the gentlemen alluded to, seem to have been impressed with the idea, not that they were to decide the question of what was the Arms of the Commonwealth, but to report such Arms as they saw proper. The result was that the plough was to be displaced by the Penn Coat of Arms, while the eagle on the crest was to stand on the keystone instead of 'on a wreath of its colours.'

"The attention of the Commissioners being called to the fact that such authority was not warranted by the resolution of the Assembly, a collection was made of impressions of the Arms of the State, as designed at various periods, as well as impressions of the Great Seal, hereafter to be described, and, in recognition thereof, the Commissioners reported to the next General Assembly, March 17, 1875, the following:

"'That they had adopted the Arms as represented by Caleb Lownes, in 1778, which represented the veritable Arms of the State, and describing the same so as to be of record in the State Department for future reference:

"'*Escutcheon*—Party per fess, azure and vert, On a chief of the first, a ship under sail. On a fess, a plough, proper. On a base of the second, three garbs, Or.

"'*Crest*—An eagle, rousant, proper, on a wreath of its colours.

"'*Supporters*—Two horses, sable, caparisoned for draught, rearing, respectant.

"'*Motto*—Virtue, Liberty, and Independence.'

"The foregoing, therefore, is the proper heraldic description of the Arms of the State of Pennsylvania, save the mention of the maize and olive branch on the sides of the shield; and, as such, it should never be deviated from in the least. As it is a very important matter, we have thus alluded to it in full, giving, as closely allied thereto, the following brief account of the Great Seal of the Commonwealth:

FIG. 386.   FIG. 387.

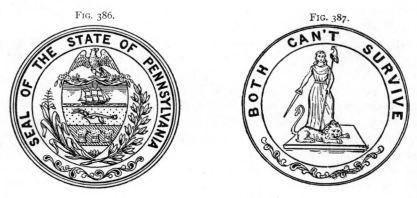

"THE GREAT SEAL OF THE STATE.

"The great Charter of Pennsylvania, given by Charles II. of England to William Penn, declares, among other things: 'Know Yee Therefore, that Wee reposing speciall trust and confidence in the fidelitie, wisedome, justice, and provident circumspeccon of the said William Penn, for us, our heires, and successors, Doe grant free, full and absolute power, by vertue of these presents to him and his heires, and to his and their Deputies and Lieutenants, for the good and happy government of the Countrey, to ordeyne, make, Enact, and *under his and their Seals* to publish any Lawes whatsoever, for the raising of money for the public use of the said Province, or for any other End apperteyning either unto the publick state, peace, or safety of the said Countrey, or unto the private utility of perticuler persons, according unto their best discretions,' etc., etc.

"The first Great Seal, therefore, of the Province of Pennsylvania contained the Arms of the Penn family, and this seal continued in use till the period of the Revolution. On the 28th of September, 1776, the first State Constitution was adopted; which, besides declaring the independence of the State of Pennsylvania, in the 16th section thereof, provided for a seal for the General Assembly to be called 'The seal of the laws of Pennsylvania.' This was to be affixed to every bill, but not to be used for any other purpose. In the 21st section of the same bill, as referred to in the historical sketch of the 'Arms of the State,' it directed 'all commissions to be in the name and by the authority of the freemen of the Commonwealth of Pennsylvania, sealed with the Great Seal, signed by the President or Vice-President, attested by the Secretary, which seal shall be kept by the Council.'

"It may, however, be remarked here that at the meeting of the Committee of Safety, August 31, 1775, it was resolved 'That Mr. Owen Biddle procure for the use of this Board, a seal about the size of a dollar, with the cap of Liberty, and the motto: "This is my right, and I will defend it," inscribed with "Pennsylvania Committee of Safety, 1775."' This was, therefore, designed and used especially on all commissions issued by that body up to, perchance, the year 1778. On the second of January of that year, however, an act was passed for establishing a new seal for the Supreme Court, etc., in these words: 'Whereas, Since the late glorious Revolution, it is become expedient and proper to have a new seal for the Supreme Court and the Courts of Oyer and Terminer and general gaol delivery of the State; be it enacted, etc. That a new seal shall be procured and made under the direction of the prothonotary or clerk of the said Supreme Court, having the Arms of the State engraven thereon, with such other devices as the justices of the said court shall direct, with an inscription round the edge and near the extremity thereof, in these words, to wit: "Seal of the Supreme Court of Pennsylvania," and the figures "1776" underneath the arms; and that the same from and after the receipt thereof by the prothonotary of the said court, shall be the seal of the said court, and used as such upon all occasions whatsoever.'

"In 1780 the seal which has come down to us and [which is] designated as the Great Seal was engraved in Paris, a copy of which in exact fac-simile is preserved in connection with this report. A letter from P. Penet to the Supreme Executive Council, writing from Nantes, under date of May 20th, 1780, says: 'I bespoke your standards in Paris; I expect them every day. They will be

FIG. 388.

sent to you by some French frigate. Capt. Samuel Smith, who has been ready to sail for some time, will deliver to you as soon as he arrives in Philadelphia, the seals representing the Arms of your State. As you desired they were engraved in Paris.' (Fig. 388.),

"From an impression of this seal in 1782, we find the following heraldic devices: On a shield, parted, by a fess of gold, charged with a plough,—a ship sailing upon a silver field above, and three sheaves of wheat or garbs upon a blue field below. These same devices

were, as has already been stated, engraved upon the first paper money issued by the State, in April, 1777. As a fuller description of this is given further on, it is here omitted. There seems to have been no innovation at any time made upon the Great Seal. When the New Constitution of 1789–90 was adopted, no provision was made for a State seal, although article 6, section 4, recognized its existence, and the first law that passed under that instrument, of date January 8, 1791, declared and established the seals of the Commonwealth, as follows:

"'Whereas, the late convention of this Commonwealth did, on the second day of September last, establish a new form of government for Pennsylvania, and no provision is therein made for public seals:

"'Be it enacted therefore, by the Senate and House of Representatives of the Commonwealth of Pennsylvania, in General Assembly met, and it is hereby enacted by the authority of the same, that from and after the passing of this act, the seal, heretofore known by the name of the "Great Seal," lately in the custody of the Supreme Executive Council, is hereby constituted the State Seal, and shall be affixed to all patents, proclamations, and other public rolls, commissions and papers of State, which require the Great Seal of the Commonwealth, and to which the same has heretofore been usually applied.

"'And be it further enacted by the authority aforesaid, that the seal lately in the custody of the Supreme Executive Council, called the "Lesser Seal," shall be henceforth deemed and taken and shall be applied as the Less Seal of this Commonwealth, and, as such, set to land-office warrants, marriage licenses, licenses to keep public houses, and such other documents, as have heretofore been issued under the Lesser Seal.

"'And be it further enacted by the authority aforesaid, that the said seals, respectively, shall be, and the same are hereby declared to be, the Great and

Less Seals of this Commonwealth, and shall be affixed accordingly, under the direction of the Governor.'

"The next we hear of the 'Great Seal' was in March, 1809, when an act was passed on the second day of that month to perpetuate the same, as it is so expressly entitled. This was owing to the fact that the seal so long used had become worn out. The act referred to provides:

"'Whereas, The Great Seal of this Commonwealth is so nearly worn out, that it is necessary to renew the same, and whereas, it appears that there is no description thereof on record, and it being proper that the said seal should be particularly described and established, so that the same may hereafter be more fully known and recognized; therefore,

"'Be it enacted by the Senate and House of Representatives of the Commonwealth of Pennsylvania in General Assembly met, and it is hereby enacted by the authority of the same, that the Secretary of the Commonwealth be, and he hereby is authorized and directed to procure the renewal of the Great Seal of this Commonwealth, and record and deposit a description thereof, in writing, in this office that the same may be made perpetual.'

"Under the foregoing act a record was made of the Great Seal, which we find in the Executive Minutes under the date of Saturday, July 1st, 1809, as follows:

"'In obedience to the directions of an Act of General Assembly passed the second day of March, one thousand eight hundred and nine, the following description of the Great Seal is recorded, that is to say:—

"'The shield shall be parted *Per Fess, Or*, charged with a plough, *Proper*, in chief; on a sea *wavy, Proper*, a ship under full sail, surmounted with a sky, *Azure ;* and in *Base*, on a field *Vert*, three *Garbs, Or*. On the *sinister* a stock of maize, and *Dexter* an olive branch. And on the wreath of its colours a bald eagle—*Proper, perched* Wings extended, for the *Crest. Motto—Virtue, Liberty*, and *Independence*. Round the margin of the seal, *Commonwealth of Pennsylvania*. The reverse, Liberty, trampling on a Lyon, Gules, the emblem of Tyranny. *Motto—Both can't survive.'*

"This, therefore, is the Great Seal of the State. Unfortunately, there seems to be some difference between the original engraving in Paris and that now in use in the office of the Secretary of the Commonwealth. We, therefore, present for the purpose of permanent record a copy of the first seal; although, as will be perceived, the heraldic description as extracted from the Executive Minutes shows some errors, as follows: First, in describing the base as vert, when the horizontal lines on the seal show that it was azure; second, in describing as on the sinister side the stock of maize and on the dexter side an olive branch, when neither were to be found upon the seal; third, in describing the eagle, when there was no eagle or wreath upon the seal; fourth, in describing the inscription around the edge of the seal as 'Commonwealth of Pennsylvania' instead of 'Seal of the State of Pennsylvania,' as was on the original seal.

"In these days when the tastes of the people have been directed to the subject of heraldry, it is certainly appropriate that not only the Great Seal of the State, but the Arms of the Commonwealth, shall be now and henceforth heraldically correct, and it is hoped that by referring in brief terms to the history of this subject, better attention thereto will hereafter be given."

FIG. 389.

Obverse.

Since this book has gone to press a new seal has been designed, which corresponds with the description, excepting that the branches upon either side are still transposed (Fig. 389), the olive branch appearing upon the sinister instead of the dexter. In the reverse, the female figure is somewhat changed in attitude, and the sword-point rests upon the lion's head.[1]

RHODE ISLAND.[2]

"'The arms of Rhode Island are a golden anchor on a blue field, and the motto thereof is the word Hope.'[3]   This is *not* a foul anchor, as often represented. (A foul anchor has a cable attached and intertwined with the anchor.)

FIG. 390.   FIG. 391.

This device is very old. At first it was described as 'an anchor,' giving no colors. Colors were assigned in 1882 for the first time. In the earliest times there was a seal in common use in Providence for sealing deeds. This seal

---

[1] Acknowledgments are due Governor Pattison and H. D. Tate, Esq.

[2] Letter of Hon. George M. Carpenter. The seal of the Newport Historical Society is a reproduction of the old seal of the Colony. The cut, Fig. 391, was furnished by R. H. Tilley, Esq., Librarian of the Society, and an impression of the present State seal by Richard W. Jennings, Esq., Executive Secretary.

[3] "Public Statutes of Rhode Island," cap. v. p. 40.

had the figure of an anchor.[1] It has been thought that the suggestion for the State arms may have come from this seal.

" The first arms of the Colony were a sheafe of arrows bound up, and in the leiss or bond this motto indented : ' Amor Vincet Omnia.'[2] The second device, adopted in 1647, as follows : ' It is ordered that the seale of the province be an anchor.' "[3]

SOUTH CAROLINA.[4]

" The device for the armorial achievement and reverse of the Great Seal of the State of South Carolina was as follows :

FIG. 392.

" ARMS. A Palmetto-tree growing on the sea-shore erect; at its base a torn-up oak-tree, its branches lopped off, prostrate; *both proper.*

" Just below the branches of the Palmetto, two shields pendent; one of them on the dexter side is inscribed $\frac{March}{26}$, the other on the sinister side $\frac{July}{4}$. Twelve spears *proper*, and bound crosswise to the stem of the Palmetto, their points raised; the band uniting them together bearing the inscription QUIS SEPER-ABIT. Under the prostrate oak is inscribed MELIOREM LAPSO LOCAVIT, below which appears in large figures 1776; at the summit of the exergue are the words SOUTH CAROLINA, and at the bottom of the same ANIMIS OPIBUSQUE PARATI.

" REVERSE. A woman walking on the sea-shore over swords and daggers; she holds in her dexter hand a laurel branch, and in her sinister the folds of her robe ; she looks toward the sun just rising above the sea, *all proper ;* on the upper part is the sky azure.

" At the summit of the exergue are the words DUM SPIRO SPERO ; and within the field below the figure is inscribed the word SPES. The seal is in the form of a circle, four inches in diameter; and four-tenths of an inch thick.

" It was not designed until after the fort at Sullivan's Island had defeated the British fleet, as all its devices will prove. The fort was constructed of the stems of the palmetto-trees (corypha palmetto) which grow abundantly on our sea islands,—which grew on Sullivan's Island at the time the fort was made, when the battle was fought, and which grow there at this day.

" The Arms were designed by William Henry Drayton, and the original executed by him with a pen, bearing great similtude to what is represented on

[1] See " Early Records of Providence," vol. i. pp. 29, 40, 42, 52.

[2] " Rhode Island Colonial Records," i. 115.

[3] Ibid., i. 151.

[4] Letter of Mrs. Caroline Le Conte, State Librarian. Seal impression was furnished by Governor Tillman.

the seal, is in the possession of his son. It, however, contains more devices, but this is easily reconciled by supposing all he had designed was not deemed by the President and Privy Council necessary for the Great Sêal. The explanation of this side of the seal is the following: The Palmetto-tree on the seashore represents the fort on Sullivan's Island, the shields bearing $^{March}_{26}$ and $^{July}_{4}$ allude to the Constitution of South Carolina, which was ratified on the first of these days, and to the Declaration of Independence, which was made by the Continental Congress on the last of them.

"The sun rising in great brilliancy above the sea indicates that the 28th of June was a fine day, it also bespeaks good fortune." [1]

"'An Act concerning the Seal of the State,' which enacts 'that hereafter there shall be two copies of the small seal of the state, one to be kept in the office of the Secretary of State in Charleston and the other in the office of the Secretary of State in Columbia; and that the copy of the seal of the state usually called the small seal which has been procured by his Excellency John L. Wilson, Governor and commander in chief in and over the State of South Carolina, shall be deposited in the office of the Secretary of State at Columbia and hereafter used in the said office as the seal of the State; any law, usage or custom to the contrary notwithstanding.'

"The seal as above described contains the arms of the State. There has, however, been used for many years at the head of advertisements of proclamations, official papers, and the like, a representation, which represents two sides of the seal, with Liberty on one side with a crown in her hand, a Continental soldier on the other side, and Fame going from Liberty to the soldier. How and when this was adopted has not been ascertained."

TENNESSEE.[2]

FIG. 393.

"The devices on the seal were adopted by the Convention of 1796, the year in which Tennessee was admitted as a State. The Roman numerals XVI were inserted to denote that Tennessee was the sixteenth State admitted.

"The only known authority for the use of the great seal of the State of Tennessee is in article 3, section 15, of the Constitution of the State of Tennessee, which says: 'There shall be a seal of the State, which shall be kept by the Governor, and used by him officially, and shall be called the great seal of the State of Tennessee.'"

[1] From "Drayton's Memoirs," 1823. 6 vol., st. p. 210.
[2] The design of seal is taken from original impression furnished by J. D. Talley, Esq., Assistant Secretary of State.

TEXAS.

FIG. 394.

"During the struggle with Mexico, Texas adopted as an official seal a white or silver star of five points on an *azure* field encircled by branches of live oak and olive. Around the outer circle were the words, 'Republic of Texas' in Roman capital letters."[1]

The present seal of the State is as shown in Fig. 394, and is described as follows: "The Seal of the State shall be a star of five points encircled by olive and live oak branches, and the words 'The State of Texas.'"[2]

UTAH.[3]

FIG. 395.

"The seal of Utah was adopted immediately after the Territory was organized, September 9th, 1850, and its device was a bee-hive with bees *volant* about it.

"The only record known to be in existence refers to a new seal approved in 1872.

"'The Auditor of Public Accounts be, and is hereby authorized and required to procure a new Seal for the Territorial Secretary's office; the pattern and design of said Seal to be the same as the original Territorial Seals, excepting the year of date, which shall be represented by figures, and not as in the original by Roman letters; said Seal to be two inches in diameter.'"

VERMONT.[4]

The seal of the State of Vermont (Fig. 396) includes "The coat of arms (Fig. 397) (excluding the crest, scroll, and badge), and with the motto and circular border around the same." The arms are described as follows: "The coat of arms of the state shall be, and is described as follows: Green, a landscape occupying half of the shield; on the right and left, in the background, high mountains, blue; the sky yellow.

"From near the base, and reaching nearly to the top of the shield, arises

---

[1] Preble.

[2] Letter of Hon. George W. Smith, Secretary of State.

[3] Letter of Charles C. Richards, Esq., Secretary.

[4] Reference is made to a paper published by the Vermont Historical Society, and acknowledgments are expressed for assistance of T. L. Wood, Esq., Assistant State Librarian, and J. H. Goulding, Esq., Secretary of Civil and Military Affairs.

a pine-tree of the natural color, and between three erect sheaves, yellow, placed bendwise on the dexter side, and a red cow standing on the sinister side of the field.[1] THE CREST. A buck's head, of the natural color, cut off

FIG. 396.

FIG. 397.

and placed on a scroll, blue and yellow. THE MOTTO and BADGE. On a scroll beneath the shield, the motto: Vermont; Freedom and Unity. The Vermonter's Badge; two pine branches of the natural color, crossed between the shield and scroll."

The exact date of the adoption of this seal is believed to have been in 1778; such belief is established by records of the bill for engraving same. The Journals of the House of Representatives and of the Governor and Council, are silent upon the subject. The description of this seal is as follows:

" The principal figure is a pine-tree rising from the centre of a thick growth of evergreens with conical tops. Above these tops start the limbs of the pine, and the bases of the evergreens extend in a horizontal line quite across the seal. A sheaf of grain stands on each side of the pine, far in the background and for want of proper perspective close up under high strata of clouds that occupy the upper edge of the seal. And below the sheaf on the right of the observer, and above the tops of the evergreens, stands a cow. Below the line of evergreens, and in the form in which they are here printed, are the words:

Vermont
Freedom
& Unity.

A sheaf of grain stands at each end of the word freedom. All is encircled

---

[1] In the impressions from official documents, furnished by Governor Fuller, it is noticed that color lines indicate the mountains to be *green*, whereas they are described as *blue*, while the cow is marked by *purple* lines (Fig. 397), or indicated as a sanguine cow (Fig. 396). As in all cases, this seal and arms are copied exactly.

by a narrow border of consecutive arrow-heads, the point of each inserted in the socket of the next."

By whatever authority adopted, this was the seal of the State used by its officers until 1821, at which time a new seal was procured substantially the same in design as the old seal; but the devices are more artistically arranged.

The sheaves of wheat, now three in number, and the cow, were taken from their aerial perch and made to stand upon the earth. The pine-tree was well clothed with foliage; and in the background, instead of the conical evergreens, were seen the mountains which gave name to the State.

Around the margin of the seal the words "Vermont Freedom and Unity." As the devices of the State seal differed greatly in detail, apparently by the fancy of every officer that had occasion to procure a new die to impress upon official documents, the Vermont Historical Society, in 1862, appointed a committee[1] to petition the General Assembly to pass a law that would not *change*, but fix and establish the seal. The petition was acted upon favorably, and a description of the seal is entered in the Statutes.[2]

VIRGINIA.

" THE COLONY OF VIRGINIA.[3]

" In the original patent of April 10th, 1606, to Sir Thomas Gates and others, for the colonization of Virginia, 'two several colonies and companies' were provided for, each to have a council of thirteen persons, to be guided by the King's instructions, and each to have a seal with the King's arms engraved on one side 'and his portraiture on the other;' on one side of the seal of the first Colony were to be the words 'SIGILLUM REGIS MAGNÆ BRITANIÆ, FRANCIÆ ET HIBERNIÆ,' on the other side 'PRO CONSILIO PRIMÆ COLONIÆ VIRGINIÆ.' The seal of the second was the same as the first except the change in the legend on one side to 'PRO CONSILIO SECUNDÆ COLONIÆ VIRGINIÆ.' There was also provision made for a council, resident in England, known as the 'King's Council of Virginia,' which should have the managing and direction of the settlement within the limit of the thirty-fourth and forty-fifth degrees of north latitude. This council was to have a seal like the others, but with the legend on one side, 'PRO CONSILIO SUO VIRGINIA.'[4] An example of this seal, with the same dimensions and devices, but with the differing legend on the reverse of 'COLONIA VIRGINIÆ—CONSILIO—PRIMA,' is in the collections of the Virginia Historical Society. It is of red wax, between the leaves of a foolscap sheet of paper, and is affixed to a patent for land issued by Sir John

---

[1] G. W. Benedict, Norman Williams, Charles Reed.

[2] General Statutes of Vermont, 1862, p. 788.

[3] From paper by Hon. J. G. Hankins, issued in the office of the Secretary of the Commonwealth.

[4] Neill's " Virginia Vetusta," pp. 4, 5, a cut of the last described seal appearing on p. 5. The cut is also given in " Narrative and Critical History of America," vol. iv. p. 140, Chapter V., " Virginia, 1606-1689," by R. A. Brock.

Harvey, Governor, dated 4th March, 1638. Another seal was proposed for the Virginia Company 15th November, 1619. An escutcheon quartered with the arms of England, and France, Scotland, and Ireland, crested by a maiden queen with flowing hair and eastern crown. Supporters: Two men in armour, beavers open, helmets ornamented with three ostrich feathers, each holding a lance. Motto: 'EN DAT [DAY] VIRGINIA QUINTUM.'[1]

"COLONIAL SEALS OF VIRGINIA.[2]

"Dr. William P. Palmer, in his introduction to the 'Calendar of State Papers of Virginia,'[3] states that the small number of documents preserved in

[1] From the "Transactions of the Virginia Company from April, 1619, to June, 1620." A cut of this seal is given in Neill's "Virginia Vetusta," p. 135. It also appears on the frontispiece to Beverley's "History of Virginia," and on the title-page of every legislative publication of the Colony to the era of the Revolution.

"This motto, allusive to five crowns (corona), was in the taste of the times. Spenser, Raleigh's friend, dedicated his 'Faerie Queene' to Elizabeth, 'Queen of England, France, Ireland, and Virginia.' After James of Scotland succeeded to the throne of England, Virginia could, in compliment, be called the fifth kingdom, and it was so called by the Rev. Patrick Copland, who, on April 8, 1622, spoke of 'this noble plantation tending so highly to the advancement of the Gospel and the honouring of our drad soueraign by enlarging his kingdome and adding a fifth crowne unto his other four, for " En dat Virginia Quintam" is the motto of the legal seal of Virginia.' As the coat of arms appears with the motto 'En dat Virginia Quintum' on the frontispiece of Smith's History, editions of 1624 and 1632, the 'Quintum' may be an error of the engraver, as " Day" undoubtedly is."—TYLER.

Mr. Hankins expresses his doubt as to whether this seal (Fig. 400) was ever used, and Professor Tyler states the following:

"The assumption, however, that any change in the Colonial seal took place in 1619 is a mistaken one. The coat of arms adopted in 1619 was for the use of the company in London, and it is so stated in their proceedings; the Colony seal was not changed at this time, nor even after the abrogation of the charter of the company in 1624. The council in Virginia was not abolished, though the company was; and so we find the old seal authorized in the original charter for the local council in use for many years later as 'the seal of the colony.' Several instances of this use as late as 1643 have come under my observation. I have two original land patents, granted by Sir John Harvey, Governor, between 1635 and 1639; one of them has the precise date torn off, the other dated August 14th, 1639, both bearing perfect specimens of the ancient seal authorized by the charter of 1606. The wax is placed between a folded sheet at the right hand upper corner, and the obverse and reverse impressions appear on the outer pages of the paper. The manuscripts are mutilated, but of beautiful chirography, and are said by Harvey to be 'given under my hand and seal of the colony.' The impressions are elliptic, about two inches and a quarter in height, and an inch and a quarter wide. There is also in the Virginia Historical Society Rooms an original land grant by Sir William Berkeley to Richard Kemp, dated April 7th, 1643; and this paper likewise bears an unmistakable impression of the same seal, though the wax in part is worn away. It may be then stated, with confidence, that the seal described in the charter for 'the first colony of Virginia' continued the recognized emblem until the treaty at Jamestown in 1652 with the parliamentary commissioners.

"As a consequence of the treaty a change of government ensued, and the royal seal was discontinued. From 1652 to 1660 the recorded copies of the land patents in the land office in Richmond are no longer declared to be under the seal of the colony, but under the hand and seal of the governor, attested by the secretary of the state; and the public papers in the state archives bear the private seals of Bennett and the other governors of the interregnum."

[2] From copies furnished by Professor L. G. Tyler.

[3] Volume i. page xxvi.

the archives of the State 'bearing impressions of the Royal, Colonial, and other official seals, is limited to the short period included between the time of James II. and the latter part of Queen Anne's reign,' and that 'the earliest of these, dated 1686, September the 1st, is a writ of election for certain members

FIG. 398. FIG. 399.

Seal of the Colony of Virginia, authorized by the charter granted April 10, 1606.[1]

of the House of Burgesses, issued at "Rosegill" (the seat of the Wormeley family, whom he was then doubtless visiting) by the governor, Lord Howard, Baron Effingham. The impression of the Colonial seal on this document (as with all others herein) (the Calendar) is upon wafer. It displays a shield in

FIG. 400. FIG. 401.

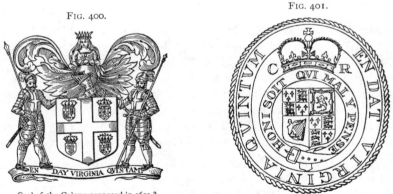

Seal of the Colony proposed in 1619.[2]

Seal used after the restoration of Charles II.

the centre field, quartering the arms of England and France first and fourth, with those of Scotland and Ireland second and third, enclosed by the Order of the Garter and its appropriate motto. In the exergue appear the words:

[1] See "Virginia Vetusta," p. 5.
[2] Design from John Stowe's "Survey of London."

"EN DAT VIRGINIA QUINTUM," the whole surmounted by the crown proper, and flanked right and left respectively by the characters "C" and "R."' This was evidently a continuation of the use of the seal of the preceding reign of Charles II., under the government of Sir William Berkeley. In the 'Richmond Dispatch,' of 15th October, 1882, appeared a communication from the editor, including one to him from Charles Dean, LL.D., Cambridge, Massachusetts, giving a proclamation from James II., dated 21st December, 1687, appointing a new seal for Virginia, as follows: 'Engraven with our Royal effigies sitting in our Royal Robes enthroned, having on each side a Landskip, and upon the Canopy, which is supported by two angels and a Cherubim

FIG. 402.   FIG. 403.

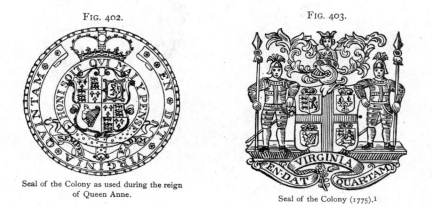

Seal of the Colony as used during the reign
of Queen Anne.

Seal of the Colony (1775).[1]

overhead, this motto: IN (EN) DAT VIRGINIA QUINTUM, with our Royal Title in the Circumference, and on the other side our Royal Coat of Arms, with the Garter, Crown, Supporters, and Mottoes, with this Inscription in the circumference: SIGILLUM DOMINI NOSTR.: VIRGIN : AMERICA.' This seal was brought from England by Colonel Bird, the first of the family in Virginia, but it does not appear to have been used.[2]

"The first use of such a seal, broad and pendent, was in the reign of Queen Anne, by proclamation dated 6th October, 1712, which veritable docu-

---

[1] As shown at the head of the "Virginia Gazette," edited by John Dixon and William Hunter.

[2] "About this time King James abdicated the throne and became a fugitive. Under William the Third no changes occurred, except the substitution of the royal letters 'W.' 'R.' for 'C.' 'R.' flanking the crown, and the addition of the arms of Nassau, placed by way of pretense upon the Stuart shield.

"On the incoming of Governor Edward Nott, in 1705, a more extensive change in the Colonial seal ensued. Anne was now Queen. A land patent dated May 1st, 1706, has in the exergue 'En dat Virginia Quintam,' and underneath the ring of the Order of the Garter. Enclosing the Stuart arms are the words 'Semper Eadem,' the Queen's motto. The escutcheon of pretense for Nassau is absent. The initial letters are also wanting, and instead of the elliptical shape the impression of the exergue is perfectly circular."—TYLER.

ment was published, with engraving of the accompanying original waxen seal,[1] and is thus described: ' Engraved on the one side with an effigy and an Indian on his knee presenting tobacco to us. This inscription, EN DAT VIRGINIA QUARTAM, being under the effigy, and around the circumference VIRGINIA · IN · AMERICA · SIGILLUM · PROVINCIÆ . . . On the other side of the said seal is engraven our arms, garter, crown, supporters, and motto, with this inscription around the circumference: ANNE · DEI · GRATIA · MAGNÆ · BRITANNIÆ · FRANCIÆ · ET · HIBERNIÆ · REGINA · FIDEI · DEFENSOR, for use to affix the said seal to all patents and grants of land, and to all public acts and instruments of government, which shall be made and passed in our name within our said colony.' On the 6th of March, 1706–7, the Queen had given her royal assent to an ' Act for an Union of the two Kingdoms of England and Scotland,' and thenceforth the motto read QUARTAM instead of QUINTUM.

" It is a quite common error, into which many writers have fallen, that Charles II. gave the motto EN DAT VIRGINIA QUINTUM in recognition of the loyalty of the colony during his exile, but the title was held as early as the reign of Elizabeth, when Virginia was the *sole* dominion of the Crown of England on the continent of America. In the inscription accompanying an admirably-engraved portrait of the ' Virgin Queen,'[2] hanging in the hall of the Westmoreland Club-house, Richmond, Virginia, in which the Virginia Historical Society has its rooms, she is entitled ' SERENISSIMA AC POTENTISSIMA PRINCEPS ELISABET D. G. ANGLIÆ, FRANCIÆ, HIBERNIÆ ET VIRGINIÆ REGINA FIDEI CHRISTIANÆ PROPUGNATRIX ACERRIMA.'

" The use of the great or broad pendent seal appears to have been common to all the colonies from the time of Queen Anne, with like designs of obverse and reverse, as have been described. They are of white wax papered, and measure about five inches in diameter and one-fourth of an inch in thickness. Documents and local commissions issued during the reigns of George II. and George III., with small pendent seals of white wax, crown-shaped, and without other insignia, are also in existence."[3]

" SEAL AND ARMS OF THE VIRGINIA MERCHANTS.[4]

" *Ar. a cross gu. betw. four escutcheons, each regally crowned ppr., the first escutcheon in the dexter chief, quarterly; France and England, quarterly; the second in the sinister chief the arms of Scotland; the third the arms of Ireland;*

---

[1] "American Historical Record," B. J. Lossing, LL.D., editor, volume v., No. 4, April, 1872, pp. 160–162.

[2] Henricus Hondius—Hague Comit : Cum Privilegio Illust.: D.D. Ord. Generalium, 1632.

[3] From " Virginia Historical Collections," vol. vii., New Series; Virginia Company, 1619–1624, vol. i., foot-notes, pp. 152–155.

[4] In Stowe's " Survey of London," edition of 1633, appears an engraving of the seal of the Virginia Company, with the cross, etc., as described. (See Fig. 404.)

fourth as the first.[1] CREST: *A maiden queen couped below the shoulders ppr., her hair dishevelled of the last, vested and crowned with an eastern crown or.* SUPPORTERS: *Two men in complete armour, with their beavers open ; on their helmets*

FIG. 404.

620 | *Temporall Government.*

Merchants of Virginia.

EN DAY VIRGINIA QVINTAM

T He Company of Merchants, called *Merchants of Virginia*, *Bermudas*, or *Summer-Lands*, for (as I heare) all thefe additions are given them. I know not the time of their incorporating, neither by whom their Armes, Supporters, and Creft were granted, and therefore am compelled to leaue them abruptly.

THE

three ostrich feathers ar., each charged on the breast with a cross gu., and each holding in his exterior hand a lance ppr. MOTTO: *En Dat Virginia Quartam."*[2]

---

[1] These arms are borne in the first quarter of shield in seal of General Society of Colonial Wars. (See Fig. 522.)

[2] Burke's " General Armory."

" SEALS OF VIRGINIA.[1]

"The celebrated State Convention of 1776 which formed the first written constitution for any State broke away from the old traditions completely. Royalty, and heraldry its accompaniment, fell into utter disrepute; the Roman and Grecian Republics, affording, as they did, the noblest exemplars of valor and grandeur known to the world at that time, became the ideals of our statesmen. One of the first acts of the Convention was to provide for a seal. The design was reported by George Mason, but is said by Girardin, under the supervision of Jefferson, to have been devised by George Wythe. The design was entirely classic, and the words of the report describing the seal are remarkable for clearness and precision: 'Virtus, the genius of the Commonwealth, dressed as an Amazon, resting on a spear with one hand and holding a sword in the other, and treading on Tyranny, represented by a man prostrate, a crown falling from his head, broken chain in his left hand, and a scourge in his right. In the exergon, the word "Virginia" over the head of Virtus; and underneath, the words "Sic Semper Tyrannis." On the reverse, a group, Libertas with her wand and pileus; on one side of her Ceres, with the cornucopia in one hand and an ear of wheat in the other; on the other side Æternitas, with the globe, and Phœnix; in the exergon these words: "*Deus nobis hæc otia fecit.*"' The Convention substituted for this last word 'perseverando' over the heads of the figures. The seal was executed in France, under the supervision of the accomplished scholar Dr. Arthur Lee, but it was not ready till September 4th, 1779. In the mean time the Governor was empowered to issue all necessary commissions under his signature without any seal; but when in 1778 William Lee was appointed Virginia's agent in France to borrow two millions of livres for the State, a seal became necessary to authenticate his power. One was improvised in America, which was not a true representation of the ideas of the Convention; to save expense it was subsequently adopted as the lesser seal of the Commonwealth, and, being far more frequently used than the great seal, has caused incorrect ideas of the figure and significance of virtus, the commanding emblem of the great seal. The original disc of the great seal itself, executed in Paris, the great centre of art, according to the most approved classic ideas, existed in 1856, when being so worn by use as to be incapable of making an impression, it was substituted by a new one, which in turn was substituted in 1884 by a third, in the preparation of which every effort was made by Colonel Sherwin McRae, then Librarian of the State, to

FIG. 405.

[1] From paper by Professor Lyon G. Tyler, Williams and Mary College.

make the figure upon it conform to the best classic models. It is claimed by Colonel McRae that no other American State has a seal equal to that of Virginia in classic beauty and appropriateness, and the fact that it was described so carefully at the beginning has been of infinite importance in securing its exact reproduction at the present time. The seal of a State, as Colonel McRae declares, 'is not a bauble, but an important and necessary element of government; indeed, the Convention of 1776 was so impressed with the truth that the great seal was made a specific constitutional provision.'"[1]

WASHINGTON.[2]

"Washington Territory was organized March 2, 1853. Its Territorial seal is two and one-fourth inches in diameter, and surrounded by the legend, 'TERRITORY OF WASHINGTON, 1853.' (See Fig. 406.) For devices, it has a female figure with flowing tresses seated in the foreground, facing to the left, and holding up her right hand; at her side is an anchor; to her right, a city with spires and domes, and a steam vessel; on her left, a log cabin and a pine forest; surrounding the head of the female is a sun with rays, and over her head, in large capitals, 'AL KI,' Indian for 'by and by.'[3] In 1889 Washington became a State, and the present seal was then adopted.

FIG. 406.   FIG. 407.[4]

"The seal of the State of Washington (Fig. 407) was adopted by the Constitutional Convention, which met in this city [Olympia] in 1889, on the 4th day of July. This Convention was held in pursuance of an Act of Congress, approved February 22, 1889, which provided for the admission of the (then) Territory of Washington into the Union."

[1] The author notes his obligations to Hon. H. W. Flournoy, Secretary of the Commonwealth; Phillip A. Bruce. Esq., Virginia Historical Society; Charles Poindexter, Esq., State Librarian.
[2] Letter of B. W. Davis, Esq., Chief Clerk and Acting Secretary of State.
[3] Design from Hough's " American Constitutions." Description from Preble.
[4] Seal is from impression forwarded upon instructions of Governor John H. McGraw.

The seal is thus described: "The seal of the state of Washington shall be a seal encircled with the words: 'The seal of the state of Washington,' with the vignette of Gen. George Washington as the central figure, and beneath the vignette the figures ' 1889.' " [1]

WEST VIRGINIA.[2]

"A Great Seal for the State of West Virginia was adopted September 26, 1863. 'The obverse bears the legend, "STATE OF WEST VIRGINIA," with the motto, "Montani Semper Liberi," inserted in the circumference. In the centre, a rock with ivy, emblematic of stability and continuance, and on the face of the rock the inscription, "June 20, 1863," the date of the foundation of the State, as if "graved with a pen of iron on the rock forever." On the right of the rock, a farmer clothed in the traditional hunting-shirt peculiar to this region, his right arm resting on the plough-handles, and his left supporting a wood-man's axe, indicating that while our territory is partially cultivated, it is still in process of being cleared of the original forest. At his right, a sheaf of wheat and corn-stalk. On the left of the rock, a miner, indicated by a pick-axe on his shoulder, with barrels and lumps of mineral at his feet. On his left, an anvil, partly seen, on which rests a sledge-hammer, typical of the mechanic arts, the whole indicating the principal pursuits and resources of the State. In the front of the rock and figures, as if just laid down by them, and ready to be resumed at a moment's notice, two hunter's rifles crossed, and surmounted at the place of contact by the Phrygian cap, or cap of liberty, indicating that our freedom and independence were won and will be defended and maintained by arms.'

FIG. 408.

"A lesser seal, an inch and a half in diameter, with the same legend, motto, devices, etc., was ordered. 'The reverse of the great seal is encircled with a wreath of laurel and oak leaves, emblematic of valor and strength, with fruits and cereals, productions of the State.

"'Device, a landscape. In the distance, on the left of the disc, wooded mountains, and on the right a cultivated slope, with the log frame-house peculiar to the region. On the side of the mountain, a representation of the viaduct on the line of the Baltimore and Ohio Railroad in Preston County, one of the great engineering triumphs of the age, with a train of cars about to pass over it. Near the centre, a factory, in front of which a river with

[1] Article XVIII., Washington Constitution.

[2] Design is taken from an impression furnished by J. B. White, Esq., Private Secretary to the Governor.

boats on the bank, and to the right of it, nearer the foreground, a derrick and shed, appertaining to the production of salt and petroleum. In the foreground, a meadow, with cattle and sheep feeding and reposing,—the whole indicating the leading characteristics, productions, and pursuits of the State. Above the mountains, the sun emerging from the clouds, indicating that former obstacles to the prosperity of the State are disappearing. In the rays of the sun the motto, 'Libertas e Fidelitate' (Liberty from loyalty), indicating that the freedom and independence of the State are faithfulness to the principles of the Declaration of Independence and the national Constitution.' "[1]

WISCONSIN.[2]

"There have been five Great Seals of the Territory and State of Wisconsin. The first (Fig. 409), designed to be 'emblematic of the mineral resources of Wisconsin," was devised by Hon. John S. Horner, the first Secretary of the Territory, in consultation with Hon. Henry Dodge, the first Territorial Governor of Wisconsin. On the 28th of October, 1836, the Territorial House of Representatives, on motion of Mr. James P. Cox, of Iowa County, voted to adopt this seal. The Territorial Council, on the second of November, adopted the report of the Committee on Territorial Affairs that 'its devices are not such as the seal of the Territory ought to be, but as a matter of expediency it had better be adopted by the Council for the present.' Official documents show this seal to have been in use as late as March 11, 1839.

FIG. 409.   FIG. 410.

"The second Great Seal (Fig. 410) was designed and engraved in pursuance of a resolution offered in the House of Representatives November 18, 1837, authorizing the Secretary of the Territory to procure a seal 'indicating the various and peculiar resources of the territory of Wisconsin.' This resolution was concurred in by the Council November 21, 1837, and December

[1] Preble, p. 625.

[2] Reference is made to "Wisconsin Blue-Book," 1880. Thanks are extended to Hon. T. J. Cunningham, Secretary of State, and Isaac S. Bradley, Esq., Librarian of the State Historical Society of Wisconsin.

14, 1838, a committee reported on the new seal to the effect that, 'while it represents the pursuits of the citizens of the different parts of the Territory, mineral, agricultural and commercial, it at the same time, by its symbols and expressive motto, "Civilitas Successit Barbarum," holds up to view in a strong light the progress of civilization and the continual regress of ignorance and barbarism. The seal shows an originality of design creditable to the artist; the more so as he is a native of our country and self-taught in his art.' March 11, 1839, Governor Dodge approved a resolution adopting the seal. This seal continued in use as late as October 1, 1849, over a year after the Territory became a State, the Legislature having passed a joint resolution June 21, 1848, adopting the seal of the Territory as the seal of the State until another could be prepared.

"The third seal was the same in design as the second Territorial seal, the word 'Territory' being changed to 'State.' This was first used March 1st, 1850, and continued in use as late as No-

Fig. 411.

vember 6th, 1851. The fourth seal was described December 31st, 1851, in the office of the Secretary of State, as follows: 'The scroll surmounting the upper part of the seal reads "Great Seal of the State of Wisconsin," followed below by thirteen stars for the original States of the Union. The shield is quartered, the quarters bearing, respectively: a plough for agriculture, an arm and held hammer for manufacture, a crossed shovel and pick for mining, and an anchor for navigation, representing the industrial pursuits of the people of the State. The arms and motto of the United States are borne on the shield, in token of the allegiance of the State to the Union. The base point of the shield rests upon the horn of plenty and a pyramid of lead ore. The supporters are a yeoman resting on a pick, representing labor by land, and a sailor holding a coil of rope, representing labor by water. The crest is a badger, the popular designation of the State, surmounting a scroll bearing the vernacular motto " Forward." '

"This seal was procured by Governor Dewey, first Governor of the State, in his second term. The motto was suggested by the motto of New York, 'Excelsior,' and presented itself successively in the words 'Upward,' 'Onward,' and 'Forward,' the latter being chosen as the best word to express the progressive character of the young and growing State. The badger was placed as the crest in compliance with the popular sobriquet for Wisconsin people, the term having grown out of the custom of the early miners to live in 'dug-outs,' suggestive of the badger's burrowing in the ground. The first three seals are not in the State Department, and their whereabouts is unknown.

"In 1881 the old seal became so worn that a perfect impression could not be taken from it, and a new seal was ordered, which has since been in use" (Fig. 411).

WYOMING.[1]

The Great Seal of the State of Wyoming was approved February 8, 1893, and described as follows: "A circle two and one-fourth inches in diameter, on the outer rim or edge of which shall be engraven the words 'Great Seal of the State of Wyoming,' and the design shall conform substantially to the following description:

"'A pedestal, showing on the front thereof an eagle resting upon a shield, said shield to have engraven thereon a star and the figures "44," being the

FIG. 412.

number of Wyoming in the order of admission to statehood. Standing upon the pedestal shall be a draped figure of a woman, modelled after the statue of the "Victory of the Louvre," from whose wrists shall hang links of a broken chain, and holding in her right hand a staff, from the top of which shall float a banner with the words "Equal Rights," thereon, all suggesting the political position of woman in this State. On either side of the pedestal, and standing at the base thereof, shall be male figures typifying the live stock and mining industries of Wyoming. Behind the pedestal, and in the background, shall be two pillars, each supporting a lighted lamp, signifying the light of knowledge. Around each pillar shall be a scroll with the following words thereon: On the right of the central figure the words "Live Stock" and "Grain," and on the left the words "Mines" and "Oil." At the base of the pedestal, and in front, shall appear the figures "1869–1890," the former date signifying the organization of the Territory of Wyoming, and the latter the date of its admission to statehood.'"[2]

"Wyoming Territory was organized July 25, 1868. The seal of the Territory has in the upper half a range of mountains, at the base of which is a railroad and train of cars; a sun in the left-hand corner gilding the mountains with its rays; over the mountains the motto 'Cedant Arma togæ, 1863.' The lower half of the shield is divided per pale; the dexter half gules, bearing agricultural implements; the sinister half or, a mailed hand holding a drawn sword."[3]

---

[1] Design is from seal impression furnished by Hon. Amos W. Barber, Secretary of State.

[2] Wyoming State Laws.

[3] Preble, pp. 654, 655.

ECCLESIASTICAL SEALS.

Ecclesiastical and corporate seals form two distinct groups, which have long held a prominent place in the heraldry of America, although they have in some instances suffered from the improper application of heraldic laws. Those of the former class generally show careful treatment, but the seals of commercial bodies, etc., are very often open to severe criticism. This difference is undoubtedly due to the fact that the clergy, as a rule, understand heraldry, and possibly dictate the arrangement of their own devices, while the seals of corporations, etc., are distinctly commercial, and their designs receive little attention, as the main object, it is apparent, is to secure something that will *make an impression.*

Ecclesiastical seals are first noted in the ninth century. In the thirteenth and fourteenth centuries they were beautiful in design and execution. Their forms have scarcely varied from the early date to the present, and usually are of pointed oval shape for both official and personal use. The most common subjects of those older seals are the figure of a bishop, sometimes the Trinity, the Virgin, or a patron saint seated under an elaborate canopy.

Records of the use of corporate seals of towns and boroughs date back as far as the twelfth century, and some of the earlier impressions bear the town gates, city walls, or some similar device. Arms were not generally introduced until later.

After the time of Constantine, the Roman emperors introduced the bullæ, or leaden seals, and their use was continued, after the fall of the Western Empire, by the Popes, who attached them to documents by bands or silk cords, hence the term the " Pope by a bull," etc.

Among the devices appearing upon ecclesiastical seals are the Pall, Cross, Keys, Crown, Sword, Pastoral Crook, Mitre, Chalice, Book, Escallop Shell, as well as the emblems of the Evangelists,—the Angel of St. Matthew, the winged Lion of St. Mark, the winged Ox of St. Luke, the Eagle of St. John. These devices, with others, are formed into achievements, and often impaled with the personal arms of bishops. Presidents of colleges and other institutions impale their personal arms with those of their office in the same manner.

The rule is invariable that the official arms shall occupy the dexter and the personal arms the sinister parts of the escutcheon. One old writer compares the form of marshalling ecclesiastical devices to the conjoining of coat-armor of a husband and wife, when he suggests that "those who have a function Ecclesiastical and possess the high honor of Pastoral Jurisdiction are supposed to be knit in nuptial bonds of love and tender care to the Cathedral Churches which they superintend 'infomuch as when a Biſhop deceaſeth, *Ejus Ecclefia dicitur, Viduata.*' Accordingly the paternal coat is always marshalled upon the sinister side of the escutcheon, the preference of position being given to the arms of their See, as these arms are perpetual, 'for they belong to a Political Body which never dieth.'"

An old seal is thus quaintly blazoned: "The Most Reverend Father in God, Dr. *William Lawde*, late Lord Archbishop of *Canterbury*, His Grace, Primate of all *England*, and Metropolitan, Chancellor of the University of *Oxford* and one of the Lords of His Majesty's most Honourable Privy Council ; Beareth these two Coats impaled, viz. :

"The Field is Jupiter, a Staff in Pale Sol, & thereupon a Cross Patée Luna, surmounted of a Pall of the last charged by 4 other like Crosses fitched, Saturn, edged and fringed as the second. This Coat belongs to the Archiepiscopal See of *Canterbury*, conjoyned with his Lordship's own Arms, Viz. : Sable, on a Chevron, Or, between three Stars, as many Crosses Patée fitchée, Gules."

A very valuable collection of seals is in the possession of Rev. Henry C. McCook, D.D., the well-known expert, who favors this volume with the following :

"The use of seals is sanctioned by custom and law. Our States all have communal seals, some of which go back to Colonial times, and have therefore direct sanction of English heraldic usages. Our cities have communal seals, some of them also Colonial. Corporations have seals, as do notarial officials, etc., and all individuals may have their own proper and legal seals.

"Here is an undeniably legitimate field for American heraldists to cultivate. It is to the seal that we should relegate the formal and public use of such ancestral arms as may be fairly established as of hereditary right. There is no good reason why one may not adopt for a legal seal the device, or some modification thereof, borne by an ancestor. Of course in its adoption good taste and good judgment as well as good genealogical science should prevail. In settling such points we need trained experts. . . . In this department, also, lies the field of ecclesiastical heraldry in the United States, and a wide field it is. Our numerous church denominations, missionary and other societies, individual congregations, bishops and other ecclesiastical dignitaries, hospitals and divers charities, educational institutions, benevolent societies, etc., etc., are for the most part chartered, and have by law the right to have and use a seal.

"Alas ! What a wilderness of inappropriate, absurd, inartistic, grotesque, and utterly unheraldic caricatures opens before one who collects and studies the seals of these different organizations. It is most unfortunate that some law, or some custom with the force of law, cannot be brought to bear upon this chaotic mass in order to reduce it to something like reasonable and scientific order. I hold it to be self-evident that if we are to have and maintain such a custom at all, it ought to be regulated by common rules pervaded by good judgment and good taste, in harmony with history and the fitness of things, and at least in sympathy with the heraldic usages of other nations.

"Does it not seem that our law-makers might well take the matter into consideration?"

The episcopal seals of America, with few exceptions, are heraldic and of remarkable interest to the student. The shape of the diocesan seals is uniform, and the reason for this is best explained in the description of the official seal of the Right Rev. William F. Nichols, D.D., Bishop of California (Fig. 413):

FIG. 413.

The seal of a diocese should be in shape what is called a pointed oval, this having been suggested by the form of the fish which, in early Christian times, was used as a symbol of Christ, from the fact that the initial letters of "Jesus Christ, the Son of God the Saviour," in Greek formed the word *IXΘΥΣ*,—a fish. The shape must be produced by the intersection of two equal circles, each of which passes through the centre of the other, producing that which is *true*. Bishop Nichols' seal consists of a golden shield, a bishop's mitre, and a ribbon with the motto, "*Pacifica et Impera*." All of this lies on a background of rich purple, the recognized color. On the golden shield is a group, composed of the Iona cross, with the circle and the key and pastoral staff; issuing from this group are rays of glory. Above this, in the upper part of the shield, is the descending dove of the Holy Spirit; and below, in the base of the shield (in natural colors), are the hills (the earth), suggested by part of the arms of the State of California. The shield, the key, and the crozier are taken from the arms of Bishop Seabury, the first Bishop of the Church in this country. The Iona cross is significant of the Scotch succession of the Episcopate, associated with Iona Island, from which succession Bishop Seabury received his consecration at Aberdeen in 1784. The legend, "The Prot: Ep: Church in the Diocese of California" is placed in letters of gold within the outlines of the border, which is also in gold. The ground of the border, on which are the letters, is of a tint in pleasing and correct keeping with the purple centre.

The official seal of His Eminence Cardinal Gibbons is composed of a shield, upon which is the figure of the Virgin Mary, over which appears the archiepiscopal cross (the sign of Metropolitan Jurisdiction); below is "Auspice Maria," which means that the hope is in the protection and intercession of the Redeemer's mother. Above all is the cardinal's hat (Fig. 414*a*). The Cardinalitial seal is shown in Fig. 414.

FIG. 414.

FIG. 414*a*.

FIG. 415.

The Right Rev. Henry Benjamin Whipple, D.D., LL.D., Bishop of Minnesota, bears a shield charged with a cross, broken tomahawk, and pipe of peace, the whole surmounted by a mitre. The motto is " Pax Per Sanguinem Crucis" (Fig. 415).

The seal of the Right Rev. Anson R. Graves, D.D., Bishop of the Platte, is a combination of his personal device and the mitre. The design (Fig. 416) is from the Scripture text, " Be ye wise as serpents and harmless as doves."

FIG. 416.

The Right Rev. Henry Melville Jackson, D.D., Assistant Bishop of Alabama, uses a personal seal made up of the official seal of his diocese and the crest from the arms of his maternal ancestor, who was a Calvert (Fig. 417).

FIG. 417.

The Right Rev. James S. Johnston, D.D., Bishop of Western Texas, combines his ecclesiastical devices with the winged spur and the motto of his family (Fig. 418).

FIG. 418.

The seal of the Right Rev. William Hobart Hare, S.T.D., Bishop of South Dakota, is symbolic of the district over which he presides.

Indians being prominent in the mission, Indian tents are represented in the seal as gathered in the angles of the cross, a cross surmounts each tent, symbolic of the emblem carried to the house of the Indian. The legend on the cross is the Greek for "That they may have life." The legend surrounding the whole means: Seal of William Hobart Hare, by the Grace of God Missionary Bishop of Niobrara (Fig. 419).

FIG. 419.

The Right Rev. Cleland Kinloch Nelson, D.D., third Bishop

of Georgia, uses a particularly well executed seal: the devices of his diocese impaled with his family arms: *Sable, upon a chevron or, between three fleurs-de-lis argent, as many roses gules* (Fig. 420).

FIG. 420.

The Right Rev. M. A. DeWolfe Howe, D.D., LL.D., Bishop of Central Pennsylvania, has a most interesting seal (Fig. 421), since from the description of the arms in Longfellow's "Wayside Inn" some of its features are taken. It is known that the arms thus described hung for one hundred and fifty years in an old inn at Sudbury, which was owned by a man "by the name of Howe" (see Fig. 18).

FIG. 421.

The well-known arms of the Potter family occupy the sinister position in the seal of the Right Rev. Henry Codman Potter, D.D., LL.D., Bishop of New York, while the devices of the diocese are as usual in the dexter (Fig. 422).

The Right Rev. Thomas M. Clark, D.D., LL.D., Bishop of Rhode Island, bears *gules a cross argent;* the shield is supported by two pastoral staffs, and surmounted by a mitre resting upon two keys in saltire. Upon either side of this achievement are the initial letters R. I., and below, the letters T. M. C. (Fig. 423).

FIG. 422.

The Most Rev. Michael Augustine Corrigan, Archbishop of New York, bears *azure, " in fesse" a barrulet argent, in chief three mountains or, the central and highest one surmounted by a cross patée* (evidently *fitchée*) of the second. In base, issuing from the sinister, a winged arm of the third, holding in the hand a sword paleways proper.*[1]*

FIG. 423.

The archiepiscopal cross surmounts the centre of the shield, a mitre and pastoral staff occupying the dexter and sinister positions upon each side of it. The archiepiscopal hat is placed over the entire group. MOTTO: "Dominus Petra Mea" (Fig. 424).

FIG. 424.

[1] The blazon is from an illuminated impression of the seal.

FIG. 425.

Although the Right Rev. Charles R. Hale, D.D., LL.D., is Bishop of Cairo and Assistant Bishop of Springfield (the jurisdiction of Cairo being part of the Diocese of Springfield), no official seal is used by him in either place, his personal signet, as shown in Fig. 425, answering that purpose.

FIG. 426.

The signet of the Right Rev. W. B. W. Howe, D.D., Bishop of South Carolina, bears a well-executed mitre (Fig. 426).

FIG. 427.

The diocesan seal of Ohio was adopted in Convention, 1891, and is described as a shield divided "*per fesse, vert and argent, on the first a sheaf of wheat, on the second a bunch of grapes, ppr.*" A bishop's mitre, key, and pastoral staff are incorporated in the design, and the motto is CREDO (Fig. 427). The two elements of the Holy Communion, Bread and Wine, are symbolized, and, as the sheaf of wheat (a staple product) is in the arms of the State of Ohio and as the grape-culture and vineyards abound in that section of the country, these emblems are added to the seal. This seal is used by

FIG. 428.

the Right Rev. W. A. Leonard, D.D., Bishop of Ohio, whose signet is as shown in Fig. 428. The devices of the diocese are impaled with those of his family coat of arms, which are introduced with the crest.

FIG. 429.

The seal of the Right Rev. John Scarborough, D.D., Bishop of New Jersey, is plain but handsomely executed. A bishop's mitre forms the central feature (Fig. 429). His private signet (Fig. 430) is composed of the arms of New Jersey impaling his family devices.

FIG. 430.

The official seal of the Right Rev. Boyd Vincent, D.D., Bishop Coadjutor of Southern Ohio, is decidedly interesting, and is composed of the following symbols: the CROSS, and gathered in its angles are the emblems of the four Evangelists,—the ANGEL OF ST. MATTHEW, the EAGLE OF ST. JOHN, the WINGED OX OF ST. LUKE, and the WINGED LION OF ST. MARK. The cross is charged with the legend of the labarum of Constantine "In Hoc Signo Vincens," and the whole is surrounded by the wording, "Sigillum Boyd Vincent Dei gratia Episcopi Ohioentis meridionalis coadjutoris," in abbreviation (Fig. 431).

FIG. 431.

Fig. 432 represents the seal of the Diocese of Springfield, as used by the Right Rev. George F. Seymour, S.T.D., LL.D., Bishop. The cross in the centre symbolizes the tree of life, whose fruit is the bread which came down from heaven. It rests on three steps, in allusion to the hill of Calvary on which the Lord suffered. The arms of the cross are expanded at the ends to show that the faith of the cross is extending through the world. The alpha and omega on either side of the cross symbolize the co-eternal deity of God the Son; they tell us also that Christ is our first and last, our all in all, the author and finisher of our faith. From underneath the cross flows forth the river which parts into four heads and goes

FIG. 432.

to the ends of the earth to carry Eden with it to all mankind. This is Christ, the well of life, and the *four* Evangelists bear him in their gospels, the *one gospel in four streams*, to the four quarters of the globe, to the *four* points of the compass, east and west, and north and south. The name of the diocese is *Springfield*. *Spring*, the living water, Christ, the Lord; the *field*, the diocese. The bishop, the clergy and laity, men, women, and children are to carry the water all over the field, and then it will bud and blossom as the rose, become as the *garden of the Lord*, a second Eden. But when clergy and laity have done all in their power by efforts and labors and offerings, all will prove of no avail unless " God giveth the increase,"—" Devs dat Incrementvm," the motto of the diocese. The young growth, which is seen starting in the field, gives promise of a full harvest hereafter.

There could be no more appropriate design for a missionary diocese, such as Springfield pre-eminently is, and the unity of teaching of the several parts is admirable. Fig. 433 shows Bishop Seymour's personal seal, the crest of his ancestor of the family of Somerset, *out of a ducal coronet, or, a phœnix of the last issuing from flames, ppr.* MOTTO: " *Foy pour devoir.*" If in England, Bishop Seymour would be a baron and entitled to a baron's coronet.

FIG. 433.

The seal of the Diocese of Tennessee, as used by the Right Rev. Thomas F. Gailor, S.T.D., Assistant Bishop, is thus described: " The seal of the Diocese of Tennessee represents our Lord seated, a bishop kneeling,

FIG. 434.

the dove lighting upon him, a mitre and pastoral staff on either side of him, and the salient symbols of the arms of the State of Tennessee, Agriculture and Commerce, on either side of the group. Around the edge is the name of the Bishop, which changes from time to time." (See Fig. 465.) Bishop Gailor's signet is a shield, supported by two keys, bearing on it a portcullis, the whole surmounted by a mitre. Beneath is the legend " Depositum Custode"

FIG. 435.

FIG. 436.

(the Vulgate rendering of St. Paul's words to St. Timothy: "Keep that which is committed to thy trust") and the date, 1893 (Fig. 434).

The Right Rev. Ellison Capers, D.D., Assistant Bishop of South Carolina, uses a seal made up of a shield charged with a tree, a cross and gloria, a scroll and motto, "Fidem Amor Spes," and initials E. C. (Fig. 435).

FIG. 437.

The seals of the Right Rev. Thomas F. Davies, D.D., LL.D., Bishop of Michigan, are shown in Figs. 436 and 437. The features of the diocesan seal and signet are the crossed keys and pastoral staff. The private seal bears the family crest and motto.

FIG. 438.

Among other seals is that of the Right Rev. William Paret, D.D., LL.D., sixth Bishop of Maryland (see Fig. 438), which is described as follows:

" QUARTERLY: *1 and 4, paly of six, Or and sable, a bend counterchanged, for* CALVERT; *2 and 3, quarterly; Argent and gules, a cross bottony counterchanged, for* CROSSLANDS,—*being the arms of Maryland; impaling a plain shield, thereon the letters W. P. in monogram for* WILLIAM PARET; *the whole ensigned with the Bishop's mitre, labelled and garnished proper; all within a cusp, double-edged and lined upon both edges plain, and inscribed " Sig. Willielmi Paret: Episcopi Maryland."*

FIG. 439.

The Right Rev. Nelson Somerville Rulison, D.D., Assistant Bishop of Central Pennsylvania, uses the same seal for both personal and official matters. The device has alpha and omega in circles in form of the beads used in the Greek Church in the consecration of the elements at the Eucharist. The form of the cross is shown, and contains in the angles the Greek letters IHXP, and below the Greek letters NIKA, meaning "Conquer" (Fig. 439).

The significance of the personal seal of the Right Rev. Daniel S. Tuttle,

S.T.D., Bishop of Missouri, is this: The dove of the Holy Spirit hovers over the bee-hive, which is a part of the Territorial seal of Utah, and the rays of the sun of righteousness are streaming across the mountains of the West (Fig. 440).

FIG. 440.

FIG. 441.

The seal of the Diocese of Milwaukee (Fig. 441), in symbolical meaning, is the *Whitsun* gift: the Holy Ghost in the form of a dove, coming down upon the Church. The motto is the opening line of the old Latin hymn, " Veni, Creator Spiritus." Above is the mitre,—symbol of the episcopal office; below are the staff and keys, crossed,—symbols of episcopal and priestly authority. The year 1847 is that of the formation of the jurisdiction. The church fabric represented in the centre of the seal is a cut of the S. Sylvanus Chapel, of Nashotah Mission House, long time the pro-cathedral of the diocese, and the place where the early ordinations were holden by the pioneer Missionary Bishop, Kemper.

The Cathedral seal (Fig. 442) of All Saints' Cathedral, Diocese of Milwaukee, symbolically represents the lily and palm-branch, crossed,—symbols of the two degrees of the Saints; the lily, those who have departed " pure and undefiled;" the palm (sign of victory), those who have been saved, passing " through great tribulations." These symbols carry out the *name* of the cathedral,—" All Saints'." The motto, in Latin, is the clause from " Te Deum,"—" to be numbered with Thy Saints in Glory Everlasting."

FIG. 442.

FIG. 443.

Below are the pastoral staff and keys, crossed. Interspersed are the " seven stars," which are " the Angels of the Seven Churches. (Book of Revelation.) Above is the mitre. These seals are used by the Right Rev. Isaac Lea Nicholson, S.T.D., Bishop of Milwaukee, whose signet is as shown in Fig. 443. *Az. two bars erm., on a chief arg. three suns ppr.*

CREST: *Out of a ducal coronet or, a lion's head erased gu. The erasure showing beneath the coronet.* This crest is placed above the sinister of the shield. A mitre occupies the dexter position.

The seal of the second Bishop of Delaware, the Right Rev. Leighton Coleman, S.T.D., LL.D., is composed of a shield azure, charged with the cross, anchor, and heart, symbolizing the three great virtues, Faith, Hope, and Charity,—the heart being surmounted by the crown, as Charity is the greatest

FIG. 444.

FIG. 445.

of the three. A mitre and the initials L. C. are placed over the whole, and the motto is "Omnia in Caritate," "Let all things be done in Charity" (Fig. 444).

The seal of the Diocese of Delaware is shown in Fig. 445, and the significance of the tree is expressed in Psalm i. 3: "And he shall be like a tree planted by the rivers of water, that bringeth forth his fruit in his season; his leaf also shall not wither; and whatsoever he doeth shall prosper."

The seal for the Diocese of Western Michigan as used by the Right Rev. George de Normandie Gillespie, D.D., is in form a *vesica piscis*, representing the sea, with a boat in which the Saviour is pictured with hand uplifted, and the word "Pax," or Peace, the meaning and symbolism of which are as follows:

FIG. 446.

The Diocese of Western Michigan is on the shore of the great fresh-water lake of the same name. This leads us at once to the one fresh-water lake or sea of the Holy Land, with which our Saviour was connected, the Lake of Gennesaret, and suggests some incident of His divine power in relation to that sea. There are two such incidents to choose from: one is the walking on the water, the other is the stilling of the tempest. We have chosen the latter because the stilling of the tempest symbolizes the work of the Church in calming the passions and tumults of the world, "the waves of this troublesome world" as the baptismal service has it. The seal then has a ship on the waves with the figure of our Saviour crowned with a cruciform nimbus, his hands stretched out over the water and the single word "Pax" above,—Peace, be still (Fig. 446).

The seal of the Right Rev. William Lawrence, D.D., Bishop of Massachusetts, represents "Joyful Service." The shepherdhood is in the text: "The Good Shepherd giveth his Life for the Sheep" in Greek.

The scroll bears the name of the Diocese and the initials of the Bishop (Fig. 447).

FIG. 447.

FIG. 448.

Fig. 448 may be described as follows:

Escutcheon bearing the coat of arms of the Right Rev. Davis Sessums, D.D., Bishop of Louisiana: a star and a plough, these symbols indicating the character of his work,—a mingling of the heavenly and earthly things, earthly labor for the attainment of heavenly things,—ministerial service of an humble and lowly sort, even with earthly and carnal weapons, to the end that men may be led to contemplate heavenly concerns; the endeavor to make the sons of toil a high and noble generation of spiritually-minded sons of God. On the lower division of the escutcheon *a pelican,* the symbol of the civil State of Louisiana, to indicate that this work is being done therein. The crest is a mitre, to indicate the episcopate. The motto, " 1891," is the date of the bishop's consecration.

Fig. 449 is from the official seal of the Right Rev. Cortlandt Whitehead, D.D., Bishop of Pittsburg, and represents our Lord seated in glory (Revelation i. 13, 14) giving his blessing to a Burg, " Ein feste Burg." On one side of his seat is the spire of Trinity Church, Pittsburg, on the other some of Pittsburg's smoky chimneys. Below this is a battlement of a castle, from which floats a flag charged with a cross, on either side of this group the Greek characters alpha and omega. The Bishop's personal seal

FIG. 449.

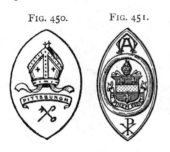

FIG. 450. FIG. 451.

bears: *az. a fesse between three fleurs-de-lis or* (Fig. 451). The Bishop's signet is shown in Fig. 450.

The Right Rev. John Henry Ducachet Wingfield, D.D., LL.D., D.C.L., F.R.G.S., Bishop of Northern California, uses, as his official seal, *Arg., on a bend gu., cotised sa. three pairs of wings conjoined in lure of the field.* CREST: *An eagle rising, arg. looking at the sun in its glory.* SUPPORTERS: *Two pegasi winged, maned, and hoofed or.* MOTTO: *Fidelite est de Dieu.* These are the arms of the family of Wingfield,

FIG. 452.

FIG. 453.

and it will be noticed that the Bishop has added a *mitre* in the *sinister chief,* and in *dexter base a key* and *staff, in saltire* (Fig. 452).

The personal seal of Bishop Wingfield is quarterly *az. and gu., in the first quarter* the letter *F, second E, third L, fourth D, over all a sinister demi-vol. or.* CREST: *A cross or supporting a rose gu.* (House of Lancaster). MOTTO: *Fidelite est de Dieu* (Fig. 453).

FIG. 454.

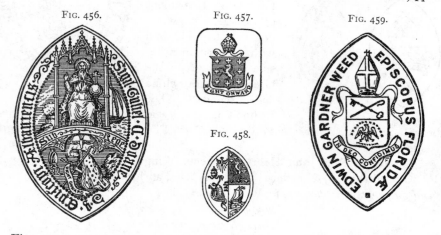

The diocesan seal of Pennsylvania, as used by the Right Rev. Ozi W. Whitaker, D.D., is shown in Fig. 454. The personal seal is shown in Fig. 455.

FIG. 455.

The Right Rev. William Croswell Doane, D.D., LL.D., first Bishop of Albany, has three very elaborate and interesting seals. Fig. 456 represents the diocesan seal. Fig. 457, his private seal, is from his family arms: *Az. crusilly or, a unicorn salient arg.* MOTTO: *Right Onward.* Fig. 458 is composed of several of the diocesan devices impaling: *per fesse, in chief* the arms of Doane, *in base* upon the sea a boat under sail, *ppr.*

FIG. 456.   FIG. 457.   FIG. 459.

FIG. 458.

Fig. 459 represents the seal of the Right Rev. Edwin Gardner Weed, S.T.D., Bishop of Florida, and is made up of a shield charged with the staff and key (indicative of episcopal office) and the American eagle. The usual mitre surmounts the group, and the motto of Florida, "In Deo Confidimus," is below.

FIG. 460.

The Right Rev. Elisha S. Thomas, S.T.D., Bishop of Kansas, bears his family arms on his signet: *Ar. a chev. lozengy, or and sa. betw. three ravens close of the last.* CREST: *On a branch of a tree lying fesseways a raven with wings expanded sa.* (Fig. 461).

FIG. 461.

The seal of the Diocese of Kansas is shown in Fig. 460.

A rainbow, a device rarely seen in heraldry, is in the shield on the seal of the Right Rev. Arthur Cleveland Coxe, D.D., LL.D., Bishop of Western New York : *Sable, a rainbow ppr. between three crosses argent* (diocesan devices), impaling : *Argent, a chevron sable between three cock's heads erased ppr.* (arms of the Coxe family) (Fig. 462).

Fig. 462. Fig. 463.

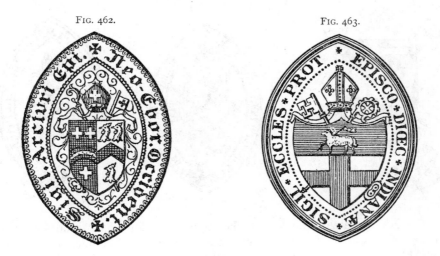

The seal of the Diocese of Indiana is :

Argent, a cross gules; on a chief azure a Holy Lamb proper. Behind the escutcheon a key and a pastoral staff in saltire, and surmounting it a bishop's mitre proper. Around the device, which has the form of the *vesica piscis*, the legend, Sigil · Eccles · Prot · Episco · Diœc · Indianæ.

The symbolism of the design is as follows : The red cross upon a white ground is the old banner of St. George, the patron saint of England, which served for centuries as the standard of the nation, from whose bishops the right reverend fathers derived their succession. The blue chief is the type of heavenly purity and innocence, and the Holy Lamb a universally recognized emblem of our Lord. The key, pastoral staff, and mitre are the insignia of the episcopal office, and indicative of the right of our bishops to assert the validity of their orders (Fig. 463). The seal thus described is used by the Right Rev. David Buel Knickerbacker, D.D., Bishop of Indiana.

Especial attention is directed to the personal seal of the Right Rev. Charles Todd Quintard, S.T.D., LL.D., Bishop of Tennessee. It will be noticed that below the shield a decoration is suspended from a ribbon. This is the Cross of the English Order of the Hospital of St. John of Jerusalem. It is an eight-pointed white cross with a gold crown above it. The Prince of Wales is the Grand Prior of the Order, and Bishop Quintard has been for more than twenty years a Chaplain. The order is that of the Knights Hospitallers of the old Crusades (Fig. 464).   The seal of the diocese (Fig. 465) is described on p. 204.

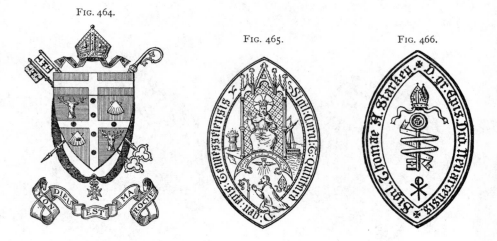

FIG. 464.

FIG. 465.

FIG. 466.

Fig. 466 represents the seal of the Right Rev. Thomas A. Starkey, D.D., Bishop of Newark.   The key symbolizes the power and commission given to the Apostles, of binding and loosing, opening and shutting.   The scroll is supposed to contain the words of the apostolic commission, conveying the power of the keys.   The device at the bottom is the symbol for "Our Lord Himself, and is placed there because He is the 'Root of David' and the Sure Foundation."

FIG. 469.

FIG. 467.

FIG. 468.

The Right Rev. Alexander Burgess, S.T.D., LL.D., Bishop of Quincy.

Official seal. The Most Rev. Patrick John Ryan, Archbishop of Philadelphia.

Seal of the Presiding Bishop of the Protestant Episcopal Church.   The seal is used to attest proceedings by the House of Bishops, and may be considered the seal of that house.

Fig. 470.

Fig. 470.

Fig. 471.

Fig. 472.

Fig. 473.

The Right Rev. Abiel Leonard, S.T.D., Missionary Bishop of Nevada and Utah.

The Right Rev. W. H. A. Bissell, D.D., Bishop of Vermont.

The Right Rev. John Williams, D.D., LL.D., Bishop of Connecticut.

The Right Rev. Leigh Richmond Brewer, S.T.D., Missionary Bishop of Montana.

Fig. 474.

Fig. 475.

Fig. 476.

The Right Rev. Alfred Magill Randolph, D.D., Bishop of Southern Virginia.

The Right Rev. Thomas Underwood Dudley, D.D., LL.D., D.C.L., Bishop of Kentucky.

Monsignor Satolli.

Fig. 477.

The Right Rev. Joseph Blount Cheshire, Jr., D.D., Assistant Bishop of North Carolina.

Fig. 478.

The Right Rev. Abram Newkirk Littlejohn, D.D., LL.D., Bishop of Long Island, New York.

Fig. 479.

The Right Rev. Alfred Augustin Watson, D.D., Bishop of East Carolina.

Fig. 480.

The Right Rev. Alexander Charles Garrett, D.D., LL.D., Missionary Bishop of Northern Texas.

Fig. 481.

The Right Rev. George Worthington, S.T.D., LL.D., Bishop of Nebraska.

Fig. 482.

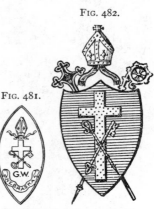

Fig. 482a.

The Right Rev. George William Peterkin, D.D., Bishop of West Virginia.

Fig. 483.   Fig. 484.

The Right Rev. Frederick D. Huntington, S.T.D., D.C.L., LL.D., Bishop of Central New York.

Fig. 485.

The Right Rev. Benjamin Wistar Morris, D.D., Bishop of Oregon and Washington.

Fig. 486.

The Right Rev. E. R. Atwill, D.D., Bishop of West Missouri.

Fig. 487.

The Right Rev. Richard Hooker Wilmer, D.D., Bishop of Alabama.

Fig. 488.

The Right Rev. T. A. Jaggar, D.D., Bishop of Southern Ohio.

Fig. 489.

The Right Rev. John Franklin Spalding, D.D., Bishop of Colorado.

FIG. 490.

FIG. 491.

Right Rev. William C.

FIG. 492.

FIG. 493.

Canterbury.

FIG. 494.

York.

FIG. 495.

London.

FIG. 496.

Durham.

FIG. 497.

Winchester.

FIG. 498.

Worcester.

FIG. 499.

Salisbury.

FIG. 500.

Bath and Wells.

FIG. 501.

Llandaff.

FIG. 502.

Norwich.

FIG. 503.

Ely.

FIG. 504.

Chichester.

FIG. 505.

Hereford.

FIG. 506.

St. Davids.

FIG. 507.

FIG. 508.

FIG. 509.

Rochester.

Bristol.

Chester.

FIG. 510.

FIG. 511.

FIG. 512.

Gloucester.

St. Asaph.

Oxford.

FIG. 513.

FIG. 514.

FIG. 515.

Lincoln.

Bangor.

Exeter.

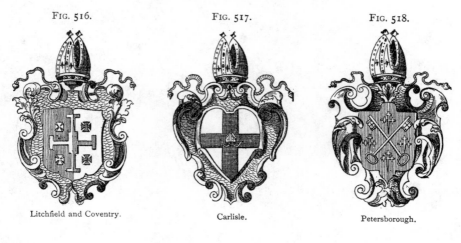

FIG. 516.   FIG. 517.   FIG. 518.

Litchfield and Coventry.   Carlisle.   Petersborough.

MISCELLANEOUS SEALS.

SEAL OF THE CITY OF SALEM, MASSACHUSETTS.

It would be useless to attempt to make even passing mention of all of America's seals in this volume, or even in more than one volume; but several miscellaneous seals are selected as examples of historic value.

The oldest of these is that of the city of Salem, shown in Fig. 519, and is unique and interesting. Three years were consumed by the City Council of

FIG. 519.

that ancient place before a design was agreed upon. Salem was the second chartered city in the Commonwealth of Massachusetts, Boston alone being before her in civic honors, and her magnates were naturally resolved, when they had a seal, to have one in every way characteristic and worthy.

An article contributed to the "Historical Collections of the Essex Institute," by Mayor Rantoul, in 1866, speaks of midnight conclaves and protracted contests of critical scholarship, and attributes the design finally adopted, in 1839, to the joint efforts of George Peabody, Esquire, and of General Henry Kemble Oliver, both members of the first City Council.

The original drawings and first wax impression of the seal are now deposited in the cabinets of the Essex Institute.

The device as ordained was as follows: "In the centre thereof, a shield, bearing upon it a ship under full sail, approaching a coast designated, by the costume of the person standing upon it and by the trees near him, as a portion of the East Indies;—beneath the shield this motto,—DIVITIS INDIÆ USQUE AD ULTIMUM SINUM, and above the shield, a dove bearing an olive branch in her mouth."

The Latin motto is probably not found, as a single phrase, in any classic author. But General Oliver's elegant and well-known scholarship is a guarantee for its correctness. "Solyma" was the word at first reported in the legend for "Salem," but the exact taste of some of the classicists in the first City Council rejected this word as of doubtful authority, and Biblical students generally express a preference for "Salem," a word adopted from the Hebrew into the Vulgate. Horace repeatedly uses the phrase *Divitis Indiæ*, and the words *Usque ad ultimum sinum* may be found in conjunction in line thirteen of the first Epode, Book V., of the same author, and perhaps elsewhere. The line referred to, singularly enough, relates to western, and not to eastern voyaging, and reads thus: "VEL OCCIDENTIS, USQUE AD ULTIMUM SINUM;" so that the Latin scholars of the opulent old seaport, who impressed this line into their service to commemorate the rich trade Salem had pushed "to the last confines of the glowing East," certainly found themselves under the necessity of wrenching a good deal away from its original meaning, a motto more fit for Columbus, who expected to find India in the west, than for explorers sailing eastward.

The dove, bearing an olive-branch in her mouth, was a very ancient device, found in use in the Essex County seal of 1687, before the deposing of Andros and the witchcraft period, and doubtless had a Biblical significance.

Mr. Peabody, whose artistic gifts and instincts were sources of great pleasure to himself and his friends throughout a long career, wrote, November 10, 1891, after examining a new die of the seal: "The dove does not look quite so calm and peaceful with the olive-branch, as usually depicted, but times have changed, and the doves, perhaps in accordance, have acquired a little more self-assertion."

From the article above cited we are permitted to embody the following passage: "The Ecclesiastical History of the town, exciting the interest of students and travellers, is common to many a New England village, though none has profited so largely as Salem by the diligence of the Annalist and the glowing pen of the Romancer." This feature of its history, too, is in some sense recognized in the dove and olive-branch surmounting the design.

Was not the then recent and almost unparalleled commercial prosperity of the place fitly chosen as its one peculiar distinction among the cities of the earth? It was the enterprise of her merchants, well commemorated in the motto, DIVITIS INDIÆ, USQUE AD ULTIMUM SINUM, which made Salem what she has been, and made her known to the world. Denied the best natural advantages for commerce, and lacking large accumulations of capital, they made her the emporium of Eastern trade. It was her shipping, fitly typified in this design, carrying the fame of her merchants as well as the flag of the country into unknown seas, that made her name, in the first half of this century, a synonym for commercial honor, enterprise, and success, throughout the other hemisphere as well as this. It is the old lesson, never to be too often repeated and enforced,—the triumph of intelligence and resolution over obstacles.

Commerce is the handmaid of Peace. The word Salem seems to stand for peace, the world over. Hebraists tell us that in Jeru-Salem, meaning the foundation of peace, and in other compounds, it served that purpose long before the Christian era. St. Paul describes Melchisedec as " King of Salem, which is King of Peace." Governor Burnett, in 1728, quarrelled with the General Court, and wishing to convene them somewhere out of Boston, the hot-bed of insubordination, said he was in doubt, on philological grounds, between Salem and Concord. Peace was his aim, and he chose Salem. So the dove and olive-branch seem not out of place on the seal of Salem.

Seal of the City of Philadelphia.[1]

This seal was approved by an ordinance of February 14, 1874, in which it is thus described :

Fig. 520.

Fig. 521.

Seal approved in 1874.

Seal of the city in 1701.

" Arms.—On a blue field, a fess golden between a plough above and a ship in full sail below; both proper. Crest.—A right arm, nude, embowed, couped at shoulder, holding a pair of scales; all proper. Supporters.— Two females, standing full face, the one on the right side of the shield habited white and purple, crowned with an olive wreath; in her right hand a scroll, charged with an anchor; all proper; the one on the left side habited white and blue; in her left hand a cornucopia; proper. Motto.—Philadelphia Maneto."

[1] Design is from impression furnished by Hon. Edwin S. Stuart, Mayor.

FIG. 522.

[See inside back cover for color plate]

Great Seal of the General Society of Colonial Wars.

What is generally acknowledged to be one of the most heraldic and correctly designed of American seals is that of the General Society of Colonial Wars, as shown in Fig. 522. This seal is a combination of the Colonial seals of the nine States represented. Virginia is known by the seal of the Virginia merchants, and New York by the seal of the New Netherlands. The seal of the Colonial Governors occupies the Massachusetts quarter and has the color indications, although no colors were shown in the original seal, or, in fact, known of; however, they have here been added in accordance with heraldic rule. New Hampshire is represented by the arms of William and Mary, Connecticut by the old "grape-vine seal," and Maryland by the well-known arms of Lord Baltimore. In the seal of Rhode Island is another example of the addition of lines to indicate the proper colors. It is presumed that it was the intent of the original designer to represent an anchor in the sea. New Jersey is represented by the arms of George I., and Pennsylvania by those of William Penn.

The entire seal is described as follows:

"SEAL OF THE GENERAL SOCIETY OF COLONIAL WARS.

"ACT XVI.

"CONSTITUTION OF THE SOCIETY OF COLONIAL WARS.

"The Great Seal of the General Society shall be: Within a beaded annulet, a title scroll '1607 : General Society of Colonial Wars : 1775,' and in base the motto 'Fortiter Pro Patria,' surrounding diaper charged with nine mullets; over all a shield, surmounted of the crown, bearing American colonial seals quarterly of nine: I. VIRGINIA: Argent, a cross gules between four escutcheons each regally crowned proper, the first and fourth escutcheons FRANCE and ENGLAND quarterly, second escutcheon SCOTLAND, third IRELAND. II. NEW YORK: Argent, a beaver bendways proper, on a border tenné a belt of wampum of the first. III. MASSACHUSETTS: Azure, on a mount between two pine trees vert, an Indian affronté or, belted with leaves of the second, holding in his dexter hand an arrow paleways, point downwards, and in his sinister hand a bow paleways, of the third; upon a scroll proper, issuing from his mouth, the legend, 'Come over and help us.' IV. NEW HAMPSHIRE: Quarterly, first and fourth grand quarter of FRANCE and ENGLAND; second SCOTLAND; third IRELAND; over all an escutcheon of pretence; azure billetée or, a lion rampant of the second, for NASSAU. V. CONNECTICUT: Argent, a dexter hand issuing out of clouds in dexter chief, holding a double scroll proper, fessways, bearing the legend, 'Sustinet qui transtulit,' in base fifteen grape vines, six, five, four, leaved and fructed proper. VI. MARYLAND: Quarterly first and fourth, paly of six or and sable, a bend counterchanged, for Calvert; second and third, per fesse and per pale argent and gules, a cross bottony, counterchanged for Crossland (Arms of Lord Baltimore). VII. RHODE ISLAND: Azure, an anchor in pale or. VIII. NEW JERSEY: Quarterly, first, ENGLAND impaling SCOTLAND; second, FRANCE; third, IRELAND; fourth per pale and per chevron, first, Gules, two lions passant guardant in pale or, for BRUNSWICK; second, Or, semée of hearts, a lion rampant azure, for LUNENBURGH; third, Gules, a horse courant argent, for WESTPHALIA; over all an inescutcheon gules, charged with the crown of Charlemagne. IX. PENNSYLVANIA: Argent, on a fesse sable, three plates (Arms of Penn)."

SEAL OF THE SOCIETY OF COLONIAL DAMES OF AMERICA.

Another entirely heraldic and historical seal is that of the above-named society, and is composed of a combination of the arms of the four leading

FIG. 523.

nations that settled this country. It is thus described: "Within a beaded annulet a title scroll bearing the inscription 'Society of the Colonial Dames of America.' A shield, surmounted of the Crown, quarterly of four: I. Quarterly; 1 and 4 azure, three fleurs de lis or, 2 and 3 gules, three lions passant guardant in pale or, for ENGLAND. II. Azure, three fleurs de lis or, for FRANCE. III. Azure, billetée a lion rampant holding in his dexter paw a naked sword and in his sinister a sheaf of arrows or, for HOLLAND. IV. Quarterly; 1 and 4 (Sweden Modern) Azure, three open crowns or, 2 and 3 (Sweden Ancient) Azure, three bendlets sinister wavy argent, over all a lion rampant or, crowned gules, for SWEDEN.

SEAL OF THE SOCIETY OF SONS OF THE REVOLUTION.

The seal of the Society of Sons of the Revolution, as prescribed by the Constitution of the Society, is as follows:

"The seal of the Society shall be one and seven-eighths inches in diameter, and shall consist of the figure of a Minute-man in Continental uniform, standing on a ladder leading to a belfry; in his left hand he holds a musket

FIG. 524.

and an olive branch, whilst his right grasps a bell-rope; above, the cracked Liberty Bell; issuing therefrom a ribbon bearing the motto of the Society, Exegi Monumentum Aere Perennius; across the top of the ladder, on a ribbon, the figures 1776; and on the left of the Minute-man, and also on a ribbon, the figures 1883, the year of the formation of the Society; the whole encircled by a band three-eighths of an inch wide; thereon at the top thirteen stars of five points each; at the bottom the name of the General Society, or of the State Society to which the seal belongs."

General Society of the War of 1812.[1]

FIG. 525.

"The seal of the Society is two and one-half inches in diameter, and consists of a rising sun, bearing on its face a representation of the bombardment of Fort McHenry by the British fleet, while above the Sun and its rays rises, displayed, the Star Spangled Banner of our country, with the motto of the Society—'FOR OUR COUNTRY'S RIGHTS'—in small Roman capital letters overhead.

"This design is surrounded by wreaths of oak and laurel (emblematic of the valor and victory of our Soldiers and Sailors), with trophies of cannon, musket, sword, and anchor on each side of and below said design. The whole encircled with a waving ribbon, one-fourth of an inch wide, bearing above, in plain Roman capital letters, the legend 'THE SOCIETY OF THE WAR OF 1812,' and below, in similar letters, the words 'FOUNDED 1854.'"

FIG. 526.

Seal of Harvard University.

FIG. 527.

Seal of Daughters of the American Revolution.

[1] From Constitution and By-Laws of the General Society of the War of 1812, published 1893.

FIG. 528.

Seal of Yale University.

FIG. 529.

Seal of the Military Order of the Loyal Legion of the
United States.

FIG. 530.

Seal of the General Assembly of the Presbyterian Church
in the United States of America.

FIG. 531.

Seal of the Historical Society of Pennsylvania.

FIG. 532.

Seal of the University of Pennsylvania.

FIG. 533.

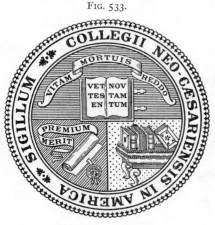

Seal of Princeton College.

AMERICAN COINS.[1]

In point of correctness, American coins may be classed above the seals, since most of them are dated and all were in circulation among the people, so that an error could not pass undetected. The coins of the early English kings nearly all bear coats of arms, and by their aid the royal arms can be traced through a number of changes.

Many of the American Colonial coins are impressed with arms and crests, among them the Virginia half-cent, which bears, QUARTERLY: *1, England impaling Scotland ; 2, France ; 3, Ireland ; 4, The electoral dominions ;* Legend: "*Virginia ;*" and the Maryland penny, which bears the crest of Lord Baltimore, *two pennants issuing from a ducal coronet.* Other Colonial coins bear devices less heraldic in character, among which the elephant was one of the most popular. The pine-tree shilling (Fig. 534) is one of the best known of the Colonial pieces ; it was coined in Massachusetts as early as 1652. The tree in the centre is so rudely engraved that it is impossible to tell whether it was originally intended to be a pine or a tree of some other kind. The emblem of the Colony was at first "a green tree," but it soon was almost universally known as a pine-tree.

FIG. 534.

After the Revolution the individual States coined money, each for itself, for some years, but in 1792 the first United States Mint was established in Philadelphia. From that time on many of the United States coins have borne the arms of the nation. The American eagle and the figure or head of Liberty have also been favorite devices. Several of the earlier coins bear the head of Washington, but it is said that Washington himself objected to this, and it has now become the rule that no man's head shall appear on the coinage of the Republic.

THE ROYAL ARMS OF ENGLAND IN AMERICA.

As the original thirteen American Colonies were under British rule, and as it has been demonstrated that the arms of some of the sovereigns were borne in Colonial seals upon old documents, the following examples may prove of value as a reference. For the sake of completeness, examples of the royal shields are shown as used from the Norman period to date. There is no certainty expressed by authorities as to several of the earlier ones. William I. is said to have assumed "Two golden leopards of his Norman duchy,"

[1] For examples of American coins the reader's attention is directed to the pamphlet issued by the United States Mint, Philadelphia.

after the Conquest, as the arms of the English kingdom. Tnese two "leopards," or lions, are believed to have been borne by later kings until 1154, when Henry II. added a third lion, since which time the royal arms of England have been *gules, three lions passant guardant, in pale or.*

Fig. 535.

Arms of William I., William II., Henry I., Stephen.

Arms of the Norman princes, 1066–1154. *Gu., two lions passant guardant, in pale or.*

Fig. 536.

Arms said to have been borne by Stephen. *Gu., a Sagittarius arg.*

Fig. 537.

Arms of Henry II., Richard I., John, Henry III., Edward I., Edward II., Edward III.

Arms of the Plantagenet princes, 1154–1340. *Gu., three lions passant guardant, in pale or.*

Fig. 538.

Edward III. laid claim to the crown of France in the tenth year of his reign, and in 1340 the French arms were introduced into the English shield by quartering; the *semée de lis* occupying the first and fourth quarters. These arms were also borne by Richard II. and Henry IV. (Lancastrian Plantagenet) during the earlier years of his reign.

QUARTERLY: *1 and 4, France Ancient (semée de lis); 2 and 3, England.* 1340–1405.

Fig. 539.

It is said that in the year 1365 Charles V. reduced the number of fleurs-de-lis in the French arms to three. The arms thus treated are termed *France Modern.* Henry IV. also reduced the number of fleurs-de-lis to three in the English arms. Henry V. and Henry VI. (Lancastrian Plantagenet princes), Edward IV., Edward V., and Richard III. (Yorkist Plantagenet princes), and Henry VII., Henry VIII., Edward VI., Mary, and Elizabeth (Tudor sovereigns), also bore the same arms about 1405–1603.

QUARTERLY: *1 and 4, France Modern; 2 and 3, England.*

Fig. 540.

Upon the enthronement of James I., the arms of Scotland and Ireland were introduced into the royal shield.

QUARTERLY: *1 and 4, France and England, quarterly; 2, Or, a lion rampant within a double tressure, flory counter-flory gules, Scotland; 3, Azure a harp or, stringed argent, Ireland.*

Arms of James I., Charles I., Charles II., James II. (Stuart), 1603–1689.

FIG. 541.

Arms of William III.

The same shield was retained by William III. As he was an elected king, he placed the arms of Nassau (*az. billetée a lion rampant or*) over it in pretence.

FIG. 542.

Mary bore the Stuart shield, and during her lifetime the arms appeared impaled. After Mary's death (1694) William bore arms as in Fig. 541.

FIG. 543.

Arms of Queen Anne (Stuart),
1707–1714.

Queen Anne bore the shield of the Stuarts (Fig. 540) from the time of her accession until the union with Scotland in 1707, when she bore,—

QUARTERLY: *1 and 4, England impaling Scotland; 2, France Modern; 3, Ireland* (Fig. 543).

FIG. 544.

The arms of Hanover were placed in the fourth quarter of the English shield upon the succession of that House. They are blazoned *Per pale and per chevron : 1, gules, two lions passant guardant, in pale or, for Brunswick ; 2, or, semée of hearts, a lion rampant azure, for Lunenburgh ; 3, gules, a horse courant argent, for Westphalia ; over all an inescutcheon gules charged with the golden crown of Charlemagne.*

Arms of George I., George II., George III., 1714–1801.

Upon the union with Ireland, in 1801, the French emblems were stricken from the English arms, and the shield appeared as in Fig. 545.

FIG. 545.

QUARTERLY : *1 and 4, England ; 2, Scotland ; 3, Ireland ; and over all in pretence, Hanover.* The inescutcheon of pretence was ensigned with the electoral bonnet of Hanover, 1801–1816 ; but from 1816–1837 the same shield was ensigned with a royal crown.

Arms of George III., George IV. William IV., 1801–1837.

FIG. 546.

HER MAJESTY QUEEN VICTORIA ascended the throne June 20, 1837 ; the arms of Hanover were removed from the royal shield, which since that time has been as shown in Fig. 546.

Queen Victoria.

CHAPTER VI.

COLONIAL SOCIETIES AND AMERICAN ORDERS.

SOCIETY OF COLONIAL WARS.

" OBJECTS.

" *Whereas*, It is desirable that there should be adequate celebrations commemorative of the events of Colonial history, happening from the settlement of Jamestown, Va., May 13, 1607, to the battle of Lexington, April 19, 1775.

FIG. 547.

" *Therefore*, The Society of Colonial Wars has been instituted to perpetuate the memory of those events, and of the men who, in military, naval, and civil positions of high trust and responsibility, by their acts or counsel, assisted in the establishment, defense, and preservation of the American Colonies, and were in truth the founders of this Nation. With this end in view it seeks to collect and preserve manuscripts, rolls, relics, and records ; to provide suitable commemorations or memorials relating to the American Colonial period, and to inspire in its members the fraternal and patriotic spirit of their forefathers, and in the community, respect and reverence for those whose public services made our freedom and unity possible." [1]

" MEMBERSHIP.

" Any male person above the age of twenty-one years, of good moral character and reputation, shall be eligible to membership in the Society of Colonial Wars, who is lineally descended, in the male or female line, from an ancestor :

" (1) Who served as a military or naval

[1] Preamble of Constitution.

officer, or as a soldier, sailor, or marine, or as a privateersman, under authority of the Colonies which afterward formed the United States, or in the forces of Great Britain which participated with those of the said Colonies in any wars in which the said Colonies were engaged, or in which they enrolled men, from the settlement of Jamestown, May 13, 1607, to the battle of Lexington, April 19, 1775 ; or,

"(2) Who held office in any of the Colonies between the dates above mentioned, either as

"(*a*) Director General, Vice-Director General, or member of the Council or legislative body in the Colony of New Netherlands.

"(*b*) Governor, Lieutenant or Deputy-Governor, Lord Proprietor, member of the King's or Governor's Council, or legislative body in the Colonies of New York, New Jersey, Virginia, Pennsylvania, and Delaware.

"(*c*) Lord Proprietor, Governor, Deputy-Governor, or member of the Council or of the legislative body in Maryland and the Carolinas.

"(*d*) Governor, Deputy-Governor, Governor's Assistant, or Commissioner to the United Colonies of New England, or member of the Council, body of Assistants, or legislative body in any of the New England Colonies.

"One collateral representative of an ancestor, such as above specified, shall be eligible to membership, provided there be no existing lineal descendant, and provided that such person be the oldest collateral representative in the male line of such ancestor, or has filed ·with the Secretary-General of the Society written renunciation from all other persons having nearer claims to representation.

"No State Society shall adopt any rule of eligibility for membership which shall admit any person not eligible for membership in the General Society ; but any State Society may, except as to members transferred from another State Society, further restrict at its discretion the basis of eligibility for membership in its own Society."

"INSIGNIA.

"The insignia of the Society shall consist of a badge, pendent by a gold crown and ring from a watered silk ribbon one inch and a half wide, of red, bordered with white and edged with red. The badge shall be surrounded by a laurel wreath in gold ; and shall consist of,—Obverse : A white enameled star of nine points bordered with red enamel, having between each star point a shield displaying an emblem of one of the nine original Colonies, and, within a blue enameled garter bearing the motto 'Fortiter Pro Patria,' an Indian's head in gold relievo. Reverse : the star above described but with gold edge, each shield between the points displaying a mullet, and in the centre, within an annulet of blue bearing the title 'Society of Colonial Wars, 1607–1775,' the figure of a Colonial soldier in gold relievo. The reverse of the crown of each insignia shall bear an engraved number, corresponding to that of the registered number of the member to whom such insignia has been issued.

"The insignia shall be worn by the members on all occasions when they assemble as such, for any stated purpose or celebration, and may be worn on any occasion of ceremony. It shall be worn conspicuously on the left breast, but members who are or have been Gentlemen of the Council of a State Society may place a rosette of regulation pattern upon the silk ribbon from which it is pendent. Members who are or have been General Officers or Officers of a State Society may wear the insignia with three jewels in the crown, and suspended from a regulation ribbon around the neck. Members who are or have been Governors, Deputy-governors, or Lieutenant-Governors of State Societies, or Officers of the General Society, may, in addition to the insignia so suspended, wear a ribbon of the Society's colors, three and one-half inches in width, extended from the right shoulder to the left hip. The insignia shall be worn only as above prescribed."

As an interesting heraldic example, the certificate of membership issued by this society is entitled to a place of record. Fig. 548 is a reduced fac-simile, the original being seventeen by twenty-two inches in size. A prominent feature is the picture of Miles Standish and soldiers, in " Morion and Casque," and a stockade in the distance. The royal crown surmounts this group, and is supported by the floral emblems of England, Ireland, and Scotland: the rose, shamrock, and thistle. The seals, as used by the nine Colonies, form a decorative accessory to the border, and an ideal Indian's head, charged upon a fleur-de-lis, symbolizes the French and Indian wars. The Colonial weapons, the flint-lock and rest, halberd, and sword, are supported by a group of oak leaves, emblematic of strength, while the flags of Sweden and the Netherlands appear amidst a cluster of corn-flowers,—the kaiser blume, Germany's national flower. The background of the border is *gules*, the scroll-work *argent*, representing the society's colors, red and white.

SOCIETY OF THE CINCINNATI.

This society was instituted on the 13th of May, 1783, by the officers of the Revolutionary army under the immediate command of General Washington, at the head-quarters of Baron Steuben on the Hudson River.

" OBJECTS.

"It having pleased the Supreme Governor of the universe, in the disposition of human affairs, to cause the separation of the Colonies of North America from the domination of Great Britain, and, after a bloody conflict of eight years, to establish them free and independent sovereign states, connected, by alliances founded on reciprocal advantage, with some of the great princes and powers of the earth ;

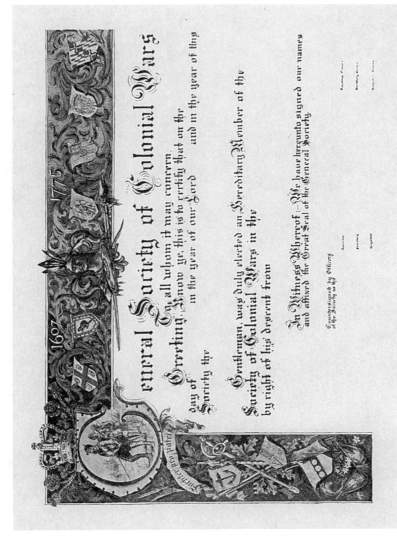

" To perpetuate, therefore, as well the remembrance of this vast event, as the mutual
friendships which have been formed under the
pressure of common danger, and, in many
instances, cemented by the blood of the parties,
the officers of the American Army do, hereby,
in the most solemn manner, associate, constitute,
and combine themselves into one SOCIETY OF
FRIENDS, to endure as long as they shall endure,
or any of their eldest male posterity, and, in
failure thereof, the collateral branches who may
be judged worthy of becoming its supporters
and members.

" The officers of the American Army having
generally been taken from the citizens of America, possess high veneration for the character of
that illustrious Roman, LUCIUS QUINTIUS CIN-
CINNATUS, and being resolved to follow his
example, by returning to their citizenship, they
think they may with propriety denominate
themselves, the SOCIETY OF THE CINCINNATI.

FIG. 549.

From one of the original insignia.

" The following principles shall be immutable and form the basis of the
Society of the Cincinnati :

" An incessant attention to preserve inviolate those exalted rights and
liberties of human nature for which they have fought and bled, and without
which the high rank of a rational being is a curse instead of a blessing.

" An unalterable determination to promote and cherish, between the respective States, that union and national honor so essentially necessary to their
happiness, and the future dignity of the American empire."

" MEMBERSHIP.

" All the officers of the American Army, as well those who have resigned with honor, after three years' service in the capacity of officers, or who
have been deranged by the resolutions of Congress upon the several reforms
of the army, as those who shall have continued to the end of the war, have
the right to become parties to this institution, provided that they subscribe
one month's pay, and sign their names to the general rules, in their respective
State Societies ; those who are present with the army immediately, and others
within six months after the army shall be disbanded, extraordinary cases
excepted. The rank, time of service, resolution of Congress by which any
have been deranged, and place of residence, must be added to each name.

And as a testimony of affection to the memory and the offspring of such officers as have died in the service, their eldest male branches shall have the same right of becoming members, as the children of the actual members of the Society. . . . And as there are, and will at all times be, men in the respective States eminent for their abilities and patriotism, whose views may be directed to the same laudable objects with those of the Cincinnati, it shall be a rule to admit such characters, as honorary members of the Society, for their own lives only: Provided always, that the number of honorary members, in each State, does not exceed a ratio of one to four of the officers or their descendants." [1]

" That the General Society conceive the true interpretation of the institution regarding the descent is, that the original member is to be the propositus from whom succession is to be derived, and that the collateral branches are those collateral to the original member, and the succession should be through the direct male line, and not through females, until all the male lines have become extinct." [2]

" INSIGNIA.

" The Society shall have an order, by which its members shall be known and distinguished, which shall be a medal of gold, of a proper size to receive the emblems, and suspended by a deep blue ribbon two inches wide, edged with white, descriptive of the union of America and France, viz. : The principal figure to be CINCINNATUS. Three senators presenting him with a sword and other military ensigns ; on a field in the background his wife standing at the door of their cottage, near it a plough and instruments of husbandry. Round the whole, *Omnia Reliquit Servare Rempublicam.* On the reverse, sun rising, a city with open gates, and vessels entering the port, Fame crowning Cincinnatus with a wreath inscribed, *Virtutis Præmium.* Below, hands joined, supporting a heart, with the motto, *Esto Perpetua.* Round the whole, *Societas Cincinnatorum Instituta, A.D. 1783.*" [3]

SOCIETY OF SONS OF THE REVOLUTION.

INSTITUTED 22D FEBRUARY, 1876.   REORGANIZED 4TH DECEMBER, 1883.

" OBJECTS.

" To perpetuate the memory of the men who, in the military, naval, and civil service of the Colonies and of the Continental Congress, by their acts or counsel achieved the independence of the country, and to further the proper celebration of the anniversaries of the birthday of Washington and of the

---

[1] Extracts from the Constitution.
[2] Resolution of 1887.
[3] Extract from the Constitution.

prominent events connected with the war of the Revolution; to collect and secure for preservation the
rolls, records, and other documents relating to that
period; to inspire the members of the Society with the
patriotic spirit of their forefathers; and to promote the
feeling of friendship among them."

FIG. 550.

" MEMBERSHIP.

"Any male person above the age of twenty-one
years, of good character, and a descendant of one who,
as a military, naval, or marine officer, soldier, sailor, or
marine, in actual service, under the authority of any
of the thirteen Colonies or States or of the Continental
Congress, and remaining always loyal to such authority, or a descendant of one who signed the Declaration
of Independence, or of one who, as a member of the
Continental Congress or of the Congress of any of the
Colonies or States, or as an official appointed by or
under the authority of any such legislative bodies, actually assisted in the establishment of American Independence by services
rendered during the war of the Revolution, becoming thereby liable to conviction of treason against the government of Great Britain, but remaining
always loyal to the authority of the Colonies or States, shall be eligible to
membership in the Society."

"INSIGNIA.

" A badge suspended from a ribbon by a ring of gold; the badge to be
elliptical in form, with escalloped edges, one and one-quarter inches in length
and one and one-eighth inches in width; the whole surmounted by a gold
eagle, with wings displayed, inverted; on the obverse side a medallion of
gold in the centre, elliptical in form, bearing on its face the figure of a soldier
in Continental uniform, with musket slung; beneath, the figures 1775; the
medallion surrounded by thirteen raised gold stars of five points each upon a
border of dark blue enamel. On the reverse side, in the centre, a medallion
corresponding in form to that on the obverse, and also in gold, bearing on its
face the Houdon portrait of Washington in bas-relief, encircled by the legend,
'Sons of the Revolution;' beneath, the figures 1883; and upon the reverse
of the eagle the number of the badge to be engraved; the medallion to be
surrounded by a plain gold border, conforming in dimensions to the
obverse; the ribbon dark blue, ribbed and watered, edged with buff, one
and one-quarter inches wide, and one and one-half inches in displayed
length." [1]

[1] Extracts from the Constitution.

THE SOCIETY OF SONS OF THE AMERICAN REVOLUTION.

INSTITUTED 30TH APRIL, 1889.

" OBJECTS.

" To perpetuate the memory and the spirit of the men who achieved American Independence, by the encouragement of historical research in relation to the Revolution and the publication of its results, the preservation of documents and relics and of the records of the individual services of Revolutionary soldiers and patriots, and the promotion of celebrations of all patriotic anniversaries; to carry out the injunction of Washington in his farewell address to the American people, 'to promote, as an object of primary importance, institutions for the general diffusion of knowledge,' thus developing an enlightened public opinion, and affording to young and old such advantages as shall develop in them the largest capacity for performing the duties of American citizens; to cherish, maintain, and extend the institutions of American freedom; to foster true patriotism and love of country, and to aid in securing to mankind all the blessings of liberty."

FIG. 551.

" MEMBERSHIP.

" Any man is eligible for membership who is of the age of twenty-one years and who is descended from an ancestor who rendered material aid to the cause of American Independence as a soldier or a seaman, or a civil officer in one of the several Colonies or States, or as a recognized patriot, provided he shall be found worthy."

" INSIGNIA.

" The insignia of the Society shall comprise (1) a cross surmounted by an eagle in gold or silver, (2) a duplicate for the same in miniature. The cross shall be of silver, with four arms and eight white enamelled points, same size as Chevaliers' Cross of the Legion of Honor of France, with a gold medallion in the centre, bearing on the obverse a bust of Washington in profile, and on the reverse the figure of a Minute-Man, surrounded by a ribbon enamelled blue, with the motto 'Libertas et Patria' on the obverse, and the legend 'Sons of the American Revolution' on the reverse, both in letters of gold. The cross shall be surmounted by an eagle in gold or silver, and the whole decoration suspended from a ring of gold by a ribbon of deep blue with white edges. The duplicate shall have all the essential features of the cross, but shall be miniature in size."

GENERAL SOCIETY OF THE WAR OF 1812.

ORGANIZED 9TH JANUARY, 1854. INCORPORATED 19TH NOVEMBER, 1892.

" OBJECTS.

"To perpetuate the memory and spirit of the men who completed the work of the Revolution by the victories of the War of 1812; to encourage research in relation to this event and the publication of the same; to the establishment of a library and museum for the preservation of documents and relics relating to said war; care and burial of veterans of War of 1812, where it is necessary, and participation in and promotion of the celebration of the anniversaries of the great events of that war; to cherish, maintain, and extend the institutions of American freedom, and foster true patriotism and love of country."

FIG. 552.

" MEMBERSHIP.

"Any male person above the age of twenty-one (21) years, who participated in, or who is a lineal descendant of one who served during the War of 1812, in the army, navy, revenue-marine or privateer service of the United States."

" INSIGNIA.

"The insignia of the Society shall consist of a badge of gold, pendant from a ribbon. Said badge shall be in the form of a Maltese cross (emblematic of faith in the justice of our cause), between four (4) golden eagles (symbolizing the four sections—north, south, east and west of our common country), and resting upon an anchor of gold (representative of the American navy, by which so many glorious victories of the War of 1812 were achieved). The arms of the cross to be enameled in scarlet, with a white border, and to bear the insignia, in gold, of the four (4) arms of service (infantry, cavalry, artillery and naval), and in the centre thereof, a medallion of dark-blue enamel, with the figures 1812 thereon in gold, surrounded by a band of black enamel, bearing eighteen (18) stars in gold, representing the number of States of the Union during the period of conflict. The anchor and cross to be suspended from the ribbon by a ring of gold.

"The ribbon shall be of watered silk, dark-blue in the centre, with white and black stripes on the sides successively, and edged with scarlet; the entire ribbon to be one and one-half inches in width and the same dimensions in displayed length." [1]

AZTEC CLUB OF 1847.

FOUNDED 13TH OCTOBER, 1847.

" OBJECT.

"This Association formed and founded in the City of Mexico, in the year 1847, by officers of the United States Army, shall be continued in perpetuity as 'The Aztec Club of 1847,' with a view to cherish the memories and keep alive the traditions that cluster about the names of those officers who took part in the Mexican War of 1846, '47, and '48.

" MEMBERSHIP.

"*First.*—Those officers who inaugurated the Aztec Club in the City of Mexico on the 13th of October, 1847, numbering 160 members and the two honorary members named in Articles I. and IV. of the Constitution published in March, 1848; and

FIG. 553.

"*Second.*—Those officers who by resolution of 1871 became eligible to membership since that date, having served in some part of Mexico during the war with that country, and who have been or may here-after be elected members. The names of members admitted upon personal application will be enrolled as Primary Members on a list (Number *One*) to be ar-ranged permanently, in numerical series, in the order of date of admittance—not to be altered except by future *additions* or by *dismissals* for cause.

"*Third.*—To extend to the memory of comrades killed in battle in Mexico or who died of wounds received in Mexico prior to the formation of our Club, all the honorable distinctions pertaining to membership in the Club, it was resolved in 1883 that upon application by the eldest son or nearest lineal descendant of the officer so killed such son or lineal descendant may be eligible to membership as representing his dead relative. When such representative has been duly elected and qualified, the name of the dead officer and the battle where he was killed should be entered on List Number *One*, in a separate group with his representative, in the order of election.

"*Fourth.*—As provided in 1887, the son or nearest blood relative of any

---

[1] Extracts from the Constitution.

deceased officer who never himself applied for membership (though eligible thereto because of personal service in Mexico during the war) may make written application for admission as the representative of his father or blood relative. . . . If elected and qualified the name of such dead officer shall also be enrolled on List Number *One*, in the same numerical series, in a separate group, and in the order of the date of admittance of the lineal descendant.

"*Fifth.*—To provide for the continuance of the Club in conformity with the resolution of September, 1874, each primary member admitted upon personal application may nominate as his successor his son or a blood relative, who during the life of the Primary shall be known as an Associate Member, and entitled to all the privileges of the Club, except that of voting, and upon the death of the Primary shall be entitled as his representative to full membership. Should a Primary die without having named his successor, his son (first) or nearest blood relative (next) may, on written application, be nominated as his representative ; . . . but no one proposed for an Associate Member or as the representative of a deceased member shall be voted for until the Examining Committee shall report him eligible and qualified to join the Club. If minors are proposed, their names will be retained for future action until they attain their majority. . . . A Representative Member may present a blood relative of the Primary Member he represents as his associate, and, if elected, he will be entitled to the privileges of an Associate Member, and upon the death of the representative may himself become a Representative Member, and in like manner nominate as his associate the nearest living blood relative of the dead Primary Member, if there be one qualified to become an acceptable representative of said Primary. When no such lineal descendant of the Primary Member exists, the succession for such member of the Aztec Club will cease." [1]

The Military Order of the Loyal Legion of the United States.

INSTITUTED 15TH APRIL, 1865.

" OBJECTS.

"To cherish the memories and associations of the war waged in defence of the unity and indivisibility of the Republic ; strengthen the ties of fraternal fellowship and sympathy formed by companionship-in-arms ; advance the best interests of the soldiers and sailors of the United States, especially of those associated as companions of this Order, and extend all possible relief to their widows and children ; foster the cultivation of military and naval science ; enforce unqualified allegiance to the General Government ; protect the rights and liberties of American citizenship, and maintain National Honor, Union, and Independence.

---

[1] Extracts from the Constitution.

FIG. 554.

"*First Class.*—1st. Commissioned officers and honorably discharged commissioned officers of the United States Army, Navy, and Marine Corps, Regular or Volunteer, including officers of assimilated or corresponding rank by appointment of the Secretary of War or Navy, who were actually engaged in the suppression of the Rebellion prior to the 15th day of April 1865, and whose names appear in the Official Registers of the United States Army and Navy and of the Volunteer Force of the United States Army, or who served under the President's call of the fifteenth day of April, 1861 ; or who, having served as non-commissioned officers, warrant officers, or enlisted men during the War of the Rebellion, have since been commissioned as officers in the United States Army, Navy, or Marine Corps, or were commissioned as officers in the Volunteer Force prior to the twentieth day of August, 1866 ; and persons who, having served as non-commissioned officers, warrant officers, or enlisted men as aforesaid, shall have become eligible to membership by inheritance from officers not members of the Order, but who were eligible as such, who shall have died prior to the thirty-first day of December, 1892. Those elected under the provisions of this clause shall be designated Original Companions of the First Class. 2d. The eldest direct male lineal descendants, according to the rules of primogeniture, of deceased Original Companions of the First Class, and of officers not members of the Order, but who were eligible as such, who shall have died prior to the thirty-first day of December, 1892; and if there are no such descendants, then the male heirs of such deceased Companions or officers in the collateral branches of their families in the order of genealogical succession according to the rules of primogeniture, disregarding intervening female lines. Provided, however, *First*, That the inheritance shall in every case of succession be traced anew from the original founder of the membership in the Order, or deceased officer as aforesaid, and not otherwise, and shall be limited in cases of collateral succession to the brothers, and descendants of brothers and sisters, of such Original Companion or deceased officer; in cases of representation through females, the elder branches shall be preferred to the younger: *Second*, That any person eligible to membership by inheritance, or by renunciation of another, may, in writing, waive and renounce his right to such eligibility in favor of the person next entitled at the time of such renunciation, excepting that no person who is a direct lineal descendant of an Original Companion or deceased officer as aforesaid, shall be allowed to waive his right in favor of a collateral relative of such Original Companion or deceased officer: *Third*, That in case a Companion of the First Class or person already eligible to membership is next in the line of inheritance from a deceased Original Companion or officer as aforesaid, the eligibility to membership derived from such deceased Companion or officer shall devolve upon the person next entitled other than such living Companion or person already eligible or the direct lineal descendants of either, but any Original Companion having no direct lineal descendants may by writing filed with the Recorder of the Commandery in which he may be enrolled, or by his last will and testament, or instrument in the nature thereof, nominate for life his successor from among his male heirs within the said limits in the collateral branches of his family: *Fourth*, That in cases of inheritance by persons under the age of twenty-one years the right of succession to eligibility to membership, or of renunciation thereof, shall remain in abeyance until they shall attain that age: *Fifth*, That the resignation, expulsion, or forfeiture of membership of a Companion who has attained such membership by inheritance shall only work as a waiver of his rights in favor of the next person in the line of inheritance from the Original Companion or deceased officer as aforesaid: *Sixth*, That no right of inheritance shall be derived from any Original Companion who has been expelled from the Order and not reinstated, but, in case an Original Companion shall have resigned or been dropped from the roll for non-payment of dues, his successor may be allowed by a vote of a majority of the members of the Commandery present at any stated meeting to revive the said right: *Seventh*, That such descendants or collateral heirs shall have first filed affidavits setting forth the facts upon which eligibility to membership is claimed.

" *Second Class.*—The eldest sons of living Original Companions of the First Class who shall have attained the age of twenty-one years. Upon the death of his father, a Companion of the Second Class shall become a Companion of the First Class, and be so announced to the Order by circular. Companions of the Second Class shall have the right to vote in all cases except in elections for membership in the First Class.

" *Third Class.*—Gentlemen who in civil life, during the Rebellion, were specially distinguished for conspicuous and consistent loyalty to the National Government, and were active and eminent in maintaining the supremacy of the same; but the number of Companions of the Third Class in any Commandery shall not exceed the ratio of one to thirty-three of those of the First Class. Provided, however, That no Companion of the Third Class shall be elected after the fifteenth day of April, 1890."

" INSIGNIA.

" The Insignia of the Order shall consist of the Badge pendant by a link and a ring of gold from the ribbon. *Badge.*—Obverse—A cross of eight points, gold, cantoned with rays of gold, forming a star—its long diameter one and three-tenths inches, its short diameter eight-tenths of an inch. The cross enameled, azure, charged with a smaller cross of like proportions, enameled white and edged with gold. In the centre thereof, within a circle four-tenths of an inch in diameter, enameled gules, the National Eagle displayed gold. On the circle, gold, one-tenth of an inch wide, in relievo, the motto, LEX REGIT ARMA TUENTUR."[1]

SOCIETY OF THE ARMY OF THE TENNESSEE.

ORGANIZED 14TH APRIL, 1865.

" OBJECTS.

" To keep alive and preserve that kindly and cordial feeling which has been one of the characteristics of this Army during its career in the service, and which has given it such harmony of action, and contributed in no small degree to its glorious achievements in our country's cause.

FIG. 555.

" The fame and glory of all the officers belonging to this Army who have fallen either on the field of battle or in their line of duty shall be a sacred trust to this Society, which shall cause proper memorials of their services to be collected and preserved, and thus transmit their names with honor to posterity."

" MEMBERSHIP.

" Officers who served with honor in said Army."

" INSIGNIA.

" SOCIETY OF THE ARMY OF THE TENNESSEE.
" 4th Meeting.   Louisville, Ky., Nov. 17, 1869.

" Report of Committee on . . . Badge :
" The undersigned were appointed at the last meeting a committee to . . . adopt and report a device for badge of the Society, and to incorporate in such device a representation of the corps badge of each corps that served in the Army of the Tennessee.

" The Committee accordingly now report . . . a device for a badge.

" It was found impracticable to incorporate the entire badge of either the 13th or 15th Corps with the others. Upon the suggestion of members of these corps the central portion of their respective badges was taken, the

[1] Extracts from the Constitution.

cartridge-box alone for the one, and the figure 13, within a circle, for the other. . . .

"We are preparing a badge, not for an existing army, but for a society of members of a disbanded army, already returned to and merged in the body of the nation. Hence the device finally adopted, and which is now reported, represents the corps badges blended with the eagle, the emblem of the nation.

*   *   *   *   *   *   *   *   *   *

"This report and badge were adopted. 13th Corps, 13; 15th Corps, cartridge-box; 16th Corps, Maltese cross in circle; 17th Corps, arrow. The above were the badges used by the corps during the war." [1]

SOCIETY OF THE ARMY OF THE POTOMAC.

ORGANIZED 5TH JULY, 1869.

"OBJECTS.

"To cherish the memories and associations of the Army of the Potomac; to strengthen the ties of fraternal fellowship and sympathy formed from companionship in that Army; to perpetuate the name and fame of those who have fallen either on the field of battle or in the line of duty with that Army; to collect and preserve the record of its great achievements, its numerous and well-contested battles, its campaigns, marches, and skirmishes." [2]

FIG. 556.

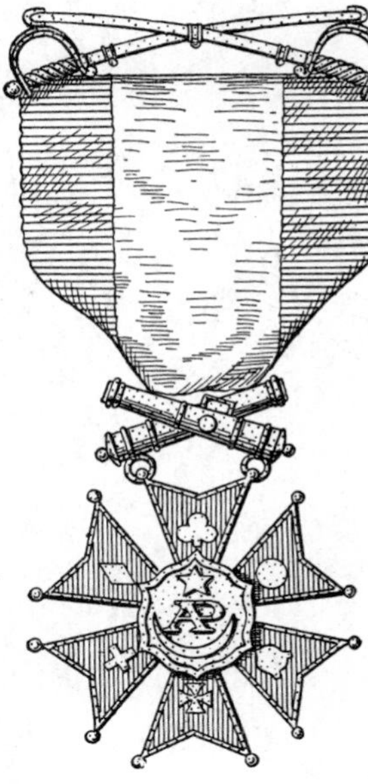

"MEMBERSHIP.

"Its membership is composed of officers and men who served with honor in the Army of the Potomac, and were honorably discharged therefrom, or remained in service in the regular Army; and also includes officers and men serving on vessels which, during the war, were in active and immediate co-operation with the Army of the Potomac, and who were honorably discharged therefrom or remained in the regular service.

"INSIGNIA.

"The cross is of six arms of branches, red enamelled to represent the first of the national colors—red. On each branch and in the centre are the insignia of the several corps of the Army of the Potomac, to wit: 1st, 2nd, 3rd, 5th, 6th, 9th, 11th, and 12th, and the crossed cannon and sabres from which the badge is sus-

---

[1] Extracts from the Constitution.
[2] Extract from the Constitution.

pended represent the artillery and cavalry corps respectively. The whole suspended from a white and blue national tri-color." [1]

GRAND ARMY OF THE REPUBLIC.
ORGANIZED MARCH, 1866. FIRST POST 6TH APRIL, 1866.
" OBJECTS.

" 1. To preserve and strengthen those kind and fraternal feelings which bind together the soldiers, sailors, and marines who united to suppress the late Rebellion, and to perpetuate the memory and history of the dead.

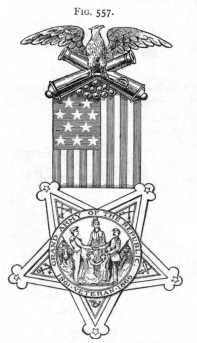

FIG. 557.

" 2. To assist such former comrades in arms as need help and protection, and to extend needful aid to the widows and orphans of those who have fallen.

" 3. To maintain true allegiance to the United States of America, based upon a paramount respect for, and fidelity to, its Constitution and Laws; to discountenance whatever tends to weaken loyalty, incites to insurrection, treason, or rebellion, or in any manner impairs the efficiency and permanency of our free institutions; and to encourage the spread of universal liberty, equal rights, and justice to all men."

" MEMBERSHIP.

" Soldiers and Sailors of the United States Army, Navy, or Marine Corps, who served between April 12th, 1861, and April 9th, 1865, in the war for the suppression of the Rebellion, and those having been honorably discharged therefrom after such service, and of such State regiments as were called into active service and subject to the orders of U. S. General Officers, between the dates mentioned, shall be eligible to membership in the Grand Army of the Republic. No person shall be eligible to membership who has at any time borne arms against the United States." [2]

INSIGNIA.

The following description of the official badge is from the report of the committee to the National Encampment at New Haven, 1873, with amendments adopted at St. Louis, September 30, 1887:

[1] Letter of General Rufus King.
[2] Extracts from the Constitution.

" That this official badge consists of a miniature strap and ribbon, to which shall be pendent the bronze star of the membership badge; that this strap be one and one-half inches in length, one-half inch in width, enameled, with a border one-eighth of an inch in width, of gold or gilt, and on it to be the insignia of official position in the Grand Army of the Republic, making use of the familiar star, eagle, leaf, and bar of the old service; that the field in enamel be, for the National and Department officers, black; for Post officers, dark blue.

" That the ribbon be one and one-half inches in length in the clear, and one and one-fourth inches in width; to be composed of the flag, as on membership badges, with a border of one-quarter of an inch on each side, the border to be in color—for National officers, buff; for Department officers, red (cherry), and for Post officers, light blue.

" That this badge be worn conspicuously on the left breast of the coat.

" That to distinguish the different departments, a miniature shield in gold or gilt, with a Coat of Arms of the State, may be worn pendent to the strap."

SOCIETY OF THE ARMY OF THE CUMBERLAND.

ORGANIZED 6TH FEBRUARY, 1868.

" OBJECT.

" To perpetuate the memory of the fortunes and achievements of the Army of the Cumberland; to preserve that unanimity of loyal sentiment and that kind and cordial feeling which has been an eminent characteristic of this army, and the main element of the power and success of its efforts in behalf of the cause of the Union. The history and glory of the officers and soldiers belonging to this army, who have fallen either on the field of battle or otherwise in the line of their duty, shall be a permanent trust to this Society, and every effort shall be made to collect and preserve the proper memorials of their services, to inscribe their names upon the roll of honor, and to transmit their fame to posterity. It shall also be the object and bounden duty of this Society to relieve, as far as possible, the families of such deceased officers and soldiers, when in indigent circumstances, either by the voluntary contribution of the members, or in such other manner as they may determine, when the cases are brought to their attention. This provision shall also hereafter apply to

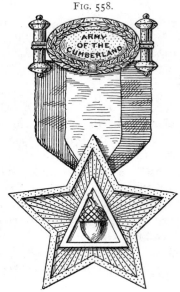

FIG. 558.

the suffering families of those members of the Society who may in the future be called hence, and the welfare of the soldier's widow and orphan shall forever be a holy trust in the hands of his surviving comrades."

" MEMBERSHIP.

" Composed of officers and soldiers who served with honor in the Army of the Cumberland."

" INSIGNIA.

" 1. *Star.*—Five-pointed. Suspended, point upward. Frosted, gold or silver, with polished edge one-twenty-fourth of an inch wide. Points of star blunt or very slightly rounded. Radius of circle of outer points, nine-tenths of an inch; of inner parts, four-and-a-half-tenths of an inch. 2. *Triangle.*— In centre of star, point upward. Frosted, gold or silver, with polished edge one-twenty-fourth of an inch wide, elevated above star one-thirty-second of an inch, or engraved if wearer chooses. Triangle of such size as to leave space around it in frosted part of the star. 3. *Acorn.*—In centre of triangle. Polished, gold or silver, with frosted cap and polished stem, in alto relievo, or engraved. Acorn of such size as to leave space around it in frosted part of triangle. Enameled natural color, if the wearer chooses. 4. *Ribbon.*—Silk— Red, White, and Blue—three-quarters of an inch wide, one and one-fourth inches long. 5. *Pin.*—Concave, oval, five-tenths of an inch long, two-and-a-half-tenths of an inch wide. Frosted, gold or silver, with polished edge raised. Laurel wreath surrounding oval, which is supported at both sides by pillars. Oval to be one-sixteenth of an inch above wreath, with ' Army of the Cumberland' engraved therein. Entire oval between pillars seven-and-a-half-tenths of an inch long." [1]

NAVAL ORDER OF THE UNITED STATES.
ORGANIZED 10TH NOVEMBER, 1890.
" OBJECTS.

" *Whereas,* Many of the principal battles and famous victories of the several wars in which the United States has participated were fought and achieved by the Naval forces,

" *Whereas,* It is well and fitting that the illustrious deeds of the great Naval commanders, their companion officers in arms, and their subordinates in the wars of the United States should be forever honored and respected;—

" *Therefore,* Entertaining the most exalted admiration of the undying achievements of the Navy, we, the survivors and descendants of participants of those memorable conflicts, have joined ourselves together and have instituted the ' Naval Order of the United States,' that we may transmit to our latest posterity their glorious names and memories; and to encourage research and publication of data pertaining to Naval art and science,

[1] Extracts from the Constitution.

and to establish libraries in which to preserve all documents, rolls, books, portraits and relics relating to the Navy and its heroes at all times."[1]

FIG. 559.

" MEMBERSHIP.

"The Companions of the Order shall be of Three Classes :

"*First Class.*—Commissioned officers, Midshipmen and Naval Cadets, in actual service in the United States Navy, Marine Corps, Revenue or Privateer services during the wars, or in face of the enemy in any engagement, in which the Navy of the United States has participated and who resigned or were discharged with honor, or who are still in the service, *provided*, however, that this clause shall not be so construed as to include officers who at any time have borne arms against the Government of the United States.

"The eldest lineal male representatives, or in default thereof, then one such collateral representative as may be deemed worthy, of *deceased* commissioned officers, Midshipmen, and Naval Cadets in actual service in the Navy, Marine Corps, Revenue or Privateer services under the authority of any of the thirteen original Colonies or States, or of the Continental Congress during the War of the Revolution, or of the United States during the War with France, the War with Tripoli, the War of 1812, the War with Mexico, the Civil War, or in face of the enemy in any engagement in which the Navy of the United States has participated, and who resigned or were discharged with honor, or who were killed in the service.

"The admission and succession to membership in the First Class shall descend to the heir male, unless, for satisfactory reasons, another be chosen, in which case the membership shall extend to the life only of the Companion so elected, and at his decease the right to representation shall revert to the then existing heir male.

"*Second Class.*—Lineal male descendants of commissioned officers, Midshipmen and Naval Cadets, who performed service in the Navy, Marine Corps, Revenue or Privateer services, as aforesaid.

"*Third Class.*—Enlisted men who have received the United States Naval Medal of Honor for bravery in face of the enemy may be enrolled, exempt from fees and dues, by the Commanderies of the States in which they reside."[2]

[1] Preamble of the Constitution.
[2] Article III. Constitution General Commandery.

" INSIGNIA.

" The Insignia of the Order shall consist of a gold Cross pattée, one and one-quarter inches in diameter, arms of blue enamel edged with gold.

" CROSS.

" OBVERSE: In the center on a circle of red enamel five-sixteenths of an inch in diameter, an eagle, wings extended, resting on an anchor surrounded by thirteen stars of five points, all of gold, representing in substance the insignia of the Navy of the United States; the whole encircled by a band of white enamel one-eighth of an inch wide, displaying in letters of gold the motto of the Order, ' Fidelitas et Patria.'

" REVERSE: The Cross as above described. In the center on a circle of red enamel five-sixteenths of an inch in diameter shall appear in gold the insignia of the United States Marine Corps, the whole encircled by a band of white enamel one-eighth of an inch wide bearing in letters of gold the legend, ' Naval Order of the United States.'

" The Cross shall be worn on the left breast suspended by a ribbon of heavy ribbed white silk one and one-half inches wide, with a red center three-fourths of an inch wide, the whole an inch and a half in displayed length.

" Officers of State Commanderies shall wear the Cross suspended by the ribbon of the Order around the neck.

" STAR.

" Officers of the General Commandery shall wear on the left breast a Star of silver of two and one-quarter inches in diameter, on which shall rest the obverse of the Cross as above described, surmounted by a Naval crown of gold and enamel; and a Cordon of heavy ribbed white silk ribbon four inches wide, with a red center two inches wide, worn from the left shoulder to the right hip, and finished with a bow-knot of the ribbon of the Order one and one-half inches wide, from which the Cross may be suspended."

SOCIETY OF COLONIAL DAMES OF AMERICA.[2]

ORGANIZED APRIL 8, 1891.

" OBJECTS.

" To collect manuscripts, traditions, relics, and mementoes of by-gone days for preservation, . . . commemorate the success of the American Revolution and consequent birth of our glorious Republic; diffuse healthful and intelligent information in whatever concerns the past and tends to create popular interest in American history, and with a true spirit of patriotism seek

---

[1] Article XIII.

[2] Since securing information in reference to the war societies, the author has deemed it important to add those composed of women, in view of the heroic services rendered by women in the Revolutionary War.

to inspire genuine love of country in every heart within its range of influence, and to teach the young that it is a sacred obligation to do justice and honour to heroic ancestors whose ability, valour, sufferings, and achievements are beyond all praise."

FIG. 560.

"MEMBERS.

"Women who are descended in their own right from some ancestor of worthy life who came to reside in an American Colony prior to 1750, which ancestor or some one of his descendants, being a lineal ascendant of the applicant, shall have rendered efficient service to his country during the Colonial period, either in the founding of a commonwealth, or of an institution which has survived and developed into importance, or who shall have held important position in the Colonial government, and who by distinguished services shall have contributed to the founding of this great and powerful nation. Services rendered after 1783 not recognized."

"INSIGNIA.

"It consists of a round disc, with centre of light blue enamel, and a figure of a Colonial Dame in gold, modeled in relief on the same. Around the centre of blue enamel is a circle of white enamel with the title of the Society, 'Colonial Dames of America,' in gold letters flush. Surmounting this is the modeled figure of an eagle in gold, and diverging from the disc are twenty gold rays arranged in four groups of five each. The three centre rays in each group are surmounted by stars of blue enamel, these, with a similar star placed immediately below the central disc, being emblematic of the thirteen original Colonies. On the reverse side of the Insignia is the motto, 'Virtutes Majorem Filiæ Conservant.' It is worn suspended (from a gold bar, on which is the name of the State) by a silk ribbon of the Continental colours used by General Washington and his staff, blue and yellow. This ribbon is one and one-half inches wide, the central section of blue being one inch, with a section one-quarter of an inch wide of yellow on each side." [1]

SOCIETY OF DAUGHTERS OF THE REVOLUTION.
ORGANIZED 9TH SEPTEMBER, 1891.

"OBJECTS.

"To keep alive among its members and their descendants, and throughout the community, the patriotic spirit of the men and women who achieved

---

[1] Extracts from the Constitution.

Fig. 561.

American Independence; to collect and secure for preservation the manuscript rolls, records and other documents relating to the war of the American Revolution, and provide a place for their preservation and a fund for their purchase; to encourage historical research in relation to such Revolution and to publish its results; to promote and assist in the proper celebration of prominent events relating to or connected with the War of the Revolution; to promote social intercourse and the feeling of fellowship among its members; 'and provide a home for and furnish assistance to such as may be impoverished, when it is in their power to do so.'"

" MEMBERSHIP.

" Any woman above the age of eighteen years shall be eligible to membership in the ' Daughters of the Revolution,' who is a *lineal* descendant from an ancestor who as a military or naval or marine officer, soldier, sailor or marine in actual service under the authority of any of the Thirteen Colonies or States, or of the Continental Congress, and remaining always loyal to such authority, or a descendant of one who signed the Declaration of Independence, or of one who as a member of the Continental Congress or of the Congress of any of the Colonies or States, or as an official appointed by or under the authority of any such representative bodies actually assisting in the establishment of American Independence by service rendered during the War of the Revolution, becoming thereby liable to conviction of treason against the Government of Great Britain, but remaining always loyal to the authority of the Colonies or States, shall be eligible to membership in this Society." [1]

INSIGNIA.

The insignia may be described as follows:

Paly of thirteen, azure and or, on a chief of the first as many mullets, argent.

CREST: *Above a scroll azure bearing the legend " Daughters of the Revolution" argent, an eagle displayed or, grasping in the dexter claw an olive branch, and in the sinister a bunch of four arrows, below the shield the motto* " Liberty, Home and Country" and " 1776–1891."

SOCIETY OF DAUGHTERS OF THE AMERICAN REVOLUTION.

ORGANIZED 11TH OCTOBER, 1890.

" OBJECTS.

" To perpetuate the memory and the spirit of the men and women who achieved American Independence, by the acquisition and protection of historical spots and the erection of monuments; by the encouragement of historical

---

[1] Extracts from the Constitution.

research in relation to the Revolution and the publication of its results; by the preservation of documents and relics, and of the records of the individual services of Revolutionary soldiers and patriots, and by the promotion of celebrations of all patriotic anniversaries.

Fig. 562.

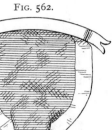

"To carry out the injunction of Washington in his farewell address to the American people, 'to promote, as an object of primary importance, institutions for the general diffusion of knowledge,' thus developing an enlightened public opinion, and affording to young and old such advantages as shall develop in them the largest capacity for performing the duties of American citizens.

"To cherish, maintain, and extend the institutions of American freedom, to foster true patriotism and love of country, and to aid in securing for mankind all the blessings of liberty."

"MEMBERSHIP.

"Any woman may be eligible for membership who is of the age of eighteen years, and who is descended from an ancestor who, with unfailing loyalty, rendered material aid to the cause of Independence as a recognized patriot, as a soldier or sailor, or as a civil officer in one of the several Colonies or States, or of the United Colonies or States; or from the mother of such a patriot; provided that the applicant shall be acceptable to the Society."

"INSIGNIA.

"The Insignia of the Society shall consist of a badge in the form of a spinning-wheel and distaff, to be worn on ceremonial occasions upon a bow of ribbon. The wheel is seven-eighths of an inch in diameter and of gold, with thirteen spokes and a field of light blue enamel upon its tire bearing the name of the Society in letters of gold. Upon its outer rim opposite the ends of the spokes are thirteen stars, which may be set with precious stones at the discretion of the owner. Underneath the wheel is a golden distaff one and one-half inches long filled with silver flax. Upon the back of the wheel the registration number of the owner shall be engraved, and her name may be added. The ribbon to be worn with the wheel is dark blue with a white edge, ribbed and watered, following the colors of Washington's staff. A rosette of the prescribed ribbon attached to a stick pin may be worn as an informal badge upon ordinary occasions."[1]

[1] Extracts from the Constitution.

CHAPTER VII.

PARTS OF AN ACHIEVEMENT.

ESPECIAL attention is directed to the several parts of a coat of arms, each individual part being known by its distinct name, and the entire composition as a *Coat of Arms* or *Achievement*. The descriptions are preliminary, and a fuller treatment will be found in later chapters.

FIG. 563.

SHIELD.

The Shield or Escutcheon, the most important part of a knight's defensive equipment, is the object upon which armorial devices are displayed (Fig. 563).

FIG. 564.

HELMET.

The Helmet or Helme was the armor for the head, and varied in different ages in form and material (Fig. 564).

FIG. 565.

MANTLING.

The Mantle or Mantling was attached to the helmet, and hung down over the armor to protect it from the weather (Fig. 565).

WREATH.

FIG. 566.

The Wreath. Bandeau, or Torse was composed of two rolls of silk or leather, of different colors, twisted together. It encircled the helmet and supported the crest (Fig. 566).

250

FIG. 567.

CREST.

Crests were borne upon helmets to distinguish military leaders and knights when engaged in battle (Fig. 567).

MOTTO.

FIG. 568.

The Motto was originally a word or sentence, which formed a war-cry. In later times it was of a religious or patriotic nature, or an allusion to the arms or crest of the bearer (Fig. 568).

FIG. 569.

SUPPORTERS.

Supporters are those figures placed upon either side of a shield as if in the act of supporting it (Fig. 569).

FIG. 570.

CROWN.

The Crown is the distinguishing ornament of kings (Fig. 570).

Royal crown.

FIG. 571.

CORONET.

The Coronet is worn by princes and nobles on state occasions (Fig. 571).

Coronet (Duke).

CHAPTER VIII.

THE SHIELD.—DIVIDING AND ORNAMENTAL LINES.

The *Shield* or *Escutcheon*, the name given to the main article of a warrior's equipment, was among the earliest of defensive arms. Shields were at first of doubled leather only, afterwards of wicker-work covered with metal, and finally of tough wood covered with leather or metal, or of metal entirely, and even of gold and silver.

The shapes and sizes varied in different ages according to the taste or strength of the bearer, and for some time before a complete system of heraldry was established they were decorated with various devices, assumed at his option.

As shields were prized very highly, it naturally followed that they should be decorated after they were proven strong and durable and a valuable means of defence. Originally the skins were stained or the metal beaten into odd shapes. Shields were also inlaid, and studded with nails of precious metal, and later the device of each warrior or knight was painted upon his shield and served to make him conspicuous and easily identified at all times.

POINTS OF THE SHIELD.

In Fig. 572, 1 is the dexter side; 2, the sinister side; 3, the chief; and 4, the base of the shield.

FIG. 572.

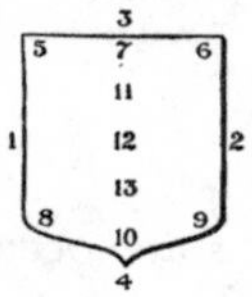

The Points of the Escutcheon or Shield, used to describe the positions of charges, are shown in the same figure: 5, dexter chief; 6, sinister chief; 7, middle chief; 8, dexter base; 9, sinister base; 10, middle base; 11, honor point; 12, fesse point; 13, nombril point.

Particular care should be given to these positions, that in blazoning the plainest description may be made of the location of each device which is borne upon the shield, since a change in the position of one charge changes the entire arms. A coat of arms with a *lion in chief* differs essentially from one with a *lion in base*.

The heraldic shield always bears its charge upon its face or external surface, and consequently the *dexter* and *sinister* sides of the shield itself are those which would severally cover the right or left side of a warrior holding the shield in front of his person. The *dexter* side of an heraldic composition or object is, therefore, opposite to the left hand of an observer, and the *sinister* opposite to his right hand.

The terms *dexter* and *sinister* are always used in heraldry.

The whole surface of the *shield* is termed the *Field*.

252

The shape of the shield may be entirely determined by the preference of the designer, but the simple forms are more desirable, and it is well to avoid the fanciful and irregular outlines of the shields so frequently appearing in the monumental architecture of the fourteenth century. When a shield has a notch cut in the dexter chief as if to form a place for a spear to pass through, it is said to be *à bouche*, but this form is not advised for decorative purposes.

It would be well to remark here that the numerous ornate and fanciful decorations and mantlings which are found surrounding the shield in painted or engraved coats of arms are entirely a matter of the artist's fancy, and *form no part whatever of the hereditary coat of arms*. The decorator, however, should be careful, as a matter of taste and technical accuracy, to confine himself in such mantling or decoration to true heraldic tinctures, remembering that while much depends upon the beauty of these ornamentations, much more depends upon absolute correctness.

PARTITION OR DIVIDING LINES.

In ancient times the surface of the shield was generally decorated with one color, but when heraldry became a distinct science, it was necessary to devise a certain system by which the shield could be decorated, in order to permit of various combinations, so that each knight might have his bearings distinct and different from any others. While shields are sometimes of one metal, color, or fur, they are often of more than one, and in this latter case are divided by a line or lines running across the surface or dividing it in a particular direction. The shield was formerly blazoned as "*parted*" or "*party per pale,*" "*party per fesse,*" etc., but this form is now generally reduced to *per pale, per fesse*, etc., as follows:

Fig. 573.

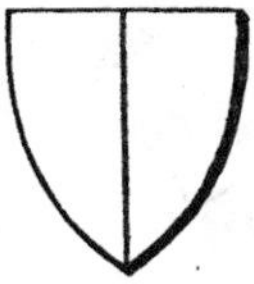

Fig. 574.

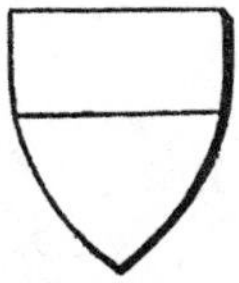

Per Pale. Divided by a perpendicular line (Fig. 573).

Per Fesse. Divided by a horizontal line through the middle (Fig. 574).

Fig. 575.

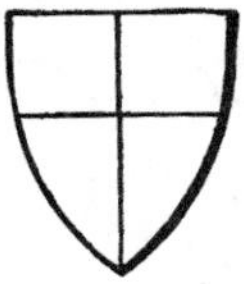

Fig. 576.

Per Cross or *Quarterly.* Divided by a perpendicular and a horizontal line crossing at the fesse point (Fig. 575).

Per Bend. Divided by a diagonal line from dexter chief to sinister base (Fig. 576).

Fig. 577.

Fig. 578.

Per Bend Sinister. Divided by a diagonal line from sinister chief to dexter base (Fig. 577).

Per Saltire. Divided by a diagonal dexter and a diagonal sinister line crossing at the centre of the shield (Fig. 578).

FIG. 579.

Per Chevron.   Divided by two lines rising from the dexter and sinister base and meeting at the fesse point (Fig. 579).

FIG. 580.

FIG. 581.

Quarterly. When a shield is divided into equal parts by lines drawn through it at right angles, it is said to be quarterly of that number, whether of four parts or more; the illustration is described as *quarterly of eight* (Fig. 580).

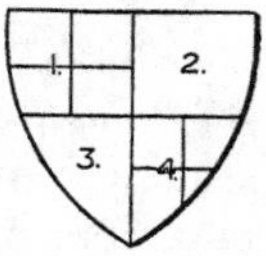

Quarterly quartered. When a coat of arms is borne with four or more quarterings, and any one or more of these quarterings are again divided into two or more coats, then such a quarter is termed a grand quarter.   In the example the grand quarters are indicated by figures 1 and 4 (Fig. 581).

ORNAMENTAL LINES.

Dividing and border lines are straight unless otherwise described, but they frequently appear curved, as in the forms shown in Figs. 582 to 591, inclusive.

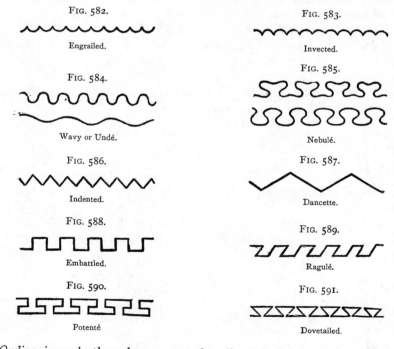

FIG. 582.

Engrailed.

FIG. 583.

Invected.

FIG. 584.

Wavy or Undé.

FIG. 585.

Nebulé.

FIG. 586.

Indented.

FIG. 587.

Dancette.

FIG. 588.

Embattled.

FIG. 589.

Ragulé.

FIG. 590.

Potenté

FIG. 591.

Dovetailed.

Ordinaries and other charges are often formed of these lines : a *Bend* may be *indented ;* a *Chevron, nebulé ;* a *Fesse, embattled ;* a *Cross, engrailed,* etc. In *engrailed* the teeth enter the field, in *invected* they enter the charge.

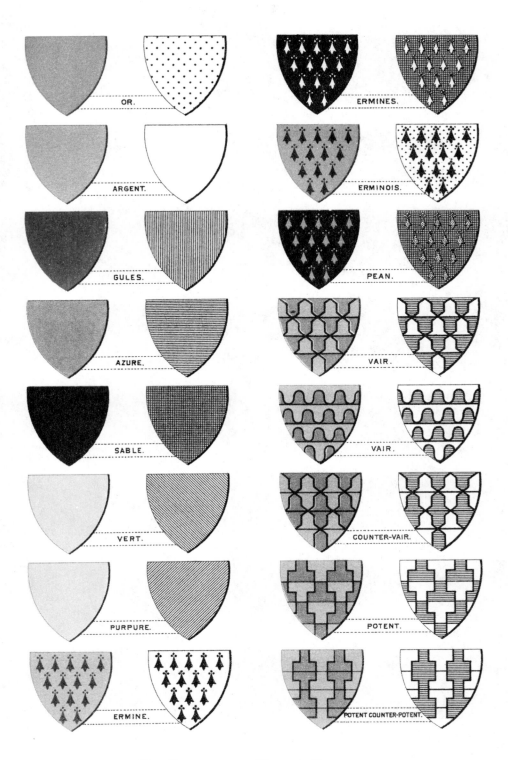

OR.

ARGENT.

GULES.

AZURE.

SABLE.

VERT.

PURPURE.

ERMINE.

ERMINES.

ERMINOIS.

PEAN.

VAIR.

VAIR.

COUNTER-VAIR.

POTENT.

POTENT COUNTER-POTENT.

THE TINCTURES AND FURS OF HERALDRY.

[See inside front cover for color plate]

CHAPTER IX.

THE TINCTURES AND FURS.

The Heraldic Tinctures comprise two metals and five colors, and are as follows:

METALS.	HERALDIC TERM.	ABBREVIATION.
Gold . .	Or . . .	Or
Silver . .	Argent . . .	Arg.
COLORS.		
Blue . .	Azure . . .	Az.
Red . .	Gules . . .	Gu.
Black . .	Sable . . .	Sa.
Green . .	Vert . . .	Vert
Purple . .	Purpure . .	Purp.

Two other colors, *Tenné* (orange) and *Sanguine* (color of cold blood), are allowed by some heralds, but are not seen in English coats of arms.

Charges or Crests represented in the natural colors of the objects delineated are denominated " proper," abbreviated " ppr."

All tinctures when correctly engraved or designed (unless in proper colors) are known by points and lines, thus:

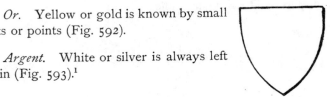

FIG. 592.

FIG. 593.

Or. Yellow or gold is known by small dots or points (Fig. 592).

Argent. White or silver is always left plain (Fig. 593).[1]

FIG. 594.

FIG. 595.

Gules. Red is expressed by lines extending from top to bottom (Fig. 594).

Azure. Blue is indicated by lines extending from side to side (Fig. 595).

[1] In proper colors Argent may be represented by silver or white.

255

FIG. 596.

FIG. 597.

Sable. Black is expressed by horizontal and perpendicular lines crossing each other (Fig. 596).

Vert. Green is indicated by diagonal lines extending from the dexter to the sinister side of the shield (Fig. 597).

FIG. 598.

Purpure. Purple is known by diagonal lines extending from the sinister to the dexter side. This tincture is not frequently used (Fig. 598).

TRICKING.

FIG. 599.

Another method of designating the tinctures in coats of arms is called "Tricking." This method is employed by artists and designers in roughly indicating the correct tinctures of all the parts of an achievement (Fig. 599).

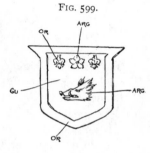

FURS.

The introduction of Furs into heraldry probably arose from the ancient custom of covering shields with the skins of beasts. Furs were also used for lining robes and garments of state. The Furs are indicated as follows:

FIG. 600.

FIG. 601.

Ermine. Black spots on a white field (Fig. 600).

Ermines. White spots on a black field (Fig. 601).

FIG. 602.

FIG. 603.

Erminois. Black spots on a gold field (Fig. 602).

Pean. Gold spots on a black field (Fig. 603).

FIG. 604.

FIG. 605.

Vair. White and blue, represented by figures of little bells or cups, ranged in a line so that the base white is opposite the base blue. Vair is said to have originated from a small beast, having a white belly and a blue-gray back, called Varus (Figs. 604, 605).

FIG. 606.

FIG. 607.

Counter-Vair. The same as *Vair*, except that the bells or cups of the same tincture are placed base against base and point against point (Fig. 606).

Potent is formed by a number of figures resembling crutch heads arranged in the same manner as *Vair* (Fig. 607).

FIG. 608.

Counter-Potent. The Potents are arranged as the cups are in *Counter-Vair* (Fig. 608).

Erminites and *Vair-en-Point* are mentioned by some heralds, but are seldom seen.

The former is similar to Ermine, but has the addition of a red hair on each side of the spots.

In Vair-en-Point, the bells are arranged with the bases in the upper line, resting upon the points of those beneath.

Vair, Counter-Vair, Potent, and Counter-Potent are always *Argent* and *Azure* unless otherwise named, in which case, if the *field* were *Or* and the bells *Vert*, it would have to be blazoned *Vairy, or and vert.*

In all cases metals precede colors unless otherwise described.

The more thoroughly to acquaint the student with the system of indicating the tinctures, they are shown in lines and proper colors in the plate.

CHAPTER X.

ORDINARIES AND THEIR DIMINUTIVES, SUBORDINARIES, AND COMBINATIONS.[1]

ORDINARIES are the earliest devices of mediæval heraldry, and derive their name from their ordinary or frequent use. They may have originated from the strips of wood or metal fastened upon the shield to add to its strength, and several are said to represent a sash or belt. While the examples show them to be formed of straight lines, they are also often formed of the various ornamental lines.

The Chief, the Bar, the Pale, the Bend, the Bend Sinister, and *the Chevron*

FIG. 609.

have diminutives which are described in regular order with the ordinaries themselves.

The Chief (Fig. 609) contains in depth the upper third part of the field; it may be borne in the same composition with any other ordinary except the Fesse. The diminutive of the Chief is the *Fillet*, one-fourth the width of the Chief, of which it always occupies the lowest portion.

FIG. 610.

FIG. 611.

The Fesse is of the same size and shape as the Chief, and differs from that ordinary only in its position in the field of the shield, of which it always occupies the horizontal central third part (Fig. 610). The Fesse may be surmounted by a Pale or a Bend (Fig. 611).

The Bar is like the Fesse, but its width is one-fifth instead of one-third of the field (Fig. 612). The Bar may be placed *horizontally* in any part of the field, except absolutely in chief or in base. A single Bar never appears in heraldic compositions without some other ordinary. The two diminutives of

FIG. 612.   FIG. 613.   FIG. 614.

---

[1] The examples are designed in black and white for the sake of distinctness, and may be blazoned argent and sable. The indications of tinctures appear in the examples of blazoning (Figs. 770 to 841, inclusive).

258

the Bar are the *Closet* (Fig. 613) and the *Barrulet* (Fig. 614), which are respectively one-half and one-fourth of the Bar itself. When either of these diminutives is placed on each side of a Fesse.or Bar, the ordinary is said to be *Cotised.*

The Pale (Fig. 615), like the Chief and the Fesse, occupies one-third of the field, but its position is vertical and always in the centre. The two di-

FIG. 615.   FIG. 616.   FIG. 617.

minutives of the Pale are the *Pallet* (Fig. 616) and the *Endorse* (Fig. 617), which are respectively one-half and one-fourth of its width.

FIG. 618.

The Cross may be defined as a combination of the Fesse with the Pale. When charged, the Cross occupies about one-third of the field, but otherwise it occupies only one-fifth of the field. It is always plain, unless otherwise specified (Fig. 618).

The Bend is formed by two parallel lines, equidistant from the Fesse Point, drawn diagonally from the dexter chief to the sinister base. When charged, this ordinary contains one-third, but when plain, one-fifth part of the field (Fig. 619).

The Bendlet (Fig. 620), which is one-half the Bend, and the *Cost* or *Cotise* (Fig. 621), which is one-quarter of the Bend, are the diminutives, and another

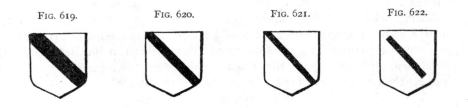

FIG. 619.   FIG. 620.   FIG. 621.   FIG. 622.

diminutive, called the *Riband* or *Ribbon*, is formed by cutting off the ends of the Cotise (Fig. 622).

Charges set on a Bend are placed bend-wise; that is, they slope with the Bend.

Two uncharged Bends can appear on one shield. When a Bend appears between two Cotises it is said to be *Cotised.*

When a Bend issues from the sinister, instead of the dexter chief, it is called a *Bend Sinister* (Fig. 623). This is frequently seen in French and

German heraldry, but avoided by English heralds, possibly because it has popularly been confused with the *Baton Sinister*.

FIG. 623.   FIG. 624.   FIG. 625.

A noted London authority thus writes under date of December 23, 1893:

" The *Bar* Sinister, properly speaking, the Bend Sinister, though sometimes it is reduced to a Baton Sinister, is often used as a difference and not as a mark of Bastardy."

There are two diminutives of this ordinary : the *Scarp* (Fig. 624), which is one-half the Bend, and the *Baton Sinister* (Fig. 628), which is one-half the Scarp, and *couped* or cut off smoothly so that its extremities do not reach the sides of the escutcheon. The *Baton Sinister* is borne as a mark of illegitimacy. This must not be confused with the *Bend Sinister* (Fig. 623), or with the *Riband* (Fig. 622), or with the *Baton* (field-marshal's staff), which are honorable charges. When a number of *Batons* appear as charges they are also honorable. The *Baton* when borne as an abatement is *borne singly*, *Sinister bendways* and *over all* other charges, as though the shield had received a broad long blot.

An erroneous impression exists in the minds of many persons, not only in the United States but in Europe, that the Baton Sinister, Bend Sinister, and " Bar Sinister" are identical, but such is not the case. The Baton Sinister is a distinct mark of illegitimacy, the Bend Sinister is defined as an " honorable ordinary," while the " Bar Sinister" is an heraldic impossibility, and the use of such a term in English or American heraldry is considered a great fault. Some French writers have used the word " Barre" to mean the Bend Sinister, from this evidently comes the English misnomer " Bar Sinister," but the leading French authorities approve the term Contrebande.

A very able critic in a recent edition of the " London Times" directs attention to the misuse of the term : " The heraldic blunders committed by gentlemen of the press and novelists—the lady ones in particular—are innumerable, and few heraldic heresies are more common than that touching the ' bar sinister.' Mr. Cussans reminds us that ignorant people often speak of the ' bar sinister' as a mark of illegitimacy ; whereas a bar sinister or dexter is a simple impossibility. As well may one speak of two parallel lines, which, meeting, form an isosceles triangle."

The definition of a Bar is as follows : " The Bar is an ordinary formed by two *parallel, horizontal* lines, and containing a fifth part of the field."

While the Bar can be placed in any part of the field (horizontally), except in chief, it cannot be placed there diagonally. See following examples:

Bar.   Bend.   Bend Sinister.
French, Barre; also Contrebande.

A *Bend* always implies a *Bend Dexter*, and a *Bend Sinister* must always be named.

The *Saltire* (Fig. 629) is a combination of a Bend with a Bend Sinister.

FIG. 629.

FIG. 630.

It contains one-fifth of the field, but one-third when charged. The Saltire may appear in the same composition as the Chief. It has no diminutive. Charges set on a Saltire slope with each of its limbs.

The *Chevron* (Fig. 630) comprises somewhat more than the lower half of a charged Saltire, and occupies one-fifth of the field. Charges set on a Chevron slope in the same manner as those set on a Saltire. *Two Chevrons* may appear in the same composition. A *Chevron* may be combined with a Chief.

FIG. 631.

FIG. 632.

The diminutives of this ordinary are the *Chevronel* (Fig. 631), which contains one-half of a Chevron, and the *Couple Close*, which is one-half the Chevronel.

The *Pile* (Fig. 632) is composed of two lines which form a wedge-shaped figure. The length depends on what other figures may occupy the shield. If it is the only charge it may extend as far as in the example. It is said to derive its origin from the stakes used in building bridges or fortifications.

The Pile may issue from various points of the shield line.

FIG. 633.

FIG. 634.

The *Quarter* (Fig. 633) is formed by a fesse line and a pale line terminating at the fesse point. It occupies one-fourth of the field, and is always placed in the chief.

The *Canton* (Fig. 634) is a square figure like the quarter, and generally occupies the third part of the chief. Unless its position is otherwise blazoned, it is situated in the dexter portion of the chief.

Of all the subordinaries the Canton alone can be placed over the Bordure. In blazoning it is named last.

FIG. 635.

The *Bordure* or *Border* (Fig. 635) generally occupies one-fifth of the field, and surrounds the edge of it. At one time the Bordure was borne as a difference, but is now frequently borne as a charge, and is always represented in relief.

The *Orle* (Fig. 636) is an inner border of the same FIG. 636. shape as the shield, which does not touch the edges, the field being seen around it on all sides, as well as within it. It is blazoned by some heralds as an *Inescutcheon voided.* In size it is one-half the width of the Bordure. Charges are sometimes arranged *in orle ;* that is, in the form and position of an *orle.*

FIG. 637.

The *Tressure* (Fig. 637) is one-half the width of the Orle, and is generally borne double. It passes around the field in the shape and form of the escutcheon. It is usually decorated with fleurs-de-lis, and blazoned *Fleury-counter-fleury* where the alternate fleurs-de-lis are reversed, as in the arms of Scotland. (See second quarter, Fig. 541.)

FIG. 638.

The *Gyron* (Fig. 638) is a triangular figure formed by two lines, one diagonally from the corner in the dexter chief and the other a horizontal line, meeting at the fesse point. When the field is divided into a number of gyron-shaped pieces the blazon would be *Gyronny,* and the number of pieces named ; thus, in Fig. 919, the thirteenth quarter is *Gyronny of eight.*

FIG. 639.

The *Inescutcheon* is a small escutcheon borne upon the shield (Fig. 639).

FIG. 640.

The *Lozenge* is a four-cornered figure, said to represent a pane of glass in old casements (Fig. 640).

The *Mascle* is by some heralds described as a lozenge voided, and is by some supposed to represent the mesh of a net; by others said to represent spots in certain flints found in Brittany (Fig. 641).

FIG. 641.

FIG. 642.

The *Rustre* is like the Mascle, except that the opening is pierced round instead of lozenge-shaped (Fig. 642).

The *Frette* (Fig. 643) is a figure resembling two sticks lying saltire-ways and interlaced with a mascle. Some writers call it a Herald's True Lover's Knot. It is probably more correct to describe it as a Bend-let, Scarp, and Mascle interlacing each other. When the interlacing is repeated so as to cover the entire field it is said to be Fretté or Fretty. The Frette is always represented *in relief* when correctly designed.

FIG. 643.

FIG. 644.

The *Fusil* is longer and more acute than the

Lozenge, and was formerly represented as a long oval, pointed at top and bottom like a spindle covered with thread (Fig. 644).

FIG. 645.

The Label (Fig. 645) is a Barrulet, with three or more pendants, placed in the upper part of the field. The Label is used for a difference of the eldest son, and supposed to have had its origin from ribbons anciently worn by a son about the neck of his helmet to distinguish him from his father.

FIG. 646.

The Billet (Fig. 646). Billets are oblong figures by some said to represent bricks, but undoubtledly derived from a letter folded in that shape. When a number of these charges appear on one shield it is described as Billetée or Semée of Billets.

The Flanch (Fig. 647) is composed of an arched line, drawn from the upper angle of the escutcheon to the base point of one side, and so on the other side. They are always borne in couples and one position.

FIG. 647.

The Flasque (Fig. 648) is like the Flanch, but smaller. These are also borne in pairs.

FIG. 648.

The ornamental lines are used in the ordinaries and subordinaries when so blazoned, otherwise the plain line is understood.

Charges are frequently placed in the form of the ordinaries, and are blazoned *in chief, in bend, in cross*, etc., which implies that they are to be arranged in the *form* or position of such ordinaries, and *not upon* them.

The ordinaries, in addition to the forms already mentioned, may be combined and borne in various ways, a few of which are illustrated and explained.

FIG. 649.   FIG. 650.    FIG. 651.

The Chief can be combined with the *Bend* and also with the *Saltire* (Figs. 649, 650).

FIG. 652.

A *Canton* and *Fesse* can be combined (Fig. 651), and can also be borne with the *Bordure*.

A *Chief Engrailed* (Fig. 652). In the example the Chief has the ornamental line, and this or any other ordinary can be formed of this or any other ornamental line.

Bends can be borne as follows:

FIG. 653.

Bend arched or archy.

FIG. 654.

Bend removed or fracted.

FIG. 655.

Bend engrailed cotised.

FIG. 656.

A Bend can also be embellished with other bearings than those with which it is charged. The example (Fig. 656) is a Bend *fleury-counter-fleury*. Bends and other ordinaries may also be composed of any of the furs.

FIG. 657.

Bend Wavy, a Bend formed of wavy lines (Fig. 657).

Two or more *Bendlets* are often borne on the same shield (Fig. 658). Bends are also subject to ornamental lines (Fig. 659). This is blazoned *three bendlets engrailed.*

FIG. 658.

FIG. 659.

A Bend can be charged with another bend.

Chevrons can be borne in any part of the field; the examples are:

FIG. 660.

Chevron abaissé.

FIG. 661.

Chevron couched.

FIG. 662.

Chevron reversed.

FIG. 663.

When a chevron is borne with its extremities cut off it is said to be *chevron couped* (Fig. 663).

Chevronels are generally borne in threes, sometimes interlaced, sometimes separately. The examples are:

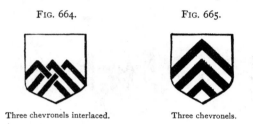

FIG. 664.

Three chevronels interlaced.

FIG. 665.

Three chevronels.

Pallets (Fig. 666) are borne in many English arms; in the example they resemble *Paly of a certain number*, but are in reality greatly different. Paly is a shield divided into stripes of alternate tinctures, all represented of the same surface, while Pallets are represented as elevated on the shield. The American shield is *Paly of thirteen argent and gules* (see frontispiece).

FIG. 666.

This also applies to three *Bars*, which is different from *Barry of six;* that is, six stripes of alternate tinctures.

Bars, Pallets, etc., may be Ondé (Wavy) or formed of any of the ornamental lines.

Piles are borne in different ways.

The following examples are blazoned:

FIG. 667.

FIG. 668.

FIG. 669.

Three piles meeting in base.

Three piles in point.

Three piles terminating in fesse.

Three Piles, one issuing between two others, transposed (Fig. 670). Piles are borne *in bend,* issuing from the sinister base or dexter chief. Piles are occasionally decorated with fleurs-de-lis, *flory on the tops.*

FIG. 670.

The Tressure is usually borne double, embellished with fleurs-de-lis, the alternate ones reversed, and is blazoned *a double tressure flory* or *fleury-counter-fleury* (Fig. 671).

FIG. 671.

When charges are blazoned *in chief, in bend, in cross,* etc., they must be placed *in the position of* the ordinary named, and not *on* it. *On a bend* signifies that a bend is placed upon the field and the charges upon the bend; but *in bend* indicates that the charges must be placed upon the field *in the position of* a bend (no ordinary interfering).

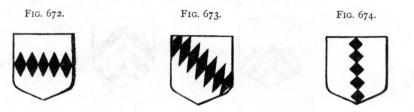

FIG. 672.   FIG. 673.   FIG. 674.

This refers as well to *on a fesse* and *in fesse*, etc.   Example (Fig. 672) is blazoned *Five fusils conjoined in fesse.*   Fig. 673, *A bend of fusils*, no number being specified.   Fig. 674, *Five lozenges conjoined in pale.*[1]

---

[1] For various combinations the writer has referred to Aveling's edition of Boutell.

CHAPTER XI.

VARIED FIELDS AND DIAPER.

In addition to ordinaries, partition lines, etc., the shield is varied by figures derived from them. The shield is not charged with these; that is, they do not rest upon it, but are in it, of the same plane or level, and are designed without shading.

FIG. 675.

Paly is when the field is divided into four or more even number of parts by perpendicular lines, and consists of two tinctures interchangeably disposed (Fig. 675).

FIG. 676.

Bendy is when a field is divided bendways into an even number of equal parts diagonally, the two tinctures alternating (Fig. 676).

FIG. 677.

Barry is a field divided by horizontal lines into an even number of equal parts, of two tinctures interchangeably disposed. The example is, *Barry of six nebulé* (Fig. 677).

FIG. 678.

When there are more than eight bars, the term *Barruly* or *Closetty* is generally used.

Paly, *Bendy*, and *Barry* all admit of an ordinary or charge being placed over them.

FIG. 679.

Paly Bendy is formed by lines perpendicular, or Paly, and by others diagonally across the shield from dexter to sinister, or Bendy (Fig. 678).

FIG. 680.

Barry Bendy is a field equally divided into four or more equal parts by lines from the dexter chief to the sinister base and from side to side, the two tinctures alternating (Fig. 679).

FIG. 681.

Gyronny is when the field is divided into six or more equal triangular parts of two tinctures, the points all uniting in the centre of the field. Fig. 680 is *Gyronny of eight*.

FIG. 682.

Lozengy is when the field or charge is divided into lozenges (Fig. 681).

Fusilly is when the field or charge is divided into fusils, similar to Lozengy except that the lines are more nearly vertical (Fig. 682).

267

FIG. 683.

FIG. 684.

Chequé, Checky, or *Chequy* is composed of small squares of two tinctures arranged alternately, the lines perpendicular and horizontal crossing each other (Fig. 683).

Fretty or *Fretté* is a field formed by dexter and sinister stripes interlacing one another (Fig. 684).

FIG. 685.

FIG. 686.

Barry Pily is composed of piles issuing from the side of shield and tapering and extending to the opposite side. Fig. 685 is *Barry pily argent and sable.*

Bendy Pily is an equal number of pile-shaped divisions arranged in the direction of a bend. Fig. 686 is *Bendy pily sable and argent.*

FIG. 687.

FIG. 688.

Compony or *Componé* is applied to an ordinary consisting of one row of small squares, of two tinctures alternating (Fig. 687).

Counter-Compony is when an ordinary is made up of two rows of squares and with the tinctures alternating (Fig. 688).

FIG. 689.

FIG. 690.

Bordure Bendy or *Bendy Bordure* is the same as Bendy, previously described, but the bends are only represented in those parts that fall within or on the bordure (Fig. 689).

In all the above it is customary that the first-named tincture occupies the dexter position.

Counter-Changing means a change of color for metal, or metal for color, and the term indicates the presence of one metal and one color, so that whatever is charged upon the metal must be tinctured of the color, and that which is charged upon the color must be tinctured of the metal (Fig. 690). *Per pale arg. and sa., a chevron counterchanged.*

DIAPER (Fig. 691).

FIG. 691.

In many heraldic designs, particularly those of the Middle Ages, diapering was introduced in various ways to add to the ornamental beauty of the shield, and consisted of geometrical patterns filled in with small decorative figures. It was chiefly employed in sculpture, seals, and stained-glass effects. While the surface of the shield was covered with many of these figures, they formed no part of the blazon, and they were always subordinate to the charges. Numerous designs in fresco and wall-paper may be said to be of the diaper pattern.

CHAPTER XII.

CHARGES, ROUNDELS, GUTTÉ.

CHARGES are figures or devices borne upon a coat of arms. Since the ordinaries and subordinaries were not of sufficient variety to give each man a different coat, various other charges were introduced, and these comprised every known object, animate and inanimate. Birds, beasts, fishes, serpents, flowers, plants, trees, fabulous creatures, planets, etc., were charged upon the shields of the warriors, each of whom took unto himself that creature "best fitted to his estate, or whose Nature and in Quality did in some Measure quadrate with his own, or whereunto himself was in some respect in Quality like or wished to be resembled unto." At other times these charges were adopted without regard to their symbolical meaning, or were borne to signalize some special event in a warrior's life, and when heraldry became systematized, they were awarded as marks of honor by sovereigns.

When a device is placed upon a shield, the latter is said to be charged with it, and this charge can be charged with another charge.

Devices are frequently blazoned as *in fesse, in pale, in cross, in orle*, etc.,

FIG. 692.

which means that they are to be disposed *in the form* of such ordinaries. Example Fig. 692 is properly blazoned as *Three escallop shells in chief*. This must not be confused with *Three escallop shells on a chief*, as example Fig. 693, which are entirely different arms.

FIG. 693.

As it would, of course, be impossible to give examples of all charges, their positions and attitudes, only a few of the most prominent will be placed before the reader.

FIG. 694.

Rampant. A term applicable to lions, bears, tigers, etc., when standing erect with head in profile, one fore paw raised above the other and one hind paw raised from the ground (Fig. 694). *Argent, a lion rampant gules.*

FIG. 695.

Rampant Guardant. Signifies animals of the above class when standing upright with head turned toward the spectator (Fig. 695). *Argent, a lion rampant guardant azure.*

Rampant Reguardant. A term used when the beast stands erect and looks

269

FIG. 696.

backward toward the tail (Fig. 696). *Argent, a lion rampant reguardant sable.*

Rampant-Addorsed. Beasts are so described when *rampant* and back to back, but when borne close together face to face they are termed *Combatant* (Fig. 708). Fig. 697 is blazoned, *Argent, two lions rampant-addorsed azure.*

FIG. 697.

FIG. 698.

Passant. In a walking position (Fig. 698). *Argent, a lion passant azure.*

Passant Guardant. A beast walking with the head turned to the spectator (Fig. 699). The three lions of England are *passant guardant.*

FIG. 699.

Passant Reguardant. Indicates a beast walking and looking behind him (Fig. 700). *Argent, a lion passant reguardant sable.*

FIG. 700.

FIG. 701.

FIG. 702.

Statant. A term used for beasts or animals when borne in a standing position with all four feet upon the ground and head in profile (Fig. 701). *Argent, a lion statant gules.* Fig. 702, *Argent, a stag statant gules.*

FIG. 703.

Salient. Applied to a beast when leaping or springing (Fig. 703). *Argent, a lion salient azure.*

Sejant. Signifies sitting, and applies to all beasts in that position (Fig. 704). *Argent, a lion sejant gules.*

Couchant. Lying on the ground. All beasts when Couchant should be represented with the head upright (Fig. 705). *Argent, a lion couchant azure.*

FIG. 704.

FIG. 705.

Dormant. Signifies a beast lying down and sleeping, and differs from Couchant by having its head resting upon the fore paws (Fig. 706). *Argent, a lion dormant azure.*

FIG. 706.

Coward (in French *Diffamé*). Defines an animal when the tail, usually borne upward, is hanging between the hind legs and the head is turned backward (Fig. 707). *Argent, a lion coward gules.*

FIG. 707.

Combatant (French *Affronté* or *Confronté*). A term applied to beasts when borne *salient, rampant,* etc., face to face. The example is *Argent, two lions rampant combatant gules* (Fig. 708).

FIG. 708.

FIG. 709.

FIG. 711.

FIG. 713.

FIG. 715.

FIG. 717.

FIG. 719.

FIG. 710.

FIG. 712.

FIG. 714.

FIG. 716.

FIG. 718.

FIG. 720.

Queue Fourché. Having a forked tail (Fig. 709). *Argent, a lion rampant sable, queue fourché.*

Tripping or *Trippant.* A term used to express a buck, antelope, or other animal of the chase when represented with the dexter foot lifted up and the other three feet on the ground, as if trotting (Fig. 710). *Argent, a stag tripping sable.*

Courant. Signifies animals of the chase, grey-hounds, etc., running or *in course* (Fig. 711). *Argent, a stag courant gules.*

Springing. A term applicable to animals of the chase in the same way as Salient is applied to beasts of prey. It is sometimes applied to fish when placed bendways. is blazoned, *Argent, a stag springing sable.*

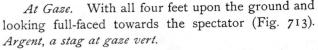
Fig. 712

At Gaze. With all four feet upon the ground and looking full-faced towards the spectator (Fig. 713). *Argent, a stag at gaze vert.*

Lodged. Refers to an animal of the chase when at rest and lying upon the ground, in the same sense that Couchant is applied to a lion (Fig. 714). *Argent, a stag lodged purpure.*

Naiant. Applied to fish placed horizontally as if swimming (Fig. 715). *Argent, a —— (name of fish) naiant azure.*

Hauriant. A fish in an upright position is blazoned *hauriant* when the head is in chief, but *uriant* when the head is in base (Fig. 716). *Argent, a —— (name of fish) hauriant gules.*

Embowed. Generally applied to the dolphin when in a bent position (Fig. 717). *Argent, a dolphin embowed azure.*

Displayed. Term applied to eagles and other birds of prey when borne with the wings spread open on each side of the head (Fig. 718). *Argent, an eagle displayed azure.* *Disclosed.* Applied to birds that are not birds of prey.

Rising. Indicates birds in a position as if preparing to take flight (Fig. 719). *Argent, an eagle rising gules.*

Volant. A term applied to a bird in a flying attitude (Fig. 720). *Argent, an eagle volant reguardant azure.*

FIG. 721.

Preying. A term used in heraldry to describe any ravenous beast or bird standing on or in a proper position for devouring its prey (Fig. 721). *Argent, an eagle sable preying on a duck azure.*

FIG. 722.

Vol. In French blazon implies two wings conjoined and expanded (Fig. 722). *Argent, a vol azure.*

FIG. 723.

Demi-Vol. A single wing is sometimes called a demi-vol, and in blazoning, mention must be made as to whether it is the *sinister* or *dexter* wing, and whether the tip is inverted (Fig. 723). *Argent, a sinister demi-vol gules.*

FIG. 724.

Erased or *Erazed.* Signifies anything forcibly torn off, leaving the parts jagged and uneven. The example is *an eagle's head erased sable* (Fig. 724).

Couped (French *Coupé*). A term used by heralds for anything that is severed with a clean cut. The lion's head in the example is said to be *couped* (Fig. 725). *Argent, a lion's head couped azure.*

FIG. 725.   FIG. 726.    FIG. 727.

Eradicated. Torn up by the roots. The tree is *couped and eradicated* (Fig. 726). *Argent, the trunk of a tree eradicated and couped, in pale, sprouting out two branches gules.*

Dismembered. Cut in parts and set in a position that retains the form (Fig. 727). *Argent, a lion rampant dismembered sable.*

ROUNDELS OR ROUNDLETS.

Roundels occur frequently in heraldry, both as charges and crests, and form a distinct group. The titles, with the exception of the Fountain, invariably denote the tinctures, which are indicated in engraving in the usual way.

The Bezant, Plate, and Fountain are represented flat, but all the others are shaded to represent their spherical shape.

FIG. 728.   FIG. 729.

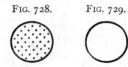

The Bezant. Or, Gold. Named from a piece of gold coin which was current in Byzantium, now Constantinople (Fig. 728).

The Plate. Argent, Silver. A round flat piece of silver without any impression (Fig. 729). William Penn's arms are *Argent, on a fesse sable, three plates.* (See Fig. 50.)

The Pomme. Vert, Green. Derived from the French *pommé*, an apple. If in plural they are called Pommeis (Fig. 730).

FIG. 730. FIG. 731.

The Torteau. Gules, Red (Fig. 731).

The Hurte. Azure, Blue (Fig. 732).

The Golp. Purpure, Purple (Fig. 733).

FIG. 732. FIG. 733.

The Pellet or *Ogress. Sable*, Black (Fig. 734).

The Fountain is of two tinctures, and is represented by wavy lines, as in the example. *Barry wavy of six, argent and azure* (Fig. 735).

FIG. 734. FIG. 735.

The Orange. Tenné or *Tawny*, Orange (Fig. 736).

The Guze. Sanguine, the color of cold blood Fig. 737).

The last two Roundels are seldom used, and by some heralds are not recognized. All, except the Bezant, Plate, and Fountain, are said to represent small cakes of different colors which were used in the Crusades.

FIG. 736.  FIG. 737.

GUTTÉ OR GOUTTES.

Gutté, derived from the Latin *gutta*, a drop, is the term for a field sprinkled with drops. In illustrations the tinctures are indicated in the usual manner.

Or . . .	Or . .	Gutté d'or . . .	Sprinkled with gold.
Argent .	Arg. .	Gutté d'eau . . .	" " water.
Gules . .	Gu. . .	Gutté de sang . .	" " blood.
Azure . .	Az. . .	Gutté de larmes .	" " tears.
Vert . .	Vert .	Gutté d'olive . .	" " oil.
Sable . .	Sa. . .	Gutté de poix . .	" " pitch.

FIG. 738.

Either the field of the shield or any charge can be Gutté, and in blazoning, either the name or the tincture can be specified. Example Fig. 738 is *Gutté de sang* or *Gutté gu.*

FIG. 739.

Gutté reversed is like Gutté, but the drops are inverted. When argent these drops are sometimes blazoned *icicles.* Fig. 739 is *Gutté de sang reversed.*

CHAPTER XIII.

CROSSES.

CROSSES figure very prominently in heraldry, and, as they have always been held in high favor, they are very frequently borne in coats of arms. They were in general use by knights during the expeditions to the wars in the Holy Land in the year 1096. There were also at that time great numbers of persons who wore crosses made of cloth or silk, which they received from the hands of bishops and priests, and sewed on their garments. From this arrangement the expeditions were named "Croisades," and by varying the forms for the devices different leaders and their followers were distinguished. As crosses were considered the emblems of Christianity, they were retained by the Crusaders to perpetuate their exploits. It will be readily seen that an immense variety of shapes and forms were thus originated, heralds differing as to the exact number. It is therefore impossible to name all, so the best known will be mentioned.

FIG. 740.

FIG. 741.

The Cross. When blazoned *a cross*, this form is understood (Fig. 740).

Cross Patriarchal. So called because it was the distinguishing cross of the patriarchs (Fig. 741).

FIG. 742.

FIG. 743.

Cross Quadrate signifies that the centre of the cross is square (Fig. 742).

Cross Nowed, Degraded, and *Conjoined.* Degraded means placed upon steps or *degrees* (Fig. 743).

FIG. 744.

FIG. 745.

Cross Patée or *Formée* is small in the centre and widens toward the ends, which are broad (Fig. 744). There are many varieties of this cross, of which example Fig. 745 is one.

Cross Patée Concaved (Fig. 745).

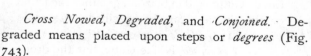

FIG. 746.

FIG. 747.

Four Fusils Cross is a cross formed by joining four fusils together (Fig. 746). Crosses may be formed in this way of fleurs-de lis, roundels, pheons, etc. (See example Fig. 747.)

Cross of Four Ermine Spots (Fig. 747).

FIG. 748.

FIG. 749.

Cross Patonce resembles the Cross Fleury at the ends, but the lines are curved (Fig. 748).

Cross Fleury or *Fleurie* signifies decorated with fleurs-de-lis, which is indicated upon the end of each arm (Fig. 749). Authorities differ as to the drawing of this cross and *Cross Flory*.

FIG. 750.

FIG. 751.

Cross Fleurettée, Fleur-de-lis, or *Flory*. Some heralds consider this the same as the Cross Fleury (Fig. 750).

Cross Urdée Voided (Fig. 751).

FIG. 752.

FIG. 753.

Cross Crosslet was very popular, and figures frequently in the heraldry of to-day (Fig. 752).

Cross Moline. A cross in the form of a Fer-de-Moline, or Mill-rind (Fig. 753).

FIG. 754.

FIG. 755.

Cross Recercellée resembles a Cross Moline, but its extremities are more expanded (Fig. 754).

Cross Engrailed. The plain cross decorated with the ornamental lines (Fig. 755)

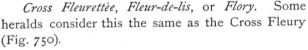

FIG. 756.

FIG. 757.

Cross Raguly. Seeming to represent two trunks of trees with branches trimmed off (Fig. 756).

Cross Flamant (Fig. 757).

FIG. 758.

FIG. 759.

Cross Double Parted (Fig. 758).

Cross Voided is the plain cross with the centre cut, leaving only thin lines between which the field is seen (Fig. 759).

FIG. 760.

FIG. 761.

Cross Tri-parted and Fretted (Fig. 760).

Cross Quarterly Pierced. The plain cross with that part cut out where the arms meet (Fig. 761).

FIG. 762.

FIG. 763.

Cross Fimbriated has a narrow border or hem of another tincture (Fig. 762).

The Latin Cross. The three top limbs of this cross are of the same size, caused by the horizontal limbs being *couped* (cut off straight) and *enhanced ;* that is, placed in a higher position than usual (Fig. 763).

FIG. 764.

FIG. 765.

Cross of St. Anthony or *Tau Cross.* A representation of the Greek letter Tau is called St. Anthony's Cross because he was always painted as wearing it upon his habit (Fig. 764).

Cross Humettée or *Couped* is so named because it is cut or shortened so that the extremities do not reach the edge of the shield (Fig. 765).

FIG. 766.

FIG. 767.

Cross Potent. So termed by reason of the resemblance its extremities bear to the head of a crutch. Potent was the old name for crutch (Fig. 766).

Cross Rayonnant is that which has rays of light behind it, darting from the centre to all parts of the escutcheon (Fig. 767).

FIG. 768.

FIG. 769.

Cross Urdée. Pointed at the ends (Fig. 768).

Cross Pommée. Applied to a cross whose extremities terminate in a ball or knob (Fig. 769).

Any crosses may be fitchée—pointed at the lower part and the entire lower arm tapering to a point. Crosses may also be formed with the ornamental lines.

CHAPTER XIV.

RULES FOR BLAZONING,[1] WITH EXAMPLES.

In heraldry the term *Blazon* or *Blazoning* is applied to the description of the tinctures, positions, and attitudes of all heraldic devices and figures, and is a very important branch of the science of heraldry, forming, with marshalling (the grouping of several coats of arms into one heraldic composition), the skill of armory.

The custom of blazoning arms preceded the system of heraldry, and arose from the tournaments held by the Germans, at which events the arms of contestants were displayed, and their various devices publicly proclaimed by the heralds. It was also the duty of the heralds to *blazon*, or blow a horn to attract attention, and from this announcing the system received its name. After the knight had been proven eligible to compete in the lists, he was permitted thereafter to bear upon his helmet horns, which indicated that his arms had been duly *blazoned*. In German heraldry these horns are frequently borne with the crest. Blazoning, in a modern sense, means a description of armorial bearings according to the rules of heraldry.

In heraldic language, which is concise and explicit, all unnecessary words are omitted, repetitions are avoided, and each and every detail is specified with great care and correctness.

RULES FOR BLAZONING.

In blazoning a coat of arms the general rule is that the tincture of the field is first mentioned. Thus, in the blazon of Fig. 795,—*Azure, a crescent between three mullets argent,—azure* is the tincture of the field. If, however, the field is divided by one or more of the partition lines, *Per pale, Per fesse, Per bend*, etc., the division line of the field, with its difference, unless straight, is mentioned before the tinctures. Thus, in the blazon of Fig. 845, *Per pale indented argent and gules*, the *per pale indented* is first named to show how the field is divided, and then the tinctures are mentioned. The first one named always occupies the dexter side, except in the case of *Per saltire*, where the tincture first mentioned occupies the upper and lower triangles. After the field the charge which lies next to the field and nearest the centre must be described, and afterwards those which are more remote : for example,

---

[1] Mainly from Hugh Clark.

Azure, a crescent between three mullets argent. Thus, the crescent is first named as being nearest to the centre of the field (Fig. 795).

When a coat of arms consists of two ·tinctures only, ás depicted in Fig. 771, it is blazoned *Argent, a fesse, in chief three lozenges sable,* which implies that both the *fesse* and the *lozenges* are sable. *Azure, on a chevron or, between three bezants, as many pallets gules.* In this example it will be noticed that the *chevron* is named *first* after the field, because it is nearest the centre ; and as the *pallets lie upon the chevron,* so they are most remote from *the field,* and must be last named (Fig. 776). When bearings are described without expressing the point of the escutcheon upon which they are to be placed, they are then understood to occupy the centre of the shield,—for example, *Argent, a lion rampant gules ;* but if the blazon is *Argent, a lion rampant in base gules,* it must be placed in the base part of the shield.

The repetition of words must be avoided, since iteration is considered a great fault in blazoning. It is correct to say, *Or, on a saltire azure nine lozenges of the first,* and incorrect to say, *Or, on a saltire azure nine lozenges or,* because the word *Or* is then named twice, which is unnecessary. The following rule will more clearly explain this important point.

If a tincture or a number occurs twice in the same sentence of any descriptive blazon, such tincture or number is to be indicated by reference to the words already used, and not by actually repeating them. If any charge be of the same tincture as the field, it is said to be "*of the field*," or, as the tincture of the field is always the *first* that is specified in the blazon, a charge of that tincture may be blazoned as "*of the first.*" Thus, in the blazoning of Fig. 773, *Argent, on a quarter sable a spear in bend of the field* (of the first), "*of the field*" means *argent.*

In the same way, when a charge is of the tincture mentioned second in the blazon it is termed "*of the second,*" when of the tincture mentioned third it is "*of the third,*" and so on. Thus, in the blazon of Fig. 791, *Per fesse sable and argent, a pale counter-changed ; on each piece of the first a trefoil slipped, of the second,* "of the first" means *sable,* "of the second" means *argent,* since those tinctures are mentioned first and second respectively. In the blazon of Fig. 776, *Azure, on a chevron or, between three bezants, as many pallets gules,* "as many" means *three.*

In printing, the position of the marks of punctuation must be carefully observed, and the rules as given near the end of this chapter should be followed.

It is a positive rule in English heraldry that *metal shall not appear upon metal, nor color upon color,*—that is, a charge of one of the metals must rest upon, or be in contact with, a surface or another charge of one of the colors,— and in like manner a charge of one of the colors must rest upon, or be in contact with, a surface or object tinctured with one of the metals.

THIS RULE ADMITS OF EXCEPTIONS when the surfaces are varied, or in the case of certain details of charges, as well as when charges are borne *proper.*

CHARGES.

In blazoning charges of any kind or description, whether animate or inanimate, if they are perceived to be of the natural colors of the animals or things they represent, they are always termed *proper* (abbreviated ppr.), and not *argent, gules*, etc.

A charge upon another charge is not mentioned until all of the charges lying next to the field have been named. Where two or more charges are of the same tincture and follow one another, the tincture should not be mentioned until all such charges have been specified.

When the same device is charged a limited number of times upon a shield, the number in each row is generally specified, the number of devices in the top row being mentioned first, as in example Fig. 805, *Or, six annulets, three, two, and one, sable;* but when a large number are borne, and the shield has the appearance of having been cut out of a pattern, it is said to be " *Semé*" of such a charge.

ORDINARIES.

Ordinaries formed of straight lines are described by the distinctive name alone, thus, *a bend az.;* but if the ordinary is *engrailed, wavy, nebuly, embattled*, etc., the difference must be stated: for example, *Argent, on a pile engrailed azure, three crescents of the first.* (See Fig. 786.)

ANIMALS: LIONS, TIGERS, DRAGONS, ETC.

The teeth and claws of all ravenous animals are called their arms, because they are their offensive and defensive weapons; when these are of a different tincture from the body of the beast they are said to be *armed*, and the tincture must be named; and when their tongues are of the tinctures of their arms they are said to be *langued. Azure, a lion argent armed and langued gules.*

The claws and tongue of a lion are always *gules*, unless the field or charge is *gules*, then they must be *azure*. This is an example of where color is permitted on color in the detail of the charge.

The bull, ox, ram, goat, etc., which are of a milder nature than the above, are endowed by nature with horns, which with their hoofs form their defensive weapons. They are said to be *armed* and *hoofed*.

As deer, etc., are by nature timorous, they were supposed to wear their antlers as ornaments and not as weapons, therefore in blazon they are described as *attired.* .

Dogs appear often in heraldic compositions, and as they were bred for exercise and hunting, the first consideration is the breed of the beast and what sport fitted for, hence the terms *beating, coursing, scenting*, etc.: for example, *Three greyhounds courant.*

BIRDS.

When the beaks and claws of birds of prey differ in blazoning from the color of the body they are said to be *armed* and *membered*; thus, *An eagle volant sable armed and membered or.* In blazoning swans, geese, ducks, cranes, herons, cormorants, etc., which are water-fowls and have no talons, instead of *armed and membered*, the correct term is *beaked and membered*. *Armed, crested, and jelloped* applies to the cock. The term *armed* signifies his beak and spurs, *crested* his comb, and *jelloped* his wattles. If he is indicated as in life he is called *a cock ppr.*, but if of any other tinctures, he is blazoned accordingly: for example, *Azure, a cock argent, armed, crested, and jelloped gules.*

The falcon is borne in the same postures as the eagle, and is described in the same terms, except when with *hood, bells, virols* (or rings), and *leashes;* it is then said to be *hooded, belled, jessed*, and *leashed*, and the colors of each must be named. *Pouncing* is a term given when he is striking at his prey.

FISHES.

In blazon fishes are described as *naiant*, swimming; *embowed*, in a bent position, head and tail down; *hauriant*, rising; *vorant*, swallowing an object whole; *uriant* or *urinant*, with head down.

When the tinctures of their fins are different from their bodies they are said to be finned of such a color, naming it: as, *A dolphin embowed gules, finned or.*

HEAVENLY BODIES.

The first consideration in the blazoning of any heavenly body, such as a planet, is the state or condition in which it appears to be, as the *sun*, whether in his *glory, splendor, rising, setting*, etc., or the *moon*, whether in her *complement*, or *in plenitude, crescent, decrescent*, or *increscent*. All descriptions should be in proper astronomical terms. This is a rule, and all blazons are more elegant when expressed in the proper terms of the arts or sciences which the figures described represent, great care being taken that no armorial term necessary to be used is omitted.

TREES AND PLANTS.

Trees and plants or their parts are blazoned first as to their condition, whether *spread* or *blasted;* what kind of a tree; whether *bearing fruit* or *not;* if a part only, what part, whether the *trunk, branches, fruit*, or *leaves;* if the former, whether *standing* or *not;* if not standing, in what manner it seems to have been felled, whether *eradicated* (torn up by the roots) or *couped* (cut evenly, as with a saw) (see Fig. 808); if the bearing consists of members, as its *branches, fruit*, or *leaves*, whether *with fruit* or *withered*, and whether *slipped, pendent* (drooping), or *erect*.

MAN.

Man and portions of the human body frequently appear in coat-armor, and in blazoning are described as *whole* or *in part;* if whole, in what *attitude*, whether *naked* or *habited;* if the latter, in what manner, whether *rustic, in armor*, or *in robes*. When the temples of a man or woman are represented as encircled with a wreath of laurel, oak, or ivy, they are blazoned as *wreathed* with *laurel, oak*, or *ivy*, whichever the case may be.[1]

The Escutcheon, or *Shield, of Pretence* when appearing in arms is blazoned last, as it surmounts all devices; and it is described in the usual way.

The *Helmet* and *Mantling* are not mentioned in a blazon, but are understood to form part of the achievement.

The following examples of coats of arms with their correct blazoning are given to acquaint the reader with the concise forms of words used, and to illustrate the foregoing rules. Some of the examples have been formed by modifying and simplifying existing coats of arms; others are arms in actual use.

No abbreviations are used in the blazoning, because the idea has been to simplify and avoid difficulties.[2]

RULES.

1. Begin the blazon of every coat or quartering with a capital letter.

2. Use no other capitals except on the occasional occurrence of a proper name (such as Katherine wheel, Moor's head, etc.).

3. Introduce only necessary punctuation, and seldom more than a comma, unless in very long and complicated blazons.

Exception. A comma (not otherwise required) may be occasionally used after the metal "or," if there is any danger of that word being mistaken for the conjunction.

4. The metals and tinctures may be either given at length, or abbreviated, as arg. az. sa. &c.

5. State always "three wolf's heads, three lion's jambs, three palmer's staves," &c., not "three wolves' heads, three lions' jambs, or three palmers' staves;" the charges representing the head of one wolf, the jamb of one lion, the staff of one palmer, &c., and it being grammatically sufficient that the nominative case "heads," &c., should agree with the numeral three.

---

[1] Too much stress cannot be placed upon the necessity of correctness in interpreting blazoning, as many different artists, from a correct blazon of arms, should be able to produce in a colored design the same result without reference to each other's work; and as in painting or engraving arms the description is frequently all that heraldic designers have to guide them, the importance of a strict knowledge of the science of blazoning is apparent.

[2] The rules for punctuation given in vol. i. of "The Herald and Genealogist," edited by John Gough Nichols, F.S.A., have been followed in printing.

6. For the heraldic numbers 3, 2, 1, 2 and 1, &c., the words "three, two, one," and "two and one" are preferable to figures, which may be confused with the numbering of quarterings.

7. In case of complicated quarterings, clearness may sometimes be produced where two coats only are quartered by the expression Quarterly, as Quarterly of France and England, of Hastings and Valence, &c.; or *Quarterly of 1 and 4, Azure, a bend or*, Scrope; and *2 and 3, Or, a chevron gules*, Stafford. Otherwise, the term Grand Quarterings is employed, and then numerals of different kinds may be used to distinguish the grand and the subordinate quarterings, thus:—

Quarterly of four grand quarterings; I. Quarterly of four: i. Quarterly, 1. Or, &c.; 2. Argent, &c. 3. Gules, &c. 4. Sable, &c.; ii. and iii. Vert, &c. iv. Ermine, &c. II. Or, &c. III. Gules, &c. IV. Azure, &c.

The student should pay particular attention to the descriptions and positions of the charges, and to the indications of the tinctures.

EXAMPLES OF BLAZONING.

FIG. 770.

FIG. 771.

Argent, on a chief gules two mullets, pierced, of the first (Fig. 770).

Argent, a fesse, in chief three lozenges, sable (Fig. 771).

FIG. 772.

FIG. 773.

Ermine, on a canton sable a harp argent (Fig. 772).

Argent, on a quarter sable a spear in bend of the field (Fig. 773).

FIG. 774.

FIG. 775.

Argent, on a fesse sable three mullets or (Fig. 774).

Ermine, three lozenges in fesse sable (Fig. 775).

FIG. 776.

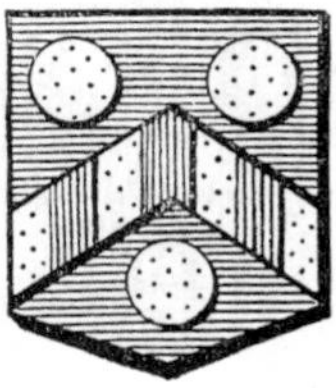

FIG. 777.

Azure, on a chevron or, between three bezants, as many pallets gules (Fig. 776).

Ermine, a chevron couped sable (Fig. 777).

FIG. 778.

FIG. 779.

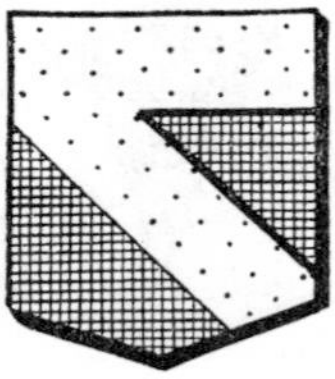

Sable, two lion's paws issuing out of the dexter and sinister base points chevron-ways argent (Fig. 778).

Sable, a bend and chief or (Fig. 779).

FIG. 780.

FIG. 781.

Sable, four lozenges in bend cotised argent (Fig. 780).

Argent, a pale and chief sable (Fig. 781).

FIG. 782.

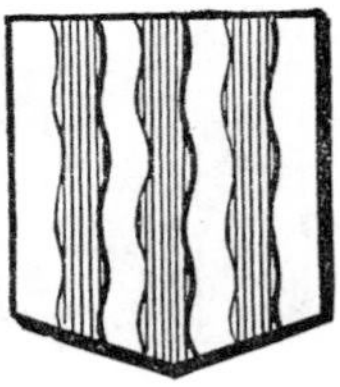

FIG. 783.

Argent, three pallets wavy gules (Fig. 782).

Gules, three tilting spears erect in pale or (Fig. 783).

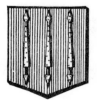

FIG. 784.

FIG. 785.

Azure, three leopard's faces in pale argent (Fig. 784).

Sable, a pile argent surmounted by a chevron gules (Fig. 785).

FIG. 786.

FIG. 787.

Argent, on a pile engrailed azure, three crescents of the first (or of the field) (Fig. 786).

Argent, three piles one from the chief between the others reversed sable (Fig. 787).

FIG. 788.

FIG. 789.

Argent, a cross vert, on a bend over all gules, three fleurs-de-lis or (Fig. 788).

Azure, five escallop shells in cross argent (Fig. 789).

FIG. 790.

FIG. 791.

Sable, two shank-bones in cross argent, that in fesse surmounting the one in pale (Fig. 790).

Per fesse sable and argent, a pale counter-changed, on each piece of the first a trefoil slipped, of the second (Fig. 791).

FIG. 792.

FIG. 793.

Sable, two shin-bones in saltire that in dexter surmounting the one in sinister argent (Fig. 792).

Per saltire gules and or, in pale two garbs argent, in fesse as many roses of the first (Fig. 793).

FIG. 794.

FIG. 795.

Gules, a saltire or, between four crescents argent (Fig. 794).

Azure, a crescent between three mullets argent (Fig. 795).

FIG. 796.

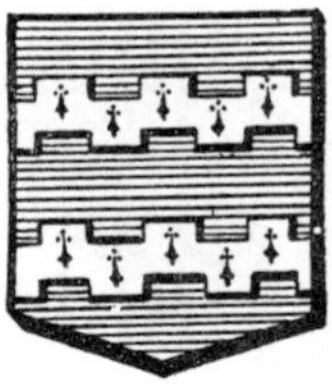

FIG. 797.

Azure, two bars counter-embattled ermine (Fig. 796).

Gules, five marlion's sinister wings in saltire argent (Fig. 797).

FIG. 798.

FIG. 799.

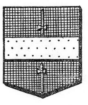

Argent, three bars-gemel azure, on a chief gules a barulet dancetté or (Fig. 798).

Sable, a fesse or, between two swords in pale the hilts toward the fesse point argent (Fig. 799).

Fig. 800.

Fig. 800.

Fig. 801.

Azure, a pile inverted in bend sinister or (Fig. 800).

Gules, a bend wavy argent, in the sinister chief point a falcon standing on a perch, of the second (Fig. 801).

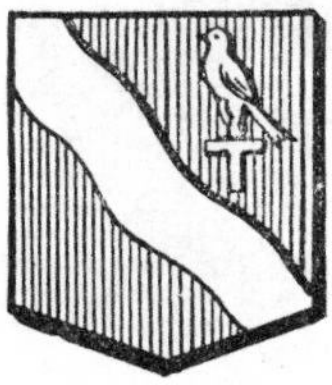

Fig. 802.

Fig. 803.

Or, a dexter arm vested issuing from the sinister fesse point out of a cloud proper, holding a cross-crosslet fitchée sable (Fig. 802).

Azure, the sun in his glory (Fig. 803).

Fig. 804.

Fig. 805.

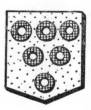

Argent, three cinquefoils gules (Fig. 804).

Or, six annulets, three, two, and one, sable (Fig. 805).

Fig. 806.

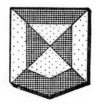

Fig. 807.

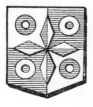

Per saltire sable and or, a border counter-changed (Fig. 806).

Quarterly argent and azure, a cross of four fusils between as many annulets, all counter-changed (Fig. 807).

FIG. 808.

FIG. 809.

Gules, the trunk of a tree eradicated and couped, in pale, sprouting out two branches argent (Fig. 808).

Sable, three scaling-ladders in bend argent (Fig 809).

FIG. 810.

FIG. 811.

Argent, a man's heart gules within two equilateral triangles voided and interlaced sable (Fig. 810).

Argent, on a chevron azure between three trefoils slipped, per pale gules and vert, as many bezants (Fig. 811).

FIG. 812.

FIG. 813.

Argent, a chevron gules between three attires of a stag fixed to the scalp proper (Fig. 812).

Or, three mullets of six points sable issuing out of as many crescents gules (Fig. 813).

FIG. 814.

FIG. 815.

Sable, a chevron rompu between three mullets or (Fig. 814).

Azure, a bull's head couped or, winged and armed argent (Fig. 815).

FIG. 816.

FIG. 817.

Argent, a man's heart gules ensigned with an imperial crown or, on a chief azure three mullets of the field (or of the first) (Fig. 816).

Gules, three bezants figured (or stamped with a head) (Fig. 817).

FIG. 818.

FIG. 819.

Argent, two chevronels azure between three flames of fire proper (Fig. 818).

Argent, three dice sable each charged with an ace of the field (Fig. 819).

FIG. 820.

FIG. 821.

Per chevron vert and argent, in chief a rose between two fleurs-de-lis of the second, in base a lion rampant reguardant azure (Fig. 820).

Gules, a lion rampant guardant double queued or, supporting between the paws a rose and branch argent (Fig. 821).

FIG. 822.

FIG. 823.

Argent, a bend engrailed azure between two buck's heads cabossed sable (Fig. 822).

Argent, three moles barways sable (Fig. 823).

FIG. 824.

FIG. 825.

Argent, two lion's gambs erased in saltire the dexter surmounted by the sinister gules (Fig. 824).

Argent, a heron volant in fesse azure between three escallops sable (Fig. 825).

FIG. 826.

FIG. 827.

Azure, on a bend cotised argent three martlets gules (Fig. 826).

Argent, on a fesse between three trefoils slipped azure as many swan's necks erased of the first (Fig. 827).

FIG. 828.

FIG. 829.

Argent, on a pale azure three pairs of wings conjoined and elevated of the first (Fig. 828).

Ermine, on two bars gules three martlets argent (Fig. 829).

FIG. 830.

FIG. 831.

Argent, three eels naiant in pale barways sable (Fig. 830).

Azure, a dolphin embowed argent, on a chief or, two saltires humetté gules (Fig. 831).

FIG. 832.

FIG. 833.

Argent, a chevron between three eagle's legs erased à la cuisse sable (Fig. 832).

Argent, six ostrich feathers, three, two, and one sable (Fig. 833).

FIG. 834.

FIG. 835.

Argent, a chevron engrailed sable between three crabs gules (Fig. 834).

Ermine, three increscents gules (Fig. 835).

FIG. 836.

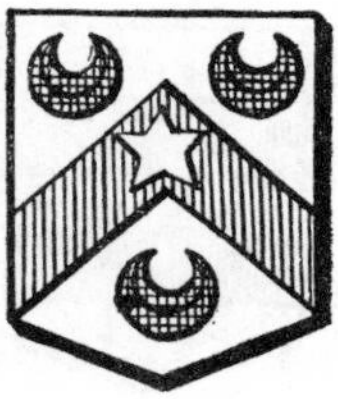

FIG. 837.

Argent, on a chevron gules between three crescents sable a mullet (for a difference) of the field (Fig. 836).

Or, on a mound in base an oak acorned proper (Fig. 837).

FIG. 838.

FIG. 839.

Or, three woodbine leaves pendent gules (Fig. 838).

Argent, three woodbine leaves bendways vert (Fig. 839).

FIG. 840.

FIG. 841.

Azure, a fesse dancetté or, between three cherubs argent (Fig. 840).

Argent, an arm sinister issuing out of the dexter chief point and extended toward the sinister base, gules (Fig. 841).

FIG. 842.

FIG. 843.

Argent, three starved branches slipped sable (Fig. 842).

Argent, three stumps of trees couped and eradicated sable (Fig. 843).

FIG. 844.

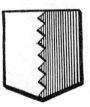

FIG. 845.

Gules, the limb of a tree in bend raguled and trunked argent (Fig. 844).

Per pale indented argent and gules (Fig. 845).

FIG. 846.

FIG. 847.

Per chevron nebulé sable and argent, three panther's heads erased, counter-changed (Fig. 846).

Argent, on a chevron gules three men's skulls of the field (Fig. 847).

FIG. 848.

FIG. 849.

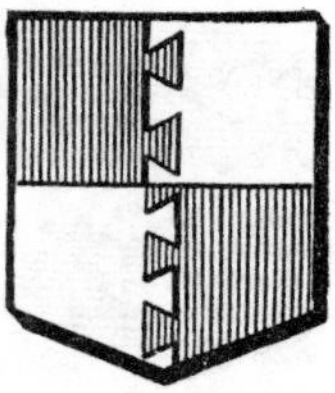

Argent, on a fesse ragulé azure three fleurs-de-lis of the field (Fig. 848).

Quarterly, per pale dove-tailed gules and argent (Fig. 849).

FIG. 850.

FIG. 851.

Per saltire or and argent, four eagles displayed in cross sable (Fig. 850).

Per fesse dancetté or and azure, two mullets pierced counter-changed (Fig. 851).

FIG. 852.

Per bend embattled argent and gules (Fig. 852).

Quarterly, I. and IV. Argent, a chevron gules between three torteaux. II. Quarterly, 1 Argent, a bend gules; 2 Argent, a fesse azure; 3 Argent, a chevron sable: 4 Argent, a pale purpure. III. Argent, a fesse between three billets gules (Fig. 853).

FIG. 853.

FIG. 854.

FIG. 855.

Gules, a chevron counter-compony argent and sable between three fleurs-de-lis of the second (Fig. 854).

Argent, a fesse checky of the first and azure (Fig. 855).

FIG. 856.

FIG. 857.

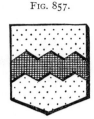

Azure, two bars indented or, a chief argent (Fig. 856).

Or, a fesse dancetté sable (Fig. 857).

FIG. 858.

FIG. 859.

Argent, a wheel of eight spokes gules (Fig. 858).

Ermine, two flanches azure each charged with three ears of wheat couped argent (Fig. 859).

FIG. 860.

FIG. 861.

Sable, a chevron ermine between three salmons hauriant argent (Fig. 860).

Or, two bars azure, a chief quarterly; 1 and 4 Azure, two fleurs-de-lis or, 2 and 3 Gules a lion passant guardant or (Fig. 861).

OBSOLETE BLAZON.

The blazon of the arms of Massachusetts (see Fig. 346) suggests the necessity of some information upon this method of describing heraldic tinctures.

"Some of those fantastic writers of the 15th and 16th centuries, who have thrown such discredit upon the science they intended to support, promulgated the absurd opinion that colours, especially when compounded, were originally intended to signify certain virtues in the bearer, viz., *gules* with *or* signifies desire to conquer, with *argent* revenge, with *vert* courage in youth, &c.

"Some, also, that Gentlemen, Esquires, Knights, and Baronets' arms should be blazoned by *metals* and *colours ;* Barons, Viscounts, Earls, Marquises, and Dukes, by *precious stones ;* Sovereign Princes, Kings, and Emperors, by *planets.* Premising that such ideas are purely visionary, and the practice of such rules mere affectation, we subjoin a table illustrating the subject—

COLOURS.			NAMES.	STONES.	PLANETS.	VIRTUES.
Yellow,			Or,	Topaz,	Sol,	Constancy.
White,			Argent,	Pearl,	Luna,	Innocence.
Red,			Gules,	Ruby,	Mars,	Magnanimity.
Blue,	which are termed in	Heraldry	Azure,	Sapphire,	Jupiter,	Loyalty.
Green,			Vert,	Emerald,	Venus,	Love loyal.
Purple,			Purpure,	Amethyst,	Mercury,	Temperance.
Black,			Sable,	Diamond,	Saturn,	Prudence.
Orange,			Tenne,	Hyacinth,	Drn. Head.	
Murrey,			Sanguine,	Sardonyx,	Drn. Tail.	

"These distinctions, however, were nowhere used but in England, being justly held in ridicule in all other countries, as a fantastic humour of our nation."[1]

[1] Planche's Clark.

CHAPTER XV.

CRESTS, BADGES, MOTTOES, AND SUPPORTERS.

THE *Crest* (from Latin *cresta*, the tuft or comb which grows upon the heads of many birds) was placed upon the top of the helmet of chieftains so that their followers might readily distinguish them in battle. Commanders alone were entitled to bear it. The helmets of esquires were decorated with feathers or scrolls, which hung down over their armor.

Among French heralds the crest is known as the *cimier*. Another name by which it is frequently called is *cognizance* (Latin *cognosco*, to know), since by it the leader was recognized. It was usually the figure of some animal or bird placed on the top of the helmet, and its height made the wearer seem taller and more imposing. Alexander the Great adopted the ram's head; Julius Cæsar was known by a star, the head of a bull, an elephant, or the she-wolf that suckled Romulus and Remus.

While crests are traceable to very early days, their use was not general until mediæval times. Many of the more ancient arms of families are borne without these cognizances. It is probable that families derived crests as badges of distinction in peaceful times, from the device which their leader had worn in recent warfare. They were originally assumed at the pleasure of their bearers, and the same coat of arms is often seen surmounted by varying crests; an illustration of this is in the arms of Fowke of Leicester, and of Fowke of Dorsetshire, London, and Staffordshire. The relation of the families is made apparent by the fact that they bear the same shield, *Vert, a fleur-de-lis argent;* the former has for a crest, *A dexter arm embowed, habited vert, cuff argent, holding in the hand an arrow or, barbed and flighted of the second point downwards,* whereas the latter has for a crest, *An Indian goat's head erased arg.*

Crests are even now less strictly under the control of the heralds than the devices on the shield, and they are so various that a classification of them is scarcely possible. The following is an abridgment of their classification by Newton, who has written very fully on the subject in his "Display of Heraldry." First, the most ancient class of crests he believes to have consisted of ferocious animals, which were regarded as figuratively representing the bearer and his pursuits. Secondly, crests were devices assumed as memorials of feats of chivalry, and for the purpose of perpetuating tradition and family legends, either in addition to or differing from charges represented on the shield. Thirdly, they served to give a more prominent place to objects already represented on the escutcheon. Fourthly, they commemorated religious vows, or expressed the religious or knightly aspirations of the bearer. Fifthly, they were whims, and were adopted for no very definite purpose.

When actually borne in battle, the crests were made of leather or some more durable material, such as metal or wood; and these devices were fastened to the helmet by leathern thongs.

Crests are now depicted on wreaths, coronets, or caps of maintenance termed chapeaus, and, when expressed without naming the wreath, coronet, or chapeau upon which they are borne (as is frequently the case), they are understood to issue from a wreath. The coronet or chapeau is always particularly named.

To face the dexter side of the shield is generally considered more honorable than to face the sinister side, and all animals, birds, or other crests that face the edge of the shield should look to the dexter, else they may be considered to have been reversed for some special reason. Palliot (French) says that the helmet when facing the sinister is a mark of illegitimacy. With the helmet thus reversed, the crest would also face sinister.

Many incompetent artists make errors in details of this nature, and coats of arms are frequently seen upon which the ignorance of the designer or engraver has placed signs of disgrace. This fact alone is a substantial reason why every one who bears a heraldic device should understand the rules of heraldry, or, at least, be well enough acquainted with them to blazon his own armorial bearings correctly. It is well to note here that the *wreath* or *roll*, ordinarily placed beneath the crest, should consist of the leading *metal* and *color* of the shield, the metal *invariably* commencing on the *dexter* side.

Originally, crests were considered personal bearings only, but leading authorities claim that they are hereditary. In the United States such seems to be the case, as the crest forms, with the shield, the distinctive family mark, and is sometimes borne alike by husband, wife, son, and daughter.

BADGES.

Badges (different from crests) were the various devices adopted by commanders and families as distinctive marks, and were borne on surcoats, military equipments, caparisons, and articles of domestic use, and also upon the coats of soldiers and liveries of household attendants, etc. This system was introduced that the followers of a chieftain might be known; and as the crest was his individual device, and his coat of arms was too elaborate for the purpose, the badge was adopted and borne without a wreath beneath it. Badges were at times selected from the devices of the shield; sometimes they resembled crests, but often were entirely different from the heraldic insignia.

Gerard Leigh says the badge was not placed on a wreath in the time of Henry V.; and for many years after no man under the degree of a knight had his badge so placed. Custom and the changes of time, however, have removed this restriction, and now quite often the badge of a retainer can only be distinguished from a crest by the careful study of pedigrees and family history.

The most famous badges in English history were the Red and White Roses; the Red, adopted by John of Gaunt, Duke of Lancaster, as the badge of his house and its followers; and the White, adopted by his brother Edmund of Langley, Duke of York. From these devices the "Wars of the Roses" received their name.

After the accession of Henry VII. and his marriage with Elizabeth of York, anno 1486, the Tudor Rose became the royal badge of England, and was represented of the two colors white and red per pale, or a white rose within a red one, and sometimes quartered, to symbolize the union of the houses of York and Lancaster. (See Fig. 5.)

KNOTS.

A distinct group of badges were formed of silk cord, which was twisted into monograms and various shapes, called *Knots*. The most prominent of these are known as the *Stafford Knot*, the *Bouchier*, the *Heneage*, the *Wake* and *Ormond*, the *Bowen*, the *Lacey*, and the *Harrington*.

MOTTOES.

Associated generally with the arms and crest is the *Motto*. This is borne in a scroll or ribbon, placed below the shield, unless it has special reference to the crest. When it has such reference, it should be placed either immediately above or below the crest. The motto is not held to be hereditary, but is supposed to be strictly personal in character. In actual usage, however, it is transmitted and borne with the shield and crest, although it may be changed at pleasure. If no motto properly belongs to a coat of arms, its bearers may, with perfect propriety, adopt one, and many instances are recorded where the same motto is borne by several different families.

Mottoes are perhaps more ancient than coat-armor, and many of the older ones were originally the war-cries of the families or clans. Later they were chosen to express the predominant passions of piety or love. In some cases the motto alludes to the name of the bearer or to some of the charges on his arms; and frequently it is merely a short quaint sentence, which pleased the fancy or caprice of the person who first adopted it, or one referring to some particular feat which it is meant to perpetuate. By the rules of heraldry women do not bear mottoes; the sovereign only is excepted. In England, bishops do not bear mottoes.

SUPPORTERS.

Supporters are exterior ornaments placed at the sides of the escutcheon. They are generally borne in pairs of the same or different figures, one standing on each side of the shield as if in the act of supporting it. Single supporters were not uncommon in early heraldry, though little used now.

Old authorities say that supporters had their origin from the custom which prevailed at tilts and tournaments, where the knights caused their shields to be carried by attendants, who were costumed as lions, bears, griffins, moors, etc. The duty of these attendants was to display and guard the escutcheons, which the knights were obliged to expose to public view for some time before the tilts commenced.

Another theory is that the introduction of supporters in achievements was due to the fancy of seal engravers of the mediæval period, who, in cutting arms on seals, introduced various figures to fill up vacant spaces.

Supporters are distinctive of high rank, and as in England they are with few exceptions borne only by the sovereign or peers of the realm, it follows that it is improper to embody them (without authority) in the arms of any American. It will thus be seen that, according to English heraldic usage, any man bearing supporters in America is supposed to express that he is a peer of the realm, or that he has been given the right to bear them by a special grant.

Burke remarks, " In England, the right to bear Supporters is confined to Peers of the Realm, Knights of the Garter and Bath, and to those who may have obtained them by Royal Grant. Garter King of Arms has not the power to grant them to any person below the degree of a Knight of the Bath, unless acting under especial direction from the Sovereign, Lord Lyon however may, by virtue of his office, do so without any such Royal warrant."

In ancient times many personages who held high offices in the state used supporters, as did various eminent though unennobled families,—viz., the Stevenings, of Sussex, the Stawells and Luttrells, of Somersetshire, the Tichbornes and Pophams, of Hants, the Fulfords, of Devon, the Savages, of Cheshire, the Trevanions, of Cornwall, etc. " Hence," says a learned heraldic writer, " it may justly be concluded, that those families who anciently used such supporters, either on their seals, banners, or monuments, and carved them in stone or wood, or depicted them on the glass windows of their mansions, and in the churches, chapels, and religious houses of their foundation, endowment, or patronage, as perspicuous evidences and memorials of their having a possessory right to such supporters, are, full and absolutely, well entitled to bear them, and that no one of their descendants of such families ever ought to alienate such supporters, or bear their arms without them, because such possessory right is by far more honourable than any other, modern grant of supporters that can be obtained from the office of arms."

It will be, to say the least, in better taste for Americans to omit supporters from their arms, excepting, of course, in the rare cases where they have a distinct right to use them.[1]

[1] As a notable instance of the existence of such a right, the Barons Fairfax may be mentioned. Thus, an American is a British peer, and may bear coronet and supporters as such.

Among other American families whose members have received titles and honors abroad are the Delafields, of New York, who are counts of the old German Empire, though long resident in the United States. The De Lanceys have been Viscounts de Laval and Nouvian; and there are other noble families here. The great scientist of the last century, Count Rumford, was a native American, and took title from his native town, Concord, N. H., then called Rumford. These Americans have had the heraldic rights of their rank, and exercised them.

Americans have been created baronets,—instance, Sir William Johnson, and the two creations in the Pepperell family. The creations were for services rendered in America during Colonial times, and carried the usual heraldic insignia of baronets.

Several Americans were knighted before the Revolution, as Sir Charles Hobby, who was knighted July 9, 1705, "for good service done the crown in New England," and who has many living descendants. Sir Charles was colonel of the Massachusetts regiment in the Port Royal Expedition, under General Nicholson, in 1710. These knights of Colonial days were entitled to bear the helmet of knighthood over their shields. Americans have also been occasionally knighted down to the present time. Professor Morse, the inventor of the telegraph, was a knight of several foreign Orders. So was the eminent physician, Dr. Marion Sims, to whom has just been raised a statue in New York. Edison, the inventor, has been knighted by the government of the French Republic for his distinguished services to the science of the world. There are several other American knights now living. These are entitled by the usages of heraldry to bear the insignia of their Orders with their coats of arms.

It is a further matter of interest that some of the most historic arms known to heraldry are borne by Americans, in consequence of the residence here of many scions of the ancient nobility of England and Europe, descended from younger sons. In some instances, at least, the actual head of the family is an American. Such is the case with the Montgomerys, one of the most celebrated of the "great houses" of the Old World, and rightful Earls of Eglinton. From 912, for many generations this family were Counts of Montgomerie in France. They also held several earldoms in England from the time of the Norman Conquest. The Scotch branch finally succeeded to the headship of the house, and became Earls of Eglinton and Barons Montgomery. The fifth earl, who died in 1612, childless, alienated the title and estates to a relative by marriage, Sir Alexander Seton, who assumed the name of Montgomery; and from him descend the present Earls of Eglinton and Winton. The sole heir of the male line of the ancient house, Sir Neil Montgomery, of Lanislaw, never recognized the rightfulness of this alienation. His eventual heir, William Montgomery, Esq., sold the estate of Brigend in 1701–2, and removing to New Jersey became seated on a new estate, "Eglinton," in Monmouth County, which long remained in possession of his descendants. The present male representative is a citizen of Philadelphia, connected by marriage with some of the best American families.

CHAPTER XVI.

MARKS OF CADENCY, DIFFERENCING, AUGMENTATION, AND ABATEMENT.

MARKS of Cadency are certain devices added to arms to distinguish members and branches of families one from the other, and are as follows:

FIG. 862.

A label for the first son. (Worn only during the lifetime of the father) (Fig. 862).

FIG. 863.

A crescent for the second son (Fig. 863).

FIG. 864.

A mullet for the third son (Fig. 864).

FIG. 865.

A martlet for the fourth son (Fig. 865).

FIG. 866.

An annulet for the fifth son (Fig. 866).

FIG. 867.

A fleur-de-lis for the sixth son (Fig. 867).

FIG. 868.

A rose for the seventh son (Fig. 868).

FIG. 869.

A cross moline for the eighth son (Fig. 869).

FIG. 870.

A double quartrefoil for the ninth son (Fig. 870).

These marks are generally placed in the chief of the shield or upon the honor point, and are also borne upon crests.

The system was invented to prevent the confusion which would arise if all the members of a family bore the same arms, and these marks were added to the family coat by the several sons in order that they might bear the family arms and still be individually identified. Marks of cadency permitted this without materially altering the original shield. According to this plan, the eldest son of a family bears, during his father's lifetime, the label as the symbol which indicates his relation to the head of the family. When he succeeds to the headship, upon the death of his father, he removes from his shield the mark of cadency, and it is transferred to his eldest son. If the eldest son of any family dies without issue, and the father is living, the second son bears the label, and when he succeeds he bears the family arms without any mark of cadency, just as his elder brother would have done. The label is always the mark of the *eldest surviving son*.

During the grandfather's life the system is sometimes extended to the grandchildren in the same way. The *first* son of the eldest son would bear the family arms charged with his father's mark,—a label,—and upon that label would be placed another label to show that he himself was an eldest son. The *second* son of the eldest son would bear the arms charged with a label, as his father's mark, and upon the label would be a crescent to show that he himself was a second son. Upon the death of the grandfather, the father's mark—the label—would be removed, and each of the latter's sons would bear the family arms with his own mark of difference.

The second son of the original family would bear the arms charged with a crescent, and his sons would bear the arms with their respective marks of cadency charged upon the crescent. The children of the third son would charge theirs upon a mullet, those of the fourth upon a martlet, and so on.

When the grandfather dies, no change is made in the marks of the second and younger sons, but each of them may become the founder of a *house*, and the mark of cadency would be retained by his descendants,—likely to change, however, if the line of one of the older houses should become extinct, since each house would then be one degree nearer the main line; the fourth would become the third, and change its martlet to a mullet, and so on with the others. Examples Figs. 871 to 880, inclusive, illustrate the system.

FIRST HOUSE.

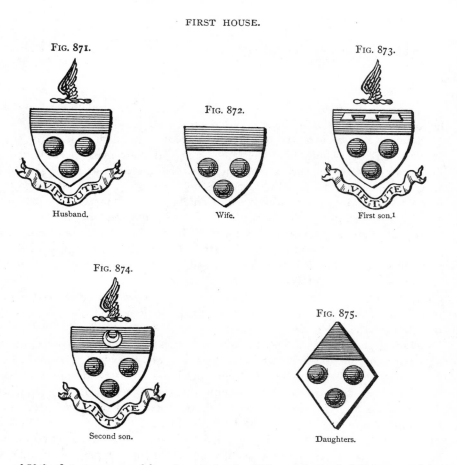

FIG. 871.

Husband.

FIG. 872.

Wife.

FIG. 873.

First son.[1]

FIG. 874.

Second son.

FIG. 875.

Daughters.

[1] If the first son marry and have issue during the lifetime of the head of the house, such issue charge their respective marks of cadency upon the label, as explained in the third paragraph on page 301. To further illustrate the system, the second house is shown in Figs. 876–880. The second son of the first house (Fig. 874) becomes the head of the second house (Fig. 876).

SECOND HOUSE.

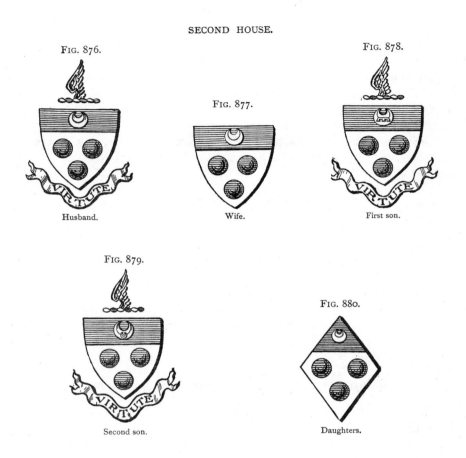

FIG. 876.

Husband.

FIG. 877.

Wife.

FIG. 878.

First son.

FIG. 879.

Second son.

FIG. 880.

Daughters.

These complicated and elaborate methods are, however, very rarely carried out, and the marks of cadency are seldom used, even by brothers during the lifetime of their father. They now serve mainly to distinguish younger branches of families from the main stem; and in many cases the mark of cadency has come to be considered an integral part of the arms.

The daughters of a family have no marks of cadency, since in English law the general rule is that all the daughters inherit equally. Hence a woman bears a mark of cadency only where it is the mark of her father or where it has become the hereditary bearing of a junior branch of the family.

The term *Differencing* is used to express certain marks which are applied to the arms of individuals and families who, while having no blood relationship are connected by marriage, or were connected in early days, through feudal dependency.

Arms may thus be differenced by adding some new charge or omitting some feature, substituting an ordinary, adding a border, changing the tinctures, reversing the tinctures of field and charges, etc.

When arms thus modified by *Differencing* are once adopted they are permanently retained, but when differenced by *Marks of Cadency* they are subject to other changes in accordance with changes in relationship. It is to be noted, however, that many old arms borne by Americans still retain marks of cadency, placed on them many years ago in England, which have now become permanent parts of the armorial achievements.

The only record of arms differenced in America known to the writer is published by " The Salem Press Historical and Genealogical Record," October, 1890, as follows :

"The Honble Benj. Lynde Esqr Sam^{ll} Curwin Esqr and Mr Henry Gibbs Executors to the last Will & Testament of Mr Wm Lynde dec^{d} to James Turner

1752			Dr.
May 14.	To 8 Escutcheons for ye Funeral of f^{d} dec^{d} at 8/ ap^{s}		£6 [torn]
	To an inscription on ye Breastplate of the coffin		8–0
June 6th.	To 9 Enamell'd Rings [1] for D^{o} w^{t} 13^{dwt}. 23 gr		4 –4–0
June 9th.	To adding a Crescent for Difference to each of the		
	Escutcheons at 2/ ap^{s}		16–0
			£11–16–0"

ARMS IN AMERICA DIFFERENCED BY THE REVERSAL OF TINCTURES.

In a number of arms inherited from early American ancestors are found the same charges which were in the original English arms, but with the tinctures reversed ; and this leads to the belief that some of the early settlers thus differenced their arms to distinguish them from their respective families in the country which they had left. This belief is strengthened by a statement of Mackenzie's explaining an established custom : " Colors have been changed upon very honorable occasions ;" and he explains that " some families upon leaving their country, retained their arms, but chang'd their colors :" for example, arms that had been *Argent, three mullets gules*, are now *Gules, three mullets argent*.

This reversal of tinctures in a number of American coats of arms must be carefully distinguished from others, more numerous, in which the tinctures have been changed by the incorrect interpretation of the blazon by designers, or by mistakes which have been made on account of the small size of the

---

[1] Rings were given at funerals in New England for at least one hundred and fifty years after the settlement of that part of the country. The custom was brought from England, as wills on record there make frequent mention of it.

original seal or engraving from which the arms have been reproduced, or, as is often the case, where the correctness of an illumination is sacrificed for more pleasing combinations of colors.

These two classes—arms properly differenced and arms which contain errors—must be treated in entirely different ways. The former may be borne as they are, without modifications; but the latter should be restored to their original condition and the tinctures and charges made to conform with the original blazon, thus avoiding "false heraldry."

AUGMENTATION.

Augmentations of arms are special marks of honor conferred by the sovereign, for a creditable act or heroic deed. They are charged upon shields or borne as crests or supporters.

An example of augmentation is shown in the arms of the family of Douglas (Fig. 13). The story is told that when King Robert of Scotland was on his death-bed he exclaimed, having previously sworn that he would go on the Crusades, "Since my body cannot perform what my heart desires, I will send my heart at least to perform my vows." He commissioned Sir James Douglas to execute this task, who set forth with the heart in a silver casket. King Alfonso of Aragon begged his aid against the Moors, and he enlisted in such behalf. The battle went against the Christians, Sir James was surrounded by the enemy, and despairing, detached the casket from around his neck and cast it far in front of him, saying, "Now thou, pass thou onward as thou were wont to do, and Douglas will follow thee or die."

Douglas was killed on the battle-field, and Sir Simon Lockhard, or de Locard, found the casket near his body and returned with it to Scotland, where the heart was buried in Melrose Abbey,—and the family of Douglas were granted an Augmentation of the Crowned Heart. Sir Simon changed his name to Lockheart. He received for an augmentation *a heart within a lock*, and bore the motto, *Corda serrata pando :* I lay open a heart shut up.

ABATEMENTS.

Abatements are mentioned by early heralds as marks whereby coats of arms were lowered or degraded in their dignity; however, no records of such arms are found, excepting those charged with marks of illegitimacy, although abatements are frequently seen in the American heraldry of to-day, the result of the indifferent treatment of blazon.

Guillim blazons the marks of disgrace, and Sir John Ferne, in his "Blazon of Gentrie" (1586), says,—

" A knight may be capable of nine vices.

  1. To reuoke his own challenge.
  2. To slea his prysoner (humblye yielding)
   with his own handes (except in time of danger)
   for so great was the compassion, mercy and
   curtesie in old times to be seene in all
   Gentlemen, farre aboue the vnnoble state
   of men (which be alwayes, vnciuell, crvel,
   vnmercifull, and inexorable) that therevpon
   in our vulgare speache we call it a man of
   mercye, compassion, and curtesie, a gentle person.
  3. To voyd from his soueraignes banner in the fielde.
  4. To tell his soueraigne false tales.
  5. Full of lecherie in his body.
  6. Full of drunklew, or subiect to Bacchus.
  7. Full of slovth in his warres.
  8. Full of boast on his manhood.
  9. Full or cowardize to his enemie."

Some heralds repudiate abatements as inconsistent with the idea of heraldry and with the spirit of chivalry that a kingly gift once given should be afterwards debased.　But they agree that there must have been a restraining influence exerted over some of the knights of old.

We have from Shakspeare a suggestion:

> " Yea, though I die the scandal will survive,
> And be an eyesore to my golden coat;
> Some loathsome dash the herald will contrive
> To cipher me."

It is most likely that those who had incurred their sovereign's displeasure or merited his punishment were at times deprived of their arms or badge, which was considered a great disgrace, since in those days every man entitled to bear arms found it necessary to guard and cherish them in order to maintain his social position.

Shakspeare's Bolingbroke, in complaining of his treatment by King Richard, says,—

> " From my own window torn my *household* coat,
> Raz'd out my *impress*, leaving me no *sign*—
> Save men's opinions, and my living blood—
> To show the world I am a gentleman."

CHAPTER XVII.

MARSHALLING.

MARSHALLING is that branch of the science of heraldry which treats of the placing in one group two or more coats of arms in strict accordance with heraldic law. In early heraldry arms were marshalled by placing the shields side by side in separate escutcheons, or the principal shield was surrounded by others containing the arms of the maternal ancestors, thereby to denote the several matches and alliances of one family with the heiresses of others. At the present time the principal methods of marshalling are by *Impalement* and *Quartering*.

IMPALEMENT.

The word *impalement* is used in heraldry to express the marshalling of arms of husband and wife (sometimes called "Baron and Femme"). In such instances the husband's coat occupies the dexter side of the escutcheon and the wife's the sinister. In this manner archbishops and bishops impale their paternal coats with the arms of their episcopal sees, placing the arms of office upon the dexter side and their own coat on the sinister. Deans, heads of colleges, and various other officers also bear their arms in this latter way.

When two coats of arms are *impaled* the distribution and size of the charges are adapted to the different spaces afforded by the impaled shield. In blazoning impaled arms they are treated separately, although the blazon is one, as in the example of the arms of Coyle and De Vere (fictitious). (See Fig. 886.) This is the coat of arms of Coyle, who married De Vere (not an heiress), who bears her father's arms. The impaled arms are not hereditary. The issue would bear the arms of the father, and the impaled arms can only be borne by husband and wife or by the survivor. The widow would bear the impaled arms in a *lozenge*, and not upon a shield. If she marries again, she naturally discards the arms of her first husband, unless he was a peer. If a widower marries a second time he can bear the arms of both wives; however, such a combination is not usual, and is naturally not considered good form, being altogether condemned by some writers.

FIG. 881.

The early form of marshalling by impalement was known as *dimidiation* (Fig. 881), which is executed by cutting *two* shields in half paleways, and conjoining the dexter half of one and the sinister half of the other. As such combinations generally produced grotesque and confusing effects, marshalling by *impalement,* as above explained, was introduced, and has since been practised.

Where the arms of a family have many additions through alliances with heiresses, marshalling is executed by quartering, and it is necessary for the herald to have before him a genealogical table, in order that he may be able to collect such quarterings in the order in which they should be borne. It will thus be readily seen that heraldry and genealogy are closely allied, and the importance of absolute correctness in every detail of each science needs no further comment.

MARSHALLING BY QUARTERING.

Quartering—the bearing of two or more coats of arms on one escutcheon, a system but little practised until the fifteenth century, but now in general use —denotes the several matches and alliances of one family with the heiresses of others. It must be remembered that the word heiress, in heraldry, does not necessarily mean an heiress of landed estates or wealth, but signifies that the lady is the only daughter in a family in which there are no sons; if there are two or more daughters and no son, they are termed *co-heiresses,* and all have equal right to the arms.

The husband of an heiress or co-heiress in event of issue is entitled to place her arms upon an escutcheon of pretence, which is then placed upon the centre of his coat of arms. The sons and daughters may, in such a case, quarter the arms of their mother with their paternal coat.

The arms of the first heiress who marries into a family are borne in the second and third quarters by the descendants, while the paternal arms of the family are placed in the first and fourth quarters. The family arms then appear as in Fig. 883, which would be blazoned *Quarterly : 1 and 4, Argent, a bend gules,* for COYLE ; *2 and 3, Or, a fleur-de-lis azure,* for DEAN.

When a second heiress marries into the family, the descendants remove the arms of heiress number one from the third quarter, and substitute those of heiress number two, the other quarters being unchanged. The arms are then as in Fig. 885. *Quarterly : 1 and 4, Argent, a bend gules,* for COYLE ; *2, Or, a fleur-de-lis azure,* for DEAN ; *3, Argent, a lion rampant azure,* for DE VERE. The arms of heiress number three would replace the original arms of the family in the fourth quarter, and the shield would then be as in Fig. 893. *Quarterly : 1, Argent, a bend gules,* for COYLE ; *2, Or, a fleur-de-lis azure,* for DEAN ; *3, Argent, a lion rampant azure,* for DE VERE ; *4, Argent, a saltire azure,* for GREENE.

When more than four coats have to be marshalled, the number of vertical lines is increased, and the divisions, though more than four, are still called quarters. The coats are then placed in the divisions or quarters in the order in which they came into the family. Where there is an uneven number of coats, the last quarter is usually filled by repeating the first.

The following will more clearly explain the system:

Example Fig. 882 illustrates the arms of *Coyle*, who married the heiress of the family of Dean, and accordingly bears her arms in the centre of his shield *in pretence*.

In event of there being co-heiresses of the Dean family, the husband of each would bear the Dean arms in the same way over his own family arms, and the issue would be entitled to bear the combined arms. For example,

FIG. 882. FIG. 883.

the issue of the Coyle-Dean family would bear the arms quartered; thus, the Coyle arms would occupy the 1st and 4th quarters and the Dean arms the 2d and 3d (see Fig. 883), and the arms thus combined would be hereditary to all succeeding descendants and lineal heirs. It is in this way that heraldry

FIG. 884. FIG. 885.

records the marriages and alliances of one family with another, and genealogists are sometimes enabled to trace pedigrees through the medium of an impression from a cut or seal of an old coat of arms.

Thus, Fig. 883 is the coat of arms of a son or descendant of Coyle-Dean, and, assuming that he marries a De Vere who is an heiress, he would bear the De Vere arms in a small shield of pretence over the arms of his family (Fig. 884), and his children would bear quartered arms, as in Fig. 885. But if the De Vere is not an heiress, the arms of the two families would then be impaled as in Fig. 886, but the issue could only bear the father's arms, as in Fig. 883.

A daughter of the De Vere heiress would bear arms, as in Fig. 885, but upon a lozenge instead of a shield, as in Fig. 887.

FIG. 886.　　　　　　　　　　FIG. 887.　　　　　　　　　　FIG. 888.

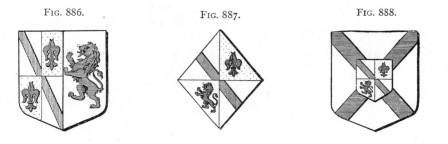

If this daughter, herself an heiress (there being no sons), were to marry a Greene, her quartered arms would be placed over his *in pretence*, as in Fig. 888; but if she be not an heiress, her quartered arms would be then impaled with his, as in Fig. 889. If she were an heiress, her descendants would bear the combined arms of Greene, Coyle, Dean, and De Vere, as in Fig. 890; but if not an heiress, they would bear the Greene arms only.

That these arms, as in Fig. 890, may be properly arranged they are marshalled by a system called quarterly quartering (see Fig. 580), and the arms of the various families are then placed in the several quarters in their regular order.

If a son of the De Vere heiress (who had married a Coyle-Dean) were to marry a Greene, he would impale the Greene arms with his, as Fig. 891, but

FIG. 889.　　　　　　　　　　　　　FIG. 890.

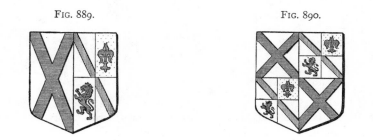

if she were an heiress her arms would be placed *in pretence* over the quartered arms of Coyle-Dean-De Vere, as in Fig. 892, and their issue would bear the quartered arms of Coyle-Dean-De Vere-Greene, as in Fig. 893. The quarters necessary for displaying later alliances would be formed by dividing the shield into a greater number of parts, as before described, the divisions or quarters being numbered from dexter to sinister as before, and the arms being placed in them in the order in which the alliances were made. (See Fig. 919.)

Where the quarterings become numerous, heralds generally select a few of the most important, especially where the arms are to be painted in a small space or engraved upon small articles.

When a man marries an heiress and their only issue is a daughter, she would bear in a lozenge the quartered arms of her father and mother. If the father had a son by a second wife, the son could bear only the father's arms, having no claim to the arms of his father's first wife. But if the second wife be an heiress, he can bear her arms with those of his paternal ancestors.

FIG. 891. FIG. 892. FIG. 893.

A shield of *pretence* must not be confused with an *augmentation of honor*, which is sometimes placed on a small shield, but is never quartered and never changes its position.

Marshalling also consists in the grouping of the various parts of a coat of arms; for instance, the shield, crest, helmet, mantling, motto, etc., when placed in one composition are *marshalled*, and called an achievement.

Arms of dominion, communities, corporate bodies, etc., are also marshalled by quartering, and the principal coat, as in all quartering, occupies the first quarter, the other coats being assigned to their proper quarters in the regular order of precedence. There are also instances of such arms marshalled by *impalement.*

ILLUSTRATION OF FOUR GRAND QUARTERS.[1]

An illustration of grand quartering is shown in Fig. 894. It includes the arms of Bellas of Bellasis, a family of whom (as has been said in time past by the heralds in their visitations of Yorkshire, Durham, and Westmoreland), "few, if any, of our British nobles can boast of a longer line than that of the great and ancient house of Bellasys, deducing, as it doth, an unbroken genealogy from the time of William the Conqueror."

These arms, in the first grand quarter, together with those of the principal alliances of the family prior to its elevation to the peerage of England as Barons, Viscounts, and Earls Fauconberg (as shown in the fourth grand quarter) quartered with those of Smith and Moore in the second and Stuart and Wemyss in the third grand quarter, are as follows: Quarterly of four grand quarters.

I. QUARTERLY: I. *Argent, a chevron gu. between two fleurs-de-lis in chief and an eagle displayed in base az. (Bellas).* II. *Or, three pallets gu., a chief vaire (Bellasis), (Eng'd ancient).* III. *Argent, a pale engrailed between two pallets sa. (Bellasis, Scotland).* IV. *Argent, a chevron gu. between three fleurs-de-lis az. (Bellasyse of Bellasis).*

II. QUARTERLY: I. *Argent, a unicorn's head erased az. armed and maned or, on a chief wavy az. three lozenges or (Smith of Scotland).* II. *Argent, on a bend sa. three crosses crosslet of the field (Charnocke).* III. *Gules, a chevron or, between two roses in chief arg. and a bugle-horn in base of the third, garnished az. (Duncan).* IV. *Argent, ten crosses potent, four, three, two, one, gu. (Moore).*

III. QUARTERLY: I. *Or, a fesse chequé arg. and az. (Stuart).* II. *Argent, three inescutcheons gu. (Haye).* III. *Argent, on a bend az. three buckles or (Leslie).* IV. *Or, a lion rampant gu. armed and langued az. (Wemyss).*

IV. QUARTERLY: I. *Or, a fesse dancetté sa. (Vavasour).* II. *Sable, an orle between six martlets, three, two, one, arg. (Le Spring).* III. *Argent, three hunting-horns sa. stringed and garnished or (Bellingham).* IV. *Argent, three bars gemelles gu. surmounted by a lion rampant sa. (Fairfax).*

CRESTS: I. *A stag's head erased per fesse indented arg. and gu., gorged with a ducal coronet and attired or, holding in mouth a fleur-de-lis az.* (for *Bellas*). 2. *A lion couchant guardant az.* (for *Fauconberg*). 3. *An arm in armor embowed throwing a spear ppr.* (for *Smith*).

MOTTOES: I. *Bonne et belle assez* (for *Bellas* and *Bellasis*). 2. *Virtute sine timore* (for *Smith*).

---

[1] This is not an achievement in use, but the authentic arms of different branches of one family marshalled as an example.

Fig. 894.

CHAPTER XVIII.

MISCELLANEOUS : HELMETS, CROWNS, CORONETS, MITRES, CAPS, MANTLE, SURCOAT,
CYCLAS, JUPON, TABARD, CONTOISE, HATCHMENTS, AND BOOK-PLATES.

HELMETS.

The Helmet, in English heraldry called also helm, casque, basinet, morion, and salade, in Latin *gales* and *cassis*, and in French *heaulim, haulme, haume,* and *casque*, has been made of various forms and compositions, to protect the head in battle.   The earlier Greek and Roman helmets were surmounted by plumes, but, unlike their modern successors, did not protect the face.   During the Middle Ages the helmet was made of the finest steel, often inlaid with gold, and provided with a visor to cover the face in action and to allow of being opened at other times.

From the form known as the Norman, the helmet at a later period varied in shape according to the degree of the person who wore it ; and helmets were set over coats of arms to indicate by their forms the rank of the bearer.

The helmet borne by the sovereign and princes of the blood royal is of gold, full faced and open, generally with but six bars, and lined with crimson (Fig. 895).   At times it is shown with a seventh bar.   The helmet borne by dukes and marquises is placed affronté, and is of steel, with five golden bars.

FIG. 895.

FIG. 896.

The helmet borne by earls, viscounts, and barons is of silver and guarded with ten golden bars, but placed in profile, so that only five of the bars show. It is lined with crimson (Fig. 896).

The helmet assigned to baronets and knights is full faced, of steel, the visor up, and without bars, ornamented with silver, and lined with crimson (Fig. 897).

The helmet of esquires and gentlemen is of steel, with the visor or beaver

314

down, ornamented with silver, and placed in profile. This is the form used when the helmet is borne as a charge upon the field (Fig. 898), and, with rare exceptions, is the only helmet that should appear in the heraldry of America.

German and other Continental heralds, who recognize the use of many crests over one shield of quarterings, place all of them upon helmets, looking from each side toward the centre one; but English heralds, when only one is

FIG. 897.

FIG. 898.

borne, ever place it, if in profile, turned toward the dexter, but when two crests are depicted, they are sometimes placed *vis-à-vis* for the sake of artistic effect.

In achievements the helmet is borne upon the top of the shield.

The helmet when borne over the shield supports the crest, but it is not mentioned in blazoning. In American arms, care should be taken in the designing of a proper helmet, as it would appear ridiculous for an American to bear the helmet of a king or noble. To the latter there are several exceptions. According to English heraldic law, a helmet should never be placed over the arms of any woman except those of the sovereign.

CROWNS, CORONETS, MITRES, AND CAPS.

Crowns have always been the distinguishing ornaments of kings, and are the emblems of sovereignty throughout Europe at the present time. Coronets are worn by princes and nobles upon state occasions, and are always represented above their coats of arms, the form of the coronet at all times indicating the rank of the bearer. In France the coronet appears above the shields of noblemen almost invariably, and little attention is paid to the crest.

The Imperial Crown of England is composed of four crosses pattée and four fleurs-de-lis, which are set upon the circlet alternately. Two arches studded

FIG. 899.

FIG. 900.

FIG. 901.

with pearls arise from within the crosses, and are surmounted by a mound, upon which rests another cross pattée. The cap is of crimson velvet (Fig. 899).

The Mural Crown is of gold; the circle is *masoned* and the top *embattled.* It was given to those who distinguished themselves in military sieges. It is drawn with either four or five points, but the form shown in Fig. 900 has the preference.

The Pallisado Crown is a golden circle, from which sharp-pointed stakes arise (Fig. 901). When the stakes arise from the inside it is called *Crown Vallery.*

The Eastern or *Antique Crown*, sometimes called *Radiated*, is represented by an indefinite number of rays, although it is generally drawn with five. It is of gold (Fig. 902).

FIG. 902.　　　　　FIG. 903.　　　　　FIG. 904.

The Celestial Crown resembles the Eastern Crown, but the rays are higher and not quite so broad, while each is surmounted by a star (Fig. 903).

The Naval Crown is a gold circle, bearing on the rim sterns of ships and sails, arranged alternately (Fig. 904).

A Duke's Coronet is a circle of gold chased and guarded by ermine. It is decorated with eight strawberry leaves, of which five are shown in representation (Fig. 905). This must not be confused with the *Ducal Coronet* (Fig. 910).

A Marquis' Coronet is a chased circlet of gold, with four pearls or balls of silver and as many strawberry leaves alternating, and set upon low points on the rim. In illustrations three leaves and two pearls are shown (Fig. 906).

FIG. 905.　　　　　FIG. 906.　　　　　FIG. 907.

An Earl's Coronet is a chased circle of gold, from which rise eight rays or spikes, and upon the top of each is a pearl. On the rim and alternating with the rays are strawberry leaves, of which four are shown in illustrations (Fig. 907).

A Viscount's Coronet is of gold, and embellished with twelve, fourteen, or sixteen pearls set upon the rim close together (Fig. 908).

A Baron's Coronet is a circle of gold, enhanced with six pearls of large size, four of which are shown in illustrations (Fig. 909).

A Ducal Coronet. Various modifications of crowns and coronets exist, and are often charged upon shields or borne with crests, etc. The most prominent is the *Ducal* or, as Boutell suggests, the "*Crest Coronet*" (Fig. 910).

FIG. 908.   FIG. 909.   FIG. 910.

This coronet has reference to no rank, but is generally borne in conjunction with the crest or upon the necks of birds or animals, which are then said to be *gorged*.

FIG. 911.

The Cap of Maintenance or *Chapeau* was for a long time an emblem of rank worn by kings and nobles. It is sometimes borne as a charge, but is generally used to support the crest in place of the wreath (Fig. 911).

The Archbishop's Mitre is often represented as rising from a duke's coronet, but sometimes the crest coronet is used as shown in Fig. 912.

FIG. 912.   FIG. 913.

The Bishop's Mitre is generally represented as in the example (Fig. 913).

The caps of the coronets of the nobility are crimson, but they are not necessarily worn with the coronets, or borne with them in heraldic achievements. The wife of a noble is entitled to bear over her arms the same coronet as her husband.

COATS OF ARMS: THE MANTLE, SURCOAT, CYCLAS, JUPON, TABARD, AND CONTOISE.

The Mantle or *Surcoat* was a loose, flowing garment, attached to the helmet, and worn over the armor to protect it from rust as well as heat, and from this arose the idea of decorating painted, engraved, or carved coats of arms with it. It is generally shown in fanciful twists and turns, said to represent the cuts received in battle, and is designed at the taste of the artist, although in earlier times it was indicated exactly as worn. The mantle was decorated with the arms and heraldic devices of the bearer, and helped to distinguish him in the field of battle.

The style of the surcoat naturally changed, and it was followed by the *Cyclas*, which was long and flowing behind, but short in front. This was probably due to the inconvenience of fighting with much material hanging over the arms. It is said that the surcoat and cyclas were worn only in battle.

The Jupon was the next fashionable garment, and probably originated from cutting the back of the cyclas to the length of the front, although it fitted the body more closely.

The Tabard was popular many years after the jupon had ceased to be worn, and may be described as like the jupon but with short sleeves, the jupon having no sleeves.

The Contoise was a scarf worn by knights upon the helmet, and is said to have been a love-token. From it the mantling seen in the decoration of shields is supposed by some to have been derived.

Ladies of rank also wore mantles, frequently decorated with their husband's arms impaled with their own, or the husband's arms only. Many dresses of the richest materials were also embroidered with heraldic devices of most elaborate execution.

HATCHMENTS.

Hatchments are the armorial bearings of the deceased, borne within a lozenge-shaped form, which is placed upon the front of the house. They are not now used in the United States, although several examples still exist. One

FIG. 914.

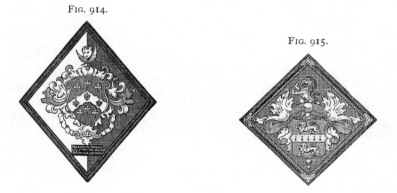

FIG. 915.

of these hangs in the Tower Room of Old Christ Church in Philadelphia, and is represented by Fig. 914. Another, that of the Dickinson family, hangs in the Philadelphia Library (Fig. 915).

Among other hatchments are those of the families of Browne, Gookin, and Thurston.

BROWNE.

Gules, on a chevron between three leopard's heads argent, as many escallops azure.

CREST: *A cubit arm vested gules cuffed argent, holding in the hand ppr. a sword erect of the last, hilted or, enfiled with a leopard's head of the second.*
MOTTO: *"Virtus curâ servabıt,"*—"Virtue shall preserve by care." [1]

GOOKIN AND THURSTON.

Quarterly 1 and 4, Gules, a chevron between three cocks or (Gookin); *2 and 3, Sable, a cross crosslet ermine, impaling: Argent, on a bend gules three mullets or, and in chief a lion statant gules.* [2]

The hatchment bearing the arms of the Izard family, related to the Drayton family, of Philadelphia, hangs in Old Goose Creek Church, South Carolina.

Each hatchment indicates whether the deceased was a private gentleman or nobleman, whether a bachelor, married man, widower, married woman, maid, widow, etc.

Hugh Clark thus describes the system:

"BACHELOR.

"When a bachelor dies, his arms and crest are painted single or quartered, but never impaled; the ground of the hatchment under the shield is all black.

"MAIDEN.

"When a maiden dies, her arms (but no crest) must be placed in a lozenge, and may be single or quartered, with the ground under the escutcheon all black, as the former.

"MARRIED MAN.

"When a married man dies, his arms are impaled with his wife's; the ground of the hatchment under his side of the shield in black, the ground under his wife's side in white; the black side signifies the husband to be dead, and the white side denotes the wife to be living.

"MARRIED WOMAN.

"When a married woman dies, her arms are impaled with her husband's (but no crest); the ground of the hatchment under her side of the shield is black, that of her husband white; which signifies the wife to be dead, and the husband living.

---

[1] This hatchment has been owned by three successive generations of William Browne, of Sudbury, Massachusetts. It is now the property of Mrs. Samuel Reed, of Ayer, Massachusetts, a grand-daughter of William Browne who died in Sudbury, 1850.

[2] These arms hung in the church of Ripple, Kent, England, and were procured by the late J. Wingate Thornton, Boston, to whose family they belong. They are now deposited with the New England Historical and Genealogical Society.

"WIDOWER.

"When a widower dies, his arms are impaled with those of his deceased wife, with his crest; the ground of the hatchment to be all black.

"WIDOW.

"When a widow dies, her arms are impaled with her husband's in a lozenge (but no crest); the ground of the hatchment to be all black.

"When a man is the last of a family, the death's head supplies the place of a crest, denoting that death has conquered all.

"When a woman is the last of a family, her arms are placed in a lozenge, with death's head on the top.

"OTHER DISTINCTIONS.

"The peer is distinguished by his coronet and supporters.

"The baronet by his peculiar badge.

"The knight-companion by the motto of his order.

"The bishop by the mitre."

BOOK-PLATES.

Whatever criticism may be expended on the bearing of arms in America, none can affect the use of the book-plate; for in the privacy of his own library the armiger may enjoy the innocent luxury of heraldry to his heart's content

FIG. 916.

and adapt his family devices in a manner both useful and decorative. From the many book-plates long used in this country, it is evident that they are a source of great pleasure to lovers of the art. The designs are endless and of all classes, displaying in many instances the owner's tastes and fancies. Some, generally heraldic, have passed as heirlooms from generation to generation, the drawing and execution bearing evidence of the time in which the plates were made. Others are of later design—fanciful, pretty, appropriate or inappropriate, as the case may be—and in many instances the name alone in script or ornamented letters answers the librarian's purpose. Book-plates (*ex-libris*) originated in Germany (the birthplace of heraldry), and are known to have been used as early as the sixteenth century. Naturally, they were most often of heraldic form, as a coat of arms within a book answered the same practical purpose as the devices upon a warrior's shield; one identified the man, the other his property.

Much has been written on this interesting subject in this country as well as abroad; and here many fine examples are in the possession of collectors, who have gathered them from all sources. It is possible that several hundred Colonial families used this system of marking their libraries; and the practice has steadily increased in favor. Probably the oldest known book-plate is that of William Penn (1702), as shown in Fig. 50. The Byrd book-plate (Fig. 916) may be mentioned as one of historical interest. From many others the book-plate of Francis Hopkinson has been selected on account of its odd and artistic style (Fig. 917).

FIG. 917.

The best-known book-plate in America is undoubtedly that of Washington, examples of which are in possession of various historical societies and individuals throughout the country. The example as shown in Fig. 918 is taken from an original impression at Valley Forge. The arms in this plate are thus blazoned in Burke:

THE WASHINGTON ARMS.

ARMS: *Arg. two bars gu.; in chief three mullets of the second.*

CREST: *Out of a ducal coronet or, an eagle issuant, with wings endorsed, sa.*

ANOTHER CREST: *A raven, with wings endorsed, ppr., issuing out of a ducal coronet or.*

Another book-plate (impaled) is a complete "heraldic achievement," and practically a genealogical table, showing the various alliances of the male lines with heiresses (Fig. 919). This is undoubtedly one of the finest specimens in use in the United States, and is thoroughly heraldic and historic in its character. No more pleasing or instructive example could be set before the student, and it is commented upon at length because it is American in every respect and detail. The arms in the quarterings are without exception those of coats borne paternally or quarterly by American Colonial families and well recorded and substantiated abroad. Of particular interest to Americans is the fact that two leading founders of the Colonies are here commemorated, in the family coat of arms of Sir Walter Raleigh and that of West, Lord Delaware. The book-plate is from the library of the Rev. Dr. C. Ellis Stevens, Rector of Christ Church, Philadelphia, and Chaplain-General of the Society of Colonial Wars. Its emblazonry is as follows:

ARMS: STEVENS—QUARTERLY OF SIXTEEN: 1. *Per chevron azure and argent, in chief two falcons rising or.* 2. *Gules, on a bend cotised argent, a bendlet wavy azure.* 3. *Or, a chevron azure between three mascles gules, on a chief of the last a wolf passant argent.* 4. *Argent, a chevron sable between three roses gules seeded and leaved proper.* 5. *Argent, a chevron engrailed gules between three leopard's faces azure, a crescent for difference of the last.* 6. *Or, a bend vaire.* 7. *Ermine, a fesse between three cinquefoils gules.* 8. *Gules, two bends wavy argent.* 9. *Or, in fesse two mullets between three bugle-horns sable, stringed gules, through that in base an arrow in pale point downward of the second, barbed and feathered argent.* 10. *Azure, a chevron or, between three bucks statant argent.* 11. *Gules, a fret and canton argent.* 12. *Argent, a fret gules.* 13. *Gironny of eight, argent and gules.* 14. *Azure, a chevron between three boar's heads couped or.* 15. *Argent, on a chevron gules, between three covered cups or, a dagger of the second tau sable.* 16. *Azure, semé of fleurs-de-lis and a lion rampant argent; impaling Aikman, quarterly of six:* I. *and* VI. *Argent, a sinister hand in base issuing out of a cloud fesseways, holding an oaken baton paleways, with a branch sprouting out at the top thereof proper, surmounted of a bend engrailed gules.* II. *Grand quarter, (1 and 4)*

EXITUS ACTA PROBAT

George Washington

Argent, a fesse dancetté sable, (2 and 3) Gules, three leopard's faces reversed, jessant de lis or. III. *Azure, two bars argent, on a chief or, three escallops of the first.* IV. *Argent, on a bend engrailed sable, three annulets or.* V. *Azure, on a terrace vert, a tree proper.*

CREST: *A demi-eagle displayed or.* MOTTO: "*Byde Tyme.*"

Below the centre of the shield is suspended the cross decoration of a Knight Commander of the Order of Christ, conferred on Dr. Stevens by the King of Portugal.

These arms are an illustration of marshalling rare in this country, and, as already said, form a complete "heraldic achievement." On the dexter side they are quartered according to the English heraldic law, and on the impaled side according to the Scottish law, which is nearly the same as that in use upon the Continent of Europe. Though the bearer of this coat of arms is a male representative of the Norman house of Fitz Stephen, dating from the reign of the first of the Plantagenet kings, Henry II., in the twelfth century, his own line (which alone holds the hereditary honors) has been resident in this country for more than two hundred and fifty years.[1] All the quarterings have been inherited from heiresses, and are preserved in seals, or in sepulchral or manorial sculptures, and recorded in Visitations of the College of Heralds prior to 1620. The quarterings are, in fact, so ancient as to illustrate many points of interest in the history of heraldry,—some of them dating from the time of the actual use of coat-armor in battle and tournament. Such, for instance, is the sixth quartering, which represents a shield of brass with a band across it of the fur called vaire. This is the oldest device of the shields of the Raleighs, of Devonshire, and has been quartered by the ancestors of the present owner since before the days of Sir Walter Raleigh, who belonged to a later generation of the same house. Space does not permit of a full description of the many points of this emblazonry; but it may be mentioned that the ninth quartering is of the family of Howley, of which was Dr. Howley, Archbishop of Canterbury; and the tenth quartering is that of the arms of Sir Robert Tresilian, Lord Chief Justice of England in 1382. Sir Robert was beheaded and attainted by the rebellious baronage for his loyalty to the king, forfeiting the right to transmit arms to his descendants. The arms are here quartered in consequence of a subsequent special royal grant of King Richard II. The eleventh and twelfth quarterings are interesting as furnishing an old example of the noting of difference in heraldic inheritance by reversal of tinctures. The first, ninth, tenth, and fourteenth quarterings illustrate ancient usages of hunting and the chase.[2] The impaled arms are those of the house of Aikman, lairds of Cairney, Rosse, and Brambleton,

---

[1] The surname Stevens or Stephens, being derived from the Christian name Stephen, is borne by many English, Welsh, and American families having no connection with this particular family.

[2] It will be noticed that the fifteenth quartering contains the apparent heraldic novelty of the use of metal on metal; but it has been borne in this way by the family since the reign of King Edward II.

which has a recorded descent of eight hundred years, in Scotland. The arms of the first impaled quarter relate to the knightly deed that gave the family its name,—which in English meaning is " Oakman." This deed of Scottish history has been rendered famous by Shakspeare in his tragedy of " Macbeth," and is therefore of unusual interest. The founder of the house was an officer of the forces which overthrew the usurper Macbeth and restored to the Scottish throne the rightful king, Malcolm III. In attacking Macbeth's stronghold of Dunsinane he planned a surprise. Each soldier advancing toward the castle through the wood of Birnam (which to the present day is magnificent with its growth of oaks) was ordered to cover himself with oak boughs so as to seem part of the forest. Shakspeare's reference to this event is in the poetic form of the supposed witch's prophecy to Macbeth by means of an apparition bearing the Aikman crest of a tree, and uttering the words,—

> " Macbeth shall never vanquished be, until
> Great Birnam wood to high Dunsinane hill
> Shall come against him."

The victory is commemorated by the arms, which show in the " *engrailed bend, gules*," flowing blood of battle, and display a left hand holding an oak branch, the right hand being supposed to be reserved for the using of sword or spear. The crest of this family is an oak-tree, and the motto, " *Sub robore virtus*,"—" Valor beneath the oak." This is one of the oldest escutcheons in Scotland. The Aikman second (impaled) quartering is an example of a " grand quarter,"—*i.e.*, a quartering of quarterings. It dates from the reign of Edward III., and is, as already mentioned, the well-known coat of arms of West, Lord De La Warr, of which family was the Lord De La Warr from whom the State of Delaware is named. The third impaled quartering is of the arms of the ancient Dukes of Charente, a French family settled in England, and, during Colonial times, in America. A descendant of this line actively co-operated with Benjamin Franklin in public works of philanthropy. The fourth impaled quartering is of the Clarksons, of Yorkshire, an ancestor of which family was appointed Secretary of the Province of New York by William of Orange. It is connected with the Van Cortlandts, Van Rensselaers, Livingstons, De Peysters, and other Colonial families of New York. All the quarterings of these impaled arms were borne in America during Colonial times, and before the War of the Revolution.

Fig. 920 is another example, and copied from a very artistic copperplate etching used by the Griffitts family of Philadelphia, who are of Welsh descent. Its continued use suggests its genealogical value. Thomas Griffitts emigrated to Jamaica, West Indies, 1714, and in the year following to Philadelphia, engaging in trade with the first Isaac Norris, whose daughter Mary he married in 1717. He was Keeper of the Great Seal of Pennsylvania from 1732 to 1734· Provincial Councillor, 1733; Mayor of Philadelphia, 1729–1733–1737;

BYDE TYME

C. Ellis Stevens, LL.D., D.C.L.

Fig. 919.

FIG. 920.

Judge of the Supreme Court from 1739 to 1743. He died in Philadelphia, 1746.

William Griffitts, born 1724, was one of the founders and earliest contributors to the Pennsylvania Hospital. He married, April 16, 1752, Abigail, daughter of Samuel Powel, and died at Philadelphia, August 25, 1762.

Samuel Powel Griffitts, M.D., born in Philadelphia, July 21, 1759, was founder of the Philadelphia Dispensary, 1786; one of the founders of Philadelphia College of Physicians; and Professor of Materia Medica in the University of Pennsylvania. He married Mary, daughter of William Fishbourne, and died in Philadelphia, 1826.

This book-plate is a copy of one used successively by Thomas, William, and Dr. Samuel Powel Griffitts from 1714 to 1826. The original is still in the possession of a descendant, and copies are in the libraries of other descendants of the families of Griffitts, Fisher, Lewis, Morgan, Rotch, Jackson, Wharton, Churchman, Emlen, Smith, Etting, and Wells.

The book-plate shown in Fig. 921 presents the arms of the Merrick family quartered with those of Vaughan. The former traces ancestry to Cydavail, Judge of the Powis Court, Wales, *circa* A.D. 1200. The family name, then spelled *Meuric*, was the Christian name of the son of Llewellyn, of Bodorgan, Anglesea, Wales, who thus became a founder. He died *circa* 1550. The descent lies through his second son, Rowland Meyrick, Bishop of Bangor (1556), and his grandson, Sir Gelly Mericke, of Lascard, County Pembroke, one of whose daughters married Sir John Vaughan, of Golden Grove, County Carew, Earl of Carberry, who died 1635. Thus the arms of these two ancient families were for the first time quartered. At subsequent periods intermarriages took place between these two families, who were near neighbors in Wales and the bordering counties of England.

The arms of the Merricks in one branch (through Sir Gelly Mericke) were: *Gules, two porcupines in pale argent, armed or ;* in another branch, *Sable on a chevron argent, between three staves raguly or inflamed proper, a fleur-de-lis azure between three Cornish choughs proper.* The original crest is *A castle argent, surmounted by a chough holding a fleur-de-lis in the dexter claw.* In 1583 a crest was granted to the aforesaid Sir Gelly Mericke of "*a lyon's hedd couped arg. on a wreath argent and gules, wounded with a broken launce Or, embraced, gules, mantled argent doubled gules :*" all as appears by a grant given under the hand and seal of Gilbert Dethocke, Garter King-at-Arms. A photographic copy of this unique document is presented in Fig. 268.

The arms of the Vaughan family as they appear quartered in the plate are, *Sable, a chevron argent between three boy's heads couped ppr. crined or, enwrapped about the necks with snakes vert.*

The arms thus quartered were first borne in America before the Revolution by Samuel Merrick, who settled in Philadelphia as a merchant. His

FIG. 921.

brother, John Merrick, married Rebecca Vaughan, a descendant of the afore-mentioned Sir John Vaughan, who was a sister of John Vaughan, Esq., the well-known philanthropist in the early days of Philadelphia. They settled in Hollowell, Maine, *circa* 1790.

The owner of the book-plate is the son of their eldest son (Samuel Vaughan Merrick, Esq., who died 1871), and their eldest grandson. He has incorporated with the quartered arms both crests, and the motto (*Christi Servitus Vera Libertas*) which belonged of long time to his own branch of the family.

The use of book-plates is by no means confined to individuals. Colleges, public libraries, societies, etc., have their book-plates, which emphasize his-torical events or are emblematic of the organization's object. Notable among these is the book-plate of the Maine Historical Society,[1] which is particularly interesting. The heraldic features are in the shield, which is quarterly of four: I. From the seal of Sir Ferdinando Gorges. II. The arms of the Popham family. III. Arms of France. IV. Arms of Edward Godfrey, first Governor of Maine, 1649. Over all is an inescutcheon charged with four dates: 1605, First Voyage to the Coast of Maine. 1649, Edward Godfrey chosen Governor. 1678, The Usurpation by Massachusetts. 1820, The Sepa-ration from Massachusetts. (See Fig. 922.)

The book-plate of the Historical Society of Pennsylvania is of the arms of Penn impaling the present arms of the State. (See Fig. 923.)

[1] For a copy of book-plate from which design is taken acknowledgments are tendered Mr. H. W. Bryant, Librarian.

FIG. 922.

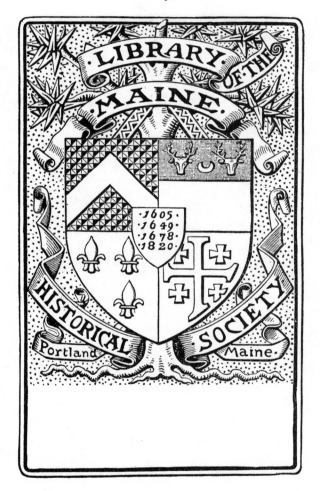

Fig. 923.

CHAPTER XIX.

FRENCH AND GERMAN HERALDRY.

THE heraldry of France and Germany differs materially from that of England, since it is more elaborate in character and governed by less exact rules. This fact was made very apparent at the Columbian Fair, where the endless display of heraldic decorations gave ample opportunity for comparison. The heraldry of Germany was particularly splendid in color and design, but so elaborate, and often so freely executed, that it became difficult to blazon it. Color appeared upon color and metal upon metal. Shields were charged with numbers of smaller ones. Charges and crests faced either the sinister or dexter. As many as ten or twelve helmets were placed over one shield, and in some instances the great number of quarterings produced confusing effects. The same characteristics were very noticeable in the Italian and Spanish exhibits also, and the free use of flags as accessories was a prominent feature. By contrast with so much that was elaborate and confused, the more simple and intelligible system of English heraldry commanded attention; and it is worthy of note that the execution of American heraldic painting seemed to conform to the English rules.

FRENCH HERALDRY.

The heraldry of France is particularly artistic and elegant, and probably approaches the English standard of accuracy more nearly than the heraldry of any other country; but there, as in the work of the other nations of the Continent, more freedom in execution is allowed. The rule that color shall not be charged on color nor metal upon metal exists, but it is avoided by terming bearings which violate it *Cousu*, or *sewed to* the field. Thus, a *mullet gules* could be borne on a *field azure* by simply inserting the word *cousu*, to imply that the mullet was not *charged upon* the field, but simply sewed to it.

The English rule that charges shall always face the dexter is violated in France, since charges borne contourné frequently occur, and in both impaled and quartered arms the charges on the dexter side sometimes face the sinister when there is a similar charge on the sinister side facing the dexter. This is probably done for the sake of artistic effect.

The crest is rarely seen in French achievements except on helmets, but its place is supplied by the coronet or *couronne*, which marks the rank of the

330

bearer. The coronet of a baron is known as *le tortil;* all others are termed *couronnes.*

Another striking difference is found in the methods of marshalling. The shields of husband and wife are not *impaled,* but are borne on separate shields, and these are then placed side by side (*accolé*). The children of the marriage bear the arms *impaled,* or sometimes quartered after the English manner.

FIG. 924.   Prince.

FIG. 925.   Duc.

FIG. 926.   Marquis.

Dimidiation is common in France, but it is used by the Germans even more often, and among them the results of it are occasionally very grotesque. The inescutcheon frequently bears the arms of an allied family, which, according to English rules, would form another quartering.

FIG. 927.   Comte.

FIG. 928.   Vicomte.

FIG. 929.   Baron.

The French shield usually has for supporters two animals of the same species,—two bears, two lions, or two eagles,—and when human figures are used for supporters they are termed by some *tenants;* Pierre Palliot (1661), however, rejects this use of the term, and uses *tenant* only where a *single* figure or one animal holds or supports the shield.

A very important difference in terms, and one that has caused some confusion in the United States and even in England, occurs in the use of the term *Barre* (French), which is used by some writers to mean the Bend Sinister. Guillim says, " A Bend Sinister is a term to which the French are unacquainted, who call this ordinary a Barre : And some authors, as *Baron* in his *l'Art Heraldique, p. 29,* observes, ' Contreband, in my opinion, is a much properer name than the former : for as Bande or Bend is universally understood to express a Bend dexter ; so Contrebande shews as plain the reverse in a Bend Sinister, which Barre I think doth not to any but themselves.' "

The outline of the shield or l'Ecu may be varied, as is the practice in England, but the better usage seems to be to use a plain form, somewhat broader at the base than the customary English one, and thus better adapted to display quarterings. The lozenge is used for the arms of maiden ladies only ; a widow retains the shields of her husband and herself *accolé.*

The *Mantling* (*Lambrequins* or *Hachements*) is especially elaborate, and as it permits the full exercise of fancy, French artists ·take advantage of the opportunity to produce the most beautiful designs. It is tinctured in accordance with the arms. The motto is placed under the shield, and is called a *Cri de Guerre* or a *Devise.*

The French helmet is placed over the shield, and *should be either affronté or facing the dexter.* The old rule was that the achievements of noblemen only should be ornamented with a helmet, but even as early as the seventeenth century the rule was abused and commoners began to bear helmets. When the strict rule is followed, EMPERORS and KINGS bear *all of gold, ornamented and damasked, affronté, with the visor open* (Figs. 930 and 931). SOVEREIGN PRINCES and SOVEREIGN DUKES bear a helmet which differs from the King's

FIG. 930.   FIG. 931.   FIG. 932.   FIG. 933.

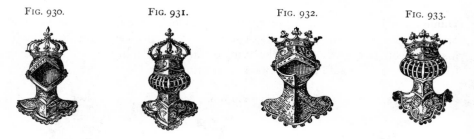

helmet only in having the visor somewhat less open (Figs. 932 and 933). In either case the helmet may be borne with bars to the number of eleven or more. PRINCES and DUKES WHO ARE NOT SOVEREIGNS, and certain high officers,—Constables, Admirals, Generals of Armies, Marshals, Governors of Provinces, Chancellors, and some others,—bear a helmet of *silver, the visor, eye-guards, nose-guard, and ventaille border and studs (or nails) of gold, affronté and with nine bars* (Fig. 934). MARQUISES *bear all of silver with seven bars affronté* (Fig. 935). COUNTS and VISCOUNTS, as well as Premiers, Presidents, Guardians of the Seal, Colonels, and Master of the Camp, if

FIG. 934.   FIG. 935.

FIG. 936.

they are Gentlemen by blood, bear *all of silver, and turned so that two-thirds of the visor is seen, thus showing only seven bars* (Fig. 936). BARONS and KNIGHTS OF OLD LINEAGE bear it of *burnished silver, turned so that two-thirds of the visor is seen, showing five bars* (Fig. 937). GENTLEMEN of three races, paternal and maternal, should bear it *of polished steel, in profile, with the visor open, nazal raised and the ventaille lowered, showing three bars* (Fig. 938). ESQUIRES bear it *of iron, placed in profile, and only slightly open at the visor* (Fig. 939). The Esquire's helmet is also assigned to those newly ennobled. The same helmet when turned to the sinister was used as a mark of illegitimacy.[1]

FIG. 937.　　　　FIG. 938.　　　　FIG. 939.

Some charges in French coats of arms differ from the English forms. Chevrons are drawn high, and where no charges appear in the chief, they often extend almost to the top of the escutcheon. The *Bordure* also occupies more space than is permitted in the heraldry of England. The Mullet is represented with six points and the Etoile with five wavy points. The names of the tinctures and furs are much the same in both French and English blazon, except *Vert*, which is termed by French heralds *Sinople*. In blazoning gutté, the French usage is to give the tincture instead of using such terms as *de sang, de larmes*, and *de l'eau*. Thus, Fig. 738 would be blazoned by an English herald *Argent, gutté de sang*, but the French blazon for it would be *D'argent gutté de geules*. The Roundel of each color has its particular name, as in English, but these names are not generally used. The custom is to blazon them *torteaux* and indicate the tincture in the usual way. Thus, a *Pellet* would be blazoned *Un torteau de sable ;* the English *Torteau* would be blazoned *Un torteau de geules ;* a *Hurt* would be blazoned *Un torteau d'azure.*

The method of blazoning was originally the same in both countries, but now there is a wide difference between English and French blazons of the same arms. This can be best illustrated by a few examples.

ABERDEEN DE CAIRNBULY. *De gu. au chev. d'arg. acc. de trois étoiles rayonnantes (6) d'or.*

ABERDEEN (Cairnbuly). *Gu. a chev. ar. betw three étoiles or.*

ADAMS (Londres). *D'herm à trois chats pass. d'azur, l'un sur l'autre.*

ADAMS (London). *Erm. three cats-a-mountain in pale az.*

BROKE DE NACTON (Cheshire). *D'or à la croix engrêlée partie de gu. et de sa.*

BROKE (Nacton, Co. Suffolk, bart.). *Or, a cross engr. per pale sa. and gu.*

---

[1] For examples of helmets reference was made to Palliot, 1661.

BROOKE.   *De gu. au chev. d'arg. ch. d'un lion de sa. cour. d'or.*

BROOKE.   *Gu. on a chev. arg. a lion ramp. sa. crowned or.*

KERR DE GREENHEAD.   *De gu. au chev. d'arg. ch. de trois étoiles du champ et acc. en p. d'une tête et col de cerf du sec.*

KER (Greenhead, Scotland).   *Gu. on a chev. ar. three mullets of the first, a buck's head erased in base, in chief a crescent of the second.*

GERMAN HERALDRY.

The distinguishing characteristic of German heraldry is, perhaps, the elaboration of detail. This is frequently carried so far that clearness is entirely lost and the arms become a confused mass of color. Quarterings are obtained not only by marriage with heiresses, but with others as well, and the result naturally is a great increase in the number of divisions of the shield and a consequent reduction in the size of the charges of each division.

The form of the shield may vary with the fancy of the artist, but a plain form is most usual. The colors used are the same as those found in English coats, and are indicated in engraving in the same way.

Roth	Gules . . .	Red	R.
Blau	Azure. . . .	Blue	B.
Grün	Vert	Green . . .	G.
Schwarz . . .	Sable	Black . . .	
Purpur . . .	Purpure . . .	Purple . . .	

and the metals :

Gold	Or	Gold	G.
Silber . . .	Argent . . .	Silver . . .	S.

The rule that color shall not be placed upon color nor metal upon metal was strictly observed in early times, but the carelessness or ignorance of later painters has caused many violations of it. Arms which do not conform with this canon, which is fundamental in English heraldry, are called Räthsel-Wappen,—Puzzle-Arms,—a term which suggests the French des Armes à Enquérir. The colors which correspond to our *Murrey* and *Sanguine* are usually mentioned in connection with the other tinctures, but are rarely used.

The furs which appear oftenest in German arms are those common in English arms, but to these have been added at least twenty others. A partial list of those used follows : Hermelin (Ermine), Gegenhermelin (Ermines), Goldhermelin (Erminois), Fehwammen or Kürsch (no corresponding fur in English), Hermelinkürsch (no corresponding fur in English), Vehem (or natural Ermine), and Feh (Vair) in many varieties, the most common of which, *Eisenhut-Feh*, is the English vair. This same general name includes Potent (Sturtzkrücken-Feh) and a modification of it (Wechsel-krücken-Feh). The German *Krücke* corresponds to our English *potent*, since both mean a crutch.

Diapering or Damascirung appears subordinate to the tinctures and charges of the field, as is the custom in English heraldry, but this ornamentation is used much more frequently by German artists, and their patterns are more elaborate.

The shield may be divided by the partition-lines,—Gespalten (per pale), Getheilt (per fesse), Geschrägt or Schräggetheilt (per bend), Linkgeschrägt or Schräglinksgetheilt (per bend sinister), Schräggeviert (per saltire), Geviert (per cross or quarterly). The ornamental lines are found both as partition-lines and forming the outlines of the ordinaries, but space will not permit of a detailed description of them.

The "ordinaries" of English heraldry are known to the Germans, but the German drawings differ in breadth from the English; thus, the Pfal occupies but two-sevenths of the breadth of the field, while the English Pale occupies one-third. The Balken corresponds to the Fesse, but it is narrower, and may be placed higher or lower than the middle. Of the other ordinaries, the Schildhaupt (Chief), Vierung (Quarter), Obereck (Canton), Kreuz (Cross), Bord (Border), Schrägbalken (Bend), Linker Schrägbalken or Schräglinkbalken (Bend Sinister), Keil (Pile), Sparren (Chevron), Schragen or Andreaskreuz (Saltire) correspond very nearly to the English forms. Der Sparren is, however, drawn much higher than the chevron. In addition to these there are the *Flanke*, resembling a pale moved to the edge of the shield; the *Shildfuss*, an ordinary placed on the base of the shield corresponding to the Chief in size; the *Deichsel*, an ordinary shaped like the letter Y; the *Göppel*, formed like an inverted Deichsel; and the *Spitze*, an inverted Pile. The Cross appears in the plain form and in the numerous fanciful variations, just as in the English arms.

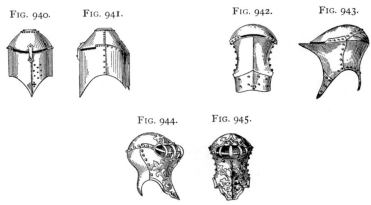

FIG. 940.   FIG. 941.   FIG. 942.   FIG. 943.

FIG. 944.   FIG. 945.

Three forms of helmets are seen, the Kübel Helme (Figs. 940 and 941), the Stechhelme (Figs. 942 and 943), and the Spangenhelme (Figs. 944 and 945). They are usually of polished iron and lined with red, but helms of gold and silver are sometimes seen, and occasionally blue or black is used for the lining. It is a general custom to place as many helmets above the shield as there are quarterings. The Mantling (Helmdecken) is attached to the helmet and colored in accordance with the tinctures of the arms.

The Crest (Kleinod) is an essential part of a German achievement, and the rule once was that no helmet should be borne without a crest, and no crest without a helmet. This rule is not now followed, however, and many arms

FIG. 946.

are borne with the crest placed on a wreath immediately over the shield. Perhaps the most common crest is the horn or pair of horns, said by some to represent the herald's trumpet, and to indicate that the arms had been duly blazoned at some tournament. Crests face either dexter or sinister, but when borne in American achievements should be subject to the English custom, and face dexter.

The crowns and coronets of the German Empire are too numerous to be given in detail, since the sovereign of each state has his own particular form of crown, and the members of the reigning houses also bear coronets as distinguishing marks of their rank. The Kaiserkrone of the new German Empire is shown in Fig. 946. A few of the other coronets are shown in Figs. 947 to 952, inclusive.

FIG. 947.

Princes and dukes.

FIG. 948.

Marquis in Austria.

FIG. 949.

Earl.

FIG. 950..

Baron.

FIG. 951.

Knight in North Germany.

FIG. 952.

Knight in South Germany.

Human figures, beasts, and birds are used as supporters (Schildhalter); and the motto (Wappensprüche), also called the Schlachtruf, or war-cry, may be placed either above or below the shield on the Spruchband.

GLOSSARY.

GLOSSARY.

In this glossary the aim has been to give a clear definition of every heraldic term in the shortest possible way. Many words quite familiar to English ears are explained at some length, since they are seldom heard in America, and in the same way some animals, common in England but rare here, are described.

Numerous French terms are included for the benefit of those interested in armorial bearings on the Continent. Those which rarely occur in English blazon are marked (Fr.).

The adjectives ending in *y* are for the most part formed from French adjectives ending in *é* or *ée*. When the French form is given, the masculine *é* has been used in all cases except where the adjective follows a *cross*; there the feminine ending *ée* has been retained, in accordance with the general usage. The accurate use of the French adjective when applied to English words would be difficult for those not deeply skilled in French genders, and, on the whole, an attempt to follow the French rule seems somewhat out of place. The adjectives have become technical words in English heraldry, and so should conform to English rules.

Many different forms of the same word, produced by the erratic orthography—or, perhaps, non-orthography—of the writers previous to the time of Elizabeth, are included for the sake of completeness as well as for the assistance of Americans interested in the heraldic terms of early English literature.

A.

A. In tricking denotes argent.

Abacot. A royal cap of state, in the shape of two crowns.

Abaissé (Fr.). Lowered; used of an ordinary when depressed below the centre of the shield.

Abatements. Certain marks of disgrace added to arms for an unworthy action committed by the bearer or his ancestor.

Abbot. The head of an abbey or monastery.

Abbot's Staff. An abbot's staff of office. Represented with a crook turned inwards. It is usually accompanied by a cloth which hangs from it and encircles it.

Abeyance. When the real owner of an estate or dignity is unascertained, the title is said to be in abeyance until the dispute is settled.

A Bouché, a Shield. One notched for a lance on the dexter side near the top.

Abouté. Used by the French heralds for *Conjoined*.

Accessories. The various parts which go with the shield to make a complete armorial bearing; among them the helm, the crest, the supporters, the motto and scroll, the wreath, etc.

Accolade. The blow given when the honor of knighthood was bestowed. It was said to be the last blow that the knight was to let pass unavenged.

Accolé. Used by French heralds to express *collared*. It also is used of two swords, etc., placed behind a shield, and of two shields placed side by side.

Accompagné (Fr.). *Between.*

Accosted. Used of a charge when flanked by other charges.

Accroché. Used by French heralds to signify that one charge is hooked into another.

Accroupi (Fr.). *Lodged.*

Accrued. Used to express a tree which has attained its full growth.

Achievement. While this word is applicable to armorial bearings generally, yet it is now commonly used when speaking of the *funeral* achievement of some deceased person. This is usually affixed to the dwelling-house to denote the death, rank, and station of the late occupant. It is composed of the shield with all the accessories,—helmet, mantle, crest, motto, etc.

Acorné (Fr.). *Attired.*

Acorned. Bearing acorns. Also called *Fructed.*

Acoté (Fr.). *Accosted.*

Addorsed or **Adossed.** Applied to beasts, etc., placed back to back.

Addossé (Fr.). *Addorsed.*

Adorned. Decorated. As when a cap, turned up, has anything set on the side of it.

Adumbrated. Represented in shadowy outline.

Adumbration. The shadow of any figure, outlined and painted of a color darker than the field. Seldom seen in English coats of arms.

Advancers. The upper branches of a stag's horns.

Affronté. (1) Facing or fronting one another. (2) Front or full-faced to the spectator.

Agneau Pastoral (Fr.). *Agnus Dei.*

Agnus Dei Lamb, or **Holy Lamb.** A white lamb *passant*, with a staff crossed at the top, and a banner bearing the Red Cross of St. George.

Aguilated or **Aigulated.** Ornamented with eagle's heads.

Aiglette. A small eagle.

Aiguisé. Sharp and pointed, or *Fitché.* Used by French and early English heralds.

Ailettes. See EMERASSES.

Aislé (Fr.). Winged.

Ajouré (Fr.). Having a part of the ordinary removed so that the field appears through it. Also applied to open windows of castles.

Alaissé or **Alisé** (Fr.). *Couped* or *Humetté.*

Alant. A short-eared mastiff dog.

À la Quise. See CUISSE.

Alb. A long white garment worn by priests.

Albany Herald. One of the members of the Lyon Office.

Alderman. A city officer, derived from old English *ealdor* (older) and man. One of the elders.

Alembic. A vessel for distilling, used originally by the alchemists.

Aliaizé or **Aliecé.** A French term applied to an ordinary when it is couped at the ends so that it does not touch the edge of the shield.

Alisé. Spherical. Also (Fr.) *Humetté.*

Allerion. An eagle displayed, without beak or feet.

Allumé (Fr.). Applied to the eyes of a beast when they glow or sparkle.

Almoner. One who distributes alms. Originally a member of a certain religious order whose vows bound them to distribute alms among the poor.

Altar. Usually borne surmounted by flames.

Alterné (Fr.). *Alternate.*

Amalthea (Fr.). *Cornucopia.*

Ambulant. Walking or *passant.*

Ambulant, Co-, Walking together.

Amethyst. A precious stone of violet color, used by ancient heralds to denote *purpure* when blazoning the arms of peers.

Amphisien Cockatrice. See BASILISK.

Ananas. The West Indian pine-apple.

Anchor. Borne in pale without a cable unless blazoned " cabled."

Anchored or **Ancred.** A cross is so termed when each of its four extremities resembles the fluke of an anchor.

Ancient or **Ancyent.** A small pointed flag, carried by an officer similar to the modern Ensign, who was also known as an Ancient.

Ancré (Fr.). *Anchored.*

Andrew's Cross. See SALTIRE.

Angenne. A six-leaved flower.

Anglé (Fr.). *Angled.*

Angled. Applied to any bearing the outline of which is turned from its straight and natural course at one or more points.

Anille (Fr.). *Fer de Mouline.*

Animé. See INCENSED.

Annelet (Fr.). *Annulet.*

Annodated. Bent like the letter S. Also applied to serpents twisted or knotted loosely together.

Annulet. A ring. Representing liberty and nobility, and, by its circular form, strength and eternity. It is the mark of difference of the fifth son.

Annulets, Conjoined. Two or more annulets interlacing each other.

Annuletté, Annnulated, etc. Having a ring or annulet at each extremity. A *Cross Annulated.*

Anserated. Parted. Used of a cross which is parted, and the extremities of which are formed into the shape of animal's heads.

Anshent. See ANCIENT.

Antarctic Star. When but one star is borne it is called the *North* or *Polar Star*, but when two are borne, opposite each other, they are termed the Polar Stars, or the *Arctic* and *Antarctic Stars*.

Anté or **Enté.** Ingrafted, or pieces let one into another, like dovetail.

Antelope. An animal of the deer kind, with horns almost straight, tapering gradually from the head up; a long and slender neck, feet, legs, and body like a deer. The *heraldic antelope* is a fabulous monster, having the body of a stag, the tail of a unicorn, a tusk at the tip of the nose, and tufts down the back of the neck and on the tail, chest, and thighs.

Anthony's Cross. See TAU, a *Cross*.

Antic or **Antique.** Ancient.

Antique Crown. See EASTERN CROWN.

Anvil. The instrument used by smiths.

Apaumé or **Appalmed.** Applied to a hand erect, open, and with the palm toward the spectator. This is the way the hand is represented unless other directions are given. The red hand apaumé is the badge of all baronets. See BADGE OF ULSTER.

Ape. An animal of the monkey tribe. Borne *saltant.*

Apostles' Emblems. The emblems which have been given to the apostles have been adopted by various ecclesiastical bodies. The keys of St. Peter are borne by the sees of York, Exeter, and Gloucester, among others.

Appalmed. *Apaumé* or *Apaumée.*

Apple. Always borne with a short stalk.

Apres. A fictitious animal, like a bull, but having the tail of a bear.

Aquilated. Ornamented with eagle's heads.

Ar. or **Arg.** The abbreviation for *Argent.*

Arazed. See ERASED.

Arbaleste. A cross-bow.

Arch. Usually the arch of a bridge, supported by pillars. Both double and single arches are used in heraldry.

Archbishop. The highest order in the English Church.

Archduke. The title of the sons of Austrian emperors.

Archduke's Crown. A circlet of gold, adorned with eight strawberry leaves, and closed by two arches of gold set with pearls, meeting in a globe, which is surmounted by a cross. The cap is scarlet.

Arched, Arché, or **Archy.** Said of an ordinary when both sides of it are curved alike.

Arctic Star. When one star is borne it is of six points, wavy, and is termed the Arctic or North Polar Star. See ANTARCTIC STAR.

Argent. The French word for silver, and in heraldry it is commonly white. It is usually abbreviated *ar.* or *arg.*, and represented in engraving by plain white.

Arm. The human arm often appears as a charge, but more frequently as a crest.

Armarium Honoris. See CABINET DES ARMES.

Armé (Fr.). *Armed.*

Armed. Signifies that the claws, or the horns and hoofs, or the beak and talons, of any beast or bird of prey are borne of a different tincture from that of its body.

Armed at all Points. Used for a man completely encased in armor.

Armes Parlantes. See REBUS.

Arming Buckles. Lozenge-shaped buckles for fastening armor.

Arming Doublet. A surcoat.

Armoiries (Fr.). *Insignia.*

Armorer. A maker of armor.

Armorial Bearings. See ARMS.

Armory. One branch of the science of heraldry, consisting in the knowledge of coat-armors, as to their blazons and various intendments.

Armoyé (Fr.). Applied to a mantling when charged with arms.

Arms. Hereditary marks of honor, composed of certain tinctures and figures, and originally either assumed by the bearers or else granted by sovereigns, to distinguish individuals, families, and communities.

Arms of Adoption. The arms of a family into which a man is adopted. He usually bears them quartered with his paternal coat.

Arms of Alliance. The arms of an heiress, quartered with those of her husband, borne by their children.

Arms, Assumptive. Such arms as a man takes to himself as distinguished from inherited arms.

Arms, Canting. Canting arms are those which allude to the name of the bearer,—a trevet, for Trevet; three herrings, for Herring; a camel, for Campbell; a pine-tree, for Pine; three harrows, for Harrow; a bolt and tun, for Bolton; and many others.

Arms of Community. Those of societies, guilds, towns, bishoprics, and other incorporated bodies.

Arms of Concession. Parts of his own regalia granted by a sovereign to such as he wishes to honor. They are borne as augmentations.

Arms of Dominion. Those which kings and emperors bear. These are attached to the lands and territories, and belong to the sovereign by virtue of his office.

Arms, Paternal and Hereditary. Those acquired by descent.

Arms of Patronage. Those that governors of provinces, lords of manors, patrons of benefices, etc., add to their family arms as a token of their rights and jurisdiction.

Arms of Pretension. Coats borne by sovereigns who have some claim to, though they are not in actual possession of, the territories which the arms represent.

Armys. Old English for arms or armor.

Armys Harnysyd. *Arms armed.*

Arondé. Rounded off.

Arondia. See ARRONDIE.

Arraché (Fr.). See ERASED.

Arraswise or **Arrasways.** Applied to any square charge when placed with one corner toward the observer, and showing the top and two of the sides in perspective.

Arrayed. Clothed or vested.

Arrayer. A mediæval military officer.

Arrière. With back toward the spectator.

Arrondie. Rounded or curved.

Arrow. Represented with point down, *barbed* and *feathered*.

Arrow Pheoned. One having a pheon instead of a spear-head or barb.

Arrows. A bundle or *sheaf* consists of three,— two in saltire and one in pale. When more than three are borne their position must be described.

Ascendant. Issuing upward.

Aseare or **Asewre.** *Azure.*

Ash Keys or **Ashen Keys.** The seeds of the ash-tree as they grow in bunches.

Asker. An egg-breeding reptile.

Aspect. Full-faced, or *at gaze*. *In full aspect* implies no part turning to either side.

Aspectant or **Aspecting.** Face to face, or opposite each other. *Combatant* is applied to lions in a similar position.

Aspersed. *Powdered* or strewed.

Ass. "The lively emblem of Patience."

Assailant, Assaultant, or **Assaulting.** Used of animals placed almost upright.

Assemblé (Fr.). Dovetailed.

Assieta or **Assiette** (Fr.). A bearing or charge.

Assis (Fr.). Sitting or *sejant.*

Assumptive Arms. Arms of a defeated knight assumed by his conqueror.

Assurgent. Rising from the sea.

Asteroid or **Astroid.** A star.

Astrolabe. An instrument for taking the altitude of the sun, stars, or other heavenly bodies.

At Bay. Applied to beasts of chase to denote that they are in a position of self-defence. Particularly applied to a stag with head lowered as if butting.

At Gaze. Applied to beasts of chase to denote that they are standing full-faced to the spectator.

At Speed. See SPEED.

Atchievement. See ACHIEVEMENT.

Athelstan's Cross. *Party per saltire, gules and azure, on a besant, a cross botonée or.* The banner ascribed to Athelstan, who expelled the Danes, subdued the Scots, and reduced his country to one monarchy.

Attire. A term for the horns of a stag or buck.

Attire. Clothing.

Attired. Applied to a stag, buck, or other animal, which wears ornamental weapons of defence, when represented with its antlers. A *bull* is *armed* of his horns.

Attires of a Stag. Both the horns affixed to the scalp.

Augmentation. A particular mark of honor added to an already existing coat of arms, and borne either on an escutcheon or on a canton.

Aulned. Bearded, applied to ears of grain.

Auré. *Gutté d'or.* Sprinkled with drops of gold.

Auriflamme. The royal standard of France. A blue banner charged with golden fleurs-de-lis.

Ave. The first word in the Romish salutation of the Virgin Mary.

Avellane, a Cross. So called because the quarters of it resemble a filbert nut.

Avellaned Pomel, a Cross. Sometimes called *Pomety avelane* or *Pomel flory.*

Averlye. *Semé* or powdered.

Aversant or **Dorsed.** Applied to a hand open but with the back toward the spectator.

Axe. The axes usually borne are: (1) *Battle-axe*, a short-handled weapon with a *convex* axe-blade to the dexter, a spear-point in chief, and another point to the sinister. (2) *Lochaber-axe*, a weapon with handle slightly curved, with a *concave* axe-blade to the dexter, broader than that of the battle-axe, and with a point to the sinister. The spear-point on the upper end of the battle-axe is absent from the Lochaber. (3) *Broad-axe*, an instrument with a broad *convex* blade to the dexter, but blunt to the sinister, and without the spear-point.

Aylets or **Sea-Swallows.** Black, with red legs and beaks.

Ayrant. Applied to eagles or other birds in their eyries or nests.

Az. or **Azure.** The color blue. In engraving it is expressed by horizontal lines.

Azur (Fr.). *Azure.*

B.

B. In "tricking" denotes blue or *azure.*

Bachelor. The first stage of knighthood. One who had not yet raised his standard on the field of battle was a knight-bachelor.

Badelaires. Crooked swords or cutlasses.

Badge. A device adopted by some families in addition to the regular coat of arms. It is not placed on the coat of arms but borne separately, and has a peculiar signification of its own.

Badge of Ulster. The badge of all baronets. It is a sinister (left) hand, couped (cut) at the wrist and colored gules (red), usually borne on a canton, or on an inescutcheon placed on the middle chief point or on the fesse point. It was given as a charge to one O'Neile who, on an early expedition to Ireland, cut off his left hand and flung it on shore, so that he or some part of him might be the first to land. From this O'Neile the ancient kings of Ulster were descended. This story explains why the *left* hand is borne rather than the right, since it was much more natural for the right hand to cut off the left, than for the left to cut off the right. This bloody left hand became the badge of baronets from the fact that James I. created the degree for the purpose of raising soldiers and money to put down rebellions in Ulster. The badge is blazoned: *Argent, a sinister hand erect, appaumé, couped at the wrist, gules.*

Badger or **Brock.** Usually borne *passant.*

Bag of Madder. This charge resembles a bale of goods.

Bagpipe. The Scotch national musical instrument.

Bagwyn. One of the heraldic monsters.

Baillonné. A lion rampant, holding a staff in his mouth.

Baldrick. A girdle worn by heralds.

Bale Corded. See BAG OF MADDER.

Bale-Fire. See BEACON.

Balista or **Ballistra.** See SWEEP. Always borne loaded with a stone.

Ball. A spherical roundel.

Ball of Fire, or **Fire-Ball.** A bomb with flames streaming from the top.

Ball, Tasselled. A ball with four tassels, radiating like a cross.

Band. The fillet by which a sheaf is bound.

Bande (Fr.). *Bend.*

Bandé (Fr.). *Bendy.*

Banded. When anything, such as a garb or wheat sheaf, is tied round with a band of a different tincture from itself, it is said to be *banded.*

Bandelette (Fr.). *Bendlet.*

Banderole. A streamer fastened by strings near the head of a *crozier* or immediately under the crook of a *pastoral staff*, and enveloping the shaft.

Banderolle (Fr.). Banner-roll. A banner three feet square, sometimes rounded at the fly.

Bandrick. A sword-belt.

Bandrol. *Banderolle.*

Banner. A square flag, standard, or ensign on which was placed the heraldic device of the higher orders of military chiefs. It served to distinguish the leader from the ordinary knight, since the latter bore only the pointed pennon.

Banner disveloped. This term is used for an ensign, or colors in the army, when open and flying.

Banneret. A knight who was permitted to bear a banner instead of a pennon, as a reward for some noble action.

Bar. An ordinary formed by two parallel, horizontal lines and containing a fifth part of the field. The bar can be placed in several parts of the field, horizontally.

Bar-Gemelle. Two parallel bars.

Barbé et Cresté (Fr.). *Barbed and crested.*

Barbed or **Bearded.** Having *Barbs.* This is also applied to a weapon with a barbed point.

Barbed or **Barbée.** A cross is so termed when its extremities are like the barbed irons used for spearing fish.

Barbed and Crested. Blazon for the comb and gills of a cock.

Barbed and Flighted. Used of an arrow when the head and feathers are different in tincture from the shaft.

Barbed Arrows. Arrows with barbed heads or points.

Barbel. A fresh-water fish. Generally borne *embowed.*

Barbelé (Fr.). *Barbed.*

Barbs. The five outside petals of the heraldic rose.

Barded. *Caparisoned.*

Barelle (Fr.). *Barrulet.*

Barellé (Fr.). *Barruly.*

Barking. The cry or noise made by a fox.

Barnacle. A large water-fowl with a flat, broad bill. Somewhat like a goose in shape.

Barnacles or **Breys.** A sort of curb placed on the upper lip of a horse when he is being broken to harness.

Baron. Next below viscount in rank, and the lowest rank in the peerage. The name and degree were introduced in England about the time of the Norman Conquest, and replaced the Saxon *thane.*

Baron and Femme. In blazoning the arms of a man and his wife marshalled together side by side, BARON expresses the husband's side of the shield, or the *dexter ;* FEMME, the wife's side, or the *sinister.*

Baronet. In rank between a knight and baron. It is the lowest title of hereditary honor, and was created by James I. in 1611.

Baronet's Badge. See BADGE OF ULSTER.

Baron's Coronet. On a gold circle bordered with ermine, six balls, of which four are shown in representation.

Barracles. See BARNACLES.

Barralet or **Barrulet.** A diminutive of the bar, one-fourth of it in size.

Barre or **Barre Une** (Fr.). A *Bend Sinister.*

Barruletté, Barruletty, Barrullé, or **Barrully.** *Barry* of more than eight.

Barry. Applied to a field divided by horizontal

lines into an *even* number of equal parts. When more than eight parts are formed it may be blazoned *barruly of ten,* etc.

Barry Bendy. Applied to a field divided into an *even* number of equal, lozenge-shaped parts by lines from the dexter chief to the sinister base, and from side to side.

Barry Indented. Applied to a field divided by bars so indented that the whole has the appearance of being covered with small triangles of alternate tinctures.

Barry Pily. When the shield is covered with piles placed barways. See chapter on VARIED FIELDS.

Barry Sinister. See BARRY INDENTED.

Barry Wavy. Similar to *Barry,* but with undulating lines instead of straight ones.

Bars (Fr.). *Barbel.*

Bar-Shot. An iron missile formed of two balls joined by a bar. It somewhat resembles a dumb-bell.

Barways or **Barwise.** Placed horizontally upon the shield.

Bas de l'Ecu (Fr.). *Base.*

Base. The bottom or lower part of the shield.

Base Esquire. This charge resembles a gyron, but may taper beyond the fesse point.

Basilisk. An imaginary animal, represented like the fictitious heraldic cockatrice, and with the head of a dragon at the end of its tail. Also called the Amphisien Cockatrice.

Basket. See WINNOWING-BASKET.

Bassenet, Bassinet, or **Basnet.** A plain, round helmet.

Baston, Baton, Batton, Etc. One-fourth of the bend sinister, but cut off at the ends so that it does not touch the edge of the shield. It is the mark of illegitimacy, and when of metal is borne by the offspring of princes only.

Bat. See RERE MOUSE.

Bath. An English order of knighthood. See KNIGHTHOOD (4).

Bath King-of-Arms. The herald of the Most Honorable Order of the Bath.

Baton. A symbol of field-marshal's authority. Sometimes borne as an honorable charge, sometimes as part of a crest.

Baton. See BASTON.

Baton Sinister. A mark of illegitimacy. The term used to distinguish it from a field marshal's *baton.*

Bat's Wing. Borne expanded, but may be placed in various positions.

Battering-Ram. An engine made of large pieces of timber fastened together with iron hoops, strengthened at one end with an iron head, and armed with iron horns like a ram's, from whence it took its name. It was suspended by two chains, and swung forwards and backwards, by numbers of men, to beat down the walls of a besieged town or castle.

Battle-Axe. See AXE.

Battled. In the form of battlements or fortifications.

Battled Arrondie. Having a circular battlement on the top.

Battled-Embattled. Having one battlement upon another. A line of partition.

Battlement of a Tower. The fortified upper part.

Batune. See BASTON.

Baudrick. See BALDRICK.

Baudrier (Fr.). *Baldrick.*

Bauteroll. See CHAPE.

Bay. See AT BAY.

Beacon, Beacon-Fire, Cresset, or Fire-Beacon. An iron basket with flames coming from it, placed on a pole against which a ladder leans. It was placed on top of a high hill and set blazing to warn the country-side of an attack or threatened invasion. In the reign of Edward III. every county had one.

Beaked. A term for birds other than those of prey when borne with their bills of a different tincture from that of their bodies.

Beam. The main horn of the attire of a stag.

Beams or **Rays of the Sun.** Sometimes borne alone in a circle, but generally surrounding some other charge.

Bear. Usually borne *passant.*

Beard. The jagged part of the point of an arrow.

Bearded. (1) *Barbed,* when applied to arrows. (2) *Blazing,* when applied to the tail of a comet.

Bearers. *Supporters.* Figures placed as if supporting or guarding the shield.

Bearing. Any figure borne as a charge.

Bearings. Coat-armor.

Beauseant. An oblong flag,—*Per fesse, sable and argent,*—the banner of the Knights Templars.

Beautified. Adorned.

Beaver. An amphibious, fur-bearing animal, with a tail covered with scales.

Beaver. The *visor* of a helmet.

Bebally. *Party per pale.*

Becqué or **Bequé.** See BEAKED.

Beddeth. Used to express the place where a roe is lying.

Bee. The emblem of industry. Borne *volant,* as a rule.

Bee-Hive. Borne generally with bees *volant* about it, but sometimes borne alone.

Beffroy. See VAIR.

Belfry. The part of the steeple in which the bells are hung.

Belic. See GULES.

Belled. Having bells affixed to some part.

Belling. The noise or cry made by the roe.

Bellowing. The noise made by the hart. Also applied to the noise of a bull. An ox or cow is said to be *lowing.*

Bellows. Borne *in pale* with handles *in chief.*

Bells. The bells common in heraldry are, (1) The round hawk's bells, and (2) Church bells.

Belt or **Girdle.** Generally borne *in pale* with buckles *in chief.*

Bend. An ordinary formed by two parallel lines drawn from the dexter chief to the sinister base; it is supposed to represent a shoulder-belt or a scarf.

Bendlet. One of the first diminutives of the bend. In size, half the breadth of a bend.

Bend Sinister. An ordinary like the bend, except that it extends from the sinister chief to the dexter base, or from left to right.

Bendways, Bendwise, or **In Bend.** Applied to charges placed diagonally from the dexter chief to the sinister base.

Bendy. Used when a field or charge is divided bendways into an even number of equal parts diagonally.

Bendy Pily. See chapter on VARIED FIELDS.

Bequé. See BEAKED.

Berly. See BARRY.

Besant (Fr.). *Bezant.*

Besaunte. See BEZANTS.

Besca. A spade or shovel.

Besom. A broom.

Betw. Abbreviation for between.

Bever. See BEAVER.

Bevil, Bevel, or **Bevile.** Formed by one line meeting another at an acute angle.

Bevy. A term applied to a number of roes together; also to a number of quails.

Bezants or **Besants.** Pieces of gold without any impression. They were the current coin of old Byzantium, now called Constantinople, and are supposed to have been introduced in arms by those who were at the Holy War.

Bezanté. *Semé* of bezants.

Bezantlier. The branch which shoots from the main beam of a stag's antlers, just above the brow-antler. The second branch of a hart's attires.

Bezantry. A cross composed of bezants.

Bicapitated or **Bicapited.** Having two heads.

Bicorporated. Having two bodies.

Bill or **Billhead.** An instrument for lopping and cutting trees.

Billets. Oblong squares, by some taken for bricks, but generally supposed to be epistles made up in that form.

Billetté (Fr.). *Billetty.*

Billettes (Fr.). *Billets.*

Billetty. Applied to a field sprinkled with billets when they exceed ten.

Billing. A term applied to birds when facing each other with beaks touching.

Biparted. Having a triangular piece cut out.

Bird-Bolt. (1) A small arrow with a blunt head. (2) A small arrow with three heads.

Bishop's Cross Staff. A golden staff terminating in a silver *Cross Patée.*

Bit or **Bitt.** Both the *snaffle* and the *manage bit* are borne in heraldry.

Biting his Tail. Serpents are borne in this position, and, making a complete circle, they represent eternity.

Bittern. A sort of heron.

Black. In heraldry, *sable.* By old systems, Saturn or the diamond. See SABLE.

Black Rod (Usher of the). One of the Garter officers, and chief Usher to the sovereign of England.

Bladed. Applied when the blade or stem is tinctured differently from the ear, head, or fruit of a plant.

Blanche. White.

Blanch-Lyon. One of the ancient pursuivants.

Blasted or **Starved.** A term for a branch when borne without leaves.

Blazing Star. See COMET.

Blazon. The proper heraldic description in words for an armorial bearing.

Blazon. To express in proper terms all that belongs to a coat of arms.

Blazoner. A herald.

Blazonry. The part of the heraldic art which relates to the blazoning of armorial bearings.

Blemished. See REBATED.

Block-Brushes. Bunches of kneeholm or myrtle used by butchers to clean their chopping-blocks.

Blood. The color representing blood is *Sanguine.*

Blood-Hound. Borne as if on scent with his nose to the ground.

Bloom or **Blossom.** A flower.

Bloomed or **Blossomed.** Bearing flowers.

Blue. In heraldry *Azure.*

Blue-Bottle. A flower of the Cyanus, somewhat like the thistle.

Blue Mantle. One of the Pursuivants of the College of Arms.

Boar. Always the wild boar with its tusks.

Boar's Head. Always borne in profile.

Bois de Cerf or **Bois de Diam** (Fr.). *Attires.*

Bole or **Head.** Applied to flowers.

Bolt and Tun or **Bolt-in-Tun.** A bird-bolt *in pale,* piercing a tun.

Boltant or **Bolting.** Springing forward.

Bolt-Hedys. Bull's heads.

Bonnet. A cap of velvet worn with a coronet.

Bordé (Fr.). *Bordered.*

Border or **Bordure.** Borders were anciently used for distinguishing one part of a family from the other. They were thus used as a difference, but now are generally borne as charges.

Bordered. Applied to a coat of arms around which a border is placed.

Bordure. See BORDER.

Boss. The ornament at the end of a bit.

Boterall or **Boteroll** (Fr.). See CHAPE.

Botoned. Having round buds, knobs, or buttons at the extremities.

Bottle. Usually leathern, but sometimes glass, with a knotted cord attached to its long neck.

Bottony. This term is applied to a cross when its extremities resemble the trefoil.

Bouchier Knot or **Bourchier Knot.** A knot of silk.

Bouckys. Ancient orthography for bucks.

Bouclé (Fr.). *Buckled.*

Bouget. See WATER-BOUGET.

Bourdon. A palmer's staff.

Bourguignote (Fr.). *Burganet.*

Bouse (Fr.). See WATER-BOUGET.

Bouterolle. See CHAPE.

Bouterolle d'une Lance (Fr.). *Bur.*

Bow. Should always be blazoned strung, unstrung, or sans strings.

Bowed or **Embowed.** Applied to a serpent when coiled, with head erect in the centre.

Bowed, Flected, or **Reflected.** Curved. When applied to an arm, bent at the elbow.

Bowed-Embowed. Bent like the letter S.

Bowen's Knot. A knot composed of four bows.

Bowl. A large, deep dish, usually containing a boar's head or something of the kind.

Braced or **Brazed.** Applied to figures of the same sort interlacing one another.

Bracelet. An ornament placed about the arm of a king as part of the insignia of royalty.

Branché (Fr.). Branched.

Branches. Generally bearing nine leaves, but when *fructed* only four. The *slip* should bear three leaves; the *sprig*, five.

Brands or **Fire-Brands.** Borne *in pale, raguly, inflamed in chief*.

Brassarts. Armor for the elbow.

Brasses. Engraved brass plates placed on tombs.

Brassetts. Armor for the arms.

Breast-Plate. See CUIRASS.

Breathing. Applied to the stag instead of "*at gaze*" by some heralds.

Brectesches. Parapets or battlements.

Brettessé or **Des Bastonades** (Fr.). Embattled on both sides. Having battlements facing each other. *Counter-embattled.*

Breys. See BARNACLES.

Brick or **Brique.** Same shape as a billet, but so placed that the thickness is shown.

Bricklayer's Axe. A tool used for cutting bricks.

Bridge. Usually of three or more arches, embattled.

Brigandine or **Brigantine.** A jacket or coat of mail.

Brimsey. A gad-fly.

Brinded, Breended, or **Brindled.** Spotted.

Brisé (Fr.). Broken.

Brisé Decouplé (Fr.). Disjointed.

Bristled. Applied to a boar when the hair on his back is different from his body in tincture.

Brisure or **Brizure.** The French term for a *difference* or *mark of cadency*. Any figure which is used to mark the "*distinctions of houses*" is a brisure.

Broad Arrow. This differs from the pheon by having the inside of its barbs plain.

Broad-Axe. See AXE.

Brochant (Fr.). *Debruised.*

Broches. Instruments used by embroiderers.

Brock. A badger.

Brocket. A stag in the second year of its age.

Brogue. A high shoe worn in Ireland.

Broken. Applied to any charge when its extremities are jagged, as if it had been violently torn apart. Also applied to a deer when being cut up.

Bronchant, Sur le Tout (Fr.). See OVER-ALL.

Bronchant. Used by French heralds of a beast borne on a field which is semé of fleurs-de-lis.

Brow-Antler. The first branch of the horn of a hart or buck that shoots from the main beam, next the head.

Brush. The tail of a fox.

Bruske. See TENNÉ.

Bubble. Borne *argent* and represented spherical. It differs from the plate or roundel *argent*, since the plate is always represented *flat*, without any shading.

Buck. The male of the deer kind. When five years old, it is termed *a buck of the first head*.

Bucket. A pail standing on three legs and having a cord handle. Borne in various other forms.

Buckle. Borne in various forms, oval, round, lozengy, etc.

Buckled. Applied to belts, etc., borne with buckles.

Buckler. A shield.

Budded. (The Cross.) See BOTTONY.

Bugle. A bull is sometimes so called. From this we have *bugle-horn* for hunting-horn, since it was made from the horn of the *bugle*.

Bugle-Horn. Borne with mouth-piece to sinister. Usually *garnished* with the rings around it, and *with strings*. See HUNTING-HORN.

Bull. A bull is *armed* of his horns, not attired.

Bullets. See PELLETS.

Bullrush. An aquatic plant.

Bunch or **Cluster.** Applied to a number of fruits or flowers borne together.

Bundle of Sticks. Usually six, *in pale*, bound with a cord.

Bur. A broad ring of iron behind the hand, on spears used in tilting.

Burelle (Fr.). *Barrulet.*

Burellé. See BARRY.

Burganet or **Burgonet.** A steel cap worn by foot-soldiers in battle.

Burling-Iron. An instrument used by weavers.

Burning Bush. Sometimes called *Moses's Bush.* A bush on fire.

Burst. Applied to anything split or open.

Bush. See BRUSH.

Bust. The head, neck, and shoulders, usually placed with face affronté.

Bustard. A kind of wild turkey of a brownish color.

Butcher's Axe or **Slaughter-Axe.** The axe used by butchers to kill steers.

Buttoned. Applied to buckles when ornamented.

Buttony. See BOTTONY.

Butterflies. Generally borne *volant*.

C.

Cabinet des Armes. A square tablet hung on the wall of the church in which a nobleman is buried, bearing on it, in the centre his *tabard*, *helm*, and *crest*, on one side his gauntlets and on the other his sword, at the bottom his spurs, and in the four angles his paternal and maternal coats of arms.

Cablé (Fr.). *Corded.*

Cable. A twisted rope, affixed to an anchor.

Cabled. Entwined by a cable.

Caboched, Caboshed, or **Cabossed.** This term is used to express the head of any beast except the leopard, when it is placed affronté or full-faced and has no part of the neck visible.

Cabossé (Fr.). *Caboched.*

Cabré or **Effray** (Fr.). Applied to a horse instead of *salient.*

Cadency. The heraldic distinction between members of a family, or between different collateral branches.

Cadet. A younger son or younger branch of a family.

Caduceus or **Mercury's Mace.** Sometimes called a *snaky staff*. It was the staff of office borne by Hermes or Mercury, the messenger of the gods, and hence was adopted as the herald's staff on account of the latter's office as messenger. It is variously represented, but usually it is a slender staff having two serpents entwined about it, the heads meeting at the top and the tails at the lower end or handle.

Calamine Stone. A mineral which forms brass when mixed with copper.

Calf. Applied to the young of the stag-kind as well as to that of the cow.

Caltrap. See GALTRAP.

Calvary, a Cross. The cross on which our Saviour suffered on Mount Calvary. It is set upon steps.

Calza. A stocking.

Camel. Usually depicted *passant.*

Camelopard. Heraldic name for giraffe.

Camelopardel. A beast of heraldic creation, formed by affixing two straight horns on the head of the camelopard.

Camp. See GOBONY.

Campaned. Applied to a file or other similar charge from which bells are pendent.

Campanes. Bells.

Canellé (Fr.). See INVECKED.

Cannet. A duck without beak or feet, placed in profile like the *martlet*, but it has a longer neck than the martlet, and has not a forked tail.

Cannon. A piece of ordnance, always borne mounted on a bed or a carriage unless otherwise described.

Canon. A church officer.

Canon. A rule or law.

Canting Arms. See REBUS. See ARMS, CANTING.

Canton. A charge generally formed at the dexter or sinister chief parts of the escutcheon by two lines meeting at right angles.

Cantoned. See CANTONNÉ. Also applied to a single charge, placed on a canton.

Cantonné. Placed between four objects or charges.

Cap. Frequently borne by ecclesiastics instead of a crown or coronet.

Cap-a-Pie. From head to foot. Applied to a knight when in complete armor.

Cap of Liberty. Always red.

Cap of Maintenance. Made of crimson velvet, lined and turned up with ermine, and worn by the nobility.

Cap of Mercury. Represented with wings.

Caparaçonné. See CAPARISONED.

Caparisoned. Applied to a horse completely furnished for the field.

Capital. The head or top of a column.

Capuchon. A hood closed on every side.

Carbuncle. See ESCARBUNCLE.

Cardinal's Hat. Pope Innocent IV. ordained that cardinals should wear red hats, to signify that those who entered into that order ought to expose themselves, even to the shedding of their blood and the hazard of their lives, in the defence of ecclesiastical liberty.

Careering. Applied to a horse instead of *saliant.*

Cartouche. The oval escutcheon of the Pope or other churchman.

Case. The stuffed skin of an animal.

Cased. Flayed.

Casque. French for *helmet*.

Castle. Usually one tower or two towers connected by a wall with a gate. This was granted as a charge to those who had reduced a fortified place or who were the first of a scaling party to mount the walls of an assaulted fortification. Also one of the pieces used in chess. See CHESS-ROOK.

Cat. The domestic animal is seldom borne in coat-armor, but the wild-cat or *cat-a-mountain* occurs frequently. It is always borne *guardant* or full-faced.

Caterfoil. See QUARTREFOIL.

Catherine-Wheel. A wheel of eight spokes with a spike at the end of each. It was an instrument of torture, and derived its name from the fact that St. Catherine the Virgin suffered martyrdom upon it.

Catoose. See SCROLL.

Caudé (Fr.). Coward, when applied to a lion borne with his tail between his legs. Also applied to a comet with a streaming tail.

Caul or **Cowl.** A monk's hood.

Cave. Rarely borne except with a wild animal issuing.

C. B. Companion of the Order of the Bath.

Ceckko. See CHECKY.

Centaur. See SAGITTARIUS.

Cercelé or **Recercelé.** When applied to a cross, signifies encircling or curling at the ends like a ram's horn.

Cercle. A circle.

Cerclé (Fr.). Surrounded by a circle or diadem.

Cerise. A torteau.

Chafant. Applied to a boar when depicted as if enraged.

Chain. Sometimes borne alone, but usually affixed to some other charge.

Chained. Having a chain affixed.

Chain-Shot. Some have taken this to be the head of a club called holy-water sprinkler; others, to be balls of fire; but it is generally supposed to be an iron-spiked shot with a chain at each end.

Chalice. A cup.

Challenger. The champion who offers to fight or contest at a tilt or tournament.

Chamber-Piece. A term for a short piece of ordnance without a carriage.

Chamberlain, Lord. An officer of the English royal household.

Chame. A French term for an annulet having a sharp point rising from one side.

Chameleon. When borne in arms it is colored a pale green.

Chamfrain or **Chamfron.** Armor to protect the head of a horse.

Champ (Fr.). *Field*.

Champain. See CLECHÉ.

Chantant. Applied to song-birds when borne as if singing.

Chape or **Crampit.** The metal ornament placed at the lower end of the scabbard to prevent the sword-point from obtruding. Termed by the French *bouterolle*.

Chapeau. See CAP OF MAINTENANCE.

Chaperon, Chaperoun, or **Chaperonne.** An old French word signifying a hood to cover the head, such as friars wear, with as much hanging down as was necessary to cover the shoulders and part of the arms. The name given to the small shields placed on the heads of horses at pompous funerals.

Chaperonné or **Shafferoné.** Hooded.

Chaperonnet (Fr.). A little hood.

Chaplet. A wreath of laurel or oak leaves interspersed with acorns. A wreath of leaves and flowers is also termed a chaplet, but more correctly a *garland*.

Chaplet of Roses. Formed of four roses, two *in pale* and two *in fesse*, placed on a wreath or circlet of leaves or branches.

Chapournet. A chief divided by a curved line. Used incorrectly by some English heralds for *Chaperonnet*.

Chappé or **Chapé** (Fr.). Cloaked. Formed by two diagonal lines drawn from the centre of the upper side, one to the dexter base, the other to the sinister base.

Characters. The letters of the various alphabets, as well as the signs of the planetary system, are frequently borne on coat-armor.

Charge. A figure borne on a coat of arms.

Chargé (Fr.). *Charged*.

Charged. Any ordinary or figure upon which there is another figure, is said to be *charged* therewith.

Charlemagne's Crown. Divided into eight parts, made of gold, and weighing fourteen pounds. Borne as a charge in arms of George I. and his successors as Arch-Treasurers of the Holy Roman Empire.

Chasuble. A priest's outer garment.

Chat (Fr.). Cat.

Chatter or **Chatterer.** The Bohemian lark. It resembles the English crested lark.

Chaussé (Fr.). Shod or wearing shoes. In blazon it is the opposite of *Chapé*, and is formed by two lines drawn from the upper corners of the field and meeting at the lowest point of the escutcheon.

Chaussé-Trappes (Fr.). *Galtraps.*

Cheapeau-wise. Like a chapeau.

Checkers. See CHECKY.

Checky. Applied to a field composed of small squares of different tinctures alternately, and when on ordinaries it differs from *compony* by having three rows instead of one.

Cheeseslip. An insect.

Chef or **Chefe** (Fr.). *Chief.*

Cheque or **Chequy.** See CHECKY.

Cherub. A child's head between two wings.

Chess Rook or **Cocke.** One of the pieces used in chess. It resembles a tower, and is sometimes called a " castle."

Chevalier. A knight or horseman armed at all points.

Chevaltrap. See GALTRAP.

Chevelé (Fr.). *Crined.*

Chevellé. Streaming. Applied to a comet which has the stream of light darting from it, which is sometimes less correctly termed *the beard.*

Chevillé (Fr.). *Attired.*

Chevron. A couple. One of the honorable ordinaries. Its shape is supposed to be taken from a pair of rafters meeting at the peak of a house. See chapter on ORDINARIES. *Per Chevron,* a field divided by such a line as helps to make the chevron.

Chevron Couped. Applied to a chevron whose ends do not reach the sides of the shield.

Chevron Reversed. Applied to a chevron placed *point down.*

Chevroné (Fr.). *Chevronny.*

Chevronel. The diminutive, and in size half the chevron.

Chevronny. Applied to a shield divided into several equal portions chevronways.

Chevrons Braced. Chevrons interlaced.

Chevrons Couched. Lying sideways.

Chevrons Contre-point. One standing upon the head of another.

Chevronways or **Chevronwise.** Applied to charges placed on the field in the position of a chevron.

Chewerond. See CHEVRON.

Cheynyd and Crownyd. Used instead of *gorged with a crown and chained.*

Chief. An ordinary formed by a horizontal line. It occupies the upper part of the shield and contains in depth one-third of the field.

Chief, In. Applied to anything borne in the chief part or top of the escutcheon.

Child's Head. Usually *couped* below the shoulders.

Chimera. A mythical monster with the face of a beautiful woman, the fore legs and mane of a lion, the body of a goat, the hind legs of a griffin, and the tail of a serpent.

Chimerical. Such figures as have no existence except in the imagination.

Chissel or **Chizzel.** A carpenter's chisel.

Chivalry. The touchstone by which honor and knighthood were tried in the Middle Ages. Derived from *cheval* (Fr.), a horse.

Chough. See CORNISH CHOUGH.

Church-Bells. Borne in pale with clapper in base. They are open at the bottom and the clapper is visible. In this way they are distinguished from hawk's bells, which are closed and spherical, closely resembling the bells used in strings for sleigh-bells.

Cimier (Fr.). *Crest.*

Cinquefoil. The five-leaved grass, borne with the leaves issuing from a ball in the centre.

Circle. A ring of light about a charge.

Circumflexant-Bent. Bowed around.

Citadel. A fortress within a town as a place of last resort. It is distinguished from the *tower* in heraldry by the fact that the wall is placed *in front.*

Civic Crown. A garland composed of oak leaves and acorns, given by the Romans as a reward for rescuing a citizen who had been taken prisoner by his enemy.

Clam-Shell. See ESCALLOP-SHELL.

Clarenceux. One of the Kings-of-Arms of the English Heralds' College. He was originally known as *Sorroy,* from the fact that he had jurisdiction over all England *south* of the Trent.

Claricord. See CLARION.

Clariné. Used by French heralds to signify *gorged with small bells.*

Clarion, Claricord, or **Rest.** A conventional figure in heraldry, by some said to be the musical instrument clarion, by others a rest for the lance of a knight.

Clasped or **Conjoined.** Applied to hands when depicted grasping each other.

Cleché. Applied to any ordinary from which the centre has been removed and the outline only left.

Clenched or **Clinched.** Applied to the hand when closely shut.

Clipping. Clasping.

Clock. Usually a table or mantel clock resting on four feet.

Clos (Fr.). *Close.*

Close. Used of a bird when the wings are down and close to the body. Also applied to a helmet with vizor down.

Close Couped. Cut off close to the head, leaving no part of the neck.

Close Girt. Applied to a figure whose garments are fastened in by a girdle.

Closet. The diminutive of the bar, and half as broad.

Closing-Tongs. A tool used by founders.

Closs. See CLOSE.

Clothed. Vested or clad.

Clouds. Frequently borne *proper* with devices *issuant.* When one of the heraldic partition-lines is meant, it is termed *nebulé.*

Cloudy. Circling toward the centre.

Cloué. Nailed; applied to *Treillé* when the nails at the crossings are specially marked or tinctured.

Cloven or **Sarcelled.** Cut in half. Birds and beasts are frequently so borne in German coats.

Cloves. The well-known spice.

Club. Usually borne in the hand of a *savage,* and frequently spiked at the end.

Cluster. Applied to fruits, flowers, etc., borne in natural bunches.

Clymant. Applied to a goat when *salient* or nearly erect on its hind legs.

Co-ambulant. Walking together.

Coat of Arms. Now applied to the whole achievement. Originally the surcoat worn over the armor and ornamented with the knight's armorial bearings.

Cobweb and Spider. Borne with the spider in the centre of the web.

Cock. Sometimes blazoned *dunghill-cock,* but this is unnecessary, since it is rarely borne with its natural plumage *trimmed* for fighting.

Cockade. Originally a badge worn by political parties. The Yorkists wore a white rose as a cockade, the Lancastrians a red.

Cockatrice. A monster with the wings and legs of a fowl and the tail of a snake.

Cocquel. See ESCALLOP.

Cod. The husk or shell in which pease or beans grow. Also a sort of fish.

Codded. Applied to pease, beans, etc., when borne in the cod or pod.

Co-equal. Applied to charges placed alike.

Co-erectant. Set up side by side

Cœur (Fr.). The heart.

Cœur. A short line of partition *in pale,* in the centre of the escutcheon, which extends but a little way, much short of the top and bottom, and is there met by other lines, which form an irregular partition of the escutcheon.

Cognizance. Sometimes used for *Crest,* sometimes for *Badge.*

Coif. A hood.

Coif of Mail. A piece of defensive armor worn under the helmet.

Coiffé (Fr.). *Hooded.*

Coiled. Applied to snakes when wound about themselves in a spiral, with head erect in the centre.

Cokke. See COCK.

Collar. A part of the insignia of many orders of knighthood. Worn about the neck as a mark of honor.

Collared. Wearing a collar. Applied to animals, birds, etc. When a coronet or crown takes the place of the collar the creature should be blazoned *gorged.*

Collared Gemelle. Having a double collar.

Collaterally Disposed. Placed side by side.

College of Arms or **Heralds' College.** The body which has charge of armorial bearings in England.

Collying. Applied to the eagle when depicted with head erect and stretching upward as if about to take flight.

Colors. In engraving, *Gules,* red, is expressed by perpendicular lines; *Azure,* blue, by horizontal lines; *Sable,* black, by horizontal and perpendicular lines crossing each other; *Vert,* green, by diagonal lines from the dexter chief to the sinister base; *Purpure,* purple, by diagonal lines from the sinister chief to the dexter base.

Colorys. See COLORS.

Columbine. The flower, represented pendent from a stalk.

Column. Both Doric and Corinthian columns are borne.

Comb. The crest of a cock.

Combatant or **Confronté.** Fighting or *rampant, face to face.*

Combattand. Assaulting, or lifting up a weapon.

Combed and Wattled. See BARBED AND CRESTED.

Combel. See FILLET.

Comet or **Blazing Star.** In heraldry, a star of six points with a tail streaming from it, *in bend.* Fairbairn gives an example of one which is a star of five points.

Commise Cross. A cross Tau. In the shape of the Greek T.

Commixt. Indiscriminately mingled.

Companions. The third rank in the Order of the Bath.

Compartment. In Scotch heraldry, a panel bearing the motto, placed below the shield.

Compartments. See QUARTERINGS.

Compassed or **Encompassed.** Surrounded.

Compasses. A tool used for drawing circles.

Complement. This term signifies the moon when at her full.

Complexed. Folded or twined together.

Complicated. Sometimes applied to the wings of birds to denote that they are somewhat raised, as if the bird were about to take flight. Birds thus borne are termed *surgeant.*

Compon or **Camp.** Used by French heralds for *Compony.*

Componé (Fr.). *Compony.*

Compony or **Gobony.** Applied to an ordinary composed of one row of squares of alternate metals and colors. When of two rows it is *Compony-Counter-Compony.* When of three it is *Checky.*

Compony-Counter-Compony. Made up of two rows of small squares alternately, a metal and a color.

Concaved. Applied to ordinaries when bowed inward like an arch.

Coney. A rabbit.

Confronté (Fr.). Facing or fronting one another. English *Combatant.*

Conger-Eel. A large sea-eel. The head alone is generally borne.

Conjoined or **Conjunct.** Applied to charges, in arms, when linked or joined together.

Conjoined in Lure. Two wings joined together, with their tips downward. This bearing is an imitation of the hawk's lure.

Conspicuous or **Conspitiant.** Applied to a charge placed in front of another.

Constable. A military officer of high rank in mediæval armies.

Cont' Escartelé (Fr.). *Counter-Quartered.*

Contoise. A scarf attached to the helmet.

Contourné (Fr.). Applied to a beast with its face to the sinister side of the shield.

Contra-Nuage. Covered with escallop-shells lying like the scales of a fish, each one overlapping parts of two placed below it.

Contrary, Contra, or **Contre.** See COUNTER.

Contrebandé (Fr.). *Bendy, per bend sinister counterchanged.*

Contrebarré. *Bendy sinister, per bend counterchanged.*

Contre-Escartelent (Fr.). *Quarterly Quartered.*

Contre-Facé (Fr.). *Barry, per pale counterchanged.*

Contre-Hermines (Fr.). *Ermines.*

Contre-Palé (Fr.). *Paly, per fesse counterchanged.*

Contre-Point. Two chevrons meeting in the fesse point, the one rising from the base, the other inverted, falling from the chief, so that they are counter or opposite to one another, point against point.

Contre-Potencé (Fr.). *Counter-Potent.*

Contre-Tenant (Fr.). *Assaultant.*

Contrevaire (Fr.). *Counter-Vair.*

Converted. Turned. Applied to the ears of a griffin or other animal *converted* into horns.

Convexed. Bowed outward.

Conyd. Counter.

Coote. A water-fowl, smaller than the duck. The feathers about the head and neck are low, soft, and thick. The color all over the body is black, deeper about the head.

Cope. A priest's garment worn over the surplice on solemn occasions.

Coppé or **Copped.** With top higher than usual.

Copper. An instrument used to wind wire upon.

Coquille (Fr.). A shell.

Coquille de St. Jacques. An *Escallop-Shell.*

Coquille de St. Michel. An escallop without " ears."

Corbie. A *Raven.*

Corbyws. Old English for ravens.

Cordals. Strings of a mantle or robe of state. Made of silk and gold thread interwoven like a cord.

Cor de Chasse (Fr.). *Hunting-Horn.*

Corded. Bound with a cord, or formed like a cord or rope.

Cordilière. A silver cord which sometimes encircles the arms of widows.

Cordirobe. A Roman garment.

Cordon. A cord with tassels worn with robes of state.

Corled. *Coiled* or wound round.

Cormorant. A sharp-billed bird in shape somewhat like a goose.

Corne d'Abondance (Fr.). *Cornucopia.*

Corned. Horned.

Corneille (Fr.). Rook, crow, or *chough.*

Cornet. A musical instrument.

Cornet. A pennon or small flag with forked end.

Cornichons. The branches of the horns of a stag.

Cornish Chough. A black bird with red beak and legs. It is considered the king of crows, and is a noble bearing of antiquity.

Cornished. Adorned with a cornice or moulding.

Cornucopia. The horn of plenty, represented overflowing with fruit.

Coronated. Adorned with a coronet.

Coronet. The crown worn by a peer as a mark of noble rank. In modern times coronets are worn with a cap of crimson velvet underneath, and they are generally so represented in arms.

Cost, Cotice, or **Cotise.** One of the diminutives of the bend. In size it is one-fourth of the bend.

Coticé. A term used by the French when an escutcheon is divided bendways into many equal parts.

Coticed or **Cotised.** Accosted, sided, or accompanied by another charge, or placed between two charges.

Cotoose. See MODILLION.

Cotoyé (Fr.). *Coticed.*

Cotton Hanks. Bundles of cotton. Generally borne in pale.

Couchant or **Couched.** Signifies a beast lying down, but with his head lifted up, which distinguishes the position from *dormant.*

Couché. Applied to a shield when suspended by a belt.

Couché (Fr.). *Couchant.*

Couched. A chevron issuing from the dexter side is so termed.

Coudière. Armor for the elbow.

Coué (Fr.). *Coward.*

Coulter. Part of a plough.

Counter. Against or opposite.

Counter-Attired. When the double horns of an animal are borne one pair facing one way and the other the other way, the animal is counter-attired.

Counter-Changed. Applied to a field parted, per one of the ordinaries, and one-half tinctured with a metal and the other with a color. The charges on the metal part of the field are tinctured with the color, and *vice versa.*

Counter-Componé. A field composed of two rows of small squares having a metal and a color alternating.

Counter-Couchant. When applied to one lion means *couchant* facing sinister. When applied to more than one, it means *couchant* with heads in opposite directions.

Counter-Embowed. Bent with elbow to sinister, or bent in opposite directions.

Counter-Fleury. Having fleurs-de-lis with the alternate ones reversed.

Counter-Passant. Used of two beasts which are passing each other, walking in opposite directions.

Counter-Potent. A fur used in heraldry.

Counter-Salient. See SALIENT.

Counter-Tripping. A term applied to deer instead of *counter-passant.*

Counter-Vair. This fur differs from vair by having the cups or bells, which are of the same tincture, placed base against base and point against point.

Countess. The wife of an earl.

Coupé (Fr.). *Party per fesse.*

Coupé et Parti (Fr.). *Quartered.*

Couped or **Coupé.** Cut cleanly off, leaving no jagged edge.

Couped or **Humetté.** When used of a cross or other ordinary, means cut or shortened so that its extremities do not reach the outlines of the escutcheon.

Couped Close. See CLOSE COUPED.

Couplé (Fr.). *Coupled.*

Couple Close. A diminutive of the chevron.

Coupled. Charges borne in pairs.

Courant. Running at full speed.

Courbé (Fr). *Embowed.*

Courlett or **Cuirass.** A breast-plate.

Couronné (Fr.). *Crowned.*

Course, in his. Applied to a beast running at full speed.

Courtesy, Titles of. Such titles as are given by custom to younger sons, but which do not raise them in rank.

Couste. See COST.

Cousu (Fr.). Sewed to. When a metal is placed on a metal, or a color on a color, the upper one is termed *cousu*, that the heraldic law may not be violated.

Coutre (Fr.). *Coulter.*

Couvert (Fr.). *Covered.*

Coward or **Cowed**. Used when a lion or other animal has its tail hanging between its legs.

Cowl. A hood worn by monks and friars.

Crab. Always borne with claws in chief.

Crampette or **Crampit**. See CHAPE.

Crampetté. Ornamented like the end of a scabbard.

Cramponné. Used of a cross when it has at each end a cramp or square piece coming from it.

Crampoons or **Cramps**. Pieces of iron hooked at each end and used in buildings to fasten two stones together.

Crancelin. A bend treflé, vert. A bend ornamented like a coronet.

Crane or **Stork**. A wading bird with long legs and neck.

Crawling or **Gliding**. Applied to snakes, and other creatures which have no legs, when represented moving forward.

Crefish. A crawfish. A small fresh-water creature like a shrimp or a diminutive lobster.

Creneaux, Crenellé, or **Enmanché**. See EMBATTLED.

Crenelles. The openings in a battlement.

Crescent. The half-moon, with its horns turned *toward* the *chief* of the shield; by this position it differs from the *increscent* and *decrescent* (q. v.).

Crescented. Used of a cross when it has a crescent at each end.

Cresset. See BEACON.

Crest. A figure placed upon a wreath, coronet, or cap of maintenance, above the helmet or shield.

Cresté (Fr.). *Combed* or *Crested.*

Crested. When a cock or other bird has its crest of a different tincture from its body it is termed crested of such a tincture, naming it. See BARBED AND CRESTED.

Crest-Wreath. The wreath upon which the crest is borne. It is formed of strands of two tinctures, usually a metal and a color.

Crêté (Fr.). *Crested.*

Crevice. See CREFISH.

Crined. A term used when the hair of an animal differs in tincture from its body.

Crochet (Fr.). A note in music. Also known as the "quarter note."

Crocodile. An amphibious animal, common in the Nile.

Croissant. See CRESCENT.

Croissant Contourné. See DECRESCENT.

Croisette (Fr.). *Crosslet.*

Croix (Fr.). *Cross.*

Croix Recroisée (Fr.). A *cross crosslet.*

Cronel. The iron head of a tilting spear.

Crose or **Drawing Board**. An instrument used by coopers.

Crosier. See CROZIER.

Cross. One of the honorable ordinaries, formed by the meeting of two perpendicular with two horizontal lines near the fesse point, where they make four right angles. First popularly used as a bearing at the Crusades, where each leader was known by the cross which he bore on his standard. It was from this fact that the Crusades or "Croisades" received their name.

Cross-Bow. An old English weapon.

Cross Crosslet. A plain cross crossed at end of each arm.

Crossed. Charges borne in such a way as to form a cross.

Crosslet. A small cross.

Crossways. Placed to form a cross.

Crossys. Crosses.

Crow. See CORNISH CHOUGH.

Crowned. When this term is applied to an animal it means that it bears on its head a "ducal coronet."

Crown of Thorns. Formed by twisting two branches into a wreath.

Crown of Rue. See CRANCELIN.

Crowns. See article on CROWNS.

Crown Vallary. See VALLARY-CROWN.

Crozier. A staff ornamented at the top with a cross. It belongs to an archbishop as an emblem of his dignity. The staff of office of a bishop or abbot is sometimes termed a crozier, but it is properly a *Pastoral staff.*

Cruceil or **Crucellette**. A *cross crosslet.*

Crusilly or **Crusuly**. A field or charge strewn with crosses.

Cry of War. Any word or sentence that became a general cry throughout an army upon its approach to battle. These were afterwards adopted as mottoes.

Crystal. Used in fanciful blazoning for *argent*. *Pearl* is more common, however.

Cubit Arm. An arm couped at the elbow. The *dexter* arm unless blazoned otherwise.

Cuffed. A sleeve with a cuff of a different tincture is so blazoned.

Cuirass. A breast-plate. Originally a leathern jerkin.

Cuisse. The thigh. *À la Cuisse.* Applied to the limb of a bird torn off at the thigh.

Cuisses, Cullivers, Culboers, etc. Armor for the thighs.

Culter. A ploughshare.

Cumbant. See LODGED.

Cup. Variously borne. *Covered Cup.* An egg-shaped vessel on a high stand.

Cupola. The dome of a building.

Cuppa. One of the heraldic furs, composed of pieces formed *potent counter-potent*. Sometimes called *varry-cuppa*.

Cuppules. *Bars-Gemelle*, since they are borne in pairs or couples.

Cuppy. By some writers held to be a fur, by others not.

Curling. Applied to snakes, etc., coiled.

Curling-Stone. Used in the game of *Curling*.

Currant, Courant, or **Coursant.** Running.

Currier's Shave. An instrument used to make leather thin. A blade between two handles.

Curvilinear. A curved line.

Cushion. This bearing is looked upon as a mark of authority, and is borne by many ancient families.

Cutlass. A sort of sword.

Cutt or **Cloven.** Animals in Dutch or German arms are frequently cut in half, and the halves borne endorsed or saltier-ways.

Cutting-Iron. A tool used by pattern-makers. A blade with a handle at one end and a hook at the other.

Cuttle-Fish. An ocean monster which, when pursued, throws out an inky fluid.

Cygnet. A young swan. *Cygnet Royal.* A swan gorged with a "ducal coronet" with a chain fastened to it and curled over the back of the bird.

Cyphers. Monograms used at funerals of women instead of crests, which they are not allowed to bear.

Cypress. The tree and its branches are used to adorn funeral achievements.

D.

Dacre Knot and Badge. An escallop-shell and a ragged staff with a cord fancifully knotted and entwined about them.

Dagger. A short sword.

Dais. The canopy hung over a throne.

Daisy. The English flower. The emblem of constancy.

Dalmatic. The distinctive garment of a deacon. Worn in early times by sovereign princes and bishops as a robe of state.

Dame. The legal term for a baronet's wife.

Dancette. A large sort of indenting, wider and deeper than that called *indented*.

Double-Dancette. The bend *double-dancette* is a mark of illegitimacy.

Danché (Fr.). *Dancette.*

Danish Axe. Similar to the broad-axe, but with an indent in the upper edge of the blade.

Dauphin. The title of the eldest son of the French king until 1830.

Dauphin's Crown. A circle of gold, set round with eight fleurs-de-lis, closed at the top with four dolphins, whose tails conjoin under a fleur-de-lis.

Death's Head. A human skull.

Debased. Applied to any ordinary or charge turned downward or lowered from its proper position.

Debruised. Used when a bend or other ordinary is placed over any animal, whereby it is debarred of its natural freedom.

Decapitated, Decapité Deffait, or **Decollated.** Having the head cut off smoothly. Differs from *estête*, which signifies with head torn off leaving a jagged edge.

Dechaussé. (1) Dismembered. (2) Without claws.

Decked. Ornamented.

Decked or **Marguette.** Used when feathers of a bird are edged with a tincture different from that of its body.

Declinant or **Declivant.** Applied to a serpent borne with its tail straight down.

Decollated. See DECAPITATED.

Decoupled, Decouplé, or **Uncoupled.** Parted or severed.

Decours, Decresnent, Decressant, or **Decrescent.** Shows the state of the moon when she declines from her full to her last quarter, and differs from the *increscent* by having the horns toward the *sinister* side of the shield.

Defamed or **Disgraced.** Applied to a creature which is represented without its tail, as if disgraced by the loss.

Defences. The natural weapons of defence which are given to a beast.

Defendu (Fr.). See ARMED or TUSKED.

Deffait. See DECAPITATED.

Degradation of Honor. See ABATEMENTS.

Degraded or **Degreed.** Used of a cross when it has steps at each end.

Degrees. Steps.

Dejected. Applied to anything cast or thrown down. Also applied to animals *despectant.*

Delf. A square clod of turf or block of coal. A *delf-tenne* is a mark of disgrace for revoking a challenge.

Demembré (Fr.). See DISMEMBERED.

Demi or **Demy.** Half. The upper or *dexter* half is understood.

Demie-Jarretière (Fr.). Demi-garter or *per close.*

Demy Vol. One wing.

Dentals, Dentels, Dentees, or **Dens.** The indents or teeth of *Indented.*

Denté (Fr.). *Tusked.*

Dentelle, Viurie. Indented.

Denticules or **Denticles.** Small square pieces taken from the entablature in Ionic architecture.

Derraché. Dismembered.

Desarmé (Fr.). *Disarmed.*

Descendant or **Descending.** Applied to an eagle volant downward.

Descending. Applied to a lion borne with head toward the base of the shield.

Descent. Applied to a beast with its hind legs toward one corner of the chief and head toward one of the base points, as if leaping down from some height.

Despectant. Looking downward.

Despouille (Fr.). The stuffed skin of an animal. See CASE.

Detranché. Applied to a line bendways from some part of the upper edge or from some part of the dexter side.

Detriment. A term for the moon when eclipsed. Sometimes also applied to her when *decrescent.*

Developed. Unfolded. Applied to a flag unfurled and displayed.

Device. An heraldic bearing.

Devouring. See VORANT.

Dewlaps or **Wattles.** The excrescences growing under the beak of a cock, cockatrice, or dragon.

Dexter. The right side of the escutcheon; that is, the side opposite the *left hand* of the observer. The supporter, and everything placed on the right hand, is termed the dexter; it is also the male side in an impaled coat of arms.

Dexter Base. The right side of the base.

Dexter Chief. The angle on the right-hand side of the chief.

Dexter Hand. The right hand.

Dexter Wing. The right-hand wing.

Dez. See DICE.

Diadem. (1) A circlet worn by kings until the crown took its place. (2) The circles of gold which meet on the top of a sovereign's crown and support the mound or globe. (3) The wreath on a blackamoor's head.

Diademed. Used of the imperial eagle with its crowned head.

Diamond. Used in blazoning "by precious stones" for *sable* (black).

Diapered. Used of a field when divided into geometrical patterns, and filled with a variety of figures.

Diapré (Fr.). *Diapered.*

Dice. Borne in pairs and represented with one angle toward the observer.

Diffamé. See DEFAMED.

Diffamed. Sometimes used for a lion going toward the *sinister.*

Difference. A figure or device introduced into heraldic compositions for the purpose of distinguishing several persons who bear the same arms.

Dilated. Open or extended. Applied to compasses, etc.

Dimidiated. Represented with one-half removed.

Dimidiation. The earliest form of impalement.

Diminution of Arms. See DIFFERENCE.

Diminutives. The *pale's* diminutives are the PALLET and ENDORSE; the *bend* has the GARTER, COST, and RIBAND; the *bar* has the CLOSET and BARRULET; the *chevron* has the CHEVRONEL and COUPLE-CLOSE; the *bend sinister* has the SCARPE and BATON, etc.

Disarmed. Lacking the natural weapons of defence,—claws and teeth, or beak and talons, etc.

Disclosed. Displayed.

Dishevelled. With loose-flowing hair.

Disjointed. Applied to a chevron whose branches do not meet at the top.

Dislodging. A term used for rousing a buck from its resting-place.

Dismembered. Signifies a cross or other charge cut in pieces, and the severed parts so placed, at short distances from each other, as to retain the original form of the figure.

Dismembré (Fr.). *Dismembered.*

Displayed. An eagle with *wings displayed* is an eagle *perched* with its wings expanded. An *eagle displayed* is not perched. The eagle borne by Russia, and that on the seal of the United States of America, is *an eagle displayed.*

Disposed. Placed in any particular position.

Distilling. Dropping.

Distinctions of Families. See article on MARKS OF CADENCY.

Disveloped. Displayed. Colors flying or spread out are in heraldry said to be *disveloped.*

Dividing Lines. Lines which divide the field into parts. They are in various forms.

Diving. See URIANT or URINANT.

Dog. The dog in heraldry signifies fidelity, affection, watchfulness, and sincerity, when such illusions, rather than whim or caprice, are consulted in the formation of armorial bearings.

Dog-Collar. The ends nearly meet, and are connected by a short chain and padlock.

Dolphin. Generally represented *embowed.* Considered the king of fishes, and frequently borne in coats of arms.

Domed. Applied to a tower with a rounded roof.

Dominion, Arms of. The arms of a sovereign, not borne without a difference by any other, even the nearest relative.

Donjonné. Applied to a castle which has an inner tower rising above its battlements.

Dormant. Sleeping, with the head resting on the fore paws.

Dors or **Dors Endorsed.** Back to back.

Dorsed. See AVERSANT.

Dosser. See WATER BOUGET.

Doublé (Fr.). Ornamented with *Doublings.*

Double-Arched. Having two arches.

Double Fitchée or **Double Fitchy.** A cross, each extremity of which has two points.

Double-Headed. Having two heads.

Double Plume. Generally composed of two rows of ostrich feathers, five in the lower and four in the upper.

Double Quartrefoil. An eight-leaved grass. The distinction for the ninth son.

Double-Queued. Having a double tail.

Double Tête. Having two heads.

Double Tressure. Composed of two tressures, one within the other.

Doublet. See TRAVERSE.

Doublings. The linings of robes or mantles of state, or the mantlings in achievements.

Dove. Usually borne in profile, holding in its bill a sprig of olive.

Dovetail. One of the partition-lines. Two different tinctures are set within one another in form of doves' tails or wedges.

Downsett or **Daunsett.** Applied to the separated parts of an ordinary when set one upon the other.

Dragon. One of the heraldic monsters with a serpent-like tail, four legs, and two wings.

Dragon (Fr.). In French heraldry a *wyvern* is so blazoned.

Dragonné. See DRAGONY.

Dragon's Head. In heraldry the color *tenné* or tawny, orange color.

Dragon's Tail. In heraldry the term for *sanguine* or murrey, the color of cold blood.

Dragony. Applied to a wyvern when its head or tail is of a different tincture from that of its body. It is then *dragony* of such a tincture.

Drapeau (Fr.). A standard or ensign.

Drawing-Board. See GROSE.

Drawing-Iron. An instrument used by wire-drawers.

Drop. Called in heraldry a *gutta* or *gutte.* See GUTTÉ.

Ducal Coronet, or *Crest Coronet.* Frequently used as a collar, and occasionally in place of a wreath.

Duchess. The wife of a duke. She is addressed "*Your Grace,*" and is styled "*Most noble.*"

Duciper. See CAP OF MAINTENANCE.

Ducks. When borne without beaks or feet termed *Cannets.*

Dufoil or **Twyfoil.** A grass with two leaves.

Duke. The highest title in English nobility. Originally the Latin *dux,* a leader of an army. Edward the Black Prince was the first English duke after the Norman Conquest.

Dung-Fork. In heraldry a three-pronged fork.

Dungeoned. See DONJONNÉ.

Duparted or **Biparted.** Cut into two parts.

Dwal. The nightshade. Used by those who blazoned by flowers instead of *sable*

E.

Eagle. Generally borne displayed, with wings and legs extended on each side of the body, which is placed affronté. It signifies magnanimity and fortitude of mind. See DISPLAYED.

Eagle, Spread. An eagle displayed or an eagle with two heads. According to Pourney, the Emperor of Germany bears an eagle with two necks, because when Roumania became a part of the empire its arms, which were *an eagle displayed sable*, were the same as those of the emperor. The two eagles were united into one body, leaving it two necks, as it has now.

Eaglet. When there are more than three eagles in a coat without some ordinary between them, they may be termed eaglets.

Eared. Applied to animals whose ears differ in tincture from their bodies. Also applied to a grain when the ear is different in tincture from the stalk.

Earl. In rank between a marquis and a viscount. It was a high rank among the Saxons, and the Normans retained the name, modifying the duties somewhat. An earl is usually styled "Right honorable and truly noble." His wife is a countess.

Earl Marshal. The officer at the head of the English heraldic system. He appoints all heraldic officers except those of the Lyon Office. The office of Earl Marshal is hereditary in the family of the Duke of Norfolk.

Earl's Coronet. A golden circlet from which rise eight points, each bearing a pearl. Between the points are strawberry leaves.

Eastern or **Antique Crown.** Formerly worn by the Jewish kings; it was made of gold with rays arising from it.

Eau. Water. *Gutté d'eau.* Sprinkled with drops of water.

Ecaillé (Fr.). *Scaled.*

Ecartelé (Fr.). Quarterly.

Ecartelé en Sautoir (Fr.). *Party per Saltire.*

Echiqueté or **Echiquier** (Fr.). *Checky.*

Eclaté (Fr.). *Jagged.*

Eclipsed. The sun and moon are sometimes so borne, the face, beams, and rays, sable. The moon when partially eclipsed is called "*in her detriment.*"

Eclopé (Fr.). *Bevel.*

Ecusson (Fr.). An *escutcheon* or an *inescutcheon.*

Edged. Applied to an ordinary when its edge has a peculiar tincture.

Eel-Basket. A wicker basket used by fishermen for holding eels and fish.

Eels. Generally borne *in pale.*

Eel-Spear. A barbed spear of three or five prongs.

Effellonie. A lion standing on his hind legs with his fore legs raised to an equal height.

Effray or **Effearé** (Fr.). See CABRÉ.

Eguisée, A Cross. One which has the two angles at the end cut off so that the arms terminate in points.

Eightfoil. Formed by eight leaves attached to a central ball. See DOUBLE QUARTREFOIL.

Electoral Crown. A scarlet cap, faced with ermine, diademed with half a circle of gold, set with pearls, supporting a globe, with a cross of gold on the top.

Elephant. Borne with or without a castle on its back.

Elevated. Applied to wings with the points turned upward.

Emanche. See MANCH.

Emaux de l'Escu. The tinctures of the escutcheon.

Embattled. See BATTLED.

Embordered. Having a border.

Embowed. Bent or flexed. Applied to fish and to the human arm when bent at the elbow.

Embraced. Bound together.

Embrassé Droit (Fr.). *Traverse*

Embroidery. Applied to a hill or mount which has several rises and falls. Also applied to a mount *embroidered* with flowers.

Embrued. Bloody or dripping with blood.

Emerald. A stone; it signifies in heraldry the color vert or green.

Emerasses. Small shield-shaped pieces on the shoulders of a full-armed knight.

Emmancé, Viuré (Fr.), or **Serrated.** *Indented.*

Emmanche or **Creneaux.** Battled.

Emmets. Ants.

Emmusellé (Fr.). Muzzled.

Emperor. The highest title of sovereignty.

Empoigné (Fr.). *Banded.*

En (Fr.). In.

Enaluron. Applied to a border charged with birds.

Enarched. Arched or flexed.

En Arrière. Borne with the back to view.

En Band (Fr.). *In bend.*

Enceppé. Fettered, chained, or girt about the middle.

Enclavé (Fr.). Square pieces let into one another. *Mortised.*

Encountering. Opposed to each other. Applied to three birds, etc., borne with their beaks touching at one point.

En Croix. (Fr.). *In cross.*

Endenché or **Endenté.** See INDENTED.

Endorse. One-fourth of the *pale.*

Endorsed. Placed between two *endorses.*

Endorsed. See ADDORSED.

Enfiled. Said of any charge thrust through or encircled by another. When any charge is placed on the blade of a sword, the sword is said to be *enfiled* with that charge.

Englanté (Fr.). *Acorned.*

Engoulant (Fr.). *Vorant.*

Engouled. Being swallowed.

Engrailé or **Engreslé** (Fr.) *Engrailed.*

Engrailed. A line of partition by which ordinaries are diversified, composed of semicircles, the teeth or points of which enter the field.

Engrossing-Block. A tool used by wire-drawers.

Enguiché. Applied to the large end of a hunting-horn when it has a rim different in tincture from the horn.

Enhanced or **Enhansed.** Applied to an ordinary when placed above its usual situation. This happens most frequently to the bend and its diminutives.

Enhendée, A Cross. *Cross potence.*

Enlevé (Fr.). Raised or elevated.

Enmanché, from *Manche.* Used when the chief has lines drawn from the centre of the upper edge of the chief to the sides, to about half the breadth of the chief. It differs from *chappé,* which comes from the top to the bottom of the chief.

En Pied. On his feet. Applied by French heralds to a bear erect on his hinder feet.

Enraged. Applied to a horse borne *salient.*

Ensanglanté (Fr.). *Imbrued.*

Ensigned. Ornamented. A shield surmounted by a crown or coronet is said to be ensigned of it.

Entangled. Bound together. Fretted.

Enté (Fr.). See ANTÉ.

Enté en Rond. One of the partition-lines, somewhat like *indented* but formed of curved lines.

Entire or **Throughout.** Attached to the sides of the shield.

Entoire or **Entoyer.** The term for a bordure charged with dead or artificial things, to the number of eight.

Entrailed, Purfled, or **Shadowed.** See ADUM-BRATED.

Entwined. Wrapped by. Usually applied to a staff or sword around which is wrapped a serpent, a cable, or a branch of laurel, etc.

Entwisted. See ANNODATED.

Enurney or **Enurny.** The term for a bordure charged with beasts.

Envecked. See INVECKED.

Enveloped. Applied to a man or a beast tightly encircled by a snake.

Environed. Bound about.

Environné or **Environed.** (1) A French term for a lion, or other figure, when surrounded with other charges, such as bezants. (2) *In Orle* or *Orle.*

Enwarped. See ENVELOPED.

Enwrapped. See ENTWINED.

Epaulette. The decoration worn on the shoulder by officers of the army and navy. It was originally a badge of great distinction.

Epaulier. Armor for the shoulder.

Epimacus. See OPINICUS.

Episcopal Staff. See PASTORAL STAFF.

Epitaph. An inscription on a tomb or monument.

Eployé (Fr.). See DISPLAYED.

Equippé or **Equipped.** Applied to a knight armed cap-à-pie or to a horse fully caparisoned.

Equisé. See AIGUISÉ.

Eradicated. A term for a tree or plant torn up by the roots.

Erased or **Arazed.** Applied to the head or limb of any creature which is violently torn from the body, so that it seems to be jagged.

Erect. Upright, or perpendicularly elevated.

Ermine. Applied to a cross formed by four ermine spots in cross.

Ermine. One of the heraldic furs. Black spots on white fur.

Ermines. One of the heraldic furs. White spots on black fur.

Erminites. One of the heraldic furs, but rarely used. Black spots with one red hair on each side, on white fur.

Erminois. One of the heraldic furs. Black spots on yellow fur.

Errant. Wandering. Knights-errant were knights who wandered in search of adventure.

Errant. In heraldry means *Hauriant.*

Escaillé (Fr.). *Scaled.*

Escallop-Shell. The pilgrims' badge in their expeditions and pilgrimages to holy places. They were worn on their hats and hoods, and were of such a distinguishing character that Pope Alexander the Fourth forbade the use of them to all except the pilgrims who were truly noble.

Escarboucle (Fr.). *Escarbuncle.*

Escarbuncle. A precious stone.

Escartelé or **Ecartelé** (Fr.). *Quarterly* or *Quartered.*

Escartelé en Sautoir (Fr.). *Party per Saltire.*

Escarteler (Fr.). A *quartering.*

Esclatté. Broken irregularly or splintered.

Escloppe. A sort of indenture.

Escrol. See SCROLL.

Escutcheon or **Shield.** The shield used in war, on which arms were originally borne. The surface of the escutcheon is termed the field, because it contains such honorable marks as anciently were acquired in the field.

Escutcheon of Pretence. The small escutcheon in which a man bears the coat of arms of his wife, if she is an heiress; it is placed in the centre of the man's coat, and indicates his pretensions to her lands.

Esquire or **Equire.** By some considered the same as the *Gyron.* Others hold that the gyron cannot extend beyond the centre fesse point, while the *esquire* runs completely across the shield.

Esquire. The title of honor between knight and gentleman. Originally the armor-bearer of a knight.

Essonier. A diminutive of the *orle.*

Essorant (Fr.). Applied to an eagle when depicted with wings slightly elevated, as if rising from the ground.

Estête. With head *erased* or torn off.

Estoile or **Etoile.** A star. It differs from the *Mullet* by having six waved points, while the mullet has five plain ones. In French heraldry the star has but five points.

Estoile of eight points. Alternately straight and wavy.

Estropie. *Dismembered.*

Etête. See ESTÊTE.

Etoile. See ESTOILE.

Evangelists' Emblems. The *angel,* the *winged lion,* the *winged ox,* the *eagle.*

Ewer. A vessel for holding liquids.

Exasperated. Represented enraged.

Exhalation. A fall of rain or a water-spout.

Expanded or **Expansed.** See DISPLAYED.

Extended. Stretched out.

Eyed. Applied to the variegated spots in a peacock's tail. Also to an animal whose eyes are of a tincture different from that of its body.

Eyes. Sometimes borne in armory as emblems of vigilance and vivacity.

F.

Face (Fr.). *Fesse.*

Facé or **Fascé** (Fr.). *Barry.*

Faced-Lined. Having a part of the lining turned outward.

Fagot. A bundle of small sticks bound together.

Faillis (Fr.). Applied to an ordinary having a splinter taken from it.

Falchion or **Faulchion.** A sword with a broad curved blade.

Falcon. This bird is borne in the same postures as the eagle, and is described in the same terms, except when with hood, bells, virols (or rings), and leashes.

False Cross. A cross *voided.*

False Escutcheon. An escutcheon *voided.*

False Heraldry. Any violation of heraldic laws.

False Roundel. A roundel *voided,* and hence an *Annulet.*

Fan or **Winnowing-Fan.** An instrument used in husbandry to separate the chaff from the grain.

Fanon (Fr.). A small standard.

Far-Roebuck. The term for a roebuck in his fifth year.

Fasce (Fr.). Fesse.

Fascé (Fr.). *Barry.*

Fasciolæ Gemellæ or **Fasciollæ Duplices.** See BAR-GEMELLE.

Fawn. A deer in its first year.

Feathered or **Flighted.** Applied to an arrow when the feathers are different in tincture from the shaft.

Feathers. Used as charges and crests. See OSTRICH FEATHERS.

Feeding. See PREYING.

Femme. Used in heraldry for wife. See BARON AND FEMME.

Fendue en Pal (Fr). Voided *per pale.*

Fer de Dard (Fr.). *Pheon.*

Fer de Fourchette. A cross is so termed when it has at each end a forked iron, like that used by soldiers to rest their muskets upon.

Fer de Mouline or **Millrind.** The cross-shaped iron in the middle of a millstone.

Fermau or **Fermail.** The buckle of a military belt.

Ferr. A horse-shoe.

Fesse or **Fess.** One of the honorable ordinaries, occupying one-third of the field ; some authors say it was a belt of honor given as a reward for services in the army. *Per Fesse.* Applied to a field or charge divided into two equal parts by a horizontal line. *Per Fesse and Pale.* Used when the field is divided into three parts by the fesse line and the pale line, from the fesse point to the middle base.

Fesse Point. The centre of the escutcheon.

Fessewise or **Fesseways.** Placed horizontally.

Festoon. A festoon of fruit is called a *fruitage ;* a festoon of flowers, a *flowerage.*

Fetlock. The fetlock of a horse.

Fetterlock, Shackbolt, or **Fetlock.** A shackle or lock. An instrument attached to the fetlock of a horse to prevent him from running away.

Fiché (Fr.). See FITCHY.

Field. The surface of the escutcheon or shield which contains the charge or charges. It must be described *first* in blazoning.

Fiery Furnace. A furnace with flames darting about it.

Figetive. Fitched or fastened.

Figured. The term used for those bearings which are depicted with a human face.

File. See LABEL.

Filet (Fr.). A narrow strip.

Fillet. The only diminutive of the chief. It contains one-fourth of the chief in area, and always occupies the lowest portion.

Fimbriated. Having a narrow bordure of another tincture.

Finned. Applied to fish whose fins are of a tincture different from that of the body.

Fire-Ball. A bomb.

Fire-Beacon. See BEACON.

Fire-Brands. See BRANDS.

Firme. Sometimes applied to a cross which has its arms fixed in the sides of the escutcheon.

Fish. When the kind is not specified, a small, somewhat conventional fish is meant. Fishes are borne *naiant, hauriant,* and *uriant.*

Fish-Wheel. A sort of net for taking fish. It resembles in shape two hour-glasses placed base to base in fesse, but is made of wicker work.

Fissure or **Staff.** A diminutive of the bend sinister, one-fourth in size.

Fitchée, Fitched, or **Fitchy.** Fixed ; in blazon, *pointed.* This term is applied to crosses when the lower branch ends in a sharp point, since such crosses were used by the primitive Christians to fix in the ground during devotion. *Double Fitchée* or *Fitchy.* A cross was so termed when each extremity had two points.

Five-Leaved Grass. See CINQUEFOIL.

Fixed. See FIRME.

Flag. The modern development of the pennon or banner. On it are represented arms just as on a shield. The depth, or distance from chief to base, is termed the *Hoist* or *Dip ;* the length, or distance from the fastened side to the free end, is termed the *Fly.* The tinctures are indicated in the same way as in a coat of arms.

Flagon. Generally borne vase-shaped, with a cover.

Flamant. Flaming.

Flambant (Fr.). *Flaming.*

Flank. The side of an escutcheon between the chief and the base.

Flanches or **Flanques.** The flanch is formed by an arched line, drawn from the upper angle of the escutcheon to the base point of that side. They are always borne in pairs, the arches almost meeting in the middle of the field.

Flanque Point of the Escutcheon (Fr.). The *Base Point.*

Flasques. Like flanches, but smaller.

Flax-Breaker. See HEMP-BREAK.

Fleam or **Flegme.** An instrument used by farriers in bleeding horses.

Flecked. A line of partition.

Flect, Flectant, or **Flected.** Bent in contrary directions like the letter S.

Fleece. A sheep's skin hung by a ring. It is usually the *Golden Fleece,* badge of a celebrated order of knighthood.

Flegme. See FLEAM.

Flesh-Hook. An instrument used for taking meat out of the seething pot or caldron. It is borne with handle in base and three hooks in chief.

Flesh-Pot. An iron pot with three legs.

Fleur-de-lis. By some this charge is called the lily, or flower of the flag. It has only three leaves, by which it differs from the lily of the garden, which has five. Others suppose it to be the top of the sceptre; some the head of the French battle-axe; others the iron of a javelin used by the ancient French. It was introduced in arms of the English kings on account of their claims to the French throne.

Fleuroné or **Fleur-de-lisé** (Fr.). *Fleury.*

Fleury, a Cross. Decorated with a fleur-de-lis upon the end of each arm.

Flexed. Bent or embowed.

Flighted. Feathered and ready for flight. Applied to arrows.

Float. An instrument used by bowyers.

Flook. A flounder.

Flory. Flowered with the French lily.

Flory, a Cross. This cross differs from the *patonce* by having the flowers at the end circumflex and turning down.

Flotant. Floating or flying in the air. Applied to a flag. Also applied to a bird flying and to anything swimming or floating in water.

Flouretté. See FLEURONÉ.

Flourished. Ornamented with flowers.

Flower of the Flag. The *Fleur-de-lis.*

Flowers. In heraldry signify hope, denote human frailty, and momentary prosperity.

Fly. See GAD-BEE.

Fly. The length of a flag from the fastened end to the free end.

Flying. Floating in the air.

Flying Column. A winged column.

Focked. Applied to animals whose hind feet differ in tincture from their bodies.

Foldage. Leaves with several foldings and turnings, one from the other.

Foliage. The leaves of a tree or branch. Also the *doubling* of a mantle, where it is turned outward.

Foliated. Bearing leaves.

Fondant (Fr.). Applied to an eagle about to seize its prey.

Fontal. See WATER-POT.

Forcené. Used of a horse rearing or standing on his hinder legs.

Fore-Staff. An instrument used by seamen.

Forest Bill. See WOOD BILL.

Forked. Branching into two parts.

Form. The resting-place of the hare.

Formée. See PATTÉE.

Fortified. Surmounted with towers.

Fountain. A roundel *barry wavy of six argent and azure.* It, like the metal roundels, is always represented flat, not *spherical.*

Fourchée or **Fourchy.** Used of a cross which is forked at the ends or divided.

Fracted. Broken.

Fraise, Frasier, Fraze, or Frazier. A strawberry plant or cinquefoil.

Framed Saw. A saw fixed in a wooden frame, with a handle at each end. It is used for cutting timber.

France Ancient. The coat of arms of the early French kings. It was a field *azure, semé of fleurs-de-lis or.* This was quartered with the royal arms of England, to indicate the claim which the English kings had to the French throne. France was borne in the first and fourth quarters, with England in the second and third.

France Modern. The change from the field *semé of fleurs-de-lis* to a field bearing *three fleurs-de-lis* was made by Charles V., of France, in honor of the Trinity, and perhaps, to distinguish the royal arms of France from the arms borne in the royal arms of England. The English kings, however, soon after adopted the new form, and bore on the field *azure, three fleurs-de-lis or.* This new shield is termed France Modern.

Franché or **Frangé** (Fr.). *Fimbriated.*

French Crown. A circle decorated with stones, and heightened with arched diadems, arising from as many fleurs-de-lis, that conjoin at the top under a fleur-de-lis, all of gold.

Fresné. See FORCENÉ.

Fret. A figure resembling two sticks lying saltireways, and interlaced within a mascle. Sometimes called the Herald's True Lover's Knot.

Frette (Fr.). A *fret.*

Fretté or **Fretty.** In attacking a walled city the ancients used a movable tower built of wood, and of such a height that it overlooked the battlements of the city. It was covered with raw hides to prevent its being burnt, and had a net-work of ropes which hung in front of it, in order to deaden the violence of the stones that were thrown against it from the city. This net-work seems to be what *fretty* was originally taken from. The term is applied to a field composed of small squares placed in rows bendwise.

Fretté Triangular. Three semicircles interlaced.

Fretted. Interlaced.

Fretted. Used of a cross when fretted and pointed in the form of five mascles.

Frightened. See FORCENÉ.

Fringed. Edged of a different tincture.

Front or **Frontal.** The fore part of anything The forehead of a man or woman.

Fructed. A term given in blazon to all trees bearing fruit.

Fulgent. Having rays.

Fumant. Emitting smoke.

Furs. See article on TINCTURES. Those in most common use are *Ermine, Ermines, Erminois, Pean, Vair, Counter-Vair, Potent, Counter-Potent.*

Furchy. Forked.

Furiosant. Applied to an animal in rage or *rangant.*

Fusée (Fr.). A *fusil.*

Fuselé (Fr.). *Fusilly.*

Fusil. A spindle of yarn.

Fusil. Derived from the French word *fusée,* a spindle; it is longer and more acute than the lozenge.

Fusillé or **Fusilly.** Applied to the field or charge when filled with fusils.

Fylot, Fylfot, or **Gammadion.** A charge of unknown origin. It has been termed "the mark of Thor's hammer," others have proved it a sacred emblem of India. It resembles a cross with the extremities of its arms bent.

G.

Gad-Bee or **Gad-Fly.** The horse-fly. Generally represented *volant.*

Gads. Curved plates of metal or small spikes on the knuckles of the gauntlet.

Galleys. Small vessels with one mast, but usually propelled with oars. Also called *Lymphads.*

Galthrap, Galtrap, or **Caltrap** A small spiked instrument thrown on the ground to injure the feet of horses in battle.

Gamashes or **Buskins.** A kind of hose or stockings.

Gamb or **Jamb.** The fore leg of a lion, or other beast, when borne in arms. If it is *couped* or *erased* near the middle joint it is called a Paw.

Game-Cock. See COCK.

Gammadion. See FYLOT.

Gantlet. See GAUNTLET.

Garb or **Garbe.** A sheaf of wheat. When of any other grain it must be so stated, as " a garb of oats," etc.

Gardant or **Guardant.** Signifies a beast of prey full-faced, looking right toward the spectator with its body in profile.

Gardebras or **Garbraille.** Armor for the elbow.

Garden-Pales. Borne in pale fitché or pointed at the top and conjoined.

Gardevisor or **Guardevisure.** That part of the helmet which protects the face. It could be raised or lowered at pleasure.

Garland. A wreath of flowers and leaves.

Garnished. Ornamented.

Garter. Half of a bendlet.

Garter. See KNIGHTHOOD.

Garter King-at-Arms. The herald for the Most Noble Order of the Garter.

Garter-Plate. See STALL-PLATE.

Gauntlet. An iron glove introduced about the thirteenth century to cover the hand of a cavalier when armed cap-à-pie. It was frequently thrown like the glove by way of challenge. When borne in arms they are usually represented without fingers, and *never* mailed on the palm.

Gaze. See AT GAZE.

G. C. B. The first class of the Order of the Bath,—Knights of the Grand Cross.

G. C. H. A Knight of the Grand Cross of Hanover.

G. C. M. G. A Knight of the Grand Cross of St. Michael and St. George.

Ged. The fish known as the *luce* or pike.

Gemelles. See BAR-GEMELLE.

Gemmel Rings. See GIMMAL RINGS.

Gem Ring. A ring set with a precious stone

Genet. A small fox-like animal, not larger than a weasel.

Gentleman. The title next below esquire

Gentry. Knights, esquires, and gentlemen. Those who possess no hereditary dignity.

Genuant. Kneeling.

George. See SAINT GEORGE.

George Badge. St. George on horseback slaying the dragon. Worn by Knights of the Garter.

Gerated or **Gerratty.** Powdered or *semé.*

Gerbe (Fr.). See GARB.

Geules (Fr.). *Gules.*

Gilly-Flower. Properly July flower. A flower of a blood-red color.

Gimmal Rings. Flat hoops of gold which fitted accurately within each other and formed but one ring. They are frequently borne in heraldry, in the position of two annulets interlaced.

Giraffe. See CAMELOPARD.

Girl. The roe in its second year.

Giron. See GYRON.

Gironetté (Fr.). Applied to towers when topped with spears.

Gironné. See GYRONNY.

Girt, Girded, or Girdled. Bound with a girdle or band.

Gisant (Fr.). *Jessant.*

Givers or **Gringalé.** Figures with serpents' heads at their extremities.

Glaziers' Nippers or **Grater.** A tool used by glaziers.

Gliding. This term is applied to serpents, snakes, or adders when moving forward.

Globe. A ball which represents the earth.

Globical. Convex.

Glory. A circle of rays.

Glove. Generally the sort used in falconry.

Goat. Frequently used as a crest or a supporter.

Gobony or **Gobonated.** See COMPONY.

Gold. One of the heraldic metals, and blazoned *or.* In engraving it is represented by dots on a plain white surface.

Golden Fleece. See FLEECE.

Golpes or **Golps.** Roundels of the purple tincture.

Gonfalon or **Gonfannon.** The banner of the Roman Catholic Church.

Gonfalonier. The Pope's standard-bearer.

Gordian Knot. A double orle of annulets linked to each other and to one in the centre, gyronwise.

Gore or **Gusset.** Formed by two curved lines, one from the sinister chief point, the other from the middle base point, meeting in the fesse point and forming an acute angle. It is one of the abatements of honor.

Goré or **Gory.** Double-arched.

Gored. Cut into arched indents.

Gorge or **Gurge.** See WHIRLPOOL.

Gorged. Applied to an animal or bird which has a crown or coronet about its neck instead of a collar.

Gorget. Armor for the neck. Also a military ornament formerly worn by officers on the breast.

Goshawk. A species of hawk.

Goutté. See GUTTÉ.

Gradient. Applied to a tortoise represented walking.

Grady. Having steps.

Grady Embattled. See BATTLED-EMBATTLED.

Grafted. Fixed in. Applied to the part of a shield which is inserted into another as one of the quarterings.

Grain-Tree. A tree whose berries are used for dyeing.

Grand Quarters. See QUARTERLY QUARTERED.

Grand Seignior's Crown. A turban enriched with pearls and diamonds.

Grappling-Iron. A four-pointed anchor used in war to fasten ships together.

Grasshopper. Among the Athenians gold grasshoppers were worn in the hair as marks of nobility.

Grater. See GLAZIERS' NIPPERS.

Gray. A badger.

Greaves. Leg-armor.

Grenade. See FIRE-BALL.

Greyhound. Usually borne *courant.*

Grices. Young wild boars.

Gridiron. Usually borne *in pale with handle in base sable.*

Grieces. Steps.

Griffin. An imaginary animal, half eagle, half lion. It expresses the union of strength and swiftness.

Griffin Male. In heraldry is represented with large ears, but no wings. It usually has rays of gold issuing from various parts of its body.

Grilleté (Fr.). *Belled.*

Gringolé or **Gringollé.** A term for crosses, saltires, etc., whose extremities end with heads of serpents.

Griping. Grasping.

Grittie. A field composed equally of metal and color.

Groaning. The noise or cry of a buck.

Grose. A tool used by coopers.

Gryfin or **Gryphon.** See GRIFFIN.

Guard. Old term for doubling.

Guardant. See GARDANT.

Guarded. Trimmed or turned up with. Applied to a mantle or chapeau whose edge is turned up and tinctured differently.

Guay or **Cheval Guay** (Fr.). A rearing horse.

Gueules (Fr.). *Gules.*

Guidon. See PENNON.

Guige. A shield-belt.

Guirlande (Fr.). *Chaplet.*

Guivre. See GRINGOLÉ.

Gu. or **Gules.** The color red. In engraving it is represented by perpendicular lines.

Gull. A sea-bird.

Gunshot or **Gunstone.** See PELLET.

Gurges. See WHIRLPOOL.

Gusset. See GORE.

Gutte. A drop. A *Gutte reversed* is a drop with the tapering part downward. This is sometimes termed an *icicle.*

Gutté or **Gutty.** From the Latin *Gutta*, a drop, is said of a field or bearing sprinkled with drops. *Gutté d'huile* or *Gutté d'olive.* Sprinkled with oil, represented by drops *vert* (green). *Gutté de larmes.* Sprinkled with tears or drops *azure* (blue). *Gutté d'eau.* Sprinkled with water or drops *argent* (white). *Gutté d'or.* Sprinkled with drops of gold or drops *or* (yellow). *Gutté de poix.* Sprinkled with drops of pitch. Represented *sable* (black). *Gutté de sang.* Sprinkled with blood. Represented *gules* (red). *Gutté reversed.* When the drops are inverted.

Guze. A roundel of sanguine or murrey color.

Gyron. A gore in a garment. In heraldry it is formed by a straight line from the dexter chief point, meeting at the centre of the shield a straight line from the dexter fesse, and forming an acute angle at the fesse point.

Gyronné or **Gyronny.** Applied to a field divided into six, eight, ten, or twelve triangular parts, of two different tinctures, and the points all uniting in the centre of the field.

Gyronways. Applied to any charge borne in the form of a gyron. A chain is the most usual.

H.

Habeck or **Habick.** An instrument used by clothiers in dressing cloth.

Habergeon. A small coat of mail, consisting of a jacket without sleeves.

Habillé (Fr.). *Habited.*

Habillement (Fr.). Garment.

Habited. Clothed. Applied to an entire figure, while *Vested* is applied to a part only. Thus, a man is *habited*, an arm is *vested.*

Hacked. Applied to an indented charge when the notches are curved.

Hackle. See HEMP-BREAK.

Hair. See CRINED.

Hake-Fish. A fish like the cod, but longer in the body.

Halberd or **Halbert.** A battle-axe. Still used at certain ceremonies.

Half-Spear or **Halk-Spear.** A spear with a short handle.

Hames or **Heames.** A piece of harness fitting on the collar of a horse.

Hammer or **Martel.** Variously borne.

Hanchet. See BUGLE-HORN.

Hand. Both right and left hands are borne, and must be blazoned dexter (right) or sinister (left). The hand open with the palm outward is blazoned *appaumé*, if borne with the back toward the spectator it is *dorsed.* Again, it may be *clenched*, grasping an object, etc. See also BADGE OF ULSTER.

Harbored. See LODGED.

Harboreth. Applied to the place where a beast of chase is lodged.

Hare. Usually borne *courant.*

Harness. Armor for a knight.

Harp. The musical instrument, commonly called a Welsh harp. It is one of the national devices of Ireland, and is borne on the arms of Great Britain in the third quarter.

Harpoon. The spear with a cable attached used in capturing whales. It is usually borne with the barbed point *in base.*

Harpy. A mythological and heraldic monster with the body of a vulture and the face and neck of a woman.

Harrington Knot. A badge of the family of Harrington. It is represented flat and in the shape of a *frette.*

Harrow. An instrument used in husbandry. Usually represented triangular.

Hart. A stag or male of the red deer from the age of six years. It is then of full growth with branching horns. The female is the *hind*, and bears no horns.

Hart Royal. A hart which has escaped the pursuit of a king or queen.

Harvest-Fly. An insect with spindle-shaped body and wide-spreading wings. A butterfly.

Hat. See CARDINAL'S HAT.

Hatchet. A short-handled axe. A charge of great antiquity.

Hatchment. The armorial bearings of a deceased person, usually placed on the front of the house.

Hauberk. A coat of twisted mail.

Hauriant. A term used to express any fish erect or upright, as if it had risen to the surface for air.

Hause or **Hausse.** See ENHANCED.

Hawk or **Falcon.** A bird of prey. Borne at times with bells, jesses, and varvels, and blazoned *belled, jessed,* or *varvelled,* as the case may be.

Hawk's Bells. Small round bells, somewhat like the bells used in strings for sleigh-bells. They were attached to the legs of hawks.

Hawk's Jesses. Small leathern thongs with which the bells were attached to the hawk's legs.

Hawk's Lure. Two wings joined together with their tips downward. To this was attached a long cord, and it was then thrown in the air to imitate a bird flying. Used as a decoy by falconers.

Hay-Fork. Represented with two prongs. Not often seen in English coats of arms.

Heads. Borne in profile unless blazoned otherwise.

Healme, Heaulme, or **Helme.** See HELMET.

Heames. See HAMES.

Heart. Represented in the conventional form. Blazoned a *human heart* or a *body heart.*

Heart's-Ease. A flower. Commonly known as the pansy.

Hedge-Hog. Borne *passant* with quills erect.

Heightened. See ENHANCED.

Heinuse. The roe in its third year.

Helmet. Defensive armor for the head. When borne as a charge it is an "Esquire's Helmet."

Helved. An axe is *helved* of its handle.

Hemp-Brake or **Hackle.** A machine formerly used to break or bruise hemp to soften it for use.

Heneage Knot. A sort of double knot of cord. One of the badges of the Heneage family.

Herald. An officer who regulates armorial bearings and directs matters of precedence, etc., on public occasions.

Heraldry. In modern times the science which treats of armorial bearings. Also used by many in the sense of "device-bearing," or the custom of distinguishing individuals and communities by some symbol.

Heralds' College. See COLLEGE OF ARMS.

Herd. Applied to a number of deer, etc., grouped together.

Herissé (Fr.). Set with long sharp points like those of a *Herisson.*

Herisson (Fr.). A *hedge-hog.*

Hermine or **Hermines** (Fr.). See ERMINE.

Hernshaw or **Heron.** A wading bird.

Herse (Fr.). A harrow, or a portcullis.

Herse. A bar or framework with upright spikes for the reception of candles. Used at funeral services and church services. Originally plain, but in the fifteenth and sixteenth centuries of great beauty. Its development into the modern hearse can be easily traced.

Heurts. See HURTS.

Hiacinth. See HYACINTH.

Highness. A title of honor.

Hill. A mound *vert.* When more than one are borne they are blazoned *hillocks.*

Hilt. The handle of a sword.

Hilted. Having a handle.

Hind. The female of the red deer. It bears no horns.

Hippocampus. Sea-horse.

Hirondelle. A swallow.

Hoist. The distance from the chief of a flag to the base.

Holy Lamb. See LAMB.

Homage. The acknowledgment of his relation to his lord made by a vassal. It is derived from the form of words used, "*Jeo deveigne vostre home,*"—I become your man.

Honor Point. The point next above the centre of the shield.

Honorable Ordinaries. See article on ORDINARIES.

Honored. Applied in old blazons to an animal borne with a crown upon its head.

Hood. The head-covering attached to the long gowns of monks and friars. Also a covering used for a hawk's head in falconry.

Hooded. Wearing a hood. Applied to hawks as well as to human heads.

Hoofed. Applied to an animal whose hoofs are different in tincture from its body. Sometimes termed *Unguled.*

Hop. The climbing plant.

Horned. Applied to an animal whose horns have a special tincture. Animals of the deer-kind are *attired.*

Horse. Blazoned *passant,* when walking; *courant,* or *in full speed,* when running; *cabré* or *effray,* when *rearing.*

Horse, Winged. See PEGASUS.

Horse-Shoes. Usually borne with the ends in base and turned up.

Hound. Usually represented as a blood-hound *on scent.*

Houssé (Fr.). *Caparisoned.*

Hovering. Applied in old blazons to the eagle when represented as if floating in the air with wings outspread.

Huchet (Fr.). *Bugle-Horn.*

Humet. A bar cut off at the extremities.

Humetté. Used of an ordinary which is cut smoothly off, so that its ends do not reach the side of the shield. It corresponds to *couped,* the term applied to charges.

Hunting-Horn. This charge appears in two forms : (1) Almost semicircular with mouthpiece to *sinister.* (2) Slightly curved in the form of the horn of an ox, and borne *in pale,* mouth-piece *in base.* The first is the more usual form, and some authorities confine the term *bugle-horn* to it alone. The second form is, however, more nearly the shape of the natural horn of the *bugle* or bull, and if there is to be a distinction between the terms it would seem better to confine the term *bugle-horn* to the second form. The first form is usually borne as if suspended by a cord, and is then blazoned *stringed.* · If ornamented with specially tinctured rings about it the horn is blazoned *garnished.*

Hure (Fr.). The head of a boar or dolphin.

Hurst. A clump of trees.

Hurts, Heurts, or **Huerts.** Blue roundels. Supposed by some to represent wounds or *hurts.* Others consider them hurtleberries, and derive the name *hurts* from this.

Hurty or **Hurté.** *Semé* of *Hurts.*

Husk. The upper part of the stalk from which a gilly-flower *blows.* It need not be mentioned unless specially tinctured.

Hyacinth. A flower originally grown in the Orient.

Hyacinth. A name given to a fine red cinnamon-stone, and sometimes to a ferruginous quartz of a blood-red color. In heraldry it was used, in the blazoning by precious stones, instead of metals and colors, to express *tenné* or tawny in the arms of peers.

Hydra. A fabulous creature resembling a dragon, with seven heads.

I.

Ibex. An imaginary beast, in some respects like the heraldic antelope, but with this difference, that it has two straight horns projecting from the forehead, *serrated,* or edged like a saw.

Icicles. *Guttes reversed.*

Imbattled. A term for a house, tower, or a wall represented with battlements. Also one of the lines of partition.

Imbordered. Applied to a field which has a border of the same tincture. Seldom seen in English coats of arms, but frequently on the Continent.

Imbowed. See EMBOWED.

Imbrued. Spotted or dropping with blood.

Impale. See article on MARSHALLING.

Imperial Crown. A circle of gold, adorned with stones and pearls, heightened with fleurs-de-lis bordered and seeded with pearls, raised in the form of a cap, voided at the top like a crescent; from the middle of the cap rises an arched fillet, enriched with pearls and surmounted by a mound, whereon is a cross of pearls.

Imperially Crowned. Surmounted by an *Imperial Crown.*

In Base. In the lower part of the field.

In Bend. Placed *Bendways.*

In Chevron. Placed *Chevronways.*

In Chief. In the upper part of the field.

In Cross. Placed in the form of a cross.

In Fesse. Placed *Fesseways.*

In Foliage. Having leaves.

In Glory. Surrounded by rays.

In her Piety. See PELICAN.

In his Majesty. Applied to an eagle when crowned and bearing a sceptre.

In his Pride. See PEACOCK.

In his Splendor. See SUN.

In Leure or **In Lure.** Applied to the wings of a bird borne without the body and joined together at the place where they would naturally meet the body. The tips of the wings are in base in imitation of a *hawk's lure.*

In Orle. Nearly in a circle.

In Pale. Placed perpendicularly.

In Pile. Placed in the form of a *pile.*

In Saltire. Placed in the form of a *saltire.*

Incensant. Applied to the boar when represented angry.

Incensed. A term for leopards and panthers when represented with fire issuing from their mouths and ears.

Increment or **Increscent.** The state of the moon from her entrance into her first quarter, having her horns toward the dexter side of the shield. It was the emblem of the Turks during the Crusades.

Indented. One of the lines of partition, in shape the same as dancette, but with smaller teeth.

Indenté. Applied to a field having teeth, not joined to each other, but set apart.

Indentilly. Applied to a field having long teeth resembling piles conjoined.

Indian Goat or **Assyrian Goat.** Resembles the English goat, but has horns more bent and ears like a hound.

Indorsed. See ADDORSED.

Inescutcheon. A small escutcheon borne within the shield. It is usually placed on the fesse point.

Infamed. See DEFAMED.

Inflamed. Blazing.

Infula. A fillet or crown ; the tiara.

Ingrailed. See ENGRAILED.

Ink-Horn or **Penner and Ink-Horn.** The emblems of a notary A pen-case and a vessel containing ink, joined by a cord. They were carried by a notary in the Middle Ages.

Ink Moline. See FER-DE-MOULINE.

Inquire, Arms to. Such coats of arms as are irregular because they violate some of the heraldic laws.

Inraced or **Racé.** See INDENTED.

Insigned. See ENSIGNED.

Interchangeably Posed. Placed in parallel lines so that the head of one lies between the tails of two others.

Interchanged. See COUNTER-CHANGED.

Interfretted or **Interlaced.** When annulets, rings, keys, crescents, etc., are linked together, they are termed *interlaced* or *interfretted.*

Interposed. Placed alternately.

Intersicants. Lines which cross each other.

Invecké or **Goaré.** Double-arched or *arché.*

Invecked or **Invected.** One of the lines of partition, the reverse of *engrailed*, since the points go into the charge.

Invelloped or **Involved.** Surrounded.

Invertant or **Inverted.** Turned the wrong way. Especially wings with points down.

Invexed. Arched.

Ire. Angry.

Iron Ring. A tool used by wire-drawers.

Irradiated. Decorated or illuminated with rays of light.

Issant (Fr.). *Issuant.*

Issuant or **Issuing.** Issuing or coming out of the bottom of the chief. When an animal is so blazoned the upper half of it alone is visible. Also applied to one charge coming out of, or rising from, another.

Issuant and Revertant. Applied to an animal borne as if *issuing* into the field at the base and going out again at the chief. The upper part of the lion is shown *in base*, the lower *in chief.*

J.

Jack. The fish known as the *pike.*

Jack. See UNION JACK.

Jagged. Used when the outlines of an ordinary are rough, as if torn or broken.

Jamb. See GAMB.

Janus. One of the earliest Latin divinities. Represented on a beaming throne with a sceptre in his right hand and a key in his left. A *Janus's Head* is a head with two faces, one aged and the other youthful.

Javelin. A short spear with a barbed point. Used for throwing.

Jellop. The comb of a cock.

Jelloped. Having a " comb" different in tincture from the head.

Jerkin. A short coat or jacket.

Jersey Comb. A comb with large teeth. Used by wool-combers.

Jessamine. A flower. Used in the obsolete blazoning by flowers, for *argent.*

Jessant. Rising or issuing.

Jessant. Applied to a lion or other beast rising or issuing from the middle of a fesse.

Jessant-de-Lis. Applied to a charge through which a fleur-de-lis is thrust.

Jessed. Applied to a hawk whose *jesses* are of a different tincture from that of his body.

Jesses. Small leathern thongs with which a hawk's bells were fastened.

Joinant. See CONJOINED.

Jousts. Tournaments.

Jowlopped. See JELLOPED.

Jugariæ Fasciolæ. See BAR-GEMELLE.

Jumelle Rings. See GIMMAL RINGS.

Jumelles (Fr.). *Gemelles.*

Jupiter. The king of the Roman divinities. Afterwards the name of one of the planets, and in heraldry used for *azure* in blazoning by planets instead of by metals and colors.

K.

K.B. Knight of the Most Honorable Order of the Bath.

K.C.B. Knight Commander of the same order.

K.C.H. Knight Commander of the Order of Hanover.

Kenelleth. Applied to the place where the fox takes up his abode.

Keys. The emblem of St. Peter. Borne in a bunch or singly.

K.G. Knight of the Most Noble Order of the Garter.

Kid. Applied to the young of the roe in its first year as well as to that of the goat.

Kings-of-Arms. Heraldic officers.

Knight. In the Middle Ages, a mounted warrior entitled to bear a *pennon* and to wear golden spurs. In modern times, when used alone, it means a rank between a baronet and an esquire. The title is not hereditary. When coupled with the name of one of the orders of knighthood, as "Knight of the Garter," it means a member of that order.

Knighthood. The various orders of knighthood have been instituted by sovereigns throughout the world as "Fraternities of Honor." The principal British orders are: (1) THE MOST NOBLE ORDER OF THE GARTER, founded very early in English history, and composed of twenty-five knights companions, exclusive of the sovereign. The *Garter* is of dark-blue velvet, lettered in gold "*Honi soit qui mal y pense,*" and having a buckle and border of the same metal. It is worn by the queen above the left elbow, and by the knights below the left knee. (2) THE MOST NOBLE AND MOST ANCIENT ORDER OF THE THISTLE, instituted in Scotland at a very early period, and consists of the sovereign and sixteen knights. (3) THE MOST ILLUSTRIOUS ORDER OF ST. PATRICK, an Irish order founded by George III., and consisting of the sovereign, the Lord Lieutenant of Ireland, who is ex officio *Grand Master* of the order, and twenty-two knights. (4) THE MOST HONORABLE ORDER OF THE BATH, a very old order revived by George I. Its members are divided into three classes,—*Knights Grand Cross* (G.C.B.), *Knights Commanders* (K.C.B.), and *Knights Companions* (C.B.). (5) THE MOST DISTINGUISHED ORDER OF ST. MICHAEL AND ST. GEORGE, founded by George IV., when prince regent, as a decoration for Malta and the Ionian Islands. The order is divided into three classes like those of the Bath. (6) THE MOST EXALTED ORDER OF THE STAR OF INDIA, founded in 1861, and composed of the sovereign, the Governor General of India, who is ex-officio *Grand Master* of the order, and twenty-five knights, with such honorary knights as the sovereign may choose to appoint. (7) THE ROYAL ORDER OF VICTORIA AND ALBERT may be classed with the other orders, but it differs from them in that it is composed entirely of ladies.

Knots. Badges formed of twisted silk cord, woven in different figures.

K.P. Knight of the Most Illustrious Order of St. Patrick.

K.T. Knight of the Most Noble and Most Ancient Order of the Thistle.

L.

Label or **File.** The *Mark of Cadency* used to difference the arms of the eldest son. By some supposed to be ribbons anciently worn by young men about the neck of their helmets, to distinguish them from their fathers.

Labels. Ribbons that hang down from a mitre or coronet.

Laced. Adorned with lace or interlaced.

Lacs d'Amour (Fr.). True-love-knots.

Lacy Knot. The badge of the Lacy family.

Lady. A title properly applicable to daughters of all peers above the rank of viscounts. By courtesy, however, it is extended to the wives of baronets and knights.

Lamb or **Holy Lamb.** A white lamb *passant*, with a staff, crossed at the top, and a banner bearing the Red Cross of St. George.

Lambeaux. A cross is so termed when borne upon a label or lambeaux.

Lambeaux. See LABEL.

Lambel (Fr.). *Label.*

Lambrequin. (1) The point of a label. (2) Sometimes used for *mantling*.

Laminated. Applied to reptiles to mean *having scales.*

Lampassé (Fr.). *Langued.*

Lancaster Herald. One of the members of the Heralds' College.

Lancaster Rose. A *red* rose was the badge of the house of Lancaster. It is represented as the heraldic *rose gules.*

Lance. A tilting spear.

Landskip or **Landscape.** A landscape represented *proper* (ppr.).

Langued. Applied to an animal when its tongue differs in tincture from its body. The tongue is *gules* unless otherwise blazoned.

Lapin (Fr.). Rabbit.

Lapped. Wound around.

Larmettes or **Larmes.** Tears. See GUTTÉ DE LARMES.

Lattice or **Lettice.** See TREILLÉ.

Launce. See LANCE.

Laurel. The emblem of victory and triumph.

Laver. A coulter or ploughshare.

Laverpot. Ewer.

Lead-Line. An instrument used to find the depth of the sea.

Leaping. Applied to reptiles borne erect.

Leash. A leather thong used in hawking to pass through the varvels and thus prevent the hawk's escape. The name is also applied to a strap attached to the collar of a greyhound.

Leashed. Applied to a greyhound when a *leash* is attached to his collar.

Leaves. Various kinds are borne. Usually placed with stem *in base.*

Leg. The human leg is borne in various ways, but always bent at the knee. The leg of a lion is a *gamb.*

Legged or **Membered.** Applied to a bird whose legs differ in tincture from its body.

Legion of Honor. The decoration of this order is given for services to the state, either military or civil. It was founded early in the century under the French Republic.

Lentally. Indented.

Leopard. Always borne full-faced in early heraldry, while the lion was always borne in profile, thus the lions in the English coat were blazoned *leopards*. In modern times it is borne in the same positions and blazoned in the same terms as a lion.

Leopard's Face. When a leopard's head appears without any part of the neck it is blazoned a *leopard's face.*

Leopard's Head. When blazoned a *leopard's head*, the neck is shown.

Leopardy or **Leopardé** (Fr.). Applied to a lion instead of *passant.*

Level. The instrument used by carpenters.

Lever. A cormorant.

Leveret. A young hare.

Lié (Fr.). *Banded* or *Stringed.*

Lily of the Garden or **White Lily.** The emblem of the Virgin Mary.

Lily of the Flag. The *Fleur-de-lis.*

Lily-Pot. See CUP.

Limb of a Tree. Borne *raguled, trunked, leaved*, etc.

Limbeck. See ALEMBIC.

Lind-Worm. A dragon without wings.

Lined. (1) Applied to an animal which has a cord attached to the collar. (2) Applied to mantles, etc., whose linings are different in tincture from the outer surface.

Lines. See PARTITION-LINES.

Linked. Applied to annulets or rings *interlaced*, as well as to chains and chain-armor.

Lion. See chapter on CHARGES. *Demi-Lion.* The upper half of a lion. A part of the tail is also shown, detached from the body.

Lion of England. *Gules, a lion passant guardant or.*

Lion of Scotland. *Or, a lion rampant gules.* It is surrounded by the well-known *tressure*, as it appears in the second quarter of the royal arms of Great Britain.

Lion of St. Mark. A winged lion.

Lionceau (Fr.). *Lioncel.*

Lionced. Adorned with lion's heads.

Lioncel. A young lion. A term used by some heralds where two or more lions are in the same field.

Lion-Dragon. Upper part like a lion and hinder part like a dragon.

Lionné (Fr.). *Rampant.* Applied to the leopard.

Lion-Poisson or **Sea-Lion.** The upper half like a lion and the lower or hinder ending in a tail like a fish. It has webbed feet.

Lions Conjoined. Several lions connected, borne symbolically, and not as a monster.

Lis. *Fleur-de-lis.*

Liston. See SCROLL.

Lists. A space enclosed for a tournament.

Litre (Fr.). The armorial cincture or funeral girdle depicted on the wall of a church with the arms of the lord of the manor.

Litvit's Skin. A pure white fur.

Livery. The color or combination of colors adopted by a family for the dress of its servants. The colors should be those of the arms.

Lizard or **Lezard.** A beast common in Denmark, resembling a wild-cat.

Lizard. A small reptile, usually represented green.

Lizaré or **Liseré** (Fr.). *Bordered* or *Edged.*

Lobster. In pale. Always represented with claws in chief.

Lochaber-Axe. See AXE.

Lodged. A term for the buck, hart, etc., when lying on the ground. It corresponds to *couchant*, which cannot be used of beasts of chase.

Lolling. Applied to a bird of prey when feeding with its wings hanging down.

Long. See PER LONG.

Looking Back. Sometimes applied to a lion *rampant* toward the sinister, with the head turned to look toward the dexter.

Loop-Holes. Borne square or elongated.

Lopped or **Snagged.** Cut smoothly off. It differs from *couped*, since the thickness is shown.

Lord. Applied to peers, and to certain high officers by virtue of their office.

Losangé (Fr.). *Lozengy.*

Loup-Cervier. A lynx.

Lowered. Applied to an ordinary debased from its natural position.

Lozenge. A four-cornered, diamond-shaped figure resembling a pane of glass in old casements, or the "*diamonds*" on ordinary playing-cards.

Lozenges, Cross of. A cross composed of five lozenges.

Lozengy. Applied to the field or charge when composed of lozenges.

Luce or **Lucy.** The fish commonly called the pike, ged, or jack.

Lumieres. The eyes.

Luna. The moon. In blazoning by the planets, Luna means *argent.*

Lunel. Four crescents in cross.

L'Un à l'Autre (Fr.). *Counter-Changed.*

L'Un sur l'Autre (Fr.). Applied to two or more charges placed one above the other *in pale.*

Lure. Two wings with their tips downward, joined with a line and ring, cast in the air by falconers to imitate a bird and thus decoy hawks.

Lute. A stringed instrument somewhat like the modern guitar.

Lutra, Loutre, or **Louterel.** Otter.

Lymphad. An old-fashioned ship with one mast, and propelled with oars. Usually borne with the sail furled.

Lynes. Roes.

Lynx. See OUNCE.

Lyon Court. The court which has jurisdiction over armorial bearings in Scotland.

Lyon King-of-Arms. The head of the Lyon Office or Heralds' Office for Scotland.

Lyre. A stringed musical instrument somewhat like a harp.

M.

Mace. Originally a spiked war-club, but now borne before dignitaries as an emblem of authority.

Macers. Officers of the Supreme Courts in Scotland.

Mâcle (Fr.). *Mascle.*

Maçonné (Fr.). *Masoned.*

Madder-Bags. See BAG OF MADDER.

Maiden's Head. The head, neck, and shoulders of a woman, and the head crowned with an antique coronet and wreathed with roses.

Mail. A chain. Armor made of linked rings.

Mailed. Clothed in *mail.*

Main. A hand.

Maintenance. See CAP OF MAINTENANCE.

Male Griffin. See GRIFFIN MALE.

Mallet. A tool used by carpenters. Borne with round head *in chief.*

Maltese Cross. So called because worn by the Knights of Malta.

Manacles. Handcuffs.

Manche. An old-fashioned sleeve with long hangers.

Mancheron (Fr.). A sleeve.

Manchet. A cake of bread somewhat like a muffin.

Mandrake. A sort of root.

Maned. Applied to animals when the hair hangs down on the neck; or when the mane is tinctured specially.

Man's Head. Always the head of an old man with a beard, and placed in profile unless otherwise blazoned.

Manteau (Fr.). *Mantle.*

Mantelé (Fr.). Like *Chapé* in form, except that the lines are drawn from the *fesse point* to the dexter and sinister base.

Mantelé (Fr.). Wearing a mantle.

Mantelet. A wide short cloak with which knights covered their shields.

Man-Tiger or **Manticora.** An imaginary monster with body like a lion, face like a man, and horns on the head.

Mantle. A military cloak worn over the armor to preserve it from rust. Also a long cloak decorated with heraldic devices, worn by ladies of rank. Mantles are frequently represented as a background for armorial achievements.

Mantling. The ornamental work surrounding an achievement. It is represented as if attached to the helm. It is supposed to represent a cloak or scarf which has been hacked in battle.

Mantling. Applied to an eagle when it is represented with one wing spread and one leg raised.

Marcassin. A young wild boar. Its tail hangs down, while the tail of an old boar is twisted into a ring.

Mariné (Fr). *Marined.*

Marined. A term for an animal which has the lower part of its body like a fish.

Marine Wolf. The seal.

Marks of Cadency. Devices added to a shield or crest to distinguish sons from the father.

Marquis. The title of the rank between duke and earl.

Marquis's Coronet. See article on CORONETS.

Mars. The Roman god of war. In blazoning by the planets Mars was used for *gules* or red.

Marshalling. (1) That part of heraldry which treats of the proper arrangement of the arms of two or more families upon one shield. (2) The grouping of different parts of an achievement.

Martel. A hammer.

Marten or **Martin.** A kind of weasel.

Martin. A kind of swallow.

Martlet. A bird, in shape like the swallow, but represented without feet. It is the *Mark of Cadency* for the fourth son.

Mascle. A figure in shape like the lozenge, but the centre is cut out and only the outline left.

Mascles, Cross of. A cross composed of five *mascles.*

Masculy. Made up of mascles.

Masoned. Divided by plain strokes representing the cement in stone buildings.

Massonné (Fr.). *Masoned.*

Match. A coiled fuse used to discharge artillery.

Match-Lock. The lock of an old-fashioned musket.

Maunche. A hanging sleeve worn about the time of Henry I.

Mayor. The chief magistrate of a city or corporate town.

Meire or **Meirre.** See POTENT or COUNTER-POTENT.

Membered. Signifies that the beak and legs of a bird are of a different tincture from the body.

Membré (Fr.). *Membered.*

Meniver. See MINIVER.

Menu of Vair or **Meniver.** Applied to a field which is like vair, except that it has six or more rows instead of four.

Merchants' Marks. Devices adopted by early traders, and used either as signatures or trademarks.

Mercury. The messenger of the Roman gods. In blazoning by the planets Mercury was used for *purpure* or purple.

Merillion. An instrument used by hat-bandmakers.

Merlette or **Merlion** (Fr.). *Martlet.*

Mermaid. A fictitious sea animal, half woman and half fish. Generally represented with a comb in one hand and a mirror in the other.

Merman. A fictitious sea animal, half man and half fish. Usually represented with a trident or three-pronged spear in his hand.

Meslé (Fr.). Mingled.

Mesne Lord. The holder of a fief who was a vassal to one above him and lord to others below him.

Metals. Gold and silver are the heraldic metals, and in blazon are called *or* and *argent*. *Or* is represented yellow, and *argent* white.

Metamorphosed. Applied to any part of an animal which is unnaturally changed into a part of another animal. Thus, a lion with head metamorphosed into that of an eagle.

Meurtrière (Fr.). Port-hole or loop-hole.

Mezail (Fr.). *Gardevisor.*

Micouppé (Fr.). Applied to an escutcheon parted half-way across, *per fesse.*

Middle Base. The middle part of the base.

Middle Chief. The middle part of the chief.

Mill-Pick. The instrument used by millwrights for dressing millstones.

Millrind or **Milrine.** See FER DE MOULINE.

Millstone. Generally borne charged with a *millrind.*

Miniver. A plain white fur used in ornamenting the parliament robes of peers.

Miparty (Fr.). Applied to a shield made up of one-half from each of two others which have been *dimidiated* or cut in half *per pale.*

Mirror. Usually represented as a hand-glass with a frame and handle.

Mi-Taillé (Fr.). Cut half-way across *per Bend Sinister.*

Mi-Tranché (Fr.). Cut half-way across *per Bend.*

Mitre. The pontifical cap worn by archbishops and bishops, and placed over the shield in their armorial achievements. The archbishop's mitre has a rim like a ducal coronet, while that of a bishop is plain.

Modillion. The scroll-like ornamental work on a pillar.

Mole. A small gray animal living almost wholly under ground.

Mole-Hill. The mound of earth made by the mole.

Molette (Fr). *Mullet of six points.*

Moline Cross. A cross in shape like the Fer-de-Mouline. It is the *Mark of Cadency* for the eighth son.

Monarch. One who rules alone.

Monche. See MAUNCHE.

Monde (Fr.). *A Mound* or the world.

Monkey. Distinguished from the ape and baboon by its long tail.

Monogram. A letter or several letters so arranged as to form a single device.

Montant (Fr.). (1) Applied to a crescent with horns upward. (2) Applied to crawfish, etc., to express *erect in pale with claws in chief.*

Montegre. See MAN-TIGER.

Moon. When at full blazoned *in her complement* or *in plenitude.* When *a crescent* her horns are *in chief.* When *increscent* or *in her increment* the horns point to the *dexter.* When *decrescent* (sometimes termed *in her detriment*) the horns are toward the *sinister.*

Moor-Cock. The male of the large black grouse.

Moor's Head. The head of a Moor, or sometimes that of a negro, placed in profile, *couped* at the neck and wearing a wreath.

Mooted or **Moulted.** *Eradicated.*

Morion. A visorless steel cap or helmet worn by foot-soldiers.

Morné (Fr.). See CRONEL.

Morné (Fr.). Blemished or rebated.

Morné or **Mortné** (Fr.). Applied to a lion borne rampant, but without tongue, teeth, or claws.

Morse. An ornamented clasp.

Morse. A sea-lion.

Mortaises (Fr.). *Mortises.*

Mortcours. Lamps used at funerals.

Mort-Head. A death's head or skull.

Mortier. A cap of state.

Mortised. Let into one another or jointed after the fashion of mortises.

Mortises. Square figures hollowed so that smaller ones may be jointed into the middle of them.

Moses's Bush. A bush in flames.

Motto. A word or short sentence inserted in a scroll under, and sometimes over, a coat of arms, some alluding to the bearings and some to the bearer's name, while others express some action, employment, or noble design, and may be taken or left at pleasure.

Moulted. *Eradicated.*

Mound. (1) *Mound Royal,* a globe having a cross on top. Part of the regalia of sovereigns. (2) A small hill on which crests are frequently placed.

Mount. When the base of the shield is represented green and curved somewhat semicircularly it is termed a *mount vert.*

Mountain-Cat. See CAT-A-MOUNTAIN.

Mounted. Applied to a horse bearing a rider.

Mounting. Applied to animals of chase instead of *rampant*.

Mourn. Blunt.

Mourned. Blunted.

Moussue. Rounded at the extremities.

Mullet. Formerly supposed to be the rowel of a spur, but the mullet appeared in heraldry before spurs were used. It is a star of five points, and sometimes pierced at the centre. If of more than five points it must be so blazoned. The points of the mullet are clear cut, while those of the estoile are wavy. The mullet is one of the Marks of Cadency, and is borne by the third son.

Mullet. A sort of fish.

Muraillé (Fr.). *Masoned* and *Embattled*.

Mural Crown. Made of gold, with battlements on the circle; it was given by the ancients to him who first mounted the wall of a besieged town or city.

Murrey. The dark-red color sometimes used in heraldry. See SANGUINE.

Muschetors. The black spots of ermine without the three dots over them.

Musimon. An heraldic animal, supposed to be a cross between a goat and a ram.

Musion. A cat.

Musseled. See MUZZLED.

Muzzled. Applied to an animal when its mouth is tied or banded to prevent its biting.

N.

Naiant. Swimming. Applied to a fish when borne horizontally across the field as if swimming.

Naissant. Rising. Used of a lion or other creature that seems to be coming out of the *middle* of an ordinary or charge. *Issuant* is used when the creature comes out from the bottom or from a coronet.

Narcissus. A flower of six petals. Each petal resembles in shape the leaf of the cinquefoil.

Natand or **Natant.** See NAIANT.

Naturel (Fr.). See PROPER.

Naval Crown. This was invented by Claudius, after surprising the Britons, as a reward for service at sea; it was made of gold, and consisted of prows of galleys, and galley-sails placed alternately upon the rim or circle. It was displayed over the gate of the imperial palace. In the modern *Naval Crown* the sterns of ships alternate with square sails.

Navetté or **Navetty.** Semé of shuttles.

Nebuly or **Nebulé.** One of the partition-lines resembling clouds. When the outlines of an ordinary or partition line run arched in and out, it is so blazoned.

Neptune. The Roman God of the Sea, represented as half man and half fish, holding a trident in his sinister hand.

Nerved. Applied to leaves whose fibres are different in tincture from the leaf

Neve or **Newe.** Fretted.

Newt. A small water animal of the lizard kind.

Nimbus. A halo or glory.

Nislé or **Nyllé.** Slender, or so narrowed as to be reduced almost to nothing.

Nobility. Dukes, marquises, earls, viscounts, and barons.

Nombril or **Navel Point.** The point next below the fesse point.

Norroy. One of the English Kings-of-Arms. He is called Norroy or North King because he has jurisdiction north of the Trent.

North Star. See under ANTARCTIC STAR.

Nourri (Fr.). *Couped.* Applied to flowers.

Nowed. Knotted.

Nowy. A round projection in the centre of an ordinary.

Nuance (Fr.). *Nebuly.*

Nyllé. See NISLÉ.

O.

O. Used in *tricking* for *Or*.

Oak. The emblem of strength.

Obsidional Crown or **Garland.** Composed of grass or twigs of trees, interwoven. Among the Romans it was a reward for him who held out a siege, or caused it to be raised, repulsing the enemy, and delivering the place.

Of the Field. Having the same tincture as the field.

Of the First, Second, etc. Having the tincture named first or second, etc., in the blazon.

Oge (Fr.). *Water Bouget.*

Ogress. See PELLET.

Olive Crown or **Garland.** The prize of a victor at the Olympic Games.

Ombré (Fr.). *Adumbrated.*

Ondé (Fr.). *Wavy.*

Ondoyant (Fr.). *Gliding.*

Onglé (Fr.). Having the feet or claws specially tinctured; not applied to carnivorous birds or beasts.

On-Sett. Used when a piece of a fesse or chevron is placed as if it had fallen or slipped out of its proper place.

Open. (1) Applied to the hand instead of appaumé. (2) Applied to a chevron separated at the point.

Opinicus. This beast is of heraldic invention; its body and fore legs are like those of a lion; the head and neck like those of the eagle; to the body are affixed wings, like those of the griffin, and a tail like that of a camel.

Oppressed. *Debruised.*

Or. Gold or yellow. Represented in engraving by small dots sprinkled over the field or charge.

Oranges. Roundels of the *tenné* or *tawney* tincture.

Orb or **Globe.** A ball.

Orbit. A circle.

Ordinaries. Those figures which by their ordinary and frequent use have become peculiar to the science,—the *cross, chief, pale, fesse, pile, chevron, saltire, bend,* etc.

Oreillé (Fr.). *Eared.*

Oreiller (Fr.). A pillow or cushion.

Orgress. See PELLET.

Oriflam. See AURIFLAMME.

Orle. A border or selvage within the shield, at some distance from the edges. *In Orle.* Placed regularly within the escutcheon, in the form of an *orle,* near the edges.

Ostrich. Usually borne with a horse-shoe in its bill, on account of its fabled power to digest iron.

Ostrich Feathers. Always borne with their tops bent over.

Ostrich Feathers in Plume. If three feathers are placed together they are termed a plume. If more than three the number should be given.

Otter. An amphibious animal, usually borne with a fish in its mouth.

Ounce or **Lynx.** An animal of the leopard kind, tawny and white, spotted with black.

Over-All. Applied to any charge which is placed over another.

Overt. Open. Sometimes used instead of *Displayed.*

Owl. This bird signifies prudence, vigilance, and watchfulness, and was borne by the Athenians as their armorial ensign. Always represented full-faced.

Owndy. *Wavy.*

Ox. The well-known draught animal.

Ox-Yoke. The harness by which a pair of oxen are attached to a wagon. It is composed of two collars connected by a bar.

P.

P. In *tricking* stands for *purpure* or purple.

Padlock. The ancient square form is usually borne.

Paillé (Fr.). *Diapered.*

Pairle (Fr.). *Pall.*

Paissant (Fr.). *Pascuant.*

Pal (Fr.). *Pale.*

Pale. An honorable ordinary, formed by two perpendicular lines drawn from the top to the base of the escutcheon. It contains the middle one-third part of the shield. *In Pale.* Placed in the position of a pale, upright.

Palé Bandé (Fr.). *Paly Bendy.*

Paleways. Vertically

Palissé (Fr.). *Pily Paly.*

Pall. A bearing which resembles the letter Y, rising from the base point to the fesse point like the lower half of a pale, and there branching out to the dexter and sinister chief angles, like the upper half of a saltire. The name is derived from the *episcopal pall,* a narrow band of white lamb's wool.

Pallé (Fr.). *Paly.*

Pallet. The diminutive of the *pale,* one half of it in breadth.

Pallissé. Applied to a fesse when it bears a range of palisades, pointed at the top, with the field appearing between them.

Palm. The broad part of a buck's horn.

Palmer's Staff. See PILGRIM'S STAFF.

Paly. Divided by vertical lines into an even number of spaces, and the tinctures of the spaces alternating.

Paly Bendy. Divided into spaces by vertical and diagonal lines, and the spaces tinctured alternately of metal and color.

Pamé (Fr.). Applied to a fish, borne with its mouth open as if gasping.

Panache. A plume of feathers, usually those of a peacock, arranged to form a crest.

Pannes (Fr.). *Furs.*

Panonceaux (Fr.). *Pennoncelles.*

Pansey, Pansy, or **Heart's-Ease.** A small tri-colored flower.

Panther. Frequently represented full-faced and *incensed*, or with fire issuing from his mouth, nostrils, and ears, to show his ferocity.

Papal Crown. See POPE'S CROWN.

Papellonné (Fr.). A field divided into variegated specks, like those on a butterfly, but ranged like the scales of a fish.

Parer. An instrument used by farriers to pare the hoof of a horse.

Park-Pales. Pointed palings close together.

Parrot. The heraldic parrot is properly green, with a red ring around the neck, and red legs. It is frequently seen in Swiss coats, since in 1262 it was the badge of one of two great factions.

Parsemé (Fr.). *Aspersed.*

Parted. See PARTY.

Parti. Divided. See chapter on DIVIDING LINES.

Parti (Fr.). *Party per Pale.*

Parti de l'Un en l'Autre (Fr.). *Counter-Changed.*

Parti Enmanché (Fr.). *Barry Pily.*

Partition-Lines. Lines which divide the shield in the direction of the ordinaries, etc.

Partitions. See QUARTERINGS.

Party per Pale and Base. Divided into three parts by the pale line, and a horizontal line in base.

Party per Pale and Chevron. Divided by two lines, one a pale line, the other a line in the form of a chevron.

Pas à Pas. Step by step.

Paschal Lamb. See HOLY LAMB.

Pascuant or **Pasquant.** Grazing.

Pasmé (Fr.). See PAMÉ.

Passant. The term applied to beasts when in a walking position with head in profile.

Passant Guardant. The term applied to a beast walking, but with face affronté.

Passant Reguardant. Applied to a beast walking and looking behind him.

Passion Nail. A sharp wedge-shaped nail used in the Crucifixion.

Pastoral Staff. The staff of office borne by a bishop or abbot. It has a curved head somewhat like a shepherd's crook, from which a streamer or banderole hangs.

Patée. Spreading. Applied to a cross whose arms are small in the centre and broad at the extremities.

Paternal. Hereditary on the father's side.

Paternoster. Applied to a cross when composed of beads.

Patonce. A cross ornamented at each extremity with a fleur-de-lis is so termed.

Patriarchal. The term for the cross which was the distinguishing mark of the patriarchs. It is a cross with the upper arm recrossed.

Patrick, St. See KNIGHTHOOD.

Patte (Fr.). *Paw.*

Pauldron. Armor for the shoulder.

Pavement. See MASONED.

Pavier's Pick. A sort of pickaxe.

Pavilion. See TENT.

Paw. The foot cut off at the first joint. If more of the leg appears the charge is termed a *Gamb.*

Pawne. A peacock.

Peacock. When borne affronté with tail spread it is termed *in pride.* When blazoned "*a peacock*" it is represented in profile, with its wings down.

Peal. A sort of wooden shovel used by bakers in taking bread from the oven.

Pean. One of the furs, the ground black and the spots gold.

Pear. Borne with stem *in chief.*

Pearched or **Perched.** Applied to birds when in a sitting posture on a branch.

Pea-Rise. A stalk of the pea-vine, leaved and blossomed.

Pearl. Used for *argent* in the obsolete blazoning by precious stones.

Pecys. *Quarters.*

Peel. See PEAL.

Peer. A nobleman who has a seat in the House of Lords.

Pegasus. The winged horse upon which Bellerophon was mounted when he was engaged in combat with the Chimera.

Pelican. The pelican is represented with her wings indorsed, her neck embowed, picking her breast. When in her nest, feeding her young, she is termed a pelican *in her piety.*

Pelican's Head. Represented with the neck embowed, as if picking her breast.

Pelleté (Fr.). *Semé of Pellets.*

Pellets. Black roundels.

Pelletys. *Pellets.*

Pencil or **Pensil.** A small *pennon.*

Pendal. The cross, composed of four round spindles, which is stamped on the coin of Harold II., is so termed.

Pendant or **Pendent.** Hanging.

Pendant. (1) A small standard. (2) The hanging part of the manche.

Penner and Ink-Horn. See INK-HORN.

Pennon. A small flag, ending in one sharp point, or two, which was placed on the end of the spear with the personal device of the bearer. The charge was so placed that it was in position when the spear or lance was levelled.

Pennonceaux (Fr.). Pennoncelles.

Pennoncelle. A small pennon.

Penny-Yard-Penny. A small coin stamped with a *cross mouline between twelve balls.* So called since it was first coined in the castle of Penny-Yard, near Ross, in the County of Hereford.

Pens. The old-fashioned quill is usually borne.

Per. See DIVIDING LINES.

Percé. Having the centre cut out by lines parallel to those of the outer edge, so that the field shows through.

Perché (Fr.). *Pierced.*

Perched. See PEARCHED.

Perclose or **Demi-Garter.** The part of the garter which is buckled and nowed.

Perculaced. Latticed by vertical and horizontal lines.

Percussant. Applied to the tail of a lion when represented as if he were beating or striking himself with it.

Perflew. See PURFLEW.

Perforated. See PIERCED.

Peri (Fr.). Perished. Reduced in size. Frequently equivalent to *couped* or *humetté.*

Per Long (Fr.). Exceeding the usual length.

Perpendiculum. A plumb-line hanging from an acute angle.

Pertransient. Passing through.

Petronel. A pistol.

Pewit. A long-legged bird.

Pheon. The barbed iron head of a spear. It is engrailed on the inner sides and borne point downward.

Pheons. A cross composed of four pheons is so termed.

Phœnix. A fabled Arabian bird which, when advanced in age, burns itself and springs, with renewed youth, from the ashes. It is always represented *issuant* from flames, so that but a portion of the bird is visible.

Picoté (Fr.). Speckled.

Pierced. Applied to an ordinary or charge which has a hole through it so that the field may be seen. The opening is round unless otherwise described. Also applied to one charge through which another passes,—a chevron pierced with a bend, etc.

Piety. See PELICAN.

Pignon (Fr.). The term for the top of a building.

Pignonné (Fr.). Turreted. Also applied to a figure which resembles two flights of steps leaned against each other and forming the outline of a pyramid.

Pike. The well-known voracious fish. In blazon it is generally called a *Luce* or *Lucy.*

Pike-staff. A pronged spear used by foot-soldiers.

Pile. An ordinary in the shape of a wedge, broad at the chief and tapering to a point. *Party per Pile in Point.* Applied to a field which is divided by a wedge borne in its normal position, point down. *Party per Pile in Traverse.* Used when the field is divided by a wedge whose point is in the centre of the dexter side of the shield, and whose broadest part occupies the sinister side of the shield. *Party per Pile Transposed.* Divided by a pile inverted so that the point of the wedge is at the middle chief and the broadest part is at the base.

Pilgrim. Represented wearing a long robe and a broad-brimmed hat ornamented with an escallop-shell.

Pilgrim's Staff. A staff such as was carried on pilgrimages. Usually represented with a knob on the top. With the staff the palmer's *script* is often borne.

Pillar. See COLUMN.

Pily Barry. Bearing *piles* placed *barways*, point to the sinister.

Pily Bendy. Bearing *piles* placed *bendways*.

Pily Paly. A division of the field into the form of piles.

Pincers. A gripping tool used by smiths.

Pineapple. Originally the pine-cone, but now the West Indian fruit.

Placcate. A piece of armor worn over the breast-plate.

Planets. In the obsolete blazoning of the arms of princes by planets, instead of with metals and colors, SOL represents *or;* LUNA, *argent;* MARS, *gules;* JUPITER, *azure;* VENUS, *vert;* SATURN, *sable;* and MERCURY, *purpure.*

Planta-Genista. The broom-plant assumed by Geoffrey Plantagenet, Count of Anjou, and retained by his descendants as the badge of the famous Plantagenet family.

Plate. The white roundel. A round flat piece of silver without any impression on it.

Platté. *Semé of Plates.*

Platted or **Plaited.** Interlaced.

Playing-Tables. Backgammon-tables.

Plenitude. Applied to the moon when at the full.

Plié (Fr.). Applied to birds to mean *Close.*

Ployé. Bowed or bent like a segment of a circle.

Plume. See OSTRICH FEATHERS.

Plumetty. Sometimes applied to a field divided into fusils and filled with the ends of feathers.

Pluming. Applied to a bird arranging its feathers with its beak.

Plummet. An instrument used by seamen to sound the depth of the sea, and by masons and others to prove perpendiculars.

Pods of Beans. Borne open and displaying the seeds.

Poing (Fr.). Applied to the hand when clenched.

Point. A wedge-shaped charge issuing from the base of the escutcheon.

Pointe (Fr.). (1) Base of the shield. (2) A *point.*

Pointé (Fr.). Leaved.

Pointed, a Cross. See EGUISÉE.

Points. The term applied to a cross which has four points at each extremity.

Points of a Label. The parts which branch down.

Points of the Escutcheon. *Fesse Point, Honor Point,* etc.

Poisson. See MARINED.

Polar Star. See ANTARCTIC STAR.

Pomée or **Pommée.** Applied to a cross with a ball or knob at each end.

Pomegranate. A foreign fruit. Generally stalked and leaved and the side of the fruit burst.

Pomeis or **Pommes.** Green roundels.

Pomel. The rounded knob at the end of a sword-handle.

Pomelt and Hyltte Anowyd. *Pomelled and hilted gold.*

Pometty or **Pommettée.** Applied to a cross with more than one ball or knob at each end.

Pope s Crown. A cap or mitre of golden cloth, from which hang two pendants fringed; the cap is encompassed with three coronets, and has on its top a mound of gold, whereon is a cross of the same. Boniface VIII. added to the cap the first coronet, Benedict II. added the second, and John XXII. added the third in the year 1411, with a view to indicate by them that the pope is the sovereign *priest,* supreme *judge,* and sole *legislator* among Christians.

Popinjay. A small parrot with green feathers and red legs and beak.

Porcupine. A small animal whose body is covered with sharp-pointed quills.

Port. The gate of a castle or tower.

Portcullis. A heavy falling door, formed of bars with sharp-pointed lower ends, hung over the *port* of a castle. It could be dropped very quickly to close the gateway in case of attack.

Portcullis Pursuivant. One of the members of the College of Arms.

Portcullised. Latticed by horizontal and vertical lines.

Port-Hole. A hole pierced in the wall of a fortified place.

Posé. See STATANT.

Posé en Sautoir (Fr.). *Saltireways.*

Posed. Placed.

Pot. A steel head-piece or hat.

Pot. Of iron, with three legs.

Potence (Fr.). A crutch-shaped charge.

Potent. One of the heraldic furs. So called because formed of little figures which resemble the heads of crutches, formerly called *potents.*

Potent. The term applied to a cross whose extremities resemble crutches or "*potents.*"

Potent-Counter-Potent. One of the heraldic *furs.*

Potenté. Applied to an ordinary whose outlines resemble a succession of crutch-shaped figures.

Pouldron. Armor for the shoulder.

Pounce. The talon of a bird of prey.

Pouncing. Applied to a bird seizing its prey.

Pourpre (Fr.). *Purpure.*

Powdered. Promiscuously strewed with small, minor charges.

Powder-Horn or **Powder-Flask.** Borne *in pale* with mouth *in chief.*

Powdyrdy. Powdered.

Poynt. *Per Chevron.*

Ppr. Abbreviation for *Proper.*

Prancing. Applied to a horse when rearing.

Prasin. Used by some heralds for *vert.* Derived from a Greek word which means a *leek.*

Prawn. See SHRIMPS.

Precious Stones. In the obsolete custom of blazoning the arms of the nobility by precious stones instead of by metals and colors, TOPAZ represents *or;* PEARL, *argent;* RUBY, *gules;* SAPPHIRE, *azure;* EMERALD, *vert;* DIAMOND, *sable;* AMETHYST, *purpure;* HYACINTH, *tenné;* SARDONYX, *sanguine.* The arms of Massachusetts are thus blazoned.

Precise Middle. See MIDDLE CHIEF.

Predable. Sometimes applied to an eagle, falcon, etc., instead of birds "of prey."

Preen. A tool used by clothiers in dressing cloth.

Prester John or **Presbyter John.** Represented in a bishop's habit, seated on a tomb, his dexter hand extended, in his sinister a mound, and in his mouth a sword fesseways.

Pretence. See ESCUTCHEON OF PRETENCE.

Preying. Standing upon its prey and devouring it.

Pride. This term is used for turkey-cocks and peacocks. When they extend their tails in a circle and drop their wings, they are said to be "*in pride.*"

Primrose. The *Quatrefoil.*

Prince. A title of honor given, in England, to members of the royal family only. In other countries it is given to the sons and grandsons of an emperor or king.

Proboscis. An elephant's trunk.

Promening. See PLUMING.

Proper. Applied to any heraldic device when borne in its natural colors.

Propre (Fr.). *Proper.*

Prospect. The term for a view or landscape; also interior views of ruined castles, theatres, etc.

Proyning or **Pruming.** See PLUMING.

Pryck-Spur. See *Spur.*

Purfled. Adorned. When applied to armor, this term means that the studs and rims are of another metal. When applied to a mantle, it means lined or bordered with fur.

Purflew. A bordure of fur.

Purpure. The color purple. In engraving it is represented by diagonal lines, from the sinister chief to the dexter base.

Purse. Borne suspended from a girdle, after the fashion of the Middle Ages.

Pursuivant of Arms. The lowest grade of officers of arms.

Pycche. *Fitched.*

Pynant and Sayland. Old term for the pomel and hilt of a sword.

Pyot. A magpie.

Pyramid. A solid figure with a broad base bounded by straight lines and tapering to a point.

Python. A winged serpent or dragon.

Q.

Quadrant. A *Canton.*

Quadrant Fer-de-Mouline. A *Fer-de-Mouline* having a square hole in the centre.

Quadrate. Square.

Quadrature, In. Placed in the four corners of an imaginary square.

Quarter. An ordinary of quadrangular form which contains a fourth part of the field. To form quarters the field is divided *per pale* and *per fesse.* The dexter chief division so formed is called the *first quarter*, the sinister chief division is called the *second quarter*, the dexter base the *third quarter*, and the sinister base the *fourth quarter.* See also MARSHALLING BY QUARTERING.

Quartered. Divided into quarters. See also MARSHALLING BY QUARTERING.

Quarterings. The several coats marshalled on one field.

Quarterly. Applied to a shield or charge divided into four parts by a perpendicular and a horizontal line, which, crossing each other in the centre of the field, divide it into four equal parts called quarters. The same term is also used to indicate a division into a greater number of parts, as *quarterly of six, quarterly of eight,* etc. The number indicating how many divisions are to be made.

Quarterly Pierced. Pierced by a square hole, through which the field is seen.

Quarterly Quartered. Applied to a shield whose *quarters* are again quartered. The original quarters thus treated are then termed *Grand Quarters.* Also applied to a saltire quartered in the centre and having its branches parted by two tinctures alternately.

Quartier (Fr.). *Quarter.*

Quatrefeuille (Fr.). *Quartrefoil.*

Quartrefoil or Quaterfoil. A four-leaved grass represented without a stalk.

Quartrefoil Slipped. A *Quartrefoil* having a stem.

Queue. The tail of an animal. Most frequently used as DOUBLE QUEUED.

Queue Fourché. Having a forked tail.

Quill. An instrument on which is wound yarn, gold thread, etc.

Quilled. Applied to a bird whose feathers are different in tincture from its body.

Quintain. A "tilting" block set firmly in the ground against which horsemen broke spears. He who broke the greatest number of spears and displayed the most agility received the prize.

Quintefeuille (Fr.). *Cinquefoil.*

Quintefoil. See CINQUEFOIL.

Quise, À la. At the thigh. Applied to the limb of a bird *erased* or *couped, à la quise,* or at the thigh.

Quiver of Arrows. A case filled with arrows.

R.

Rabbit. Blazoned a *Coney.*

Racé. See INDENTED.

Rack-Pole Beacon. See BEACON.

Racourci (Fr.). Shortened or cut off so that the extremities do not reach the sides of the escutcheon.

Radiant or Rayonnant. Applied to a charge which is represented with rays or beams glittering around it.

Raguled or Raguly. Jagged or having irregular projections.

Raguly. Applied to a cross made of two tree-trunks stripped of their branches.

Rainbow. Borne issuing from clouds in its natural colors.

Ram. Represented conventionally with thick curving horns. See also BATTERING-RAM.

Ramé (Fr.). Branched or *Attired.*

Rampant. Standing upright on the hind legs, and shown in profile.

Rampant Guardant. Standing upright on the hind legs, the body in profile, but the head turned so that the face is affronté.

Rampant Reguardant. Upright on the hind legs and body in profile, but with the head turned so that the face is toward the tail.

Rampé or Ramped. See ROMPU.

Ramping. See RAMPANT.

Rangant. A term for the bull or buffalo when depicted in a rage.

Rangé (Fr.). Arranged in order.

Raping. Devouring or *Vorant.*

Rased, Rasé, or Razed. Broken or splintered. *Erased.*

Rasie. Having *Rays.*

Rasyd. *Erased.*

Raven. A black, carnivorous bird, very common in England.

Ravissant (Fr.). *Vorant.*

Ray. A stream of light from any luminous body. When drawn around the disk of the sun, the rays are sixteen in number; when round a star there are but six.

Rayonnant or Rayonné. See RADIANT.

Razed. *Erased.*

Rebated. Used of a weapon when the top or point is broken off.

Rebatements. See ABATEMENTS.

Rebending. *Bowed-Embowed,* or bent like the letter S.

Rebounding or Reboundant. In early drawings the tip of a lion's tail was turned in, and the term *rebounding* was applied when the tail was represented in the way which is now customary.

Rebus. A coat of arms that by its device alludes to the name of the person; as, *three salmons* for Salmon; a *pine-tree* for Pines; a *bolt* and *tun* for Bolton.

Recercellé. Curled. See a CROSS RECERCELLÉE.

Reclinant. Bending backward.

Recopyd or Recouped. See COUPED.

Recoupé (Fr.). Divided *per fesse* into equal parts and one of those parts divided *per fesse.*

Recourcie. See RACOURCI.

Recroiseté (Fr.). *Cross-Crosslet.*

Recrossed. *Cross-Crosslet.*

Recursant. Facing directly away from the spectator. The opposite of *affronté.*

Recurvant. *Bowed-Embowed.*

Red Hand. See BADGE OF ULSTER.

Redout or **Redoubt.** The *Cross potent rebated* is sometimes termed the Cross redout, from its resemblance to a bulwark or fortification.

Reed. An instrument used by weavers.

Reflected or **Reflexed.** Bent back. Applied to a chain or line which is attached to the collar of an animal and curved over its back.

Regalia. The ensigns of royalty. Also the name for the ensigns of any office of dignity.

Reguardant or **Regardant.** Applied to an animal looking behind, having its face turned toward its tail.

Reindeer. As drawn in armory,—a stag with double attires, or antlers, one pair erect, the other hanging down.

Remora. In heraldry a serpent. There is also a small fish of this name which adheres to the bottoms of ships.

Removed. Fallen or removed from its proper place. Usually placed lower.

Remply or **Rempli.** Filled up; denoting that the chief is almost filled up with a piece of another tincture, so that the chief appears only as a bordure about it.

Rencontre or **Au Rencontre** (Fr.). A head *Cabossed.*

Renversé (Fr.). *Reversed.*

Re-passant. See COUNTER-PASSANT.

Rere Mouse. A bat. Always borne with wings expanded.

Resarcelé. See RECERCELLÉ.

Resignant. Applied to the tail of a lion when it is hidden.

Respectant or **Respecting.** A term for two fishes or tame beasts when placed face to face, rampant.

Resplendent. Surrounded with *rays.*

Rest. This bearing is termed by some a rest for a horseman's lance, by others a clarion or claricord.

Retaillé (Fr.). Divided into three parts by lines in *bend sinister.*

Retiercé (Fr.). Divided into three parts fesseways, and each part again divided into three parts in the same direction.

Retorted. When serpents are woven together as a wreath or fretwise, they are called *retorted.*

Retracted. Applied to several charges placed *fesseways,* each of which is shorter than the next, as if cut off by a line *bendways.*

Retranché (Fr.). Cut into three parts by two lines bendways.

Reverberant. See REBOUNDANT.

Reversed, Renversed, or **Reversie.** Placed with the head downward, or contrary to its natural position, as a chevron with the point downward or a beast when laid on its back.

Revertant or **Reverted.** Bent like the letter S.

Revestu. See VESTU.

Reveyns. Ravens.

Rhinoceros. A huge African beast of great strength armed with a horn on the nose.

Riband or **Ribbon.** The eighth part of the bend, but does not touch the escutcheon at either end.

Rising. Applied to birds preparing to fly.

Risom or **Rizom.** The ear at the top of an oat-stalk.

Roe. A small species of deer about two feet three inches high at the shoulder and of about fifty pounds weight. Its color is a shining tawny brown with the under parts white.

Roebuck. The male of the roe bears erect, branching horns eight or nine inches in length.

Rompé or **Rompu.** Broken.

Rond (Fr.). (1) A circle. (2) Circular.

Roofed. Having a differently tinctured roof.

Rook. A black bird. Sometimes in blazon confused with *Chess-Rook* or *Castle.*

Rose. Represented in heraldry in a conventional form and without the stalk. It usually has ten petals, but sometimes only five.

Rose-en-Soliel. A white rose surrounded with rays.

Rouelle Spur. See SPUR.

Rouge. Red.

Rouge-Croix. Red-Cross. One of the Pursuivants of the English College of Arms. So named from the Cross of St. George.

Rouge Dragon. One of the Pursuivants of the English College of Arms. Named for one of the *supporters* of Henry VII., by whom he was created.

Roundels, Roundles, or **Roundlets.** Round figures. In English blazonry the yellow roundel is called a *bezant,* from the gold coin which was current in Byzantium at the time of the Crusades. The yellow roundel is represented flat, as is also the *plate* or white roundel. When the white circular charge is represented spherical it is called a bubble. All the other roundels are represented spherical, and are called, when green, Pomeis; when blue, Hurts; when red, Torteaux; when purple, Golpes; when black, Pellets; when *tenné*, Oranges; when *sanguine*, Guzes.

Roussant or **Rowsand.** See RISING.

Rowel. Part of a spur.

Rowt. A company of wolves together.

Royal Antler. The third branch of the attire. It shoots from the rear of the main beam above the *bezantlier*.

Roys. Roes.

Ruby. Used, in the obsolete blazoning of the arms of nobles by precious stones, for *gules*.

Rue, Chaplet or **Wreath of.** *A bend treflé vert.* This bearing resembles a coronet placed in bend, or a bend ornamented with trefoils.

Rundel. See ROUNDEL.

Rustre. A lozenge pierced in the middle by a round hole, through which the field may be seen.

Rye. An ear or head of this grain is generally blazoned a *stalk of rye* or a *rye-stalk*, since the ear is not borne without the stalk.

S.

S. In "tricking" denotes *sable* or black.

Sable. The color black. In engraving it is represented by horizontal and vertical lines crossing each other.

Sacre or **Saker.** A kind of falcon.

Sagittarius. A centaur or imaginary creature half man, half horse. It is the ninth sign of the zodiac, and was probably borne by King Stephen of England.

Sail. Usually borne with a part of the yard-arm and mast showing.

Saillant (Fr.). *Saliant.*

Saint Andrew. The patron-saint of Scotland. The St. Andrew's banner is a white saltire upon a blue field.

Saint George. The patron-saint of England. His banner is white bearing a red *cross*, known as the Cross of St. George.

Saint Patrick. The patron-saint of Ireland. His banner bears a red saltire on a white field. These three banners, St. George's, St. Andrew's, and St. Patrick's, are combined in the present British Union Jack.

Salamander. An imaginary animal generally depicted surrounded by flames proper. The animal is drawn in various ways in heraldry.

Salient or **Saliant.** Springing. Applied to a beast erect on its hind legs. It differs from *rampant*, since when *saliant* two paws are raised equally as if the beast were about to spring upon its prey. *Counter-Salient.* Leaping in opposite directions.

Salled Head-Piece or **Sallet.** A mediæval helmet.

Salmon-Spear. A spear barbed like a harpoon.

Saltant. Leaping. Applied to small animals only.

Saltier or **Saltire.** This cross is an ordinary, which is formed by the bend dexter and bend sinister crossing each other in the centre at an acute angle, like the letter X. When uncharged it contains the fifth, and when charged, the third, part of the field. *Per Saltire.* Applied to a field which is divided into four equal parts by two diagonal lines, dexter and sinister, that cross each other in the centre of the field. *In Saltire.* Applied to small charges placed in the form of a saltire.

Saltireways. Applied to swords, spears, etc., when placed to form a saltire. The sinister one generally surmounts the dexter.

Saltorels. Small saltires.

Salts or **Salt-Cellars.** Small cups with salt falling from the sides.

Sandal. A protection for the foot, bound on with strings.

Sang. Blood. See GUTTÉ DE SANG.

Sanglant. Bloody, torn off, or erased.

Sanglier (Fr.). The wild boar.

Sanguine. The murrey color, or dark red. It is represented in engravings by lines diagonally from the dexter to the sinister side, crossed by lines from the sinister to the dexter.

Sans. Without.

Sans Nombre. Without number. Powdered over with small charges, all of which are entire.

Sapphire. Used in the obsolete blazoning by precious stones for *azure*.

Saracens. The opponents of the Christians on the Crusades. A *Saracen's head* became a frequent bearing in European armory at that time. It is usually represented wreathed.

Sarcelled or **Sarcellé.** Cut through the middle.

Sarcelly. See CERCELLÉ.

Sardonyx. In blazoning by precious stones this stood for *sanguine.*

Saturn. A Roman god, the father of Jupiter. In blazoning by the planets it was used instead of *sable.*

Satyral. A fictitious animal having the body of a lion, tail and horns of an antelope, and the face of an old man.

Sautoir (Fr.). *Saltire.*

Savage. A naked man wreathed about the temples and waist and holding a club.

Sawtry. *Per Saltire.*

Scaled or **Escalloped.** Covered with scales like a fish.

Scaling-Ladder. A ladder with hooks on the upper end, used to scale the walls of besieged castles and cities. Usually placed bendways.

Scallop. See ESCALLOP.

Scalp. The skin of the forehead of a beast to which its *attires* are attached.

Scarabæus or **Scarabie.** A beetle held sacred by the Egyptians and used for seals and seal-rings.

Scarf. A small ecclesiastical banner, usually borne attached to a crozier, but when borne alone it is placed *in bend.*

Scarpe or **Escarpe.** Supposed to represent a shoulder-belt or an officer's scarf. It is a diminutive of the bend sinister and one-half its breadth.

Scatebra. See WATERPOT.

Sceptre. A staff, the symbol of royal authority.

Scimitar. The sword of the Saracens. It is like the falchion, but narrower and more curved.

Scintillant. Sparkling.

Scorpion. One of the largest of the insect tribe. Borne with the head in chief.

Scotch Spur. See SPUR.

Scrip. The pouch or bag used by pilgrims.

Scrog. A small branch of a tree.

Scroll. The label or ribbon which bears the motto. It is placed below the shield, unless the motto has special reference to the crest. When it has such reference it is placed either between the shield and crest or above the whole achievement.

Scruttle. See WINNOWING BASKET.

Scut. The tail of a rabbit.

Scutcheon. See ESCUTCHEON.

Scythe. The instrument used in husbandry. It should be borne with blade in chief to the dexter.

Sea-Dog. In shape like the talbot, but with a tail like that of a beaver, a scalloped fin continued down the back from the head to the tail; the whole body, legs, and tail scaled, and the feet webbed.

Sea-Horse. The upper part is formed like a horse, with webbed feet and a fin in place of a mane. The lower part is formed like a fish.

Sea-Lion. Half lion, half fish.

Sea-Mew. A sort of *Sea-Gull.*

Sea-Pie. A water-fowl of a dark-brown color, with white breast.

Sea-Swallows See AYLETS.

Sea-Wolf. A *Seal.*

Seal. Usually borne in its natural position.

Seax. A scimitar notched at the back.

Secretum. A private seal or personal seal used by officers of high rank in addition to their official seals.

Sedant. See SEJANT.

Seeded. Applied to roses, etc., to express the color of their seeds.

Segment. A portion of a coronet, etc.

Segrant (Fr.). Segreant.

Segreant. Used of a griffin, erect on its hind legs, with the wings indorsed and displayed as if ready to fly.

Sejant. Sitting.

Sejant-Addorsed. Sitting back to back.

Semé. Sprinkled with small charges some of which are cut by the edges of the shield, thus looking as if the field had been cut out of a larger surface.

Semé-de-lis. *Semé* of fleurs-de-lis, or having fleurs-de-lis scattered over it.

Senestrochere (Fr.). An arm issuing from the sinister side of the escutcheon.

Sepurture. *Endorsed.*

Seraph's Head. A child's head adorned with three pairs of wings, one pair *in chief,* one pair *in fesse,* and one pair *in base.*

Sergent or **Serjant.** See SEGREANT.

Serpent. Borne coiled and twisted in various forms.

Serrated. Notched like a saw.

Serus or **Cerise** A torteau.

Severed. See DISJOINTED.

Sexfoil. See SIXFOIL.

Shack-Bolt. See FETTERLOCK.

Shackle. An iron shaped like a horse-shoe, with a bolt across the opening.

Shadowed. See ADUMBRATED.

Shafferoon. See CHAPERON.

Shafted. Having a shaft or handle. Applied to a spear-head, arrow-head, etc. A feather is also termed *shafted* when the quill is of a different tincture.

Shake-Fork. A two-pronged fork resembling the *pall* as a charge, except that it is pointed at the ends and does not reach the sides of the escutcheon.

Shambroughs. A kind of ship.

Shamrock. One of Ireland's national emblems. It is a *trefoil* or three-leaved grass.

Shapewined. In a curved line.

Shapourned. In a curved line.

Shapournet. See CHAPOURNET.

Shave. See CURRIER'S SHAVE.

Sheaf. A bundle of three arrows. A sheaf of wheat is blazoned *a garb.*

Shears. Large scissors.

Sheldrake. A sort of duck.

Shield. A piece of defensive armor borne on the arm and emblazoned with the devices of the knight.

Shield of Pretence. See ESCUTCHEON OF PRETENCE.

Shin-Bones. Human shin-bones are frequently borne, placed *in saltire.*

Ship. Originally borne in the form of an ancient galley, but more modern forms are now used.

Shivered. Broken or splintered.

Shoveller. A species of water-fowl, somewhat like the duck, but distinguished by a tuft of feathers at the back of the head and another on the breast.

Shrimps. Borne as if crawling on the shield.

Shuttle. An instrument used by weavers.

Sickle and Garb. The Hungerford badge. A wheat-sheaf and a sickle.

Side. A portion of the field, not exceeding one-sixth of the whole, cut off from either the dexter or the sinister side.

Signet Royal. See CYGNET.

Silk Hanks. Small parcels of raw silk twisted into a knot.

Single. The tail of a deer.

Sinister. The left. The side of the shield opposite the right hand of the observer.

Sinister Base. The left-hand part of the base.

Sinister Chief. The left side of the chief.

Sinople (Fr.). *Vert,* the color green, represented in engraving by diagonal lines from the dexter chief to the sinister base.

Siren. A mermaid.

Sixfoil. A six-leaved grass or flower.

Skean, Skeen, Skein, or **Skene.** A dagger or short sword.

Skipping. Applied to reptiles when borne erect.

Slashed. Used of the sleeves of garments when cut lengthways and filled in with another color.

Slay, Slea, or **Reed.** An instrument used by weavers.

Sledge. A sled.

Sling. An instrument used for hurling missiles.

Slip. A twig bearing three leaves. See BRANCHES.

Slipped. Applied to a flower or branch torn from the stalk, with a portion of the stalk still clinging to it.

Slipped. Having a stalk.

Slipped. Applied to plants instead of *erased.*

Slughorn or **Slogan.** A Scotch war-cry.

Snagged. See LOPPED.

Snail. Borne crawling, with the shell on its back.

Snake. See SERPENT.

Soarant or **Soaring.** Flying aloft.

Sol. The sun. In the obsolete blazoning by planets, *Sol* was used for yellow instead of *or.*

Soldering-Iron. A tool used by plumbers.

Soleil. The sun, used especially in the pharse, "*a rose en soleil,*" meaning a rose *radiant.*

Somerset Herald. One of the members of the English College of Arms.

Sommé (Fr.). *Attired.* The number of branches is always mentioned unless more than twelve.

Sore. The young of the buck in its fourth year.

Sorel. The young of the buck in its third year.

Soustenu or **Soutenu.** Applied to a chief when supported by a small part of the escutcheon beneath it, of a different color or metal from the chief, and reaching as the chief does from side to side.

Spade-Iron. The shoeing used to protect the edges of the spade.

Spancelled. *Fettered.* Having one fore leg and one hind leg fastened by fetterlocks.

Spayade. A stag in his third year.

Spear. A long-handled weapon with an armed point for thrusting.

Speckled. Spotted over with another tincture.

Spectant. *At gaze* or looking forward.

Speed, At. Applied to a beast of chase when represented running.

Spellers. The small branches shooting from the flat part of a buck's horn at the top.

Spervers. Tents.

Sphinx. A fabulous monster with head, face, and breast like a woman, body and claws like a lion, and wings like a bird.

Spired. Having raised points.

Splayed. *Displayed.*

Splendor, In. Surrounded by *rays.*

Spotted. Speckled with some other tincture.

Spread Eagle. An eagle *displayed.*

Sprig. A branch with *five* leaves. See BRANCHES.

Springing. Applied to beasts of chase, as *saliant* to those of prey. Also applied to fish when placed *in bend.*

Spur. The earliest spur was the *Pryk Spur,* which had a single point. Then a large round plate was used, and this soon after was replaced by the Rouelle Spur, a spur with a smaller wheel, with a serrated edge.

Square Pierced. *Pierced* by a square hole, through which the field is seen.

Squirrel. The well-known animal, always depicted *sejant,* and consequently that term is omitted in blazoning.

Sruttle. A winnowing fan or basket.

S.S. Collar. Instituted by Henry IV., and the letters are supposed by some to be the repeated initial of his motto, *Soverayne.* Others hold that the Collar of S.S. is much more ancient, and borne as a badge of the Society of St. Simplicius, from which the S.S. is derived.

St. See SAINT.

Staff. See PILGRIM'S STAFF, CROZIER, PASTORAL STAFF.

Stafford Knot. An ordinary single knot, borne as one of the badges of the Stafford family.

Stag. The general name given to all kinds of deer.

Staggard. A stag in his fourth year.

Stag's Attires. The antlers of a stag.

Stall-Plate. A brass plate bearing the arms of a knight placed in the chapel of the order of knighthood of which he was a member.

Stamand. The colors murrey and tawney are sometimes so called.

Standard. A square banner bearing an achievement. It was allowed to none lower than the rank of knight banneret. In modern times it is applied to the flag of cavalry, while that of a regiment of infantry is called its *colors.* All standards were split at the end except those of princes of the blood royal.

Staple. An iron door fastening. It is usually represented square.

Star. See ESTOILE.

Star of India. See KNIGHTHOOD.

Starved. Stripped of its leaves. See BLASTED.

Statant. Applied to an animal standing on its feet, both the fore and hind legs being in a direct line.

Staves. See STAFF.

Steel Cap. A close-fitting head-piece.

Stern. The rear of a ship. The tail of a wolf is also so called.

St. George's Cross. A plain cross gules on a field argent.

Still. See ALEMBIC.

Stilts. Anciently used for the scaling of walls, castles, etc.

Stirrup. The word alone means stirrup with leather. To blazon a stirrup alone, the expression *stirrup sans leather* must be used.

Stock. The stump or trunk of a tree.

Stole. A priest's garment.

Stone Bill. See WEDGE.

Stooping. Applied to the hawk when darting down upon its prey.

Stork. This bird is the emblem of piety and gratitude.

Streaming. Used of the tail of a comet.

Stretchant. Applied to beasts when represented standing as if stretching after having been lying down.

Stringed. Having strings of a different tincture. The bugle-horn is always borne with strings unless blazoned *sans strings.*

Studded. Ornamented with studs.

Sub Ordinaries. Common charges, but less simple than the *Ordinaries.*

Subverted. See REVERSED.

Succeedant. Following one another.

Sufflue. A *Clarion* or *Rest.*

Sun. In heraldry represented with a human face, environed with rays, and termed the sun " in his splendor."

Super-Charge. A figure charged or borne upon another.

Supported. Applied to an ordinary which has another ordinary under it by way of support. It differs from *Surmounted.*

Supporters. Figures, animals or birds, which stand on each side of the shield and seem to support it.

Suppressed. See DEBRUISED.

Sur. On, upon, or over.

Surcoat. A loose coat emblazoned with the armorial devices of the wearer. It was worn over the armor.

Surgiant. See RISING.

Sur le Tout (Fr.). See SURTOUT.

Surmonté (Fr.). *Surmounted.*

Surmounted. When one charge is placed over or upon another.

Surposé (Fr.). *In Pale.*

Surroy. The ancient title of *Clarenceux.*

Surroyal Top. The broad top of a stag's horn with small branches from it.

Sursuant. Sometimes applied to beasts of chase instead of *rampant.*

Surtout (Fr.). *Over all.* It signifies a small escutcheon placed over or upon the shield.

Suspectant. Looking upward.

Sustained. Having a narrow border on the lower edge.

Swan. Usually represented with wings raised as if swimming. When blazoned *proper* it is white with a red bill.

Sweep or **Swepe.** An engine used in ancient times to cast stones into towns or fortified places of an enemy.

Swivel. Two iron links which turn on a bolt.

Sword. The heraldic *sword* is represented with a straight blade and sharp pointed.

Sykes. Fountains.

Synettys. Swans.

Syren. See MERMAID.

T.

T. In "tricking" *tawny* or *tenné.*

Tabard or **Tabert.** A military coat with large sleeves, worn over the armor and emblazoned with armorial bearings.

Tabernacle. A pavilion or tent.

Tail. A deer's tail is blazoned *the single ;* a boar's, *the wreath ;* a fox's, *the brush ;* a wolf's, *the stern ;* a hare's, *the scut.*

Taillé (Fr.). *Party per Bend Sinister.*

Talbot. A hunting-dog somewhat like a beagle-hound. It has a thick muzzle and long, thick ears.

Tanke. A deep round cap worn by Roman slaves.

Tapping. A charge or bearing.

Taré de Front (Fr.). *Affronté.*

Targant. Twisted like the letter S.

Target or **Targe.** A round buckler or shield.

Tasces or **Tasses.** Armor for the thighs.

Tassel. A bunch of silk or gold fringe, added to the strings of mantles and robes of state.

Tasseled. Decorated with tassels.

Tau, a Cross. So called from the Greek letter T, *tau.* Also known as *St. Anthony's Cross,* because St. Anthony, the monk, is always painted with it upon his habit.

Tavalures (Fr.). Ermine spots.

Tawny. See TENNÉ.

Teal. A water-fowl.

Teazel. The head or seed-vessel of a species of thistle, used by clothiers in dressing cloth.

Tenans (Fr.). Human figures which are used as supporters are sometimes termed tenans or tenants, but the better usage in French heraldry would seem to be to apply the term tenant when only one animal supports the shield.

Tenant (Fr.). A challenger.

Tenant. Holding.

Tenné or **Tenney.** Tawny or orange color. In engraving some represent it by diagonal lines, from the dexter to the sinister side of the shield, traversed by perpendicular lines; others, by diagonal lines from the sinister to the dexter crossed by horizontal lines. The latter system is favored.

Tent. Usually represented round, and with a pennon flying from the top.

Tergant or **Tergiant.** Having the back turned to the spectator.

Terras. The representation of ground at the base of the shield. Usually *Vert.*

Teste (Fr.). The head.

Teste à la Queue. Applied to fish so placed that the head of each is between the tails of two others.

Tête (Fr.). The head.

Tetragonal Pyramid. A *pile* represented as a solid figure with a square base.

Thatch-Rake. An instrument used in thatching.

Thistle. The national emblem of Scotland. See also KNIGHTHOOD (2).

Thoulouse (Fr.). Applied to a cross whose arms bear circles at the end.

Three, Two, and One. Three in the topmost line, two in the middle, and one in the lowest.

Threstle or **Trestle.** A three-legged stool.

Throughout. Extending to the sides of the shield.

Thunderbolt. A twisted bar *in pale* inflamed at each end, surmounting two jagged darts, in saltire, between two wings displayed with streams of fire ; this was the ensign of the Scythians.

Tiara. See POPE'S CROWN.

Tient de Sang (Fr.). *Imbrued.*

Tiercé. Tierced or divided into three equal parts.

Tigé. Bladed.

Tiger. The heraldic *Tyger* differs materially from the natural beast. It is a fictitious animal, with a hooked talon at the nose and with a mane formed of tufts.

Tilt. A *Tournament.*

Tilting Helmet. A heavy helmet worn over the basinet and attached to the other armor by a chain.

Tilting Spear. A heavy lance used in tournaments.

Timbré (Fr.). Having a helmet.

Timbre (Fr.). Properly all the accessories of the shield in an achievement, but generally used for the helmet when placed over the shield.

Tinctures. The metals and colors used in coats of arms.

Tirret. A modern term for manacles or handcuffs.

Toad. Always represented sitting in water with head projecting.

Toison d'Or. The Golden Fleece.

Tomahawk. An Indian war-axe.

Topaz. A precious stone of a yellow color, used in the blazoning by precious stones instead of *or*, for yellow.

Torce (Fr.). A wreath.

Torch. Generally borne *inflamed.*

Toret. A ring moving on a swivel.

Torgant. See TARGANT.

Torn. A spinning-wheel.

Torqued. See TARGANT.

Torse. A wreath.

Torteau. A *Roundel* of a red color. Represented spherical.

Torteau (Fr.). Any *Roundel.*

Torteys. Torteaux.

Tortillé. Curling, knotted, twisted, or wreathed.

Tortoise. Borne as if walking on the shield, with head to the dexter and feet and tail outstretched.

Tournament. A trial of skill in arms. Tournaments were made occasions of great pomp and ceremony, and magnificent prizes were awarded to the victors.

Tournant d'Eau (Fr.). *Whirlpool.*

Tourné (Fr.). *Reguardant.*

Tower. Usually represented as a circular embattled building, with a door.

Towered or **Turreted.** Applied to walls or castles having towers or turrets.

Tract or **Traile.** See TRESSURE.

Trade-Mark. A peculiar device adopted by a manufacturer to distinguish his products from those of other men.

Tranché (Fr.). *Party per Bend.*

Trangle (Fr.). A bar or closet.

Transfixed. Applied to a wounded animal when the weapon remains in the flesh.

Transfluent. Flowing through.

Transmuted. See COUNTER-CHANGED.

Transposed. See REVERSED.

Traverse. A triangular bearing formed by two lines issuing from the chief and base corners of one side of the shield and meeting in a point near the middle of the opposite side, but not touching the edge.

Traversed. Facing *Sinister.*

Trecheur (Fr.). *Tressure.*

Trefle (Fr.). *Trefoil.*

Treflé. Ornamented with *Trefoils.*

Trefoil. A three-leaved grass.

Treillé. Latticed. It differs from *fretty* in that the pieces which cross each other are not interwoven, but are nailed at the intersections.

Tressure. The diminutive of the *Orle,* one-half of it in breadth. The tressure follows the outline of the shield. It is a bearing rarely granted except to those of royal descent.

Trestle. A three-legged stool.

Trevet. A tripod or three-legged frame of iron used to set over a fire for the support of a pan or pot. Sometimes triangular, sometimes round.

Trian Aspect. Showing three-fourths of the body.

Tri-Arché. Formed of three arches.

Trick. To outline or sketch a coat of arms, labeling the tinctures.

Tricorporated. Having three bodies. A lion with three bodies issuing out of the three corners of the escutcheon, all meeting under one head in the fesse point, was borne as a device by Edmund Crouchback, Earl of Lancaster, brother to King Edward I.

Trident. A three-pronged spear borne in the hand of Neptune.

Trien. Three.

Triparted. Divided into three equal pieces.

Triple Plumes. Three rows of feathers, one above another.

Trippant or **Tripping.** Applied to beasts of chase when represented with one foot raised. Thus it corresponds to *passant*, which is applied to beasts of prey. *Counter-Tripping* is used when two beasts are *trippant* and passing each other in opposite directions.

Triton. A *Merman.*

Triumphal Crown. A crown of laurel granted to those Roman generals who vanquished their enemies.

Trompe (Fr.). *Hunting-Horn.*

Tronçonné (Fr.). Broken into many pieces, but preserving the general form.

Tron-onné. See DISMEMBERED.

Tronque (Fr.). *Trunked.*

Trowel. The flat trowel used by masons is usually borne.

Trumpet. A long straight horn.

Truncated. See TRUNKED.

Truncheon. A short staff.

Trundles. Quills of gold thread used by embroiderers.

Trunk of a Tree. When a tree is torn up by the roots and stripped of its branches it is called the *trunk of a tree.*

Trunked. When the main stem of a tree is borne without roots or branches it is termed a *tree trunked.* Also applied to a tree whose trunk is specially tinctured. When applied to animals it means *Cabossed.*

Trussed. *Close.*

Trussing. Applied to a bird *preying.*

Tuberated. Knotted or swelled out. Applied to a serpent when swollen at the middle.

Tudor Rose. The rose formed by the union of the White Rose of York and the Red Rose of Lancaster, which symbolized the union of the two factions by the marriage of Henry VII. with Elizabeth of York. It is usually represented as a rose (1) *per pale argent and gules;* (2) a rose *quarterly argent and gules;* or (3) a white rose within a red one. It is curious that the *argent* of York should occupy the parts of the rose which correspond to the *husband's* portion of the shield in impaled or quartered arms. The white rose within the red one may be likened to a shield of pretence, since Elizabeth was an heiress, but the other forms seem contrary to the ordinary heraldic laws.

Tuft. A bunch of grass.

Tun. A large vessel for holding liquids.

Turkish Crown. See GRAND SEIGNOR'S CROWN.

Turned Up. Having the edge specially tinctured and folded outward so that the tincture is seen.

Turnpike. A frame of three vertical and three horizontal bars revolving on the central upright bar, which has a handle for turning.

Turnstile. A turnpike placed on a foot-frame.

Turret. A small tower.

Turreted. Having small turrets on the top.

Tushed or **Tusked.** Applied to an animal when its tusks are different in tincture from its body.

Two and One. Two in chief and one in base.

Twyfoil or **Dufoil.** A two-leaved grass, sometimes borne with a flower between the leaves, and then blazoned *flowered.*

Tyger. See TIGER.

Tymbre. See TIMBRE.

Tynes. The branches of a stag's attires.

Tyrwhitt. The lapwing.

U.

Ulster Badge. See BADGE OF ULSTER.

Ulster King-of-Arms. The heraldic "king" who has jurisdiction over Ireland.

Umbraced. See VAMBRACED.

Umbrated. See ADUMBRATED.

Undatyd. See WAVY.

Undé or **Undy.** See WAVY. One of the partition-lines.

Un Demi-vol (Fr.). A wing.

Unfructed. Without fruit.

Unguled. Having hoofs of a different tincture from that of the body.

Unicorn. A very beautiful heraldic beast, with a long twisted horn on its forehead; its head and body are like those of a horse; but it has cloven feet, and hair under the chin, like a goat, with a tail like a lion.

Unifoil. A one-leaved grass.

Union Jack. The first British Union Jack was devised to symbolize the union of England and Scotland. The red cross of St. George was charged upon the banner of St. Andrew, a white saltire on a blue field, and the red cross was *fimbriated argent* to prevent a violation of the rule that color must not be placed upon color. This was declared by James I. to be the national ensign of Great Britain in 1606. After the union with Ireland the red saltire of

St. Patrick was charged upon the white saltire of St. Andrew, and the cross of St. George over all. The flag is thus blazoned by Mr. Cussans : "*Azure ; the Saltires of St. Patrick and St. Andrew, quarterly per Saltire, counterchanged, argent and gules ; the latter fimbriated of the second ; surmounted by the Cross of St. George of the Third, fimbriated as the last.*"

Upright. Erect *in pale.*

Urchant or **Urchin.** A hedge-hog.

Urdé. See CLECHÉ.

Uriant or **Urinant.** The reverse of *Hauriant.* Applied to fish borne *in pale* with head in base.

Urvant or **Urved.** Turned or bowed upward.

Usher of the Black Rod. See BLACK ROD.

V.

V. Used in "tricking to indicate *Vert* or green.

Vache (Fr.). Cow.

Vair. One of the heraldic furs. Represented as composed of small shields alternately reversed.

Vair Ancient. Represented by lines nebulé, separated by straight lines *in fesse.*

Vair, a Cross. One composed of four pieces of vair, their points turned one to another, in the form of a cross.

Vaire (Fr.). *Vair.*

Vairé (Fr.). Having the same figures as *Vair,* but of various tinctures.

Vairé or **Vairy.** A fur like *Vair,* except that the divisions which have the same tincture are placed directly under each other. Also called *Counter - Vair.*

Vair-en-Point. A rare fur in which the shield-shaped pieces are placed base to point.

Vallary Crown. A circle of gold, with palisades fixed against the rim ; it was given by the general of the army to the captain or soldier who first entered the enemy's camp by forcing the palisades.

Vambrace. Armor for the arm.

Vambraced. Applied to an arm habited in armor.

Vamplate or **Vamplet.** A funnel-shaped piece of steel placed on the handle of a tilting spear just in front of the hand to protect it.

Vamplate. A gauntlet.

Vamps or **Vams.** Short hose reaching to the ankle only.

Vannet. The escallop without ears.

Variegated. Tinctured with numerous colors.

Varriated. Cut in the form of *Vair.*

Varries or **Varreys.** Separate pieces of *Vair,* in shape resembling a small shield.

Varry. See VAIRÉ.

Varvelled. Used when the jesses of a hawk are *flotant,* with rings at the end.

Velloped. A cock is termed *armed, crested,* and *velloped* when his spurs, comb, and gills are specially tinctured.

Venant (Fr.). *Assaultant.*

Venice Crown. The cap of state worn by the Doge ; it is made of cloth of gold bound by a circle of gold covered with precious stones, and has two long lappets, pointed at the end, which hang down one on either side.

Venus. The Roman Goddess of Love. In blazoning by the planets Venus was used for green instead of *Vert.*

Verbley. A hunting-horn, edged round with metal of a different tincture from that of the horn.

Verdé. Powdered or strewed with leaves or plants.

Verdon Knot. A *fret* with the ends cut off.

Verdoy. Applied to a bordure charged with any kind of leaves or plants.

Vergetté (Fr.). *Pallet.*

Verry. See VAIRÉ.

Versant. Erected or elevated.

Versé (Fr.). *Renversé.*

Vert. The color green, represented in engraving by diagonal lines from dexter to sinister.

Vertant and Revertant. Bent like the letter S.

Verules. The rings which encircle hunting-horns. When these are specially tinctured the horn is blazoned *Veruled.*

Vervels. Small rings to which the *jesses* of a hawk are fastened.

Vested. Clad. Applied to a part of the body, while *Habited* is used when the whole figure is covered.

Vestu. Applied to an ordinary which has some division in it by lines only, and signifies clothed, as if some garment were laid upon it.

Vexillum. A scarf attached to the head of a pastoral staff, and wrapped about its shaft.

Victoria Cross. A decoration given for eminent personal valor.

View. The track of a buck.

Vigilant. Watching for prey.

Vilainie. The lower half of a *lion rampant*.

Viper. A venomous snake.

Vires (Fr.). Annulets one within another.

Virolé. The hoop, ring, or mouthpiece of a hunting-horn.

Virolled. Applied to a horn when the rings about it are specially tinctured.

Virols. Falcon rings.

Visard. See VIZARD.

Viscount. The fourth degree in rank in the British peerage, in rank below an earl and above a baron.

Viscount's Coronet. A circlet of gold upon which are placed fourteen pearls, nine of which are shown in representation.

Visiere (Fr.). *Gardevizor.*

Viudé (Fr.). *Voided.*

Viure. A narrow band.

Vivre (Fr.). (1) Dancetté. (2) *Gliding*, when applied to serpents.

Vizard. A mask.

Vizor. See GARDEVIZOR.

Voided. Applied to an ordinary when it has nothing but an edge to show its form; all the inner part is supposed to be cut out so that the field appears through.

Voiders. These figures are formed like the flanches and flasques, but are smaller than either, since the arch does not reach so near the centre of the field.

Vol. Both wings of a bird displayed and conjoined.

Vol, Demi. A single wing.

Volant. Flying.

Volentes Volare. *Essorant* or *Rising*.

Vorant. A term for any fish, bird, beast, or reptile swallowing any other creature.

Vulned. Wounded and bleeding. When the weapon remains in the wound the beast is "*transfixed.*"

Vulning. Wounding. Applied to a pelican when wounding her breast.

W.

Wake's Knot or **Wake and Ormond Knot.** A badge formed from the initials W and O, with two lengths of ribbon or cord intertwined. It is borne in chief.

Walled. *Masoned.*

Wallet. A pilgrim's pouch.

Wamays. See VAMS.

Warden. A sort of pear.

Warwick Badge. The *Bear and Ragged Staff*

Wastels or **Wastel Cakes.** Round cakes.

Water-Bouget. A vessel made of two leathern pouches, and suspended on the ends of a yoke. Anciently used by soldiers to carry water to the camp.

Water-Pot. The vessel from which a river god pours a stream over which he presides.

Watery. *Wavy* or *Undé.*

Watching. See VIGILANT.

Wattled. A term for a cock when its gills or wattles are of a different tincture from that of its body.

Waved. WAVY.

Wavy. Formed like waves, undulating. It has always three risings, and is a line of partition.

Weare or **Weir.** A sort of dam made of stakes and twigs wattled together. It is used to catch fish.

Wedge. Like the *pile* in form, but does not touch the edge of the shield.

Weel. A sort of net used to catch fish.

Welke or **Whelke.** A sort of shell-fish.

Well. Borne masoned and, as a rule, round, though square wells are sometimes seen in coat-armor.

Well-Bucket. A bucket with three legs.

Welsh Harp. See HARP.

Welt. A narrow border.

Were. *Vair.*

Werwels. *Vervels.*

Wharrow Spindle. An instrument sometimes used by women to spin as they walk, sticking the distaff in their girdle and whirling the spindle round, pendent at the thread.

Wheat-Sheaf. Blazoned a *Garb.*

Wheel. Usually of eight spokes. See CATHERINE-WHEEL.

Whet-Herys. Wheat-ears.

Whirlpool or **Gurges.** Represented by two lines, azure and argent, commencing at the fesse point and alternately encircling each other to the outer edge.

White. In heraldry *argent.* Represented in engraving by plain white.

White Spurs. The spurs of an *esquire* were

of silver, and hence termed *white spurs* to distinguish them from the gold ones of a knight.

Wild Man. A *Savage* or *Saracen.*

Windsor Herald. One of the officers of the English College of Arms.

Wine-Piercer. An instrument used for boring holes in casks.

Winged. Having wings. It also signifies that the wings are different in tincture from the body.

Winnowing-Fan, -Van, or **-Basket.** A basket for separating the grain from the chaff.

Wisalls or **Wisomes.** Carrot tops.

Wiure. See VIURE.

Wolf. When borne ppr. it is brown. Usually represented as if springing on its prey, and then blazoned *salient.*

Wood. See HURST.

Wood-Bill. A sort of axe.

Woodman. A *Savage.*

Wool-Cards. Instruments used for carding wool.

Wound. The *Hurt* or purple roundel.

Woydyd. *Voided.*

Woydyrs. Four quarters.

Wrapped. Wound about.

Wreath. An attire for the head, made of linen or silk of two different tinctures twisted together, which knights wore when equipped for tournaments.

Wreathed. Wearing a wreath.

Wyvern or **Wivern.** A kind of flying serpent, the upper part resembling a dragon and the lower an adder or snake. It differs from a dragon in that it has but two legs.

Y.

Yates. Gates.

Yellow. See OR.

Yeoman. A freeholder or man having lands of his own to live upon, the annual value of which was equal to or greater than a certain sum fixed by statute at various times.

Yoke. See OX-YOKE.

York Herald. One of the officers of the English College of Arms.

York Rose. The *White* Rose was adopted as its badge by the House of York.

Z.

Zodiac. The different signs of the zodiac are frequently borne as charges, and there was also a system of blazoning by the signs of the zodiac, which is fortunately now obsolete. In this *Or* was Leo; *Argent,* Scorpio and Pisces; *Gules,* Aries and Cancer; *Azure,* Taurus and Libra; *Sable,* Capricornus and Aquarius; *Vert,* Gemini and Virgo; *Purpure,* Sagittarius and Pisces.

Zule. A German bearing which closely resembles a chess-rook.

INDEX.

A.

393

B.

C.

D.

E.

F.

G.

H.

I.

J.

K.

L.

M.

N.

O.

P.

Q.

R.

S.

T.

U.

V.

W.

Y.

Z.